Financial Reporting Using Computer Graphics

SUBSCRIPTION NOTICE

This Wiley product is updated on a periodic basis with supplements to reflect important changes in the subject matter. If you purchased this product directly from John Wiley & Sons, Inc., we have already recorded your subscription for this update service.

If, however, you purchased this product from a bookstore and wish to receive (1) the current update at no additional charge, and (2) future updates and revised or related volumes billed separately with a 30-day examination review, please send your name, company name (if applicable), address, and the title of the product to:

    Supplement Department
    John Wiley & Sons, Inc.
    One Wiley Drive
    Somerset, NJ 08875
    1-800-225-5945

For customers outside the United States, please contact the Wiley office nearest you:

Professional & Reference Division
John Wiley & Sons Canada, Ltd.
22 Worcester Road
Rexdale, Ontario M9W 1L1
CANADA
(416) 236-3580
1-800-263-1590
FAX 1-800-675-6599

John Wiley & Sons, Ltd.
Baffins Lane
Chichester
West Sussex, PO19 1UD
UNITED KINGDOM
(44) (243) 779777

Jacaranda Wiley Ltd.
PRT Division
P.O. Box 174
North Ryde, NSW 2113
AUSTRALIA
(02) 805-1100
FAX (02) 805-1597

John Wiley & Sons (SEA) Pte. Ltd.
37 Jalan Pemimpin
Block B # 05-04
Union Industrial Building
SINGAPORE 2057
(65) 258-1157

Financial Reporting Using Computer Graphics

1995 Cumulative Supplement

Irwin M. Jarett
PhD, CPA

John Wiley & Sons, Inc.
New York • Chichester • Brisbane • Toronto • Singapore

Library of Congress Cataloging in Publication Data:
Jarett, Irwin M.
    Financial reporting using computer graphics / Irwin M. Jarett.
      p.   cm.
    Includes bibliographical references and index.
    ISBN 0-471-57408-2
    ISBN 0-471-10256-3 (Supplement)
    1. Financial statements—Graphic methods—Data processing.
2. Corporate reports—Graphic methods—Data processing. 3. Computer
graphics. 4. Management information systems.   I. Title.
HF5681.B2J34   1993
657'.32'028566—dc20   92-33434

Printed in the United States of America

10 9 8 7 6 5 4 3 2 1

CONTRIBUTORS

GREG ALTON received his B.S. in Accounting from Eastern Illinois University in 1980. Since then he has been heavily involved in the use of computers in accounting. He formed Alton & Associates in 1989, and his firm specializes in the custom design and modification of accounting systems to meet the wide-ranging needs of his clients. He installs and supports accounting systems that operate on PC networks. Current clients range from manufacturing to distribution to creative arts and from large to small firms. He has been an SBT Gold Reseller for the past three years.

Prior to forming his consulting firm, Mr. Alton developed and installed cost accounting and accounting-based information systems for the health care industry. He also worked extensively in manufacturing and distributions environments.

CHRIS BENNETT has degrees in both Computer Science and Political Science from the University of Oregon. Over the past 12 years, he has specialized in the development of accounting software applications. He is currently the Accounting Products Manager for SCS/Compute, a leading supplier of microcomputer software for accountants, where he supervises the design and development of accounting applications, as well as giving speeches and presentations at software users' groups and accounting seminars.

F. ANDREW BEST, a practicing CPA and Internal Auditor for 30 years, with degrees from Indiana University and University of Illinois, is Chief Statistician and cofounder of Med-Intell, Inc. Since 1976 he has been engaged in turnaround management activities for hospitals, savings and loans, and senior retirement and health care facilities. He has served as consultant to health care consulting firms specializing in strategic planning and aggressive marketing.

Mr. Best has been an Assistant Director of Audit for the U.S. Post Office Department and the Department of Agriculture. He developed programs for audit of statistical systems for these departments. He developed the computer audit curriculum for the Inter-Agency Auditor Training Center of the Department of Commerce. He was President of the Strata Users Association—Touche Ross & Co. computer audit software. He participated in the development of the Computer Audit and Computer Audit Guidelines used by the AICPAs and the Canadian Charter Accountants.

RODNEY S. BRUTLAG has ten years of authoritative consulting as president of Brutlag & Associates, Inc. Mr. Brutlag has spent over 28 years staffing and consulting to nationally recognized associations of all sizes. Prior to forming his consulting firm in 1984, he spent nine years of innovative turn-around management as CEO of three associations. He has served for 25 years as a leader, a speaker, and a writer at various associations such as the American Society of Association Executives, Chicago Society of Association Executives, and Association Economics Council.

MICHAEL J. BUDNICK, MHA FACHE, is President of Med-Intell, Inc. A graduate of St. Louis University, Mr. Budnick has been in the health care industry for 20 years. He has spent the last nine years as CEO of two Catholic hospitals and is currently CEO of Alliant Management Systems, Inc. of Louisville, Kentucky, a firm specializing in managing small rural hospitals.

CYNTHIA A. FROWNFELTER is Assistant Professor of Accounting and Information Systems at The University of Texas at San Antonio. She has also taught at the University of Delaware, Drexel University, and Louisiana State University. A graduate of Loyola University—New Orleans, she received her M.S. and Ph.D. from Drexel University. Her research focus is on the efficacy of graphical presentations of financial information.

A Certified Public Accountant, Frownfelter formally practiced in management advisory services, specializing in microcomputer training and installations and litigation support in the form of computer modeling. Ms. Frownfelter served on the Computer Education Committee of the Louisiana Society of Certified Public Accountants. She is presently a member of the American Institute of Public Accountants and the American Association of Accountants.

KENNETH L. THYGESEN is a software professional specializing in support and development of accounting applications. He has been in charge of the McGladrey & Pullen National Microcomputer Support since February of 1989, and has been involved in all phases of the software business since 1980.

Since joining the firm, Mr. Thygesen has been involved in the Task Force on Micros and Communications, which is in the process of setting standards for the firm's purchase of hardware and software products. He was one of the originators of McGladrey's joint venture with Sequel Software Corporation, Sequel/McGladrey Software, which will produce and market software to the accounting industry.

He graduated from the University of Iowa in 1978 with a Bachelors of Business Administration in Accounting and Finance, and holds a CPA certificate from the state of Iowa.

PREFACE

Introduction

The responses to the new edition and the 1994 supplement are most pleasing. In my conversations with the readers, two points persist.

A. You always tell us why the financial graphic standards are good. Tell us why some charts are bad!

B. You always tell us we should use tabular, text, and charts together. Yet, you only display the charts. Show us how to organize a presentation using all three presentation formats!

Here are my first responses to the two requests.

Section One: What You See Is -Not- What You Get - WYSI-Not-WYG

The new graphical user interfaces ("GUIs") tout the WYSIWYG process (What You See Is What You Get). The point of the WYSIWYG is that you can format material on the screen and the system will print it just as you see it. If you have a color printer, you will get a color print that approximates the colors on the screen. Some color printers come much closer to the screen colors than others. The more expensive color printers offer the widest range of colors. The ink jet printers are inexpensive now and offer good quality color printing. They are slow and are not considered "production" printing. Like everything else in computing, the price will come down and the value will come up in time.

The tabular formats you set up in the new spreadsheets and Windows™-based report writers print just as you see them. The fonts, lines, highlights, and other formatting print exactly as you draw them. Even the colors will be close.

The charts are easy to make. If you do not like one format, just click on the icon and change the format. If you do not like the colors, click on the icon and change the color. If you want 3D charts, click on the icon and choose a 3D chart. The system will do whatever you ask it to do. You get what is on the screen.

But you may get more. You may distort the information you provide the user to the point where it is useless. The so-called 3D charts are not 3D. A three-dimensional chart results only when a third variable is added to the normal Cartesian coordinates. The *only way* to build a 3D chart is to add a third variable. For example, time (Z) can be added to a cost (X) and volume (Y) chart to show how costs and volumes react over time.

In most cases, the so-called 3D charts in the drawing and spreadsheet packages simply add a perspective to the lines or bars. They do not allow you to add a third variable. The picture you see is an object that appears to have volume. Such graphic "artistry" adds distortion, it does not add a third dimension—**WYSI-Not-WYG.**

The viewers get value (numbers) into their brains from the surface of the area they see in a chart. The average viewer cannot see the surface values when they are distorted by an incomprehensible volume. The overriding goal of adding charts to financial and accounting information is to enhance communications and improve understanding. Fake 3D charts kill any possibility of meeting such a goal —**WYSI-Not-WYG.**

There are two chapters in this section. The first chapter describes a two-year comparative study of how 16 public companies use (or misuse) graphs to present financial data in their annual reports. The results are startling. For example, 11 of the companies showed their **PROFITS IN RED!** Such obliviousness to accounting and financial usage suggests that *taste* defeated *knowledge* and *accuracy.*

The second chapter uses three sets of tabular data to draw charts on a Windows-based spreadsheet. The tables range from simple to complex. All but a few of the available chart types appear at least once. The charts are evaluated by how accurately they depict the data. Hints are provided so that the reader can properly display similar data.

Chapter 23A—Charting Simple Data Sets Using a Windows Spreadsheet

A. The data sets, and how they were designed to produce the graphics
B. The graphics with a discussion of the problems found
C. The "good" graphics that resulted from the effort
D. How to keep from creating charts that distort instead of support

Chapter 23B—The Annual Report Study

A. The goals of the study
B. Number of company reports reviewed
C. Analysis of the study data tables
D. Samples of the bad charts with description of the potential problems
E. Summary

Section Two: The New Business Communication Page—WYSIWYG (What You See Is What You Get)

As noted earlier, the overriding goal of adding charts to financial and accounting information is to enhance communications and improve understanding. Communication depends on the accuracy and internal consistency of how the presentation stimulates all four parts of the brain. For example: The tabular data must be precise, not too much but enough to be complete; the graphic presentation must reflect the identical relationships shown in the tabular report; the written analysis must precisely report the critical results; and the verbal report must properly synthesize the operational results. The whole presentation must properly reflect the information presented to the users, who may get the numbers and the relationships into their brains, but may not understand how the numbers reflect the business.

Understanding depends on the ability of the reader to link the data presented to their reality of the business's operations. A tabular report titled "Manufacturing Costs" should reflect the manufacturing costs related to the company's manufacturing process. If the tabular report describes smelting costs and the company is a machine shop, understanding is suspended. If the tabular report shows the proper manufacturing costs, but the written analysis reflects a retail store's operation, understanding is suspended. If the tabular and the written portion of the report properly reflect manufacturing costs, but the chart distorts the information, understanding is suspended. If all three parts of the report fully support each other, but the person presenting the report puts the wrong "spin" on the information, understanding is suspended.

In short, all four parts of the presentation must be in harmony if communication and understanding are the result. Distortion perceived by any part of the brain will suspend the process until the distortion is reconciled.

One other component of communication and understanding is *consistency*. Consistency is the underpinning of accounting and financial reporting and is the underpinning of good reporting. As noted in the Annual Report study, there was trivial consistency in the charts used by a company from year to year. Except for the companies who accidentally used a common graphing tool the second year, there was no conscious consistency among the companies. If financial reporting is to shed the albatross of confusion, the entire presentation format must be consistent.

The following exhibit shows a new business reporting idea suggested in Chapter 24A of this section. There are three components to the report: the chart on the left, the tabular report on the top right, and the written analysis on the bottom right. These placements take advantage of how the eye processes information to the brain. The left eye sends information to the right side of the brain and the right eye sends information to the left side of the brain. The chart gets into the right side of the brain that is the graphics processor. The tabular data gets into the upper-left side of the brain that is the data processor. The written data gets into the lower-left side of the brain that is the word processor.

Chapter 24A in this section describes how the presentation works. The amount and level of the data and the supporting analysis must be carefully matched. The result is that the three parts of the brain stimulated by the presentation receive a consistent message, enhancing the communication process. When you describe the information, the fourth part of the brain is activated. The result is called "Intellectual Multimedia"™ because all four parts of the brain are activated toward understanding a common data set.[1]

Chapter 24A—The New Business Communication Page—WYSI-WYG (What You See Is What You Get)

A. How data, graphics, and words tie together in accounting
B. The basic reporting "page"
C. Examples of the "pages" that result from the data set
D. Examples of the "pages" that result from an accounting report
E. How Intellectual Multimedia results from a printed report
F. The next step in presentations

Chicago, Illinois   IRWIN M. JARETT
March 1995

	1995	ACTUAL	Financial Graphic	CHART: 1014
	1994	ACTUAL	Standards	December, Year to Date
			Statement of	In Thousands
			Revenue & Expenses	

Percent Variance

Total Revenues
1484.3
1227.1

Total Revenues
21.0

Total Cost of Goods Sold
771.4
621.9

Total Cost of Goods Sold
24.0

Total Gross Profit
712.9
605.2

Total Gross Profit
17.8

Operating Expenses
408.2
294.5

Operating Expenses
38.6

General & Administrative
222.7
196.3

General & Administrative
13.4

Income Before Income Taxes
82.1
114.3

Income Before Income Taxes
(28.2)

0   500   1000   1500   2000   -80%   -40%   0%   40%   80%

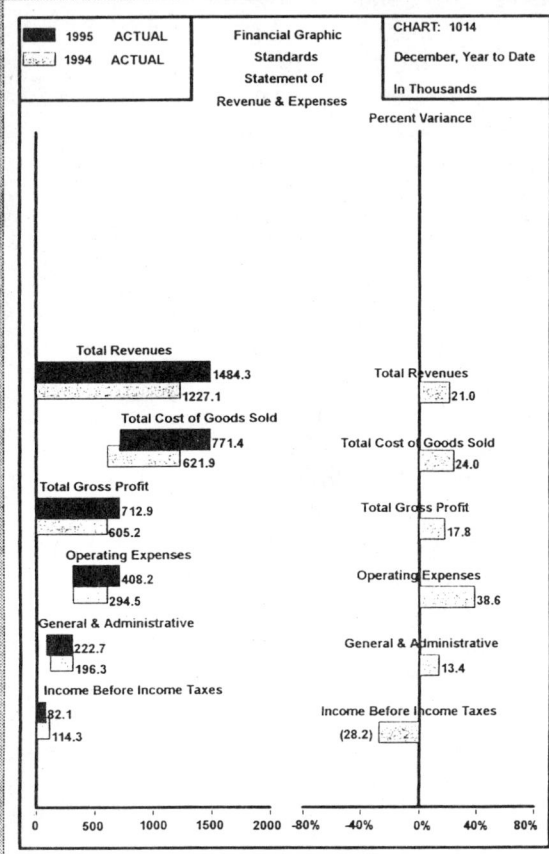

Financial Graphic

Standards

Statement of Revenue & Expenses

	1995	1994
Total Revenues	$1,484,300	$1,227,100
Total Cost of Goods Sold	771,400	621,900
Total Gross Margin	$ 712,900	$ 605,200
Operating Expenses	408,200	294,500
General and Administrative	222,700	196,400
Income Before Income Taxes	$ 82,000	$ 114,300

The chart confirms that the Cost of Goods Sold are growing at a faster rate than sales. The operating expenses expanded at an even greater rate than either sales or COGS. The result is a substantially lower Net Before taxes than the previous year. Two actions appear appropriate: review the sales mix to determine why the cost of goods sold increased faster than sales; cut operating costs.

CONTENTS

Note to the Reader: Materials that appear only in the supplement and not in the main volume are indicated by the word (New) after the title.

CHAPTER 4

FINANCIAL GRAPHIC STANDARDS—THE GROWING BUSINESS COMMUNICATION PROBLEM

Page 47, add the following new sections:

4.6 FINANCIAL GRAPHICS—COMMUNICATIONS FOR THE 1990s, THE NEED FOR FINANCIAL GRAPHIC STANDARDS, THE ILLINOIS CPA SOCIETY (New)

Introduction

The Illinois CPA Society study is one of the classic studies in the quest for financial graphic standards. This landmark study has weathered the test of time and rational, thorough reviews. The CICA study presented in Chapter 2 is, in many respects, a replication and confirmation of the study process developed by the Financial Graphics Subcommittee of the Computer Information Systems Committee, Illinois CPA Society. Both studies reviewed the literature, both studies used the annual reports of significant corporations to identify how graphics were being used, and most important, both studies called for the profession to take the responsibility for setting financial graphic standards.

The Illinois CPA Society has graciously allowed me to reproduce the "EXECUTIVE SUMMARY" with several additional quotes to support the conclusions contained in the EXECUTIVE SUMMARY. The additional quotes are included in the appropriate position in the material. Each quote is supported by a historical perspective of how the information was collected and why the committee felt the material was important.

It is not possible in a limited review of such a comprehensive report to provide the full flavor and import of all the material they have produced. The only way to properly understand the power of the information they have reported is to read the report. The reports are available from:

The Illinois CPA Society
222 S. Riverside Plaza
Chicago, IL 60606
Phone: (312) 993-0393
Fax: 312-993-9954

Executive Summary

The following section is quoted from the Executive Summary. The committee recognized the overwhelming need for financial graphic standards. They also recognized that there was sufficient material in the official literature to support a set of financial graphic standards if they were researched properly. The Executive Summary repeats the conclusion of SECTION Six of the report. Among other suggestions, the Committee emphasizes the need for formal studies by professional groups to operationalize financial graphic standards. The Committee foresight understood and saw the implications of the computer graphic revolution we are all experiencing.

Section 1—Executive Summary

The summary of this report can best be described by the final three paragraphs of Section 6 "FINANCIAL GRAPHIC STANDARDS—A MYTH OR REALITY."

Conclusion and Suggestions for Future Work

At this time, the profession has not yet addressed the need for accounting financial graphics standards. Therefore, the standards are more a myth than a reality, or an unfulfilled need. The boards must set the standards, not the market or the graphic artist. The market, if this is not done, will eventually de facto determine these standards. Indeed, existing hardware and software already constrain the use of graphical presentations, at the same time that they provide a tremendous advance over hand-prepared graphics.

The first, and probably the most essential step in this direction, is the recognition by the profession of the need for graphical accounting standards and guidelines. Once such a need is realized, the profession should set up commissions and/or committees who will study in more depth the issues that have been raised above, as well as other aspects of the problem, such as the legal and professional liability that is related to form and format of accountants' reports. Such study, in turn, will hopefully lead to development and adoption of the appropriate standards by the profession, such as those presented in this article:

But the time is short, and particularly in face of the very rapid, and even revolutionary developments in the computer graphic hardware and software facilities. Thus it is essential that the required steps as outlined above will be taken as soon as possible. And when this happens we will be able to claim that "we came, we (graphically) saw and we conquered"—"Veni, Vidi, Vici." (P. 65)

These conclusions are supported by each of the sections of this report.[1]

Section 2—A Summary of the Accountant's Responsibility in the Presentation and Use of Graphs in Financial Reporting

This summary section highlights the complete literature review performed by committee members of the then current official pronouncements regarding statement presentations:

---

[1] *Financial Graphics—Communications for the 1990's—The Need For Financial Graphic Standards;* The Illinois CPA Society, p. 2 (1988).

A. The overall search for relevant IRS, SEC, FASB, and AICPA pronouncements.

B. An Accountant's Liability to Form/Format of Statements, AICPA pronouncements.

C. An Accountant's Liability to Form/Format of Statements, SEC pronouncements.

The formal statements include comments regrading graphic representations and the accountant's responsibility. The following quotes were taken from the summary and are indicative of the material presented and the conclusions of the committee.

Four paragraphs from Section 2 are presented here as support for the need for financial graphic standards.

> The accounting profession recognizes the value and importance of presentation form and format. The accounting form/format issues, though are related most to the (textual and numerical) format of financial statements. SAS number 8 states, however, that "the auditor . . . should read *other information* (in financial statements) and consider whether such information, or the *manner of its presentation* is materially inconsistent with information appearing in the financial statements."

> While specific financial graphical standards have not yet been specified by the profession, the Security and Exchange Commission issued several rules that relate graphical representation of financial data to Rule 14a-3 of the General Rules under the Securities Exchange Act. Negligence in graphical presentation by professionals was also deemed a cause for monetary damages by the courts, e.g., as was the case in Moyer vs. Graham, the Florida Supreme Court, 285 So. 2d at 399, 1973.

> It is also worth noting that the proposed new SAS will considerably broaden the auditor's responsibility, and require improved auditor reporting and communication. The new auditor's report states that 'reasonable assurance regarding the (audit) evaluation is achieved . . . *by assessing the appropriateness of the overall financial statement presentation.*' (P. 5, paragraphs 5–8)

The following material is considered one paragraph, but was broken into subparagraphs for ease of presentation. The import of this section cannot be overemphasized, for as early as 1979, the SEC recognized the accountant's and auditor's potential liability for the ". . . form and format of financial statements . . ."

> Accountant's and auditor's potential liability as to form and format of financial statements as expressed by the Security and Exchange Commission rulings:

> "Accounting Series Release (ARN) No. 268 of July 27, 1979 states—'would also apply to any financial information such as tables, charts, graphic illustrations and ratios presented in annual reports to shareholders —.'

> And, ASR No. 279 of September 2, 1980 (Any pictorial or graphic representations shall comply with the provisions of Guide 8 of the guides for Preparation and Filing of Registration Statements' (Securities Act Release No. 5171 (July 20, 1970))"

> The above SEC pronouncements strongly tie in graphic representations to financial statement presentations and thus require CPA's to be very much aware of accurate overall presentation of all financial data. (P. 5, 2nd column, paragraph 3)

Section 3—A Study of the Use of Financial Graphics in the Annual Reports of the Fortune 500

Committee members performed an extensive survey on the use of financial graphics in the annual reports of the Fortune 500. The study was a statistical sample of the Fortune 500, accurate with regard to size and industry. The Committee received 375 responses with 499 annual reports. Each report was analyzed for graphic content, and the results were recorded on the questionnaire shown in the report. The results were analyzed and reported in Section 3 of the Illinois report. The results included in Section 3 are in four sections.

I. Summary. This section defines the study and summarizes the major findings. The Survey design is summarized and the numerical responses are reported. Each of the sections supports the need for financial graphic standards as concluded by the following paragraphs. The following paragraphs are from Section 1—Summary.

I. B. Charts and Standards Used in Annual Reports

"The survey clearly demonstrated a preference for relatively simple graphical formats: time series and simple bar charts are the preferred type of charts, followed (though not closely) by stacked bar charts. Pie charts are a remote third, while special financial graphs that are mentioned in the enclosed report are still not used.

"The survey demonstrated that there is no clear, or accepted, standard for clarity of presentation and graphical legend. At the same time, there seem to exist some "de facto" standards, all related to simplicity of presentations. Similar "de facto" standards, that agree with our recommendations in the enclosed report, exist for pie charts, time series, and simple bar charts. The result for stacked bar charts are unclear, and such charts are more rarely used.

"Graphical presentation is not confined to financial results of the current year. Rather, many graphs present multi-year selected data, but few take any serious effort to compare the overall financial results in different years. The presentation of financial data is an area where the special financial reporting graphs, described in the enclosed report, can be particularly useful."

I. C. Graphic Presentation is an Art

"The survey's results suggest that graphical presentation is currently an art, performed by an artist, rather than a formal accounting presentation with specific guidelines and standards. This result is reflected in the attention to form, rather than to financial substance, clarity and legibility.

"We found that the graphical presentation was informative, but not overwhelmingly so. The graphics presentation differentiates between financial reporting and presentation of other information, enhances the value of transferred information, and improves the quality of presentation of the financial reports. Furthermore, it seems that the evaluation and perception of graphical presentation by different reviewers is quite uniform and similar. All of these observations point to the value of charts and graphics."

I. D. Summary. The summary calls for a commission to be formed to research and define the financial graphic standards. (P. 8, begins with paragraph 6)

II. The Financial Annual Reports Survey. This section clearly defines the details of the survey methodology and the results therefrom.

A. The Methodology of the Study—the details of the research methodology.
B. The Survey Form—a detailed description of the survey form and the questions included.
C. Sections 2 and 3: General Characteristics Applicable to All Charts. Describes the general characteristics of all the charts recorded in the survey.
D. Sections 4 through 6: Characteristics of Specific Types of Charts. Specifically identifies each of the chart types and the characteristics of those charts.

E. Section 7: The Graphic Impression of the Whole Financial Report. This section deals with the "impression" the report makes on the reader. The methods used to assure reasonable objectivity are included in the discussion.

F. Section 8: Financial Reporting. Describes what financial data was described using the graphics.

III. Analysis of Survey Results. This section provides the numerical results of the survey as described in the following outline.

A. General Discussion—Scope and Included Questions

B. Statistical Summary of Results—Format of Presentation

C. Summary and Analysis of Results

IV. References. This section provides the references used to develop the methodology.

Section 4—A Brief Review of the Classic Articles in Graphic Research

Section 2 concentrates on the official statements regrading the accountant's and auditor's responsibilities in the form and format of the financial statements. Section 4 concentrates on the classical research in how humans respond to the use of graphics to display numbers. This section is, by nature, a summary of the work performed, and Dr. Frownfelter's work (Chapter 3) is a most conclusive presentation of graphic effectiveness for business information.

A Brief Review of the Classic Articles in Graphic Research. Research should also look for the effects of training on the user's ability to use graphics. Given the increasing use of graphics by management, it would be helpful to know how much and what type of training is most effective (and least costly) in helping users reach their maximum utility in the use of graphics. Section 4 provides us with a historical review of the classical articles in graphic research. Two specific conclusions can be reached from this brief summary.

1) The form of the graphics used to present financial information is absolutely essential to the clear understanding of financial data.

2) Training the users how to use graphics in the presentation of financial information is essential to understanding. This is no different than it is in the presentation of tabular statements. In both cases there is no "intuitive" understanding of the financial presentations. Therefore, the profession is obligated to create standards and help establish the process by which the training will become effective. (PP. 36–37)

Section 5—The Impact of Computer Technology on the Use of Graphics

This section is the result of several members researching the futurist literature to establish how computers will affect the practice of accounting, with special emphasis on the graphic capability of the emerging computers. The interesting part of this chapter is that the papers accurately predicted what is occurring.

Section 5 describes the impact of computer technology on the use of graphics. The most important quote in the section is: "The printing press is to the alphabet as the microcomputer is to graphic presentation" (P. 40, paragraph 2).

The rest of Section 5 develops the following premise: As the printing press forced standards in the use and presentation of type fonts in printing, the unbridled power of the micro computer will force the standards of financial graphic presentation. The alternative is chaos.

Section 6—Financial Graphic Standards—A Myth or Reality, the Committee's Description of the Need for Financial Graphic Standards

Section 6 is a complete position paper that establishes the committee's representation of the financial graphic standards proposed by the committee. The majority of the information was reproduced (with permission) from an earlier edition of my book; see Chapter 6 in the original text. This section was designed to act as a foundation and directory for future study.[2]

4.7 USING RATIOS AND GRAPHICS IN FINANCIAL REPORTING, THE CANADIAN INSTITUTE OF CHARTERED ACCOUNTANTS, 1993 (New)

Introduction

The Canadian Institute of Chartered Accountants (CICA) has taken a giant step forward as the first national accounting association to step up to the task of formally recommending that the accounting profession establish financial graphic standards. The CICA has been most gracious in allowing me to quote the following: their conclusion regarding the need for financial graphic standards; their conclusions from the three graphic chapters (Chapters 5, 6, and 7) that describe their work and their conclusions regarding the presentation of financial information in graphic form; three of the graphic exhibits that show how the annual reports originally displayed the data and how the research committee recommended the data should be shown; and a brief outline of the graphic section of the report.

It is not possible in a limited review of such a comprehensive report to provide the full flavor and import of all the material they have produced. The only way to understand properly the power of the information they have reported is to read the report. The reports are available from:

The Canadian Institute of Chartered Accountants
277 Wellington Street West
Toronto, Ontario
Canada, M5V 3H2
Phone: (416) 977-3222
Fax: (416) 977-8585

The following quote is so important, it is moved to the front of this summary. It is found in Chapter 7, starting with the third MAJOR heading.

---

[2] Ibid, pp. 2–3.

NEED FOR GENERAL STANDARDS ON FINANCIAL GRAPHICS

"The efficacy, the credibility and the raison d'être of financial reporting is based on the fact that financial statements are prepared according to strict standards which allow the trained eye to make accurate comparisons either from one year to the next, or between one company and another. Without these standards, comparisons would be confusing, if not impossible.

"Standards are usually the hallmark of a mature and stable technology. Interactive computer graphics, in spite of impressive growth and major technological gains over the past several years, is neither. Yet, it is a vehicle used in communicating financial information that is becoming more widespread in company annual reports every year.

"Graphical presentation is an area of financial reporting which, so far, has not been considered by the authoritative accounting bodies, but which in the foreseeable future will revolutionize the way in which financial information is communicated. At the present, however, there are no "standards" for preparing graphics. Even within companies, the "standards" vary from year to year. The absence of "standards" or guidelines for preparing graphics means there is significant potential for misleading representations as evidenced by the discussion in Chapter 6 of this Report. The need for such guidelines is clear and has also been raised in a number of US surveys[1] and, more recently, in a UK survey.[2] The Study Group maintains, therefore, that the CICA's Accounting Standards Board should consider the desirability of issuing Accounting Guidelines to standardize financial reporting practices regarding the preparation and presentation of financial graphics."[3]

The following general outline, discussion, and chapter conclusions provide an overall picture of the immense work performed by the CICA committee. I made no attempt to summarize the material, for that would not be within the spirit of their support of my work. Rather, I have tried to provide briefly what the reader can expect to find in the report when they obtain their copy.

---

[1] Further discussion of the need for general standards on graphics is set out in the following materials: P.J. Steinbart, "The Auditor's Responsibility for the Accuracy of Graphs in Annual Reports: Some Evidence of the Need for Additional Guidance," *Accounting Horizons* (September 1989) pp. 60–70; Illinois CPA Society, *Financial Graphics— Communications for the 1990's: The Need For Financial Graphic Standards* (1988); I. M. Jarett and Y. Babad, "Guidelines and Standards for Accounting Graphics," *Journal of Accounting and EDP* (Summer 1988) pp. 4–14; B.J. Taylor and L.K. Anderson, "Misleading Graphs: Guidelines for the Accountant," *Journal of Accountancy* (October 1986) pp. 126–135; J.R. Johnson, R.R. Rice, and R.A. Roemmich, "Pictures That Lie: The Abuse of Graphs in Annual Reports," *Management Accounting* (October 1980) pp. 50–56.

[2] Refer to V.A. Beattie and M.J. Jones, *The Communication of Information Using Graphs in Corporate Annual Reports*, Research Report 31 (London: Chartered Association of Certified Accountants, 1992). The survey findings are discussed in several articles, including: "The Use and Abuse of Graphics in Annual Reports: A Theoretical Framework and Empirical Study," *Accounting and Business Research* (Autumn 1992); "Graphic Accounts," *Certified Accountant* (UK) (September 1992) p. 101.

[3] The Canadian Institute of Chartered Accountants, *Using Ratios and Graphics in Financial Reporting,* Research Report (October 1993) pp. 3, 4, and 7.

USING RATIOS AND GRAPHICS
IN FINANCIAL REPORTING

RESEARCH REPORT
(Final Text - June 1993)

Canadian Institute of Chartered Accountants

Chapter 5: Graphical Presentations in Financial Reporting

The advantage proposed by this method is not that of giving a more accurate
statement than by figures, but it is to give a more simple and permanent idea
of the gradual progress and comparative amounts, at different periods,
by presenting to the eye a figure, the proportions of which correspond
with the amount of the sums intended to be expressed.
William Playfair[4]

Introduction
The three chapters on Graphics are a part of the Institute's report on Ratios and
Graphics. The introduction to this section of the report defines the overall struc-
ture of the three chapters.

The Role of Graphics in Financial Reporting
This is one of the major sections of the report, for it sets the foundation for the
rest of the study. The section sets the rationale for using graphics to enhance the
transfer of information. They narrow the discussion to the use of graphics in
financial presentations. Throughout this chapter and the other two chapters, the
critical statements are footnoted with appropriate references to guide the user to
more details if required. The document is a model of research reporting.

Benefits of Graphics—This section defines why and how graphics are useful
in transferring information, and is broken into seven specific areas where graphics can help. Each subsection defines the potential benefit to utilizing the appropriate graphics.

Limitations of Graphics—This section is the counterbalance to the previous
section and defines the limitations of graphics. The potential drawbacks are listed
and described.

Current Practice in Canada
This section of Chapter 5 describes the purpose of the company survey and the
numerical results. The purpose of the survey is to describe the current reporting
practices in Canada, and the specific objectives are defined for the reader. The
survey is similar to the Illinois CPA Society survey reported in Section 4.6 of this
supplement. The remainder of this section is broken into the following results categories. Each section is supported with tables and charts where appropriate. The
reader will find a clear and concise result. The headings used are self-
explanatory. The detailed results of the survey are contained in Appendix D,
Current Practice on Graphics.

Overview of Findings
Type and Frequency of Graphics

---

[4] Stated by William Playfair, *The Commercial and Political Atlas* (London: J. Wallis, Third
Edition, 1801) pp. ix–x. Playfair single-handedly invented most of the forms of the statistical
graphic repertoire used today, including the bar chart, line chart, surface chart, and pie chart.

Location of Graphics in the Annual Report
Nature of Information in Graphics
Information on Financial Ratios
Colours Used in Graphics

Literature Review

The literature search is a short summary defining the work performed. The details of the material searched is evident throughout the three chapters with endnotes supporting the critical statements. The list of materials included in the end of each chapter is impressive and covers a wide range of topics, including research into how graphics are used in decision making, financial graphic presentations and other relevant studies.

Conclusion

This chapter reviewed the role of graphics in financial reporting, including their benefits and limitations. In the Study Group's view, graphics are an effective communication technique because they are easily understood by both financial and nonfinancial readers. Graphics are also a useful and flexible medium for explaining, interpreting, and analyzing numerical facts. They make possible the presentation of quantitative data in a simple and effective manner, facilitate comparison of specific items, and reveal trends and relationships. They can also be misleading, however.

Current practices of 200 Canadian public companies were surveyed, with the results indicating that the vast majority of companies now include graphics throughout their annual reports to shareholders. A review of the current literature completed the chapter. In this regard, the Study Group maintains that, through a systematic program of research, substantial understanding of the role of graphics in decision-making can be achieved. Priorities with regard to research endeavors are difficult to establish, but a central issue should be to identify specific contexts in which certain kinds of graphics may be most useful to decision-makers.

In conclusion, this chapter has examined the role of graphics in financial reporting, current practices in Canada and the research literature. Together, they provide the context for using graphical presentations in financial reporting. In the next chapter, the Study Group takes a look at the graphical display of financial information and, in particular, how chart graphics can be potentially misleading.

Chapter 6: Displaying Financial Information Graphically

Introduction

As in all three chapters, the introduction defines what each section in the chapter is designed to present.

Impact of Information Technology

This section clearly outlines technology's present and future role in the use of graphics by accountants. The committee is clear in their understanding that the technology must not override the sound judgment of the accountant.

Basic Form of Graphics

Graphical Presentation Alternatives

This section defines the graphics that are available and differentiates between graphics and financial graphics. Examples are used with complete descriptions, showing acceptable uses of the various graphic formats and the types of information they best describe. The following categories of charts were defined:

Chart Graphics
Financial Statement Graphics
Multivariate Graphics

Misleading Aspects of Chart Graphics

This section is one of the most powerful sections in the report. Selected graphs included in the annual reports collected for the survey are shown and critiqued. The committee presents alternative representations that would make the presentations more useful and eliminate potential misleading aspects of the presentations. Exhibits 6.11, 6.14, and 6.17 taken directly from the report are self-explanatory.

Conclusion

This chapter assessed the impact of information technology on the graphical display of financial information. The Study Group noted that computer graphics systems now provide an opportunity to more effectively and efficiently communicate financial information to users. An integrated software package and a few days of practice on a microcomputer can produce business graphics that would have been astounding a few years ago. Nevertheless, the proper use of such sophisticated software requires at least a fundamental knowledge of the basic form of graphics, the various graphical presentation alternatives, and the potentially misleading aspects of financial graphics.

Presentation alternatives include chart graphics, financial statement graphics, and schematic faces. Generally, chart graphics are used to analyze and interpret selected items of financial data, such as sales or earnings, while financial statement graphics portray the financial statements themselves. In contrast, schematic faces can be an efficient means of portraying multivariate data, such as a series of financial ratios.

Based on an evaluation of chart graphics included in 1991/1992 Canadian annual reports, the Study Group identified and discussed many ways in which graphics can potentially mislead the reader. A number of examples, drawn from these reports, were used to illustrate significant concerns related to improperly drawn graphs that can easily misrepresent the underlying financial data. In the Study Group's view, preparers would benefit from an orderly approach to preparing financial graphics. This is discussed further in Chapter 7.

Chapter 7: Preparing Graphical Presentations

Introduction

Defines the structure of this chapter and the objectives.

Communicating Useful Information

In Chapter 4, Exhibit 4.1 of this CICA study, the committee defined how information becomes useful. The following criteria as defined in the previous chapter were expanded to include graphics.

Understandability
Relevance
Reliability
Comparability

Need for General Standards on Financial Graphics

This section is quoted in the beginning of this chapter.

Financial Highlights

Comments

- *overcomplicated chart — four types of data*
- multiple zero baselines
- multiple scales on vertical axis
- *order of time series is reversed*
- trendy 3–dimensional visual effects
- negative numbers obscure on data markers and scale
- *optical illusion caused by multiple zero baselines*

Revised Chart

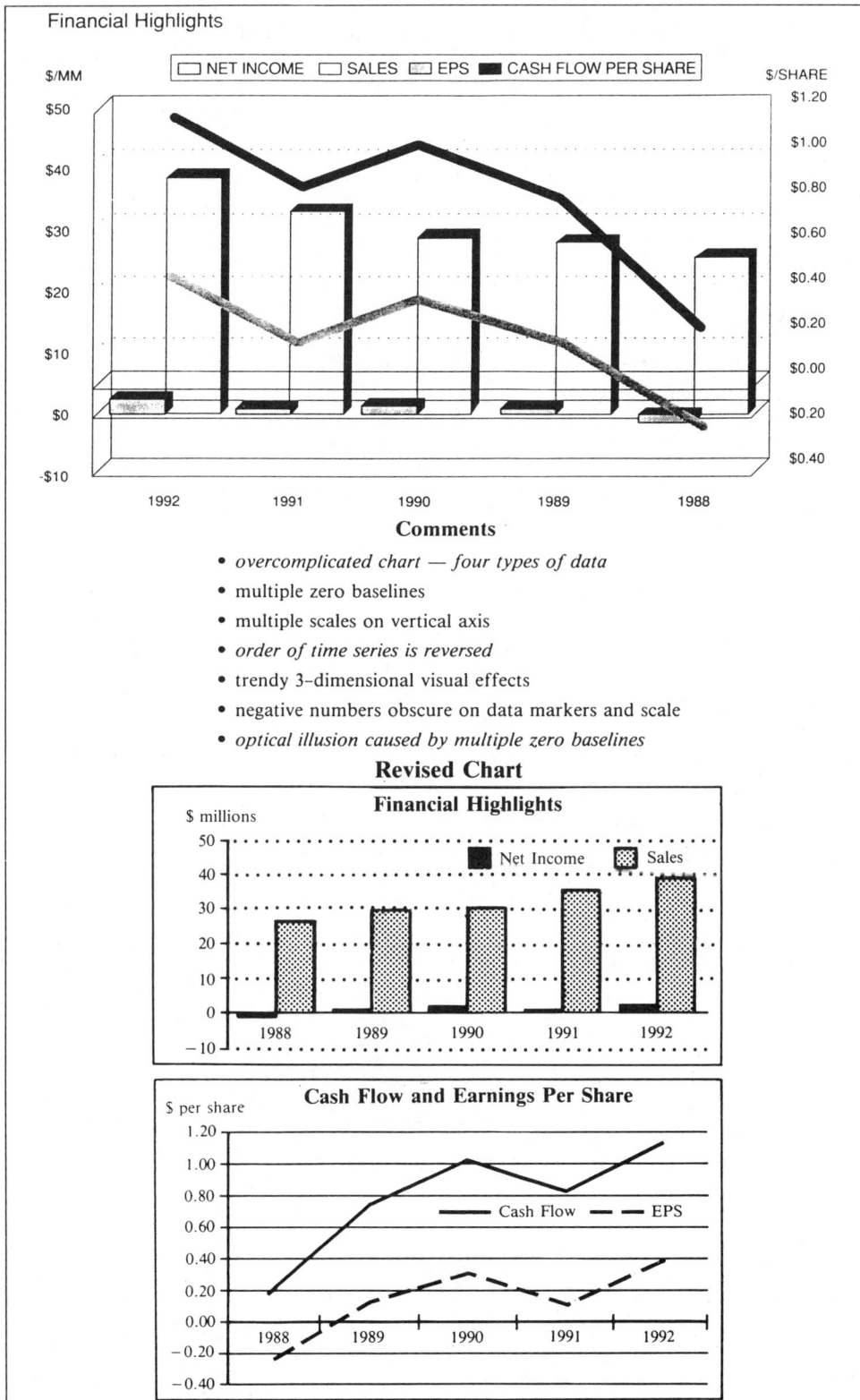

EXHIBIT 6.11   Financial Highlights and Cash Flow and Earnings Per Share
Adapted with permission from *Using Ratios and Graphics in Financial Reporting,* © 1993, The Canadian Institute of Chartered Accountants, Toronto, Canada.

Income (loss) from continuing operations
(millions of dollars)

Comments

- obtrusive background
- *overextended scale*
- *order of time series is reversed*
- trendy 3–dimensional visual effects

Revised Chart

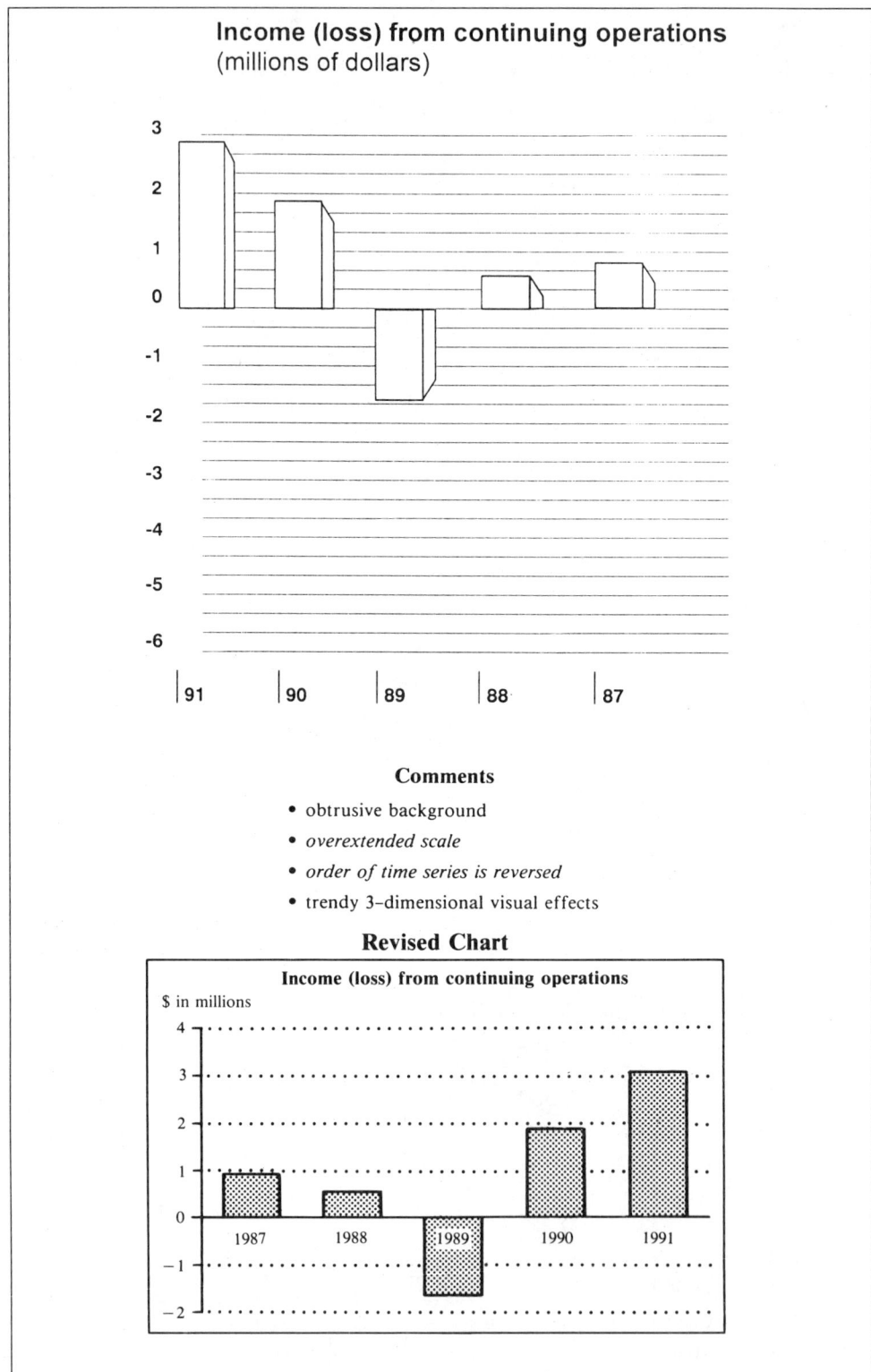

EXHIBIT 6.14   Income (Loss) from Continuing Operations

Adapted with permission from *Using Ratios and Graphics in Financial Reporting,* © 1993, The Canadian Institute of Chartered Accountants, Toronto, Canada.

Cash Surplus (Shortfall) before Financing Activities

$ in millions

887

389

217

113

(172)

87   88   89   90   91

Comments

- missing vertical and horizontal axes and gridlines
- missing zero baseline
- *1991 data marker does not begin at zero baseline*
- *optical illusion caused by shadows*
- trendy visual effects using pictorial symbols
- negative numbers obscure

Revised Chart

Cash Surplus (Shortfall) before Financing Activities

$ in millions

```
900                  887
800
700
600
500
400                         389
300
200   217
100                                113
  0
-100                                            1991
-200                                            -172
      1987    1988    1989    1990    1991
```

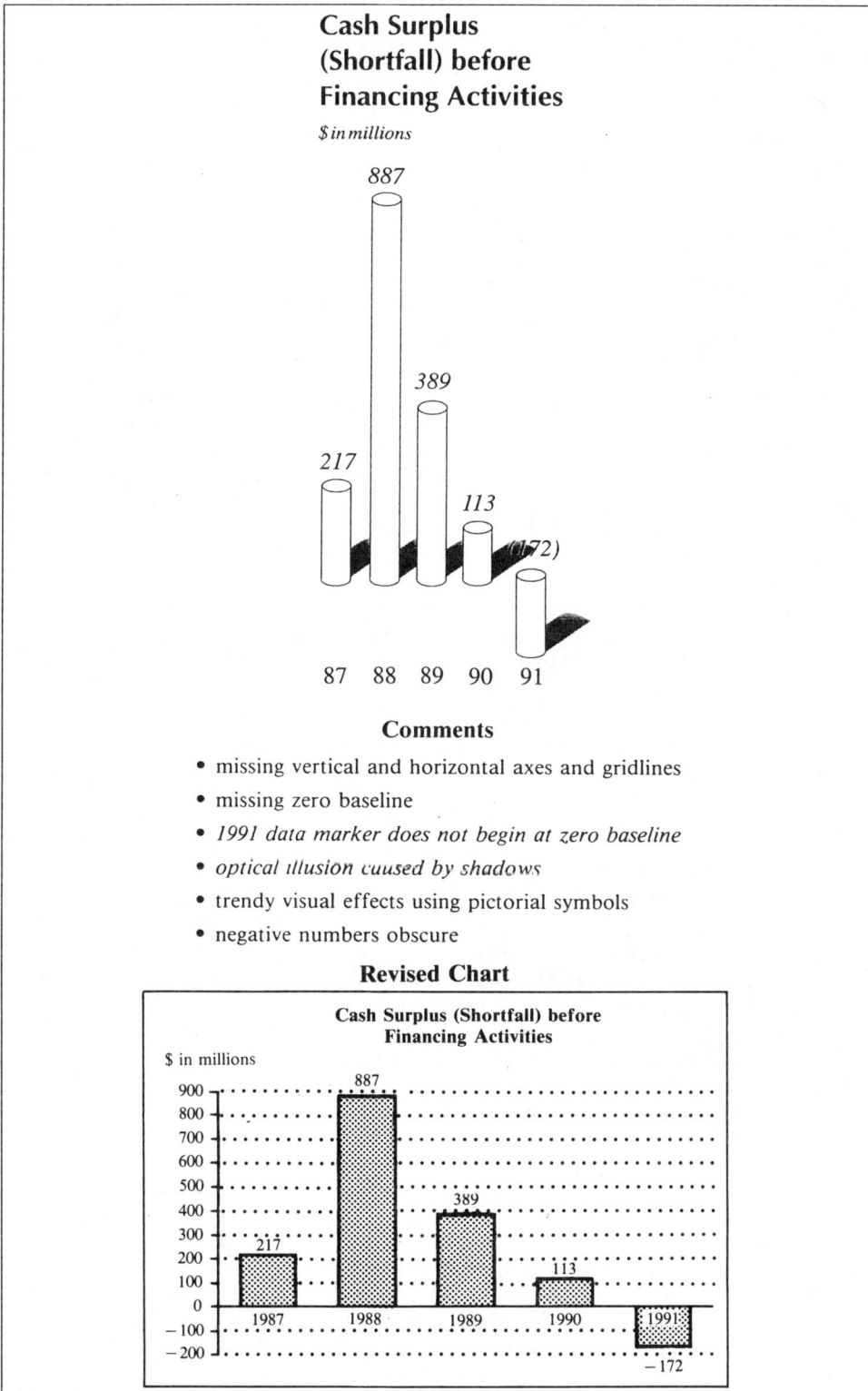

EXHIBIT 6.17   Cash Surplus (Shortfall) before Financing Activities

Adapted with permission from *Using Ratios and Graphics in Financial Reporting,* © 1993, The Canadian Institute of Chartered Accountants, Toronto, Canada.

Preparing Financial Graphics

This section puts the responsibility for the appropriate graphic presentation of financial information on the individual preparing the graphics. They provide a clear plan of action with lists of positive and negative aspects of each chart type. Decision trees are provided to assist the accountant in the selection process. The following subsections are self-explanatory and basically describe the graphic design process.

Determine the Message to be Conveyed
Select an Appropriate Chart Form
Design and Construct the Chart

Conclusion

This chapter discussed how graphics can be used to communicate financial information effectively and examined the characteristics that make such information useful—understandability, relevance, reliability and comparability. The chapter reiterated the need for general standards and presented a three step approach for preparing financial graphics.

The first step is to determine the message to be conveyed. In this regard, the Study Group cautions that too much information in a graphic makes it difficult for the reader to understand the message. Accordingly, the graphic must be kept simple, avoiding unnecessary detail, and the number of messages must be kept to a minimum.

The second step is to select an appropriate chart form. Here, the Study Group maintains that the form of the chart used to convey the message must be appropriate for the task at hand. Generally, column and surface charts are used to show variables over time, while bar and pie charts are used to show variables at a point in time. Surface charts are particularly suitable for showing change over an extended time period, such as ten years. The column chart can also be used for that purpose and for making comparisons over time. The bar chart can be used to compare items with one another to compare parts with the total. The pie chart can be used to show component relationships.

The final step is to draw the chart. The Study Group concludes that, if the message conveyed by the initial visual impression of the graphic is altered by a closer examination, then the design and construction of the chart is likely inadequate. Accordingly, the Study Group recommends that preparers follow the conventions set out in Exhibit 7.3 covering titles and labels, scales, spacing, shading and colour, and data display. Special care must be exercised when charting negative values.

The Study Group encourages the use of innovative graphics as a way of helping ordinary investors understand complex financial data. In this regard, graphical misrepresentation can be avoided if preparers are aware of the more common pitfalls and take a viewer's perspective when creating financial graphics. After all, if graphical presentations in annual reports do not accurately portray the underlying accounting numbers, they erode the reliability of financial statements and undermine the potential of graphs to communicate effectively.

Because graphics are widely used to convey financial information in interim and annual reports, and because there are significant deficiencies in this area of financial reporting, the Study Group concludes that the CICA's Accounting Standards Board should consider the desirability of issuing Accounting Guidelines to standardize financial reporting practices regarding the preparation and presentation of financial graphics. The above-noted proposals by the Study Group should help provide a focal point for the content of such guidelines.

Appendix D: Current Practice on Graphics

This Appendix describes the survey details. A series of tables summarizing and analyzing the results of the study are provided for the reader.

Appendix E: Literature Review on Misleading Graphics

This appendix describes the literature review on misleading graphics. The complete set of misleading factors and their source are summarized in a table of Graphic Design Factors/Criterion.

Appendix F: Graphical Presentation of Financial Statements

This Appendix describes and displays (with written permission) the five financial graphics that describe the financial statements in the body of this handbook.
   Balance sheet (See p. 84 in main body of handbook)
   Operating statement (See p. 116 in main body of handbook)
   Statement of cash flows (See p. 85 in main body of handbook)
   Changes in working capital (See p. 85 in main body of handbook)
   Statement of retained earnings (See p. 87 in main body of handbook)

4.8   REVIEW OF THE RESEARCH LITERATURE: GRAPHICS AS A PRESENTATION FORMAT FOR BUSINESS DECISION MAKING (New)

Cynthia A. Frownfelter, PhD, CPA

Introduction

Information technology can be used to enhance the communication of accounting information. With new capabilities available, the traditional boundaries set on accounting information presentation and content can be reassessed to determine a new direction for the profession as information providers. The communication of financial information, to decision makers, is continuously mentioned as a major objective of an accounting system. Communication has been defined as "an attempt to establish a commonness or a relationship between source and destination."[1] The principle focus of accounting should be the communication of information, about the firm, to decision makers in a manner that facilitates decisions. Even if users are assumed to be knowledgeable, information itself can have different degrees of comprehensibility. Communicating financial information that is useful to decisionmakers is the primary responsibility of the accounting profession. The purpose of this chapter is to provide an introduction and overview of the literature to date, which examines the effects of graphical presentation of accounting and financial information.

Prior Research

Research on graphics and graphical presentations is not new. There have been research studies conducted by different disciplines dating back to the 1920s.[2] Management scientists have only studied the effects of the presentation format of business information on decision makers for just over a decade. There

---

[1] See (Li, 1963).
[2] For example, see Eells (1926) and Von Huhn (1927).

has been practically no research on graphics in the accounting literature. The research studies in accounting, which have addressed the presentation of accounting information, have concentrated on comparing multidimensional graphics with more traditional tabular presentation.[3] There have been normative papers written on communication and communication theory in the accounting literature,[4] and some positive research effort devoted to information presentation in accounting, but even very little of this research has evaluated the presentation of accounting information, now provided, in light of recent technological changes.[5] Also, of these studies, few have looked at the issue of the communicative effectiveness of accounting report design.

The research that has been conducted in the management sciences area has examined the effect of presentation format of financial information on user decision accuracy and speed. Differing presentation methods have been evaluated in terms of the effect on the decisions made by users of the information. This type of research falls within the confines of Human Information Processing research (HIP). HIP research examines individual decision processing using information. It has its roots in cognitive psychology, economics, and statistics. The literature in this area is by its very nature, *interdisciplinary.*

General Findings of Prior Research

There are some general findings from the research. Two studies found that cognitive type moderates the relationship between report format and decision quality. Some researchers also found that task type moderates the relationship between report format and decision quality.[6] Significant learning effects were found among subjects using graphical formats. In addition, some preliminary evidence has been found on the efficacy of the paradigm of cognitive fit.[7] A review and analysis of the empirical research on the effects of modes and format of information presentation on decision making found five specific corresponding issues: (1) line graphs are superior to tables only when a task of medium complexity is performed; (2) for simple tasks, tables perform better; (3) line graphs are less effective, and bar charts are slightly better, than tables for information precision, especially for simple tasks; (4) Chernoff faces (pictics) are more relevant than tables; and (5) task acts as a moderator between line graphs and tables.[8] The conclusions found graphical presentation formats to be slightly better than the tabular presentation formats when evaluated in terms of information precision or accuracy. The face chart is better than the tabular representation when evaluated

---

[3] Although multidimensional graphics (Chernoff faces) may be an interesting research topic, it is unlikely that this type of graphics would be accepted widely for use in business.

[4] For example, see Lev (1969a, 1969b, 1970), Lee and Bedford (1969), Nakano (1972), Haried (1972), Ronen and Falk (1973), Abdel-khalik (1974), Babich (1975), Gorelik (1975), Belkaoui (1976, 1980) and Pendlebury (1980).

[5] Although much research has been performed in the 1980s, most of it has been performed by utilizing mainframe computers as opposed to microcomputers, which often contain more efficient and sometimes more powerful new graphics capabilities.

[6] See Lucas and Nielsen (1980), Dickson, DeSanctis, and McBride (1986), and Hard (1988).

[7] See Vessey and Galletta (1991).

[8] See Montazemi and Wang (1988).

in terms of information relevance. Task environment was found to act as a moderator between presentation format and decision accuracy and speed.

Synopsis of Prior Studies

There are two major types of studies in this area: studies that examine presentation formats across different tasks, and studies that examine them using one task. The earliest studies examined presentation format in a single-task environment. As the research proved to be conflicting and task was thought to moderate the presentation format-decision performance relationships, the studies moved to multitask settings. The single decision setting study allows the experimenter to control for task effects but is unable to provide information on the effects of presentation formats across task settings. The independent variables used in the single decision setting studies varied, but all included differing formats of presentation: graphical versus tabular (of some form). Other independent variables included: (1) mode of presentation: hard copy versus CRT; (2) decision style: using one of several tests;[9] (3) multicolor versus monocolor;[10] and (4) learning: several trials or time periods. Although decision time or speed was most often utilized as a dependent variable, one study limited the decision time and used it as an independent variable. Many dependent variables have been used to measure decision performance. Table 4.6.1 provides a listing of the dependent variables most often used.

TABLE 4.6.1   Major Dependent Variables in Graphics Research and the Rationale for Their Use (adapted from DeSanctis (1984))

Dependent Variable	Rationale
Interpretation accuracy	Data displayed in a graph should be understood correctly by the reader. This is a prerequisite to achieving any other positive outcome following the use of graphics as a decision aid.
Problem comprehension	Unlike a table, a graph has dimensionality. This provides the reader with a "different" and "better" perspective on the data. Understanding of the information in a display thus improves, and the user is more likely to identify problems when they exist.
Task performance	Because comprehension of data is better, performance on a task involving that data will tend to improve.
Decision quality	Because the user can better understand the problem, he or she is more likely to make a good decision when viewing a graph than when viewing a table.
Speed of comprehension	Graphs have a summarizing effect. They reduce information overload and can be processed faster by the brain than tables. A picture is worth a thousand words.

---

[9] For example, Lucas (1981) used analytic versus heuristic (measured by a test developed by Barkin), and Benbasat and Dexter (1985) used field-dependence versus field-independence (measured using the GEFT).

[10] See Harper and Hartman, 1992; Benbast and Dexter 1985, 1986; Benbasat, Dexter, and Todd 1986.

Dependent Variable	Rationale
Decision speed	Because information can be comprehended faster with a graph than with a table or narrative, the time required to make a decision will be reduced.
Memory for information (recognition and recall)	Graphs can be remembered better than tables because the spatial aspect of a graph provides additional information to a reader beyond the data itself. The information serves as a "cue" during recall.
Viewer preference	Users prefer graphs to tables or narratives. The spatial aspect of a graph makes it visually appealing. Special features, such as color, shading, realism, and complexity, can be added to a graph to make it even more appealing to the viewer.

Although each study utilized a single task, numerous tasks were examined across the studies. Many used simulated decision settings. One author constructed a case in which subjects had to decide how many cases of product to order each December. Another asked the question: Will graphical or tabular decision aids yield lower costs for a paint factory production scheduling problem? The subjects used also varied among the studies. Many studies used students while others used managers.

One author found results that suggest that the graphics groups developed a better understanding of the problem than the nongraphics groups. The best simulation value on the CRT was greater for the groups using graphics. Tabular groups on the hard copy printing terminal had the best performance scores in the experiment. The author concluded that this may have been due to the subjects' lack of experience with graphics and CRT terminals. Remus (1984) found the tabular displays generally yielded costs that were lower, although not significantly lower, than those of graphical displays.

Benbasat and Dexter (1986), in one of their studies, found that performance improvement over time was largest for multicolor graphical subjects over monocolor graphical subjects. No differences were found between graphical and tabular reports in terms of the quality of decision making. They concluded that for graphical reports to aid in decision making, they should be in a form to assist the task directly, not just a duplicate of the information contained in a tabular report.

Benbasat and Dexter (1986), in another study, which used time as an independent variable, found no differences in profit performance by information presentation in the 5 minute treatment. But there were statistically significant differences in the 15 minute treatment for decision performance. Subjects with graphical reports in the 15 minute treatment took less time than those with tabular reports. The authors suggested their results were due to the nature of the information displayed in a tabular report. A tabular report is considered a finer[11] information presentation than a graphical report. Even if a graph is in a form that directly supports the required problem-solving approach, it is expected that given enough time those using tabular reports will perform at least as well as those using

---

[11] Information is considered to be finer than other information if one set can be derived from the other but not vice versa.

graphical reports. Presentation formats are more likely to affect decision quality in terms of decision time than in terms of decision accuracy. The potential advantage to graphical presentation is reducing decision time. The authors concluded that a given presentation method is better than others only if it provides an important additional perspective leading to the solution of the task.

Benbasat, Dexter, and Todd's (1986) findings, reported in their study, indicate that graphical presentations are more useful when evaluating information in order to determine promising directions in the search for an optimal solution. When the task requires the determination of the exact discrete values for computational purposes, graphical reports are less useful than tabular reports.

Some of the single task studies showed advantages of graphical formats over the more traditional tabular formats. There were no consistent results found by all of the studies. The reasons for this are varied and will be examined later in the chapter. One of the primary issues was the moderating effect of task type on presentation format. Later studies examining the usefulness of differing presentation formats added task type or task setting as an independent variable. These studies allowed for information on the differing effects of information presentation across task settings. The independent variables did not vary significantly from those of single task studies; the main addition was of task type as a variable.

Dickson, DeSanctis, and McBride (1986) investigated the overall role of task environment in the use of graphics. This paper contains the results of three individual experiments. The primary difference in each experiment was the task type utilized. Each experiment used one task to test the impact of presentation format on decision performance. The tasks examined ranged from structured to unstructured. Results showed that for structured tasks, the use of graphical displays has the same effect on interpretation accuracy and decision quality as that observed when using traditional tabular reports. Users appeared to prefer tabular reporting (one with which they are familiar). In the moderately structured task they found that data presentation using graphics enhanced decision quality. In the unstructured task, tables were compared to graphs for their effects on the ability of decision makers to "get the message." The authors concluded that graphs showed an advantage over the tabular form for enhancing decision performance when a large amount of material was presented with interpretative uses. It was found that the effects of presentation formats are moderated by task complexity. Therefore it may not be appropriate to generalize about the superiority of a particular method of data presentation across task environments.

Hard (1988), in her dissertation, examined several task activities: (1) abstracting information, (2) recognizing relationships, (3) developing trends, and (4) making projections.[12] She found that for the abstraction of information task and the development of specific trends, decision quality was significantly better for subjects using tabular reports than those using graphical reports. In recognizing relationships, decision quality was not significantly different for subjects using either format. Decision quality was significantly better for subjects using graphical rather than tabular reports for developing general trends. The results of her research support the conclusion that the effectiveness of a subject's use of a report format changes as the task changes.

---

[12] These four tasks were modeled after the four subprocesses put forth by Einhorn and Hogarth (1981). The subprocesses were defined as: information acquisition, evaluation, action, and feedback.

Hwang (1990) also tested the moderating effects of task complexity and time pressure between graphics presentation and decision-making quality. The purpose of his research was to determine whether graphics enhance performance for decision makers under time pressure. He conducted a series of three experiments with varying task complexities. He defined task complexity as the number of variables processed for each task. Task content and task structure were also varied. In order to simulate time pressure, different time limits were imposed on task performance. His results indicated that graphical formats lead to better performance only in the medium complex task. As time pressure increased, performance generally decreased. However, deterioration in performance was only significant among subjects using the tabular format. In one instance, more time pressure led to significantly better performance among the subjects using graphics. Hwang concluded that graphical formats may be better than tabular formats when time pressure is high. He also determined that the advantage of graphical formats for tasks with intense time pressure suggests that time pressure may have an impact on task complexity.

Implications of Prior Research

Because this type of research and the technology supporting it is new, much of the research in the area has been atheoretical or exploratory. The conclusions reached by these studies have often been conflicting. Numerous studies conclude that graphical presentations are superior to tabular presentations. However, there are also many that conclude the opposite. Two primary reasons for conflicting results in the empirical research are: (1) lack of a theoretical base and (2) differences in measurements between studies. Prior research shows that task characteristics moderate or act with presentation characteristics to impact the user's (judge) decision performance. Research also provides some evidence that judge characteristics mediate the relationship between presentation and task characteristics.

Recommendations for Future Research

By examining the pieces of evidence obtained from prior research, it is possible to derive a basic theoretical framework portraying these relationships. Exhibit 4.6.1 illustrates these proposed theoretical relationships. In order to identify clearly the relationship between the presentation format and decision performance future financial graphics research has to match task to format (task characteristics to format characteristics) and has to control extraneous subject characteristics (judge characteristics). Each variable used in a research study should be strictly and carefully defined so that the presentation format-decision performance relationship can be isolated. There have been several specific problem areas identified in prior research. These include: (1) the use of poor graphical formats, (2) content differences between graphical and tabular formats, (3) uncontrolled task effects, (4) omitted correlated variables, (5) uncontrolled learning effects, (6) differing or subjective measures of decision quality, and (7) univariate tests of related dependent variables. Each of these will be discussed. Table 4.6.2 provides a summary and examples of these deficiencies from the prior research.

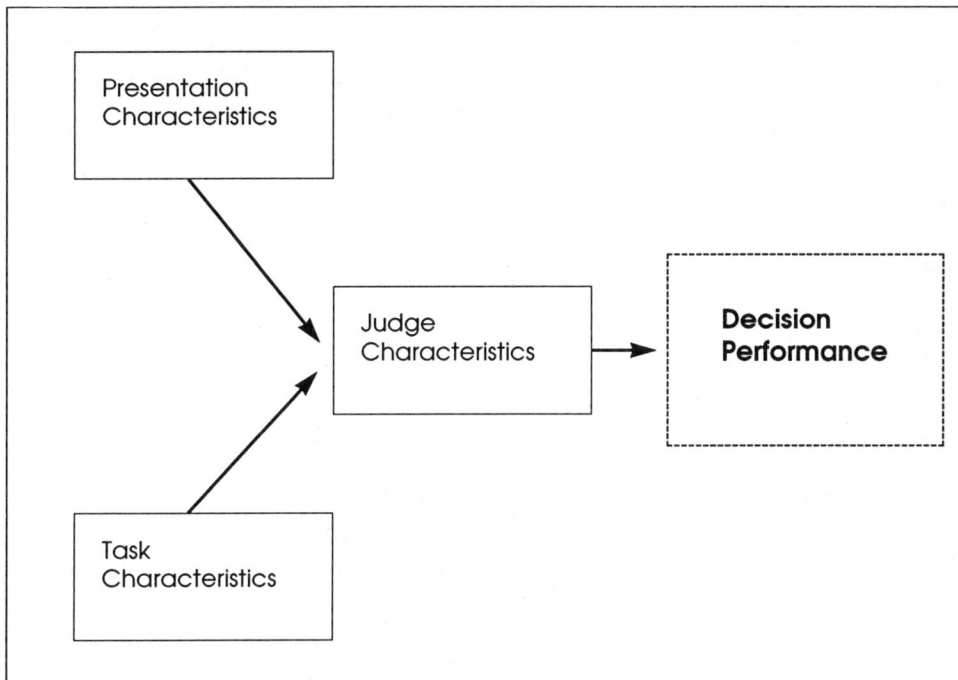

EXHIBIT 4.6.1 Theoretical Framework

TABLE 4.6.2 Summary and Examples of Methodological Deficiencies in the Presentation Format Literature

Methodological Problem
Internal validity issues
Poorly designed graphics
Lack of theoretical basis
Learning effects have not been properly controlled in some studies
Lack of a task classification scheme or taxonomy for this research
Content differences between presentation formats
Differing or unobjective measures of decision quality
Omitted Correlated Variables
Univariate tests of relevant dependent variables that measure decision quality
External validity issues
Lack of realistic tasks that are not generalizable outside of the experimental setting

Use of Poor Graphical Formats and Content Differences

One of the limitations of prior research has been that the graphical formats, used in some studies, may not have been good surrogates. A graphical format is not a good surrogate for research purposes if the graphics are of poor quality or do not follow standards for good graphics. Research examining differences in tabular and graphical presentation formats needs to be internally valid. Therefore, several precautions should be taken. First, the graphics developed should follow general guidelines for good graphics. Second, the graphics and tabular formats should be of the highest quality available. These two precautions should reduce the chances of confounding within the design of the study. Two studies in particular reported that the similarity between the graphical and tabular formats may have resulted in no significant differences being reported on subjects' decision quality. If the information given to the subjects differs in content, it will be impossible to separate format effects from information effects.

Due to the problems with research validity and the increasing use of graphics for the presentation of business information, recently there has been a call for standardization of presentation formats for financial data by graphics researchers and advocates. At present, there are no mandated standards for the creation and presentation of graphics in business. Several experts in the field of presentation graphics have outlined guidelines for the design of good graphics.[13] Graphical presentation guidelines will become increasingly important as graphics are used more often. There are few empirical studies that provide support for graphical guidelines. More are certainly needed.

Following general guidelines is important. It is also important to fit the type of graphs to the data being presented. A recent survey concluded that 75% of all business graphs were of time-series data. The most common forms of graphic presentation are: bar charts, line graphs, and pie charts. Anderson (1983) and Douglas and Beed (1986) judged the line graph and bar graph to be the most appropriate graphical presentation format for financial data. They further suggested that vertical columns best present values at a point in time and horizontal columns best present values over a time interval. At the present time, the only standard for comprehensive graphical financial statements has been developed by Jarett.

Uncontrolled Task Effects

It is also possible that the types of graphs presented were not appropriate for the task being tested. Hard suggests that different decisions require different formats. She recommends different formats be designed for specific tasks. Hard attempted to overcome some of the methodological deficiencies of prior research, specifically in the examination of presentation formats across tasks. Her study examined which subprocesses of a decision-task were supported by a particular presentation format. In her study, tasks were identified as subprocesses of the decision process. Therefore, her results may not be extendable to tasks, where more than one of these subprocesses is included. Her study was limited in that it did not provide evidence of which format was better for any overall decision-task, either simple or complex. While her approach may be appropriate for specific management tasks, general purpose financial statements are provided for a variety of decision-tasks. The one best format for all of these tasks has yet to be determined.

There has been little consensus among any of the researchers as to the definition of *task complexity.* Most researchers can agree on what components make up a task, but not on how to define task complexity. The components of a task are: the task acts, information cues, and the task product. Most definitions of task complexity are based on the task acts and the information cues needed to perform the task. Exhibit 4.6.2 is a graphical representation of the components of a task. While it is commonly accepted that the task affects the format and decision effectiveness relationship, the definition and measurement of task type or complexity has not been resolved. Although a taxonomy of tasks and their relationship to presentation formats would be the answer, this taxonomy has not yet been developed.

---

[13] See Jarett, (1983, 1985, 1993); and Tufte (1983) for good graphical guidelines.

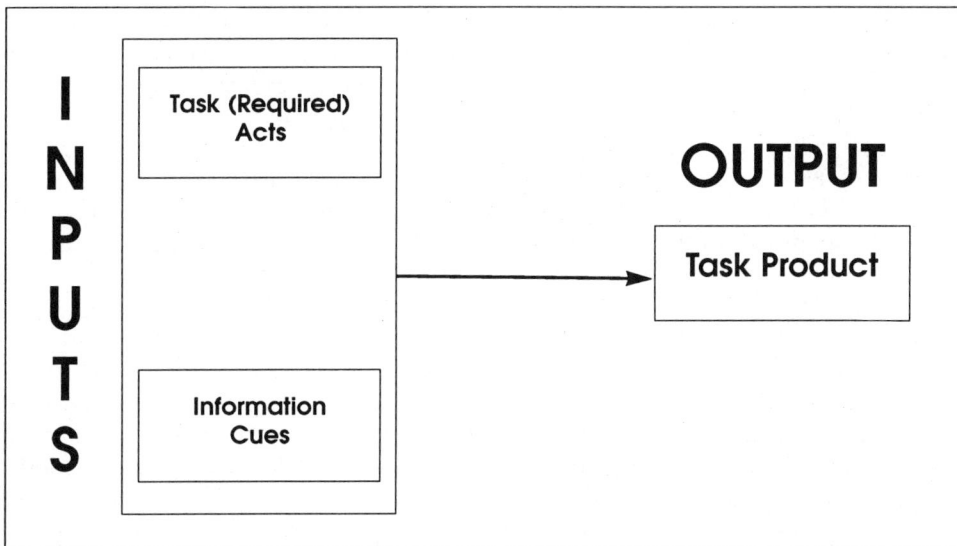

EXHIBIT 4.6.2   Components of a Task

Recently, there has been some theoretical development relating tasks to presentation format research. Vessey (1991) related task type directly to presentation format research. In her definitions of tasks and task categories, she relies on task acts as a foundation. Vessey concluded that if both the problem representation and the problem-solving task involve the same cognitive style, then there is a *cognitive fit* between them. Cognitive fit between the problem representation (presentation format) and the problem-solving task is "when the problem-solving aids (problem representation among them) support the task strategies required to perform that task."[14] This relationship is shown in Exhibit 4.6.3.

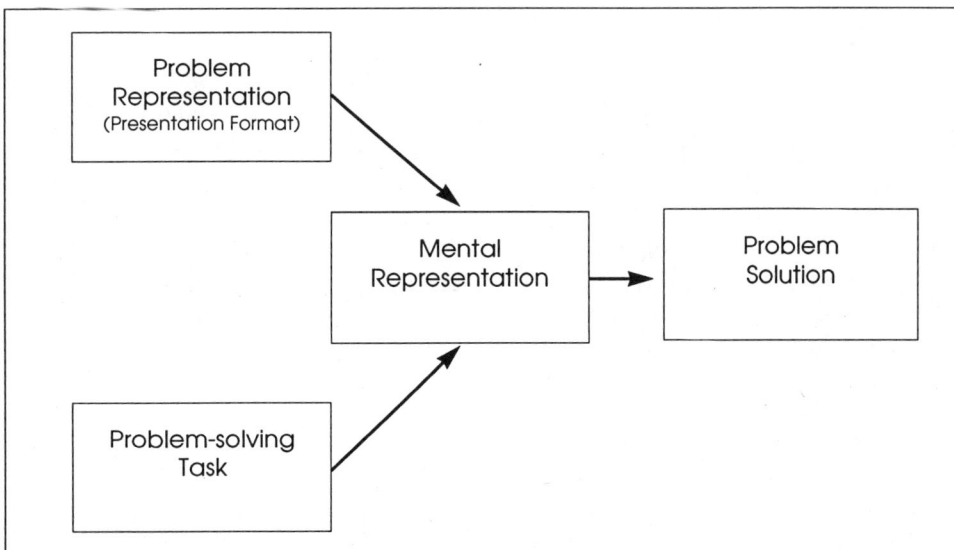

EXHIBIT 4.6.3   General Problem-Solving Model (adapted from Vessey (1991, p. 221))

_____

[14] Vessey, 1991, p. 220.

Vessey (1991) argued that the development of a link between presentation format and task characteristics would be difficult, if not impossible, due to the large numbers of characteristics and the many ways in which they have been described, in a traditional sense. Her solution to this problem was to move to a two-category classification based on cognitive style and task requirements. Both presentation format and tasks were broken down into two categories. She classified presentation format into two cognitive types: *spatial* and *symbolic.* Graphics are considered spatial problem representations, while tables are symbolic problem representations. She then divides tasks into two categories: (1) *elementary tasks* and (2) *decision-making tasks.* Elementary tasks require only one operation on the data. She states that these tasks are "principally information acquisition tasks and tasks involving comparison of two data values."[15] Decision-making tasks are "more complex tasks that may be decomposed into several subtasks."[16] Decision-making tasks are those tasks that usually involve judgment or inference and involve both information acquisition and information evaluation.[17] Both elementary tasks and decision tasks may be classified by the type of presentation that would best fit the task. Table 4.6.3 presents a matrix summarizing Vessey's relationship between presentation format, task categories, and task types.

Table 4.6.3 Matrix of Vessey's (1991) Task Types

Task Category	Task Type	
	Spatial	Symbolic
Elementary	Compare two data values	Extraction of a specific amount
	Compare trends	
	Assess relationships	
Decision-making	Combination of one or more elementary spatial tasks	Extraction and manipulation of one or more specific amounts
Presentation format type	Graphical	Tabular

Vessey's paradigm of "cognitive fit" has been examined for validity against past research.[18] Her theory was also validated using information acquisition tasks. Where decision-making tasks are involved, they must be broken down into subtasks to classify. These subtasks can be used to classify whether the task is of similar or dissimilar subtasks. Although neither of the problem representations will have a distinct advantage over the other concerning accuracy, graphical formats may allow for a quicker or less-timely decision. Bettman and Zins (1979) found differences in the time of performance but not accuracy. Vessey and Galletta (1991) suggest that decision makers adapt the time to complete a task while keeping accuracy constant.

---

[15] Ibid (p. 225).

[16] Ibid.

[17] Vessey (1991) limits the paradigm of cognitive fit to the elementary tasks and the simpler decision-making tasks. She refers to these task types as information acquisition and (simple) information evaluation tasks, respectively.

[18] The past studies used in this validation, for the most part, used information acquisition tasks.

Vessey and Galletta (1991) suggest that research be conducted using more complex problem-solving tasks.

> We should, . . ., concentrate on determining the characteristics of the tasks that problem solvers must address, and supporting those tasks with the appropriate problem representations and support tools.[19]

Jarvenpaa, Dickson, and DeSanctis (1988) call for a taxonomy of tasks that will provide a theoretical basis for the presentation format-task relationship.

> Future research efforts will keep producing contradictory results unless researchers develop some type of taxonomy of tasks and start interpreting the results within the taxonomy.[20]

Vessey and Galletta also conclude that the effectiveness of the format presentation must be considered in the context of the task to be performed.

Omitted Correlated Variables

Many studies have been oversimplified and have not controlled for many of the variables shown to have an effect on the format-decision relationship. Lusk (1973) and Remus (1984) were criticized for this. Remus included only presentation format as an independent variable. Many of the other variables such as cognitive style or task-related characteristics were omitted. Weick (1983) demonstrated that the increase in the complexity of communication has a differential impact on the ability of individuals to process the information. It is necessary to control for cognitive type in individual subjects, in order to avoid confounding effects in presentation format research. As such, it is widely recommended that cognitive style be used as a control measure. Cognitive style has been measured, in prior literature, using three distinct dimensions: cognitive complexity, analytic-heuristic,[21] and field independence dependence.[22, 23]

Much of the previous accounting research examining the impact of perceptual skill on decisions has used either field-independence or field-dependence. This classification provides a useful measurement dimension in predicting behavior. Specifically, it may allow researchers to measure a particular dimension of individual cognitive differences that is sensitive to accounting information. Field-dependence has shown consistency in its predictability and it has also been shown to be a useful dimension for use in accounting research. Many studies on information presentation in the management sciences have also used this classification.

---

[19] Vessey and Galletta (1991, p. 82).

[20] Ibid (p. 144).

[21] Cognitive complexity, field independence-dependence, and analytic-heuristic were the most important descriptions of cognitive style in this type of research via a survey in Lee's (1988) dissertation on presentation format frameworks.

[22] Bariff and Lusk (1978) provide an evaluation of all tests for cognitive style.

[23] "Field independence is the ability of an individual to arrive at a correct perception by ignoring interfering context. Field dependence is the inability to exclude irrelevant and misleading information when attempting to form an opinion." (Siegel and Ramanauskas-Marconi, 1989, p. 344) Field-dependent persons manage ambiguous information and problem situations better than field-independent persons. In addition, they tend to be more confident of their decisions than field-independent persons (pp. 344–345).

Uncontrolled Learning Effects

There has been evidence of a learning effect when using graphical presentation formats. The satisfaction and confidence ratings of graphics users improved over time, while they did not improve for the tabular users. This supported the conclusion of Schutz (1961), who reported that the time to complete a task improved for subjects using graphics presentations over several trials. Many studies have not controlled for this effect.

Differing or Unobjective Measures of Decision Performance

Objective measures of decision performance will perform best in the evaluation of presentation formats. Decision performance has typically been measured using two separate variables, *decision accuracy* and *decision speed.*

Decision accuracy is measured in many different ways. The differences in the measurement of decision accuracy across studies make comparisons of results difficult. Some of these have been: the magnitude of the errors, the percentage of correct responses, profit in a task, and consensus of opinion. Dickson, DeSanctis, and McBride (1986) measured accuracy in two ways: questions that measured "getting the message," and questions that measured interpretation accuracy. Other studies have measured accuracy in terms of profit.[24] Table 4.6.1 summarizes the major dependent variables, which have been used in graphics research.

While accuracy is an important measure in the quality of judgment decisions, there are cases for which the criterion for accuracy is unknown. In these cases, judgment consensus[25] has been used as a surrogate of judgment accuracy. Unfortunately, the research on consensus has provided mixed results. Recent research, which has examined the judgments of experts, has found consensus to be low.[26] Ashton's (1985) results indicate a consistent, highly positive correlation between consensus and accuracy. However, she cautions researchers from being overconfident that consensus is a surrogate for accuracy.

> . . . overconfidence in consensus as a surrogate for accuracy should be avoided. . . . it is conceivable that "all of the people could be wrong all of the time." Further, there is a possibility that an oddball genius, who does not agree with anyone else, could be proved correct. . . .[27]

She provides a conservative approach to using consensus as a surrogate for accuracy.

> If an individual's predictions agree strongly with those of others in a group, then that individual will tend to be among the most accurate in the group.[28]

[24] For example: Lucas and Nielsen (1980) and Benbasat and Dexter (1986).

[25] Judgment consensus is but one of three ways in which judgment agreement can be measured. The other two are stability and convergence. Consensus has been the most commonly used. See Ashton (1982) for a discussion of all three measures.

[26] See, for example: Hoffman, Slovic, and Rorer (1968), and Slovic, Fleissner, and Bauman (1972).

[27] Ashton (1985, p. 185).

[28] Ibid.

Murray and Regel (1992) reexamine Ashton. They used the data from Ashton's (1985) study to reanalyze her results. Their analysis was motivated by their concern that the construct consensus was not consistent with the underlying concept of consensus. They cite Webster for a definition of consensus. "Consensus refers to 'general agreement' or 'agreement across individuals using the same data.'[29]."[30] Therefore, consensus reflects the degree to which all the group members share a common judgment regarding a decision.

Consensus has been measured typically as the *mean pairwise correlation*. This measure is the average of all pairwise correlations between the decisions of all the possible subject pairs. Murray and Regel (1992) compared a group's accuracy and consensus across decisions. They used mean square error (MSE) as an indicator of accuracy. They calculate MSE as:

$$MSE_j = \sum_{i=1}^{n_j} (S_{ij} - Y_j)^2 / n_j$$

where: S_{ij} is subject i's prediction, based on case j information
          Y_j is the actual number.
          n_j is the number of subjects

Then MSE was decomposed into two parts: (1) the *variance* (VAR) and (2) the *bias* (BIAS). Both MSE and BIAS were used as accuracy measures. MSE is relevant if each individual's decision is implemented by the individual. BIAS is relevant if the group average decision is implemented.[31] Murray and Regel's (1992) empirical results show a positive association between VAR and MSE. They also show a positive association between VAR and BIAS, but only at quite high levels of consensus. The implications of Murray and Regel's results are very important in cases where a group's average judgment is used. "Only at very high consensus levels is consensus a valid proxy for accuracy."[32]

Interpretation accuracy is used frequently as a dependent variable in graphics research to surrogate for decision effectiveness/accuracy. The rationale for the use of interpretation accuracy is that it "is a prerequisite to correct problem comprehension and improved decision quality."[33] Interpretation accuracy is measured by computing correct responses to a general set of questions designed to assess the subjects' understanding of the material.

Conclusion

Many suggestions have been provided in the literature to improve the methodology used in these studies. There are two main issues. First, which types of graphics should be studied. In the past, each researcher chose a graphical representation that seemed to suit the purpose or one that was easily produced. This made it very difficult for research results to be compared across studies. If standards were adopted, researchers would be able to focus on one type or several types of

---

[29] Goldberg and Werts, 1966.

[30] Murray and Regel, 1992.

[31] Ibid, p. 137.

[32] Ibid.

[33] Jarvenpaa, Dickson, and DeSanctis (1985), p. 147.

graphs. Secondly, a task taxonomy or theory of tasks needs to be developed so that researchers may begin to construct theories to support the use of graphics for individual tasks. A summary of the other issues discussed in the form of guidelines for future research are:

1. Researchers should assure that their graphs and tables are of the highest quality available, use good graphical guidelines, and keep the content of the graphs and tables as consistent as possible.
2. Researchers should attempt to measure or control factors that are known from previous research to influence decision performance.
3. Learning effects should be controlled so as to avoid unwanted familiarity biases with tabular versus graphical presentation.

The findings and suggestions of prior research should be utilized to strengthen both the internal and external validity of any future study. In order to form a sound theoretical basis a priori predictions on all the major research variables should be made based on prior research. Table 4.6.4 summarizes the methodological problems identified in Table 4.6.2 and solutions provided for in the chapter discussion.

TABLE 4.6.4 Summary of Methodological Issues and Solutions in Graphical Presentation Research

Methodological Problem	Solutions to the Methodological Problem
Internal validity issues	
Poorly designed graphics	Use the highest quality graphics available and follow standards for good graphics found in Tuft (1983) and Jarett (1993).
Lack of theoretical basis	A priori predictions should be made based on prior research for all variables of interest.
Learning effects have not been properly controlled for in some studies.	Use of a repeated measures design to measure and control for learning effects.
Lack of a task classification scheme or taxonomy for this research.	At this time, there is no accepted task classification scheme. Future research should either test one of the existing classification schemes like Vessey (1991) or develop a testable task classification scheme.
Content differences between presentation formats	All formats should contain the exact information.
Differing or subjective measures of decision quality.	The measures of decision quality should be objective and chosen according to the qualities of the tasks to be performed.
Omitted correlated variables	Variables that have been shown to be significantly correlated in prior studies should be controlled.
External validity issues	
Lack of realistic tasks that are not generalizable outside of the experimental setting.	Tasks to be used should be designed in order to closely approximate real world tasks and decisions.

References

Abdel-khalik, A. R., "The Entropy Law, Accounting Data, and Relevance to Decision-Making," *The Accounting Review,* April 1974, pp. 271–283.

Anderson, Anker, *Graphing Financial Information—How Accountants Can Use Graphs to Communicate,* New York: National Association of Accountants, 1983.

Ashton, A. H., "Does Consensus Imply Accuracy in Accounting Studies of Decision Making," *The Accounting Review,* April 1985, pp. 174–185.

Bariff, M. L., and E. J. Lusk, "Designing Information Systems for Organizational Control: The Use of Psychological Tests," *Informational and Management,* Vol. 1, 1978, pp. 113–121.

Belkaoui, A, "The Entropy Law, Information Decomposition Measures and Corporate Takeover," *Journal of Business, Finance, and Accounting,* Autumn 1976, pp. 41–52.

Belkaoui, A, "The Interprofessional Linguistic Communication of Accounting Concepts: An Experiment in Sociolinguistics," *Journal of Accounting Research,* Autumn 1980, pp. 362–374.

Benbasat, Izak, and Albert S. Dexter, "An Experimental Evaluation of Graphical and Color-Enhanced Information Presentation," *Management Science,* Vol. 31, No. 11, 1985, pp. 1348–1364.

Benbasat, Izak, and Albert S. Dexter, "An Investigation of the Effectiveness of Color and Graphical Information Presentation Under Varying Time Constraints," *MIS Quarterly,* March 1986, pp. 59–81.

Benbasat, Izak, Albert S. Dexter, and Peter Todd, "The Influence of Color and Graphical Information Presentation in a Managerial Decision Simulation," *Human Computer Interaction,* Vol. 2, 1986, pp. 65–92.

Benbasat, Izak, and R. G. Schroeder, "An Experimental Investigation of Some MIS Design Variables," *MIS Quarterly,* Vol. 1, 1977, pp. 37–49.

Bettman, J. R., and M. Zins, "Information Format and Choice Task in Decision Making," *Journal of Consumer Research,* Vol. 6, September 1979, pp. 141–153.

Campbell, Donald J., "Task Complexity: A Review and Analysis," *Academy of Management Review,* Vol. 13, No. 1, 1988, pp. 40–52.

Davis, Donald Lamar, *An Experimental Investigation of the Form of Information Presentation, Psychological Type of the User, and Performance Within the Context of a Management Information System,* Unpublished Doctoral Dissertation, University of Florida, 1981.

DeSanctis, Gerardine, "Computer Graphics as Decision Aids: Directions for Research," *Decision Sciences,* Vol. 15, 1984, pp. 463–487.

DeSanctis, Gerardine, and S. L. Jarvenpaa, "An Investigation of the 'Tables versus Graphs' Controversy in a Learning Environment," In *Proceedings of the Sixth International Conference on Information Systems in Indianapolis, Indiana, December 16–18, 1985,* by Society of Information Management and The Institute of Management Sciences, 1985, pp. 134–144.

Dickson, Gary W., Gerardine DeSanctis, and D. J. McBride, "Understanding the Effectiveness of Computer Graphics for Decision Support: A Cumulative

Experimental Approach," *Communications of the ACM,* January 1986, pp. 40–47.

Douglas, P. P., and T. K. Beed, *Presenting Accounting Information to Management,* New York: National Association of Accountants, 1986.

Eells, W. C., "The Relative Merits of Circles and Bars for Representing Component Parts," *Journal of the American Statistical Association,* Vol. 21, 1926, pp. 119–132.

Ghani, J. A., and E. Lusk, "Human Information Processing Research: Its MIS Design Consequences," *Human Systems Management,* Spring 1982, 1981.

Goldberg, L. R., and C. Werts, "The Reliability of Clinicians' Judgments: A Multitrait-Multimethod Approach," *Journal of Consulting Psychology,* Vol. 30, 1966, pp. 199–206.

Gorelik, G., "On the Nature of Information," *International Journal of Accounting Education and Research,* Spring 1975, pp. 109–125.

Gul, Ferdinand A., "The Joint and Moderating Role of Personality and Cognitive Style on Decision Making," *The Accounting Review,* April 1984, pp. 264–275.

Hard, Nancy J., *Empirical Research of Decision-Making Effectiveness When Using Differing Presentation Formats Under Varying Decision Tasks,* Unpublished Doctoral Dissertation, University of North Texas, 1988.

Haried, A. A., "The Semantic Dimensions of Financial Statements," *Journal of Accounting Research,* Autumn 1972, pp. 376–391.

Harper Jr., Robert M., and Bart P. Hartman, "An Experimental Evaluation of the Effects of Learning on Alternative Display Formats of Accounting Information," *Proceedings of the American Accounting Association Western Region, Twenty-Seventh Annual Meeting,* April 30–May 2, 1992, pp. 64–71.

Hoffman, P. J., P. Slovic, and L. G. Rorer, "An Analysis-of-Variance Model for the Assessment of Configural Cue Utilization in Clinical Judgment," *Psychological Bulletin,* May 1968, pp. 338–349.

Huber, G., "Cognitive Styles as a Basis for the Design of DSS and MIS: Much Ado about Nothing?," *Management Science,* May 1983, Vol. 29, No. 3, pp. 567–579.

Hwang, Mark I., *An Investigation of the Effects of Presentation Format and Time Pressure on Decision-Makers Performing Tasks of Varying Complexities,* Unpublished Doctoral Dissertation, University of North Texas, 1990.

Ives, Blake, "Graphical User Interfaces for Business Information Systems," *MIS Quarterly,* Special Issue, 1982, pp. 15–47.

Jarett, Irwin M., *Computer Graphics and Reporting Financial Data,* New York: John Wiley and Sons, Inc., 1983.

Jarett, Irwin M., *Computer Graphics and Reporting Financial Data,* New York: John Wiley and Sons, Inc., 1987.

Jarett, Irwin M., *Computer Graphics and Reporting Financial Data,* New York: John Wiley and Sons, Inc., 1993.

Jarvenpaa, S. L., G. W. Dickson, and G. DeSanctis, "Methodological Issues in Experimental IS Research," *MIS Quarterly,* Vol. 9, No. 2, 1985, pp. 141–156.

Lee, Jong-Sung, *State of Development of Experimental Research on the Mode of Presentation in Management Information Systems,* Unpublished Doctoral Dissertation, University of Mississippi, August 1988.

Lee, L. C., and N. M. Bedford, "An Information Theory Analysis of the Accounting Process," *The Accounting Review,* April 1969, pp. 256–275.

Lev, Baruch, *Accounting & Information Theory Studies in Accounting Research #2,* Sarasota, FL: American Accounting Association, 1969a.

Lev, Baruch, "An Information Theory Analysis of Budget Variances," *The Accounting Review*, October 1969b, pp. 704–710.

Lev, Baruch, "The Informational Approach to Aggregation in Financial Statements: Extensions," *Journal of Accounting Research,* Spring 1970, pp. 78–94.

Li, David H., "The Semantic Aspect of Communication Theory and Accountancy," *Journal of Accounting Research,* Spring 1963, pp. 102–107.

Lucas, Henry C., "An Experimental Investigation of the Use of Computer-Based Graphics in Decision Making," *Management Science,* July 1981, pp. 757–768.

Lucas, H.C., and N. R. Nielsen, "Impact of the Mode of Information Presentation on Learning and Performance," *Management Science,* October 1980, pp. 982–993.

Lusk, E. "Cognitive Aspects of Annual Reports: Field Independence-Dependence," *Empirical Research in Accounting: Selected Studies, 1973, Supplement to Journal of Accounting Research,* Vol. 11, pp. 191–202.

Lusk, E. "A Reply: Cognitive Aspects of Annual Reports: Field Independence-Dependence," *Empirical Research in Accounting: Selected Studies, 1973a, Supplement to Journal of Accounting Research,* Vol. 11, pp. 215–224.

Lusk, E. J., and M. Kersnick, "Effects of Cognitive Style and Report Format on Task Performance: The MIS Design Consequences," *Management Science,* Vol. 25, 1979, pp. 787–798.

Montazemi, A. R., and S. Wang, "The Effects of Modes of Information Presentation on Decision-Making: A Review and Meta-Analysis," *Journal of Management Information Systems,* Winter 1988–89, Vol. 5, No. 3, pp. 101–127.

Murray, Dennis, and Roy W. Regel, "Accuracy and Consensus in Accounting Studies of Decision Making," *Behavioral Research in Accounting,* Vol. 4, 1992, pp. 127–139.

Nakano, I., "Noise and Redundancy in Accounting Communications," *The Accounting Review,* October 1972, pp. 693–708.

Nibbelin, Michael Charles, *The Effects of Mode of Information Presentation and Perceptual Skill on Bond Rating Change Decisions: A Laboratory Study,* Unpublished Doctoral Dissertation, The Florida State University, Fall 1988.

Pendlebury, M. W., "The Application of Information Theory to Accounting for Groups of Companies," *Journal of Business, Finance and Accounting,* Spring 1980, pp. 105–117.

Remus, William, "An Empirical Investigation of the Impact of Graphical and Tabular Data Presentations on Decision Making," *Management Science,* May 1984, pp. 533–542.

Ronen, J., and F. Falk, "Accounting Aggregation and the Entropy Measure: An Experimental Approach," *The Accounting Review,* October 1973, pp. 696–717.

Schutz, Howard G., "An Evaluation of Methods for Presentation of Graphic Multiple Trends - Experiment III, *Human Factors,* Vol. 3, 1961, pp. 108–119.

Siegel, Gary, and Helene Ramanauskas-Marconi, *Behavioral Accounting,* Cincinnati, Ohio: South-Western Publishing Co., 1989.

Slovic, P., D. Fleissner, and W. S. Bauman, "Analyzing the Use of Information in Investment Decision Making: A Methodological Proposal," *Journal of Business,* April 1972, pp. 283–301.

Tufte, E., *The Visual Display of Quantitative Data,* Cheshire, Connecticut: Graphics Press, 1983.

Vessey, Iris, "Cognitive Fit: A Theory-Based Analysis of the Graph versus Tables Literature," *Decision Sciences,* Vol. 22, 1991, pp. 219–240.

Vessey, Iris, and Dennis Galletta, "Cognitive Fit: An Empirical Study of Information Acquisition," *Information Systems Research,* March 1991, pp. 63–84.

Von Huhn, "Further Studies in Graphic Use of Circles and Bars: A Discussion of the Eells Experiment," *Journal of the American Statistical Association,* Vol. 22, 1927, pp. 31–36.

Webster's New Collegiate Dictionary, Springfield, Massachusetts: G. Merriam and Company, 1974.

Weick, K. E., "Stress in Accounting Systems," *The Accounting Review,* April 1983, pp. 350–369.

White, Gilbert Fowler, *Choice of Adjustment to Floods,* University of Chicago, Department of Geography, Research Paper No. 93, 1964.

Zmud, R. W., "An Empirical Investigation of the Dimensionality of the Concept of Information," *Decision Sciences,* Vol. 9, No. 2, 1978, pp. 187–195.

4.9   SOME SUGGESTIONS FOR FURTHER RESEARCH

The Problem

The one point that is absolutely clear in the Illinois CPA Society report as in the CICA report (see Chapter 3) is that both professional organizations call for the profession to establish *financial graphic standards.* Why has the profession ignored this call? It is too soon for the CICA to respond, the call just being issued in 1993. Based on preliminary comments, it appears the CICA will respond to the call. But what is the AICPA doing to respond to the call issued in 1988?

The Illinois CPA Society report clearly concludes that interpretation of financial information in graphic form is *not intuitive* and thus has to be learned, just as interpretation of tabular information has to be learned. What are the accounting professors doing to help the profession prepare itself for the paradigm shift that has already left us behind? Based on the literature search reported by Professor Frownfelter, NOTHING! The research on the effectiveness of graphics to communicate accounting and/or financial information is being performed by nonaccountants.

Further, the research that Professor Frownfelter reports in her literature search is fraught with problems that range from scope, technique and, most important, relationship to the real issues in using graphics to communicate information. If the same research methodologies had been used centuries ago to test the validity of the graphic representation of human speech, we still would not have the alphabet!

The Problem is that accountants are not concerned about the graphic representation of their work, and, as a result, no one else is. The only way that true financial graphic research will be completed is for the accounting profession to get involved and sponsor the research. This chapter proposes a research methodology that could jump start the Profession toward a leadership role.

The "Task"

Professor Frownfelter reports that several research studies concluded that the "Task" was the critical factor in the research design. Yet in all of the research the tasks were severely limited, even when the research included several tasks. The reason for the limitation was "control" of the research subjects and the time constraints of the researchers. Most of the reported research used students or selected groups who had limited time to understand the task assigned, much less to understand the task and the graphics presented to perform the task. Just as disturbing, the various researchers did not use similar graphics to test similar tasks.

The Task of graphic research for the presentation of accounting and financial reports is immense. Chapters 1 and 2 in the main body of the text outline the Task of the accounting language. Simply stated, "The Task of accounting and financial reporting is to support all business activities." Graphics are a part of that task.

The "Task" is *not* to show that people make better or worse decisions using graphics rather than tabular. The "Task" *is* to show how people make better decisions when the information is presented in all four forms of input to the human brain—Tabular Data, Written Interpretations, Graphic Representations, and Sound. To limit research to testing the subjects' ability to make an unreal decision in an unreal setting totally ignores the human capacity to learn, to adapt, to expand and to utilize their wide range of knowledge and experiences to solve the most trivial or the most complex problem.

The "Task" is *not* to show that people do not learn in a business situation. The "Task" *is* to show how people from all disciplines learn more about how the firm responds to external variables when they can observe the immense change in the subject firms operations by showing how all the financial components react to changes in the business variables. The use of the Charnoff Faces was an attempt to do just that. But the practicality of showing a series of faces to active managers defies practical considerations.

Therefore, the tasks to be researched are:

A. How do people make better decisions when the information is presented in all four forms of input to the human brain—Tabular Data, Written Interpretations, Graphic Representations, and Sound.

B. How do people from all disciplines learn more about how the firm responds to external variables when they can observe the immense change in the subject firms operations by showing how all the financial components react to changes in the business variables.

There is one other assumption present in most of the reported literature, whether the assumption is stated or unstated, and that is that the graphic representations need not be accurate representations of what accountants do. In my opinion, that is simply not true. How can you expect a research subject to understand all the implications of a change in an external variable if the graph forms are limited in the number of impacts that can be shown and are not reflective of the accounting implications of the data representations? If the subject cannot see and understand the impact of a change in a single variable (such as interest, or health care costs) on all the major components of a Balance Sheet, the Revenue and Expense Statement, the Cash Flow Statement, the Retained Earnings Statement, and the Change in Working Capital, how will they ever learn to make good decisions based on financial information? The task includes testing learning, experience, and eventually knowledge.

If the research is to learn how graphics impact the ability of the user to utilize the information inherent in the accounting data, the graphics *must* reflect the accounting presentations. In short, the graphics must show what accountants do so that the graphic is, in fact, a replication of the tabular data.

The Illinois CPA Society report and the CICA report both acknowledge that the only graphic representation of the financial statements are those utilized by TFGA. Therefore, it seems appropriate that the proposed research start with these formats as the basis for the research. Consider researching how people read. What form would you use for representing the sounds we make when we speak? Probably the Western alphabet. Why? Because we all learned the alphabet, and we can use it to communicate among a wide range of disciplines. We simply accepted the alphabet because it was provided to us, we all learned it, and it works. How many of you reading this text challenged your parents, your kindergarten or first-grade teacher when they said, "This is an 'A'?"

The Financial Graphic Alphabet works. The case studies shown in this supplement and in the main volume prove that. What we need to do now is learn how to use the alphabet to improve communications in the business world.

The Research Design

Purpose: The purpose of the research is to learn the impact of integrating financial (accounting-based) graphics in the normal operations of a firm, or in the normal learning environment of business students.

Timing and Content: The research should include enough material to support the results defining the impact of including graphics as an integral part of the learning and business environment. Therefore:

1. The financial graphics should be included in the entire first year of students learning accounting. The starting point is necessary to prevent any previous bias from entering the experiment from the first year of accounting.

2. The content should be all of the material and concepts that would normally be included in a first year accounting curriculum. The only difference is that the test group would have the financial graphics seamlessly integrated into the learning process while the control group would have no graphics other than those normally included (such as break even charts.) The scope is to assure that learning has occurred.

3. The test group and the control group should be located in different parts of the country in different schools where little or no cross learning would occur. It is most critical how the students are informed about the study.

The rest of the design should include details specifying how to inform the test and control groups, how to make sure that both groups are relatively equal in academic scores, right brain and left brain dominance, and other more accepted baseline controls. Because of the immense size of the project, a multidisciplinary group of researchers should be involved to assure an accurate and acceptable research design, implementation, analysis, and reporting of the results.

Note. *To aid in this research, I am willing to allow the researchers to use The Financial Graphic Alphabet as the starting point and to work on the project as an integral part of the research team or as a consultant to the team or as an interested but uninvolved observer.*

CHAPTER 9

USING FINANCIAL GRAPHICS IN INTEGRATED APPLICATION SYSTEMS

Page 139, add new material after section 9.4

9.4A BUILDING A HEALTH CARE DECISION SUPPORT SYSTEM (New)

by
F. Andrew Best, CPA
Michael J. Budnick, MHA FACHE

Introduction

As we approach the twenty-first century, the board members and CEOs who lead the health care industry will need different, more action-based information to help them make the critical decisions. The hospital was the primary leader and fiscal beneficiary of the health care system from the end of World War II until the mid-1970s. Since then the individual hospital market share has been eroded constantly from all sides, and the health care industry suffers from massive overcapacity, reactionary thinking, and me-too-ism.

Strategic planning of the past, with its long-term goals, is giving way to strategic improvement and improvising in the *real time*. Organizational renewal through incremental changes is being replaced by continual reengineering of the organization. These rapid fire changes result in Board Members, their CEOs, and the medical staffs being asked to take increasingly larger risks with no protection from the greater downside risk that occur due to lower volumes, reduced reimbursement levels, or newly developed and competing services.

During the 1970s and 1980s financially driven management led the hospital to unusual financial successes. However, the era of cutting costs, downsizing, raising prices, and/or duplicating services proved that such actions were not effective solutions for an excess capacity industry. With the changes in the reimbursement policies of both industry and government, increased competition and changing delivery arrangements, hospital management has been forced into market-driven thinking. Hospital management must learn to think and act differently if they want to be around tomorrow.

This chapter suggests that there are formal, structured processes that can turn the reams of *data* that surround us into *information* utilizing advanced financial graphic formats and, if properly used, can materially reduce the risks. Health care institutions, like other industries, have accumulated massive amounts of data. Hospitals report information to federal and state agencies, national and state associations, trade and professional groups and data collection services. Only a limited number of not-for-profit hospital organizations and contract management firms are starting to tap into this data-rich environment to extract vital information.

Such critical information can be shown graphically and used for planning, service development, recruitment, financial management, account control, and overall decision making. Appropriate use of such visualized information will help boards, CEOs, medical staffs, and other interested parties reduce their risk through better management using proven marketing-based management techniques.

The processes are available for the large health care systems as well as the small and rural hospitals and small group systems, and, most important, the current employee base can be trained to operate and maintain the systems. But ongoing support needs to be readily available to train replacements, because people with these skills will quickly move on to other opportunities.

Moving from Data to Action

The goal of this chapter is to describe a graphic reporting system that helps hospital management move from data to action utilizing advanced design techniques and financial graphics. In the current environment and market, no resource can be ignored or overlooked. Significant opportunities are waiting to be found in the mountains of unused data resources. Med-Intell, Inc. has developed and utilizes a structured approach to help hospital management draw upon the potential associated with strategic improvising. Exhibit 9.4A.1 is a representation of the steps we take to move from Data to Action.

MOVING FROM DATA TO ACTION!

by
MED-INTELL, INC.

DATA
INFORMATION
UNDERSTANDING
KNOWLEDGE
ACTION

EXHIBIT 9.4A.1 Moving from Data to Action
Copyright © by Med-Intell, Inc.

In this process, there is a danger that presenting the information in graphic formats will cause an immediate leap to action, thereby passing over understanding and knowledge. It is critical that the two processes of developing understanding before assuming knowledge and building knowledge before starting action be completed before decision making is affected. Once the process is in place, it will become iterative as management continually moves from data to action. This systematic approach to the conversion of a largely unused asset—raw data—into a major corporate resource for rural and small hospitals, physicians, and health care systems will help the health care professional learn to strategically improvise and establish sustainable competitive advantages.

The balance of this chapter is divided into five sections:

Section 1—Identify and assemble available data.
Section 2—Design the system that turns the data into information.
Section 3—Train the health care professionals to understand the information.
Section 4—Help the health care professionals turn their understanding into knowledge.
Section 5—Help the health care professionals turn their knowledge into action.

Section 1—Identify and Assemble Available Data

The first step is to assemble the various databases and data sources that will provide the crucial and valuable data necessary to support the Health Care Decision Support System. The mainframe files of *Patients Financial and Medical Records* and the hospital's *Trial Balance* are the core sources of the raw data. A rich source of raw data can be assembled into what we call the *Reference Data Bases.* Such databases contain information about various hospitals, that is, their costing, profit results, patient and procedure mix, physician contribution, and other revenue, cost, and performance results from local, state, and national sources. This reference information is used to help measure the performance of the target hospital.

The Reference Data will be found in manually prepared reports and the electronic-based databases available in the hospital and from external databases sources. Internal resources include data collected from selected data fields from patient medical records, patient financial records, and/or physician profiles. Cross-reference of patient medical and financial records for matching purposes must be accomplished with full patient confidentiality. Data from the general ledger trial balances and cost report files provide an additional source of data. Monthly reports showing physician activities, inpatient, outpatient, and emergency department volumes, ordered tests and procedures, and Diagnostic Related Group (DRG) profiles are also significant sources of information.

Monthly reports of DRG outpatient activities and outpatient service lines, with zip code and census tract, payor, and employer information provide exceptional marketing information. Other internally prepared reports with a wealth of pathology and comparative information include Joint Commission on Accreditation of Hospitals (JCAH) reports, state hospital association reports, state board of health survey reports, incident reports, employee turnover, and physician/professional support staff recruitment expenses.

External resources include the following sources: 1. Competitor analysis from Hospital Competitor Information Analysis (HCIA); 2. Financial analysis from Healthcare Financial Management Association (HFMA); 3. Healthcare Finance

Administration (HCFA) cost reports; 4. State databases on hospital patient data origin; 5. State databases on DRG's cost, charges, reimbursements; 6. Mapping boundaries—county and census tract; 7. Simmons Market Report; 8. Health care industry reports.

Section 2—Design the System That Turns the Data into Information

The Health Care Decision Support System—Exhibit 9.4A.2 is a top-level flow chart that outlines the computer-based processes and resources used to convert data into action-based visualized information. The objective of the computer-based visualization analysis is to respond to the statements: "I don't know what I want or need until I see it!"; and/or "I must see it to manage it." If the response to these statements is to be successful, the hospital must be willing to spend the time required to train their staff to use the new systems and to understand how to make all of the different relationships work. Even after the system is fully implemented, common sense indicates that ongoing, outside, telephone and on-site support must still be available to the hospital.

Designing the Graphics to Form the Basis of the System. The most important part of the installation is the original design process for the charts that form the basis of the graphic library. The design process must be closely monitored and approved by the CEO, the Chairman of the Finance Committee, the Board Chairperson, the Chief of the Medical Staff, and other appropriate senior management personnel. While the tasks are not simple, a number of people in the organization can be trained to perform the graphic designs and to help the computer department build the appropriate databases. In most organizations this task could be split among job descriptions.

All graphs are to be produced using the financial graphic standards defined in the handbook, "FINANCIAL REPORTING USING COMPUTER GRAPHICS."[1] We found that the financial graphic standards apply equally to financial, marketing, and/or operational graphics. These standards were selected to prevent distortions in the information being generated.

The Grouping Categories

The graphics will present the status of the organization in four major groupings:

Groupings	Description
Doing good	Service to customers
Doing well	Financial viability
Planning	Marketing
	Operational
	Financial
Controlling	Real time feedback with resultant corrective action (The familiar Plan Do Check Act (PDCA) found in Continuous Quality Improvement (CQI) Articles)

---

[1] See the main body of this handbook.

HEALTH CARE DECISION SUPPORT SYSTEM

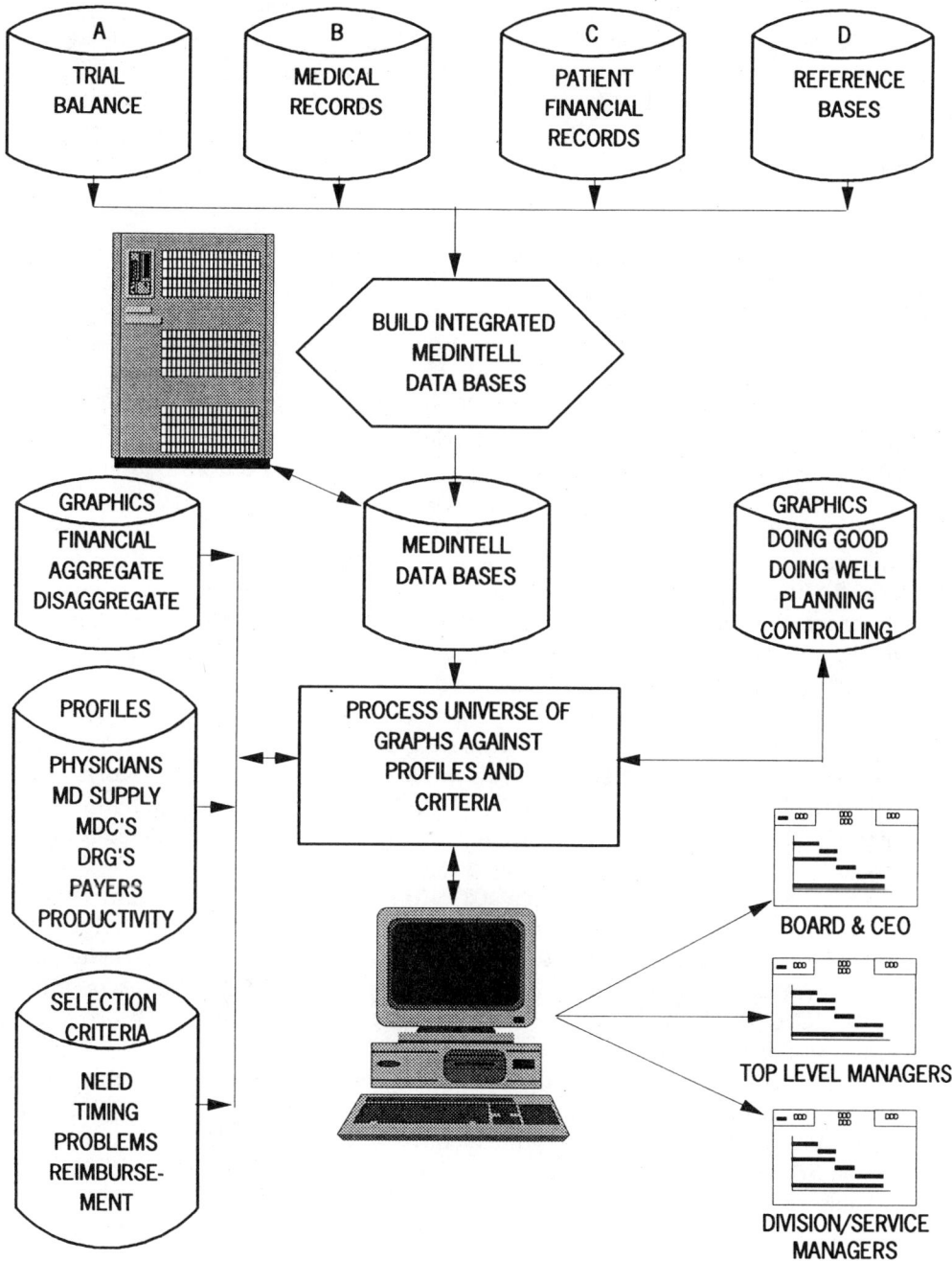

EXHIBIT 9.4A.2   Health Care Decision Support System

The information delivered by this visualization system is based on a number of publications and business concepts. *The Directors Information Guidelines* are published by The Compliance Division of the Office of Thrift Supervision of the U.S. Department of Treasury and were issued in December 1989. These guidelines focused on 34 critical information indicators for reporting to the boards. The 34 indicators were combined into six areas of concern for presentation: Financial Reports, Asset Quality, Asset/Liability Management, Internal Reports, External Reports, and so on. The authors know of no similar health care industry information guidelines. The Health Care Decision Support System described herein utilizes the concepts proposed in this landmark document.

Ernst and Whinney in their monographs on *A GUIDE TO THE BOARD'S ROLE IN HOSPITAL FINANCE* and *A GUIDE TO THE BOARD'S ROLE IN STRATEGIC BUSINESS PLANNING* define a number of hospital financial ratios to monitor performance. They make extensive use of charting in the planning guide. The American Hospital Association's *MONITREND* and the Health Care Financial Management Association's Financial Analysis Service and Strategic Operating Indicators, and the HCIA's Hospital Financial Analysis all contribute to the growing number of information resources that can be used by the hospital to develop its internal director information guidelines.

The four classifications of Doing Good, Doing Well, Planning, and Controlling originate with *Strategic Choices for American's Hospitals* by Stephen M. Shortell, Ellen M. Morrison and Bernard Friedman, published by Jossey-Bass Publishers, San Francisco-Oxford, 1990. There are some differences in perspective because Shortell combines Planning and Controlling while others, including Med-Intell, treat them as separate functions.

The reengineering concept is fully described in *Reengineering The Corporation—A Manifesto for Business Revolution* by Michael Hammer and James Champy, published by Harper Collins Publishers, Inc., New York, 1993. The strategic improvising concept is described in *Real Time Strategy* by Lee Tom Perry, Randall G. Stott and W. Norman Smallwood, published by John Wiley & Sons, Inc., 1993.

Continuous Quality Improvement (CQI) originated with Dr. Edward Deming and is described extensively in a number of well-known publications. CQI is the formal process of identifying and structuring the organizational process to measure and impact the quality of the products produced. PDCA is an acronym for *PLAN DO CHECK ACT*, used by many management consultants. It provides a mental model for controlling the processes of planning, doing, follow-up, and correction. It is a long-standing model that can be used to reenergize the system as described in the series of texts on MANAGEMENT originating with Harold Koontz and Cryil O'Donnell and published by McGraw-Hill, New York.

In addition to the four Groupings noted above, the graphs will also fall into at least three distinct levels: Level 1—Board and the CEO graphics; Level 2—the CEO, top management and medical staff leadership graphics; Level 3—and the top management, department, and individual physician graphics. Each level provides a different set of graphics to match the needed information with the level of responsibility. Additional detailed levels are available on demand to meet specific information needs.

The graphs can also be divided into an aggregate–disaggregate continuum. This continuum provides the criteria to assure the appropriate amount of information for each of the management levels. At the Board and CEO level, overall direction and appropriate responses require in-depth analytical support to events such as: (1) Managed care products coming to the community with the resulting redirecting of patients, or (2) Where a competing hospital in a neighboring city establishes a walk-up emergency center next door to your hospital. At the disaggregate end of the continuum, top management and department personnel need to know the overall status as well as the details picturing how their service or department is doing in specific performance areas.

Exhibit 9.4A.3 describes which of the management groups is most likely to use the graphics at the Aggregate and Disaggregate levels. The Board and CEO are Most likely (HIGH) to use the Aggregate level graphics while the Department managers and Individual physicians are least likely (LOW). On the other hand, the Board and CEO are least likely (LOW) to use the disaggregate level graphics while the Department managers and Individual physicians are most likely (HIGH).

A Sample Graphic System

The Fingraph aggregate and disaggregate system is conceptualized in Exhibits 9.4A.4 through 9.4A.7.

Exhibit 9.4A.4—The four principal data groupings are shown in Exhibit 9.4A.4. This exhibit shows the significant areas of concern for hospitals at several levels of governance and management.

A.   The first grouping is "Doing Good" and is concerned more with the impact on basic human needs.[2] All of the human and social values must be measured and considered. Such measurements are shown starting at a level 1 graphic. The categories described at this Overview level describes three Level 2 categories: (1) Service Analysis, (2) Customer Analysis for patient-related customers, and (3) Customer Analysis for the payor customers.

AGGREGATE/DISAGGREGATE
GRAPHIC UTILIZATION

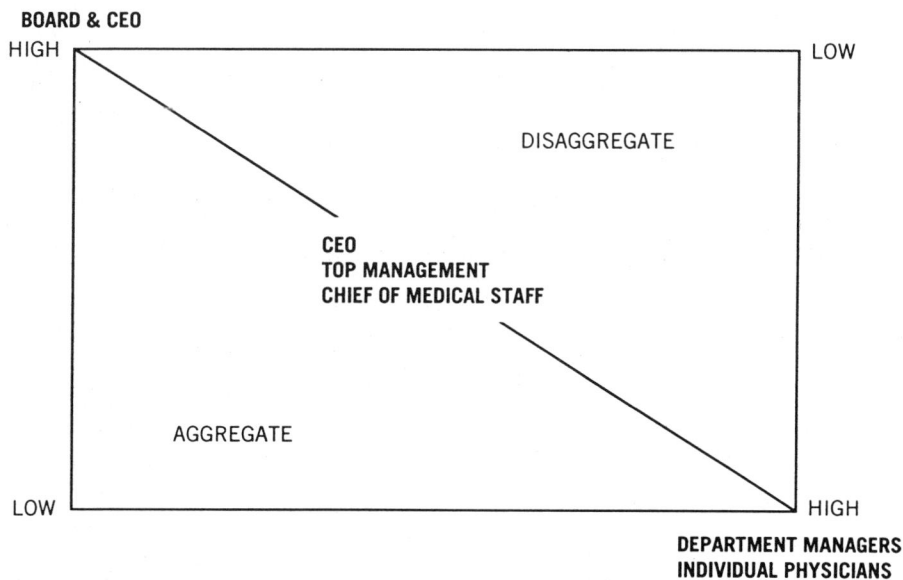

EXHIBIT 9.4A.3   Aggregate/Disaggregate Graphic Utilization

---

[2] For more information on the presentation of Doing Good, see *Key Factor Analysis, A Logic Leading to Social Accountability,* Irwin M. Jarett, Patricia A. Brady, Editors; Southern Illinois University Press, Carbondale & Edwardsville, Illinois; 379+ pp., 1976.

HEALTH CARE DECISION SUPPORT SYSTEM GRAPHICS
OVERVIEW

	Level 1	Level 2	Level 2	Level 2	Level 3	Levels 4 & 5
A	Doing Good	Service Analysis	Customer Physicians Patients Families	Customers 3rd Party Payors Employers Employees		
B	Doing Well	Financial Analysis	BS Charts P&L Charts Fund Bal. Cash Flow	Disaggregate Each Area		
C	Planning	Internal External	Market Share % of Market Prod. Analysis Service Line	Technology Capital Use Pricing Case Mix	Market Plan Business Plan Operational Plans	
D	Controlling	Feed Back	Incident Rate Variance Trend			Internal Audit External Audit State Exams JCAH Review

EXHIBIT 9.4A.4 Health Care Decision Support System Graphics Overview
Copyright © by Med-Intell, Inc.

B. The second grouping is "Doing Well" and is mostly concerned with the organization's financial performance starting at a level 1 graphic. The main emphasis in Doing Well is the Income Statement, Balance Sheet, Equity or Fund Balances, and Cash Flow. Doing Well has been the principal concern of the Board and CEO for a number of generations.

C. The third grouping, Planning, now includes a high level of interest for market-driven concerns and management activities starting at a level 1 graphic. Planning includes both internal and external indicators. For example, the external indicators include Market Share and Technology measurements. Internal indicators include Capital Use, Pricing relationships, and Case mix. The indicators are summarized into the three major planning areas: Market, Business, and Operational. Planning has been oriented to long-range and strategic planning but now must respond with strategic improvising and real time improvements. Real time improvements require an ongoing response to the comments noted earlier: "I must see it to manage it." One of the key benefits of creating a "war room" of appropriate level graphics is the ability to support the need to monitor and control the real time reengineering of the organizational processes.

D. The final grouping, Controlling, has historically received considerable attention by the Board and the CEO. This grouping deals with operational activities starting at a level 1 graphic with a high emphasis on productivity of employees—reducing the number of FTEs being one of the primary goals. Recently the area of controlling has been broadened to include quality control, competitive analysis, internal and external audit with examination, and certification reports.

Exhibits 9.4A.5, 9.4A.6, and 9.4A.7—Exhibit 9.4A.5 is another way of showing the four groupings by individual graphic types rather than the data level for the graphics. For example, Doing Good has specific sets of graphs for Patients, Physicians, Employers, Employees, Community, and Public Health. Doing Good and Doing Well are detailed further in Exhibits 9.4A.6 and 9.4A.7, respectively. Exhibit 9.4A.6 describes the graphics that will identify a series of key indicators to measure the hospitals efforts in Doing Good. Exhibit 9.4A.7 shows how the more familiar financial graphics fit into the health care schema.

Exhibit 9.4A.8—Exhibit 9.4A.8 is an example of a Doing Good chart. It is an item chart that describes a set of key indicators for a 300-bed hospital. The primary bar (solid bar) shows the Actual 1993 performance; the first comparative bar shows the mean performance and the second comparative bar shows the control performance for the 300-bed hospital category. The variances show how the client hospital is performing.

Exhibit 9.4A.9—Exhibit 9.4A.9 is one of the premier financial graphics used to measure Doing Well, the Balance Sheet. The primary bar is Actual 1993 and the first comparative bar is the 1992 Actual bar for the 300-bed client hospital.

Exhibit 9.4A.10—Exhibit 9.4A.10 is another of the premier financial graphics used to measure Doing Well, the Income Statement. Primary bar is Actual 1993 and the first comparative bar is the 1993 Forecast. The variances demonstrate the hospital's performance.

Exhibit 9.4A.11—Exhibit 9.4A.11 is a third type of Doing Well graphic, that displays a series of financial indicators: 1993 Actual to the Mean and the Control data.

Exhibit 9.4A.12—Exhibit 9.4A.12 is a Planning graphic that shows how the client hospital performed against a wide range of critical planning indicators.

Exhibit 9.4A.13—Exhibit 9.4A.13 is a Controlling graphic that shows a wide range of control indicators.

GRAPHIC AGGREGATE AND DISAGGREGATE

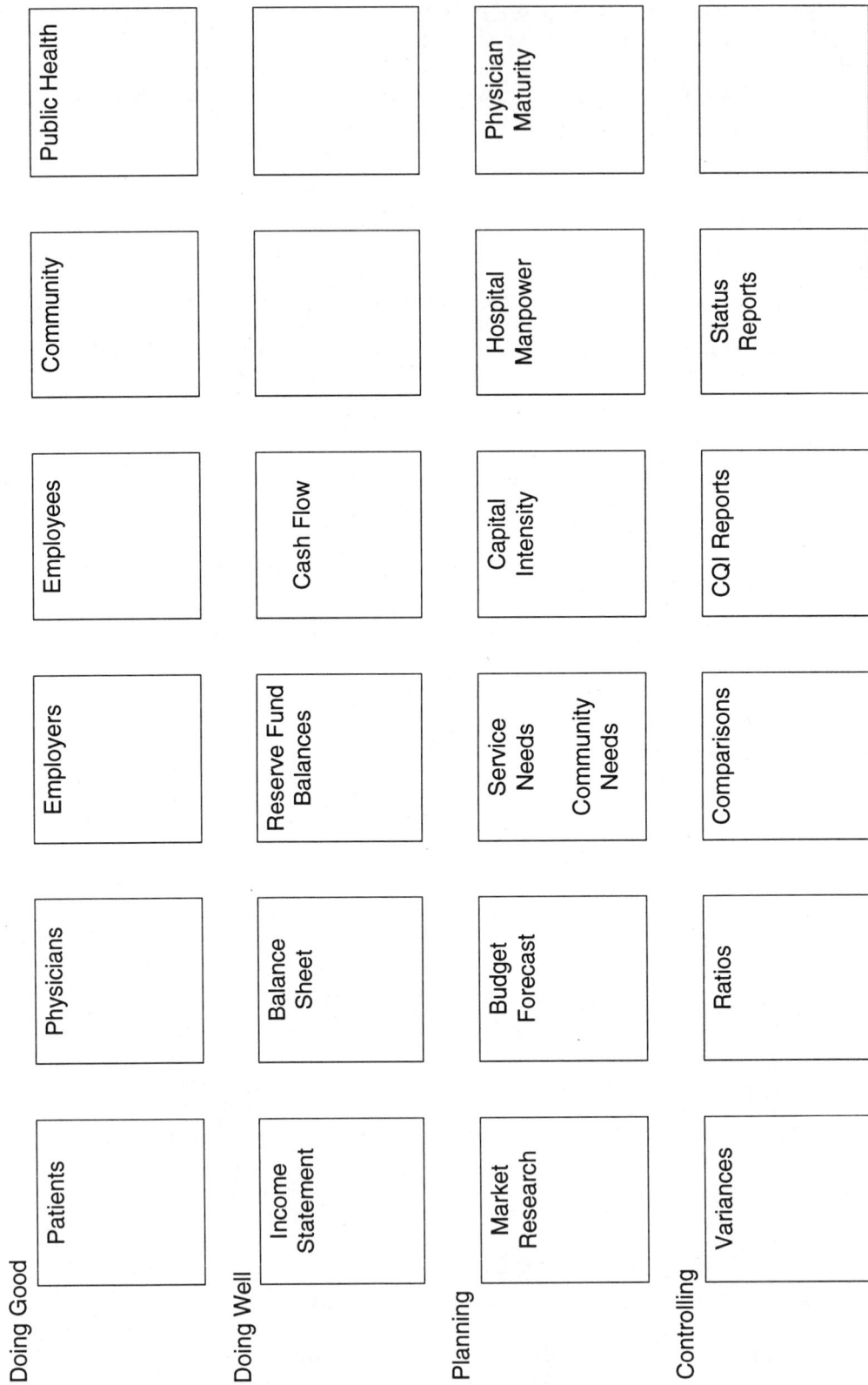

Doing Good

Patients	Physicians	Employers	Employees	Community	Public Health

Doing Well

Income Statement	Balance Sheet	Reserve Fund Balances	Cash Flow		

Planning

Market Research	Budget Forecast	Service Needs / Community Needs	Capital Intensity	Hospital Manpower	Physician Maturity

Controlling

Variances	Ratios	Comparisons	CQI Reports	Status Reports	

EXHIBIT 9.4A.5 Graphic Aggregate and Disaggregate
Copyright © by Med-Intell, Inc.

GRAPHIC AGGREGATE AND DISAGGREGATE
DOING GOOD—SERIES—PATIENTS

	Level 1	Level 2	Level 2	Level 3	Level 3	Levels 4 & 5
A	Patients IP-OP Emergency Home Health DME	Types of Freebees Charity Free Service	Patient Satisfaction Family Satisfaction	Patient Travel Time Distance		
B	At Home RT PT Rehab Industrial	Discounts Religious County Govt.	Focus Group Survey Tract. Ltr & Phone Waiting Time			
C						
D						

EXHIBIT 9.4A.6   Graphic Aggregate and Disaggregate Doing Good—Series—Patients

GRAPHIC AGGREGATE AND DISAGGREGATE
DOING WELL SERVICES

	Level 1	Level 2	Level 2	Level 3	Level 3	Levels 4 & 5
A	Income Expense	Income	Expense	Profitability Ratios / Deductability Ratios	Case Mix Index / Level of Acuity	Allowance for Bad Debt
B	Balance Sheet	Assets	Liabilities	Current Assets / Fixed Assets	Current Liabilities / Long-Term Liabilities	
C	Equity Reserve &/or Fund Balances	Bond Designated Reserves / Free	Capital Ratios			
D	Cash Flow	Sources	Uses	Days of Cash on Hand	Day in A/R Net & Gross	Days in Accounts Payable

EXHIBIT 9.4A.7 Graphic Aggregate and Disaggregate Doing Well Services
Copyright © by Med-Intell, Inc.

▅ 1993 ACTUAL	YOUR HOSPITAL	CHART: 620
▅ 1993 MEAN	———	January
▓ 1993 CONTROL	DOING GOOD - 300 BED HOSPITAL	

Difference Variance

MEDICARE DISCOUNT
74.0
110.7
50.0

CHARITY CARE
49.0
55.0
50.0

ACUTE CARE SERVED
90.0
77.8
50.0

OUT PATIENT SERVED
59.9
96.2
50.0

INPATIENT SERVED
0.0
86.6
50.0

MEDICARE DISCOUNT
36.7
60.7

CHARITY CARE
6.0
5.0

ACUTE CARE SERVED
(62.2)
(22.2)

OUT PATIENT SERVED
36.3
46.2

INPATIENT SERVED
86.6
36.6

0   40   80   120   160   -160   -80   0   80   160

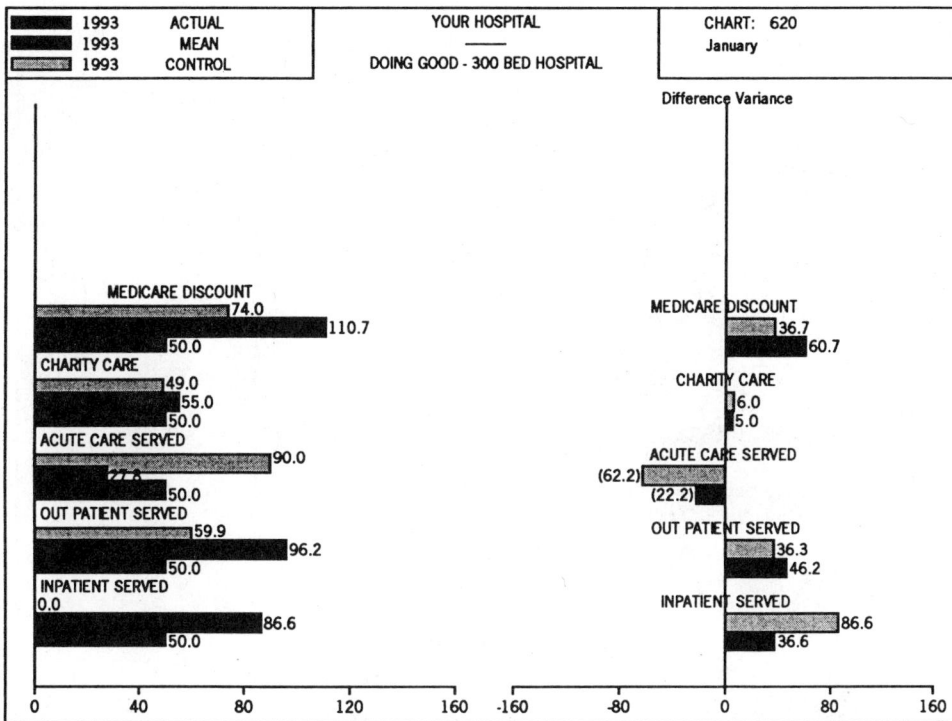

EXHIBIT 9.4A.8   Your Hospital—Doing Good—300-Bed Hospital

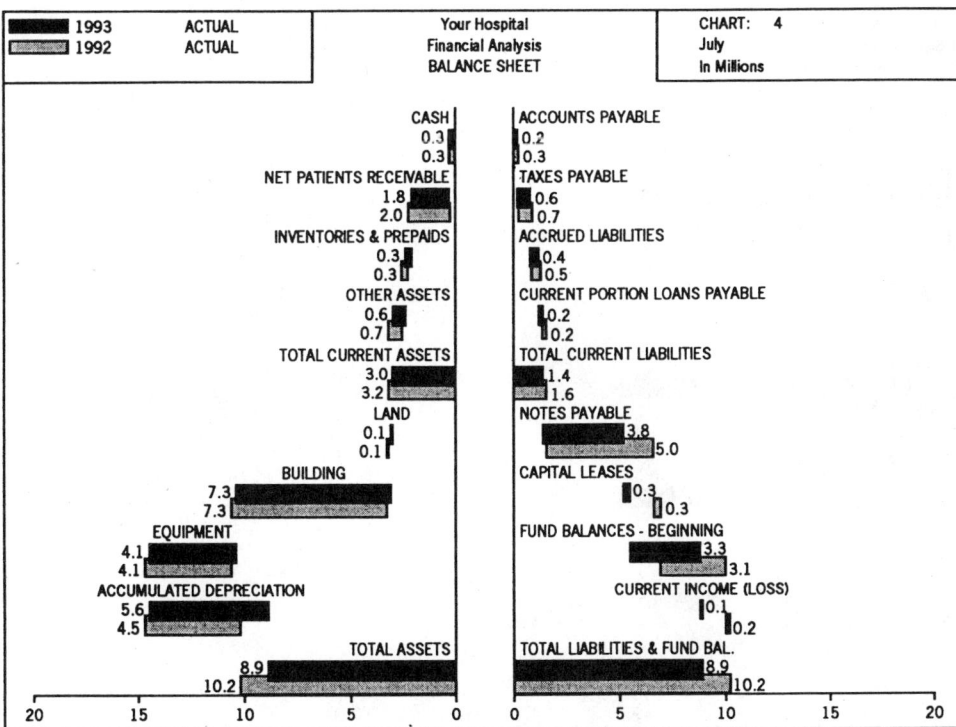

▅ 1993 ACTUAL	Your Hospital	CHART: 4
▓ 1992 ACTUAL	Financial Analysis	July
	BALANCE SHEET	In Millions

CASH
0.3
0.3

NET PATIENTS RECEIVABLE
1.8
2.0

INVENTORIES & PREPAIDS
0.3
0.3

OTHER ASSETS
0.6
0.7

TOTAL CURRENT ASSETS
3.0
3.2

LAND
0.1
0.1

BUILDING
7.3
7.3

EQUIPMENT
4.1
4.1

ACCUMULATED DEPRECIATION
5.6
4.5

TOTAL ASSETS
8.9
10.2

ACCOUNTS PAYABLE
0.2
0.3

TAXES PAYABLE
0.6
0.7

ACCRUED LIABILITIES
0.4
0.5

CURRENT PORTION LOANS PAYABLE
0.2
0.2

TOTAL CURRENT LIABILITIES
1.4
1.6

NOTES PAYABLE
3.8
5.0

CAPITAL LEASES
0.3
0.3

FUND BALANCES - BEGINNING
3.3
3.1

CURRENT INCOME (LOSS)
0.1
0.2

TOTAL LIABILITIES & FUND BAL.
8.9
10.2

20   15   10   5   0   0   5   10   15   20

EXHIBIT 9.4A.9   Your Hospital—Financial Analysis—Balance Sheet

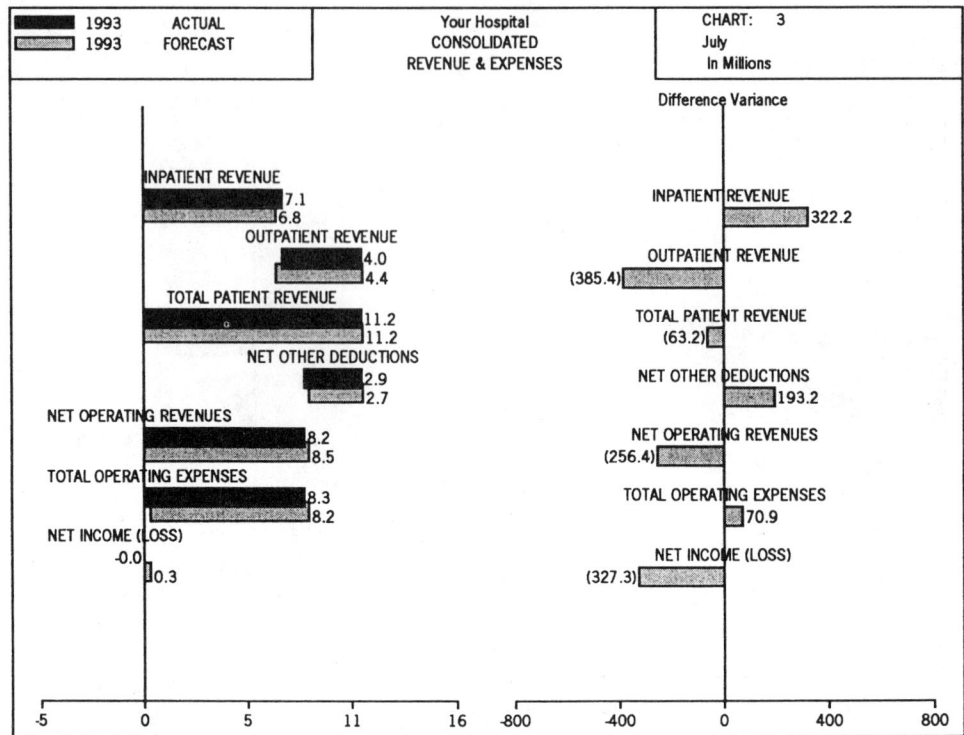

EXHIBIT 9.4A.10 Your Hospital—Consolidated Revenue & Expenses

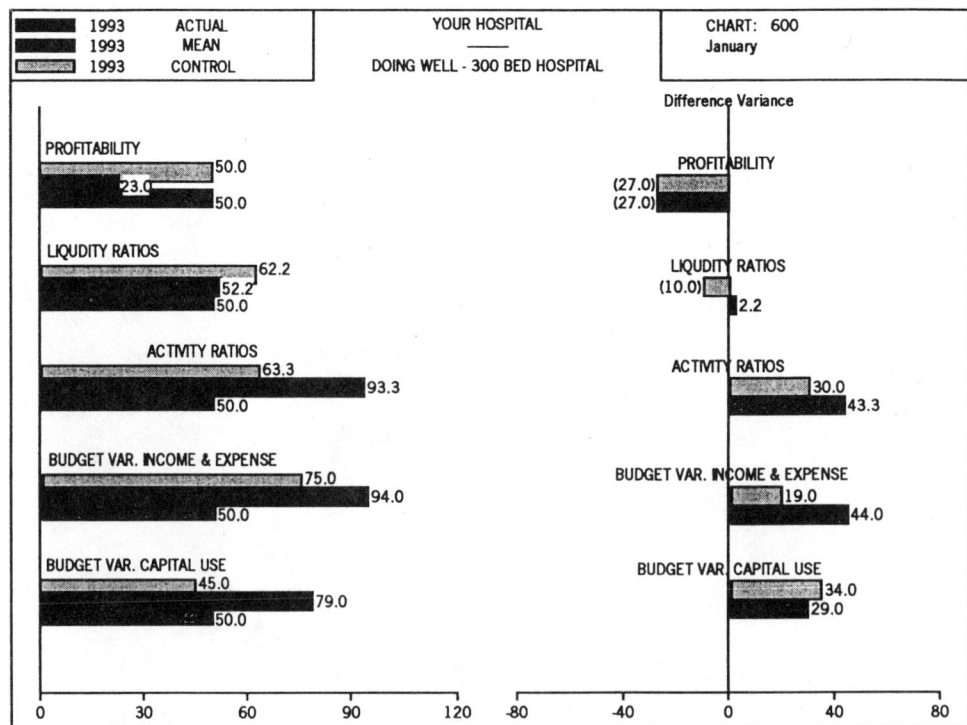

EXHIBIT 9.4.A11 Your Hospital—Doing Well—300-Bed Hospital

			YOUR HOSPITAL	CHART: 610
1993	ACTUAL		——	January
1993	MEAN		PLANNING - 300 BED HOSPITAL	
1993	CONTROL			

Difference Variance

VOLUME RATIOS
70.0
54.4
50.0

VOLUME RATIOS
(15.6)
4.4

CAPITAL STRUCTURE RATIOS
56.6
50.0
50.0

CAPITAL STRUCTURE RATIOS
(6.6)
0.0

OTHER FUNCTIONS RATIOS
38.8
32.2
50.0

OTHER FUNCTIONS RATIOS
(6.6)
(17.8)

LIQUDITY RATIOS
62.2
52.2
50.0

LIQUDITY RATIOS
(10.0)
2.2

NET PRICE RATIOS
99.9
78.8
50.0

NET PRICE RATIOS
(21.1)
28.8

PROFIT INDICATORS
5.1
6.1
50.0

PROFIT INDICATORS
1.0
(43.9)

ACTIVITY BASED COST INPUTS
67.0
79.9
50.0

ACTIVITY BASED COST INPUTS
12.9
29.9

0   30   60   90   120   -80   -40   0   40   80

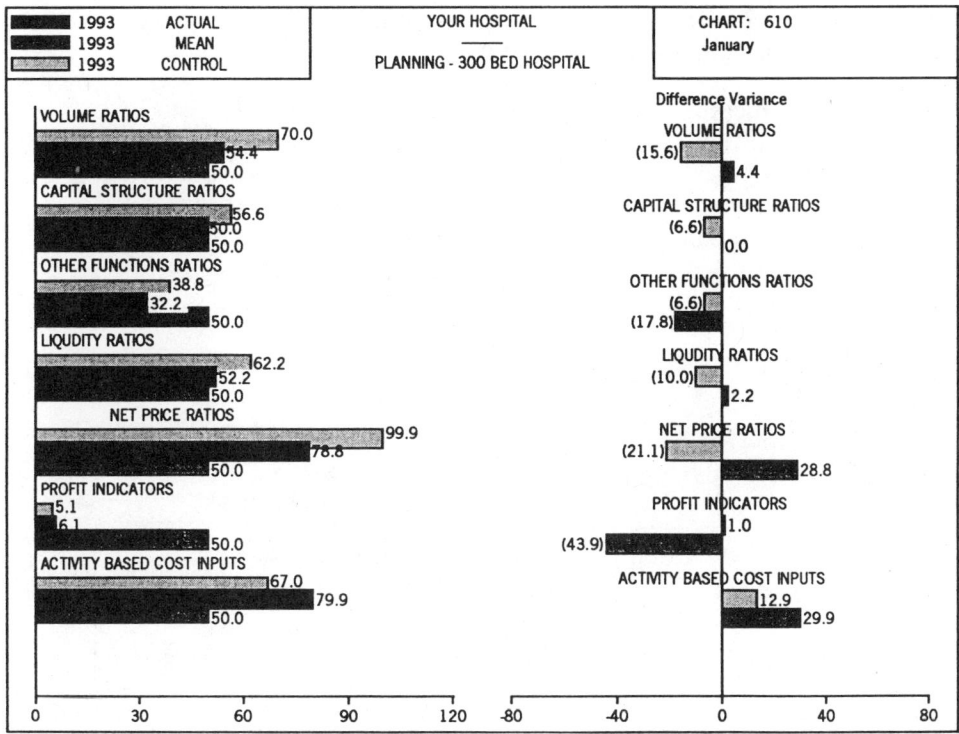

EXHIBIT 9.4A.12   Your Hospital—Planning—300-Bed Hospital

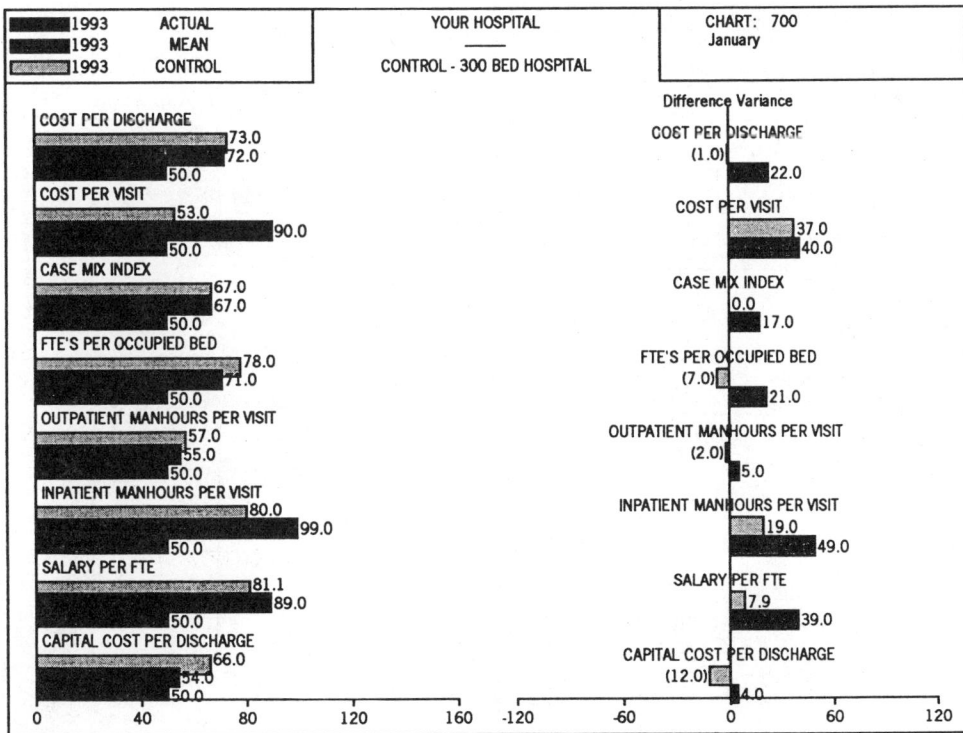

			YOUR HOSPITAL	CHART: 700
1993	ACTUAL		——	January
1993	MEAN		CONTROL - 300 BED HOSPITAL	
1993	CONTROL			

Difference Variance

COST PER DISCHARGE
73.0
72.0
50.0

COST PER DISCHARGE
(1.0)
22.0

COST PER VISIT
53.0
90.0
50.0

COST PER VISIT
37.0
40.0

CASE MIX INDEX
67.0
67.0
50.0

CASE MIX INDEX
0.0
17.0

FTE'S PER OCCUPIED BED
78.0
71.0
50.0

FTE'S PER OCCUPIED BED
(7.0)
21.0

OUTPATIENT MANHOURS PER VISIT
57.0
55.0
50.0

OUTPATIENT MANHOURS PER VISIT
(2.0)
5.0

INPATIENT MANHOURS PER VISIT
80.0
99.0
50.0

INPATIENT MANHOURS PER VISIT
19.0
49.0

SALARY PER FTE
81.1
89.0
50.0

SALARY PER FTE
7.9
39.0

CAPITAL COST PER DISCHARGE
66.0
54.0
50.0

CAPITAL COST PER DISCHARGE
(12.0)
4.0

0   40   80   120   160   -120   -60   0   60   120

EXHIBIT 9.4A.13   Your Hospital—Control—300-Bed Hospital

Exhibit 9.4A.14—Exhibit 9.4A.14 is another way of describing the disaggregate process inherent in the graphic information system design.

Level 1—The Income Statement shown in Exhibit 10.
Level 2—**Exhibit 9.4A.15** is a detailed chart showing selected income and expense totals by Department with variances from the forecast data.
Level 3—**Exhibit 9.4A.16** is a level 3 presentation of expenses only by department (Radiology) with variances from the Forecast data.
Level 4—**Exhibit 9.4A.17** is a level 4 presentation of Radiology Volume.
Level 5—**Exhibit 9.4A.18** is a level 5 detailed presentation of Physician Referrals.

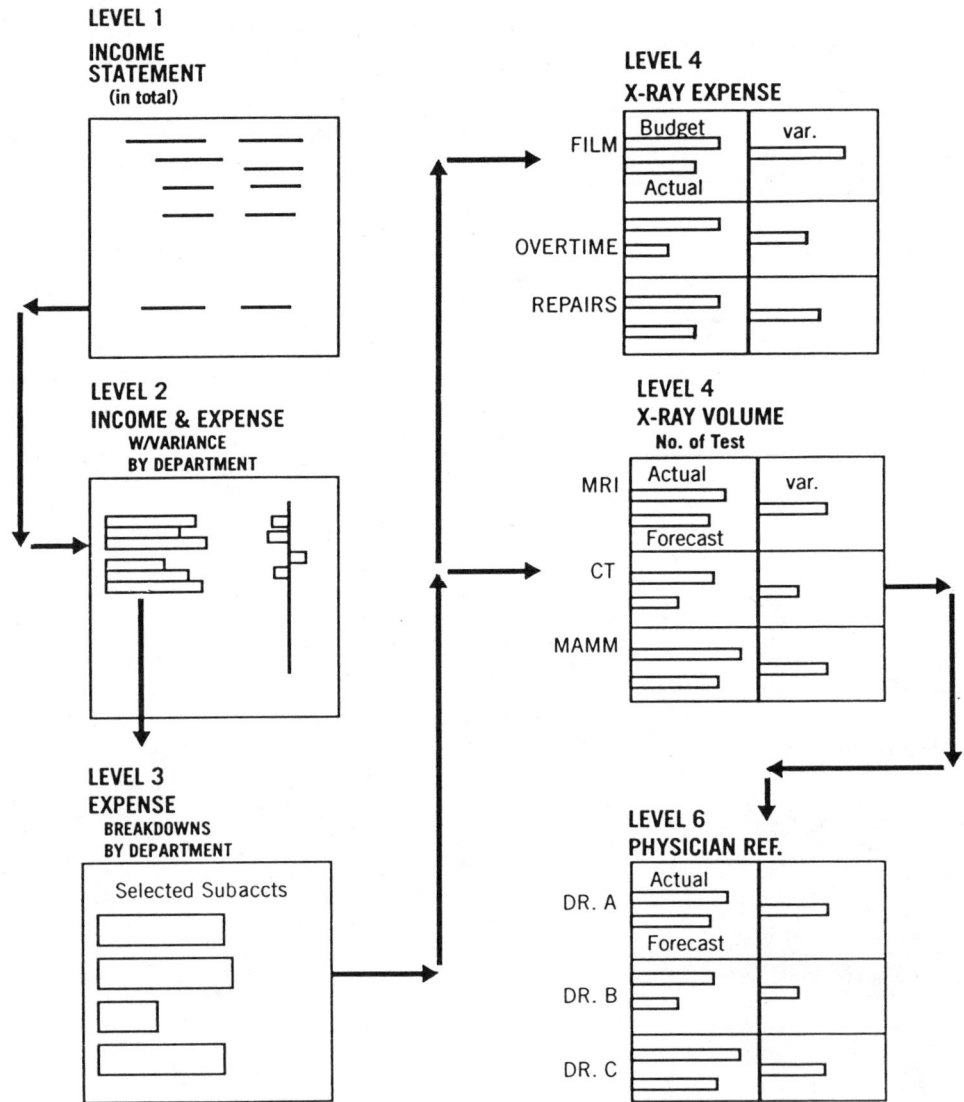

EXHIBIT 9.4A.14   The Disaggregate Process

1993 ACTUAL	Your Hospital	CHART: 5
1993 FORECAST	Financial Analysis	July
	1-Nursing, 2-Clinical, 3-Radiology	In Thousands

Difference Variance

1 - TOTAL PATIENT REVENUE
2658.9
2791.8

1 - TOTAL OPERATING EXPENSES
1005.1
1055.4

1 - NET INCOME (LOSS)
1653.8
1736.5

2 - TOTAL PATIENT REVENUE
1417.8
1488.6

2 - TOTAL OPERATING EXPENSES
447.8
470.2

2 - NET INCOME (LOSS)
969.9
1018.4

3 - TOTAL PATIENT REVENUE
1352.0
1419.6

3 - TOTAL OPERATING EXPENSES
631.1
662.7

3 - NET INCOME (LOSS)
720.9
757.0

1 - TOTAL PATIENT REVENUE
(132.9)

1 - TOTAL OPERATING EXPENSES
(50.3)

1 - NET INCOME (LOSS)
(82.7)

2 - TOTAL PATIENT REVENUE
(70.9)

2 - TOTAL OPERATING EXPENSES
(22.4)

2 - NET INCOME (LOSS)
(48.5)

3 - TOTAL PATIENT REVENUE
(67.6)

3 - TOTAL OPERATING EXPENSES
(31.6)

3 - NET INCOME (LOSS)
(36.0)

0   900   1800   2700   3600   -240   -120   0   120   240

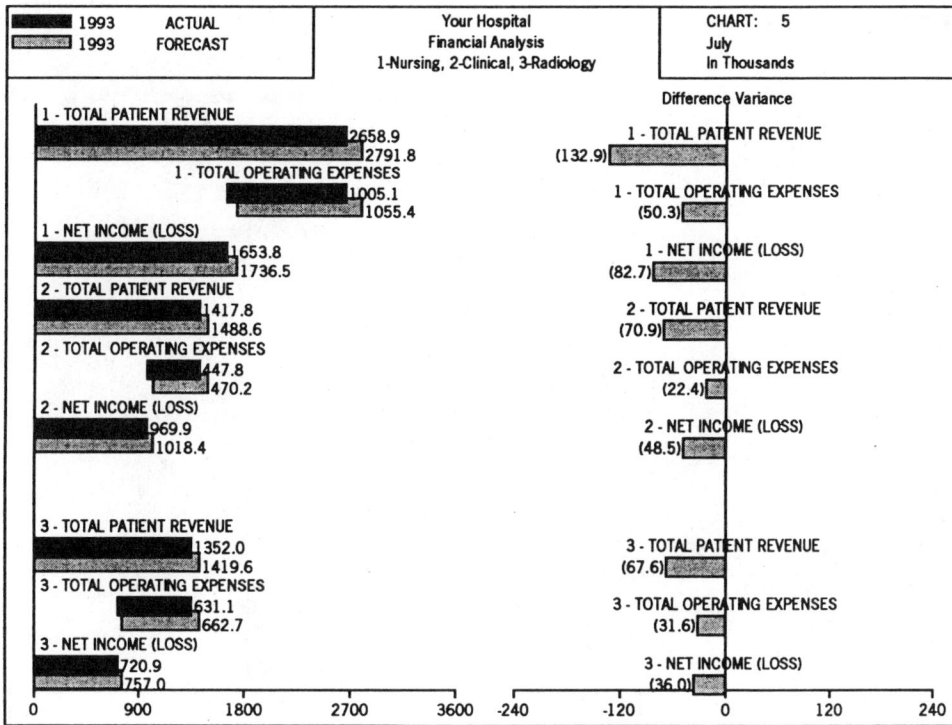

EXHIBIT 9.4A.15   Your Hospital—Financial Analysis—1-Nursing, 2-Clinical, 3-Radiology

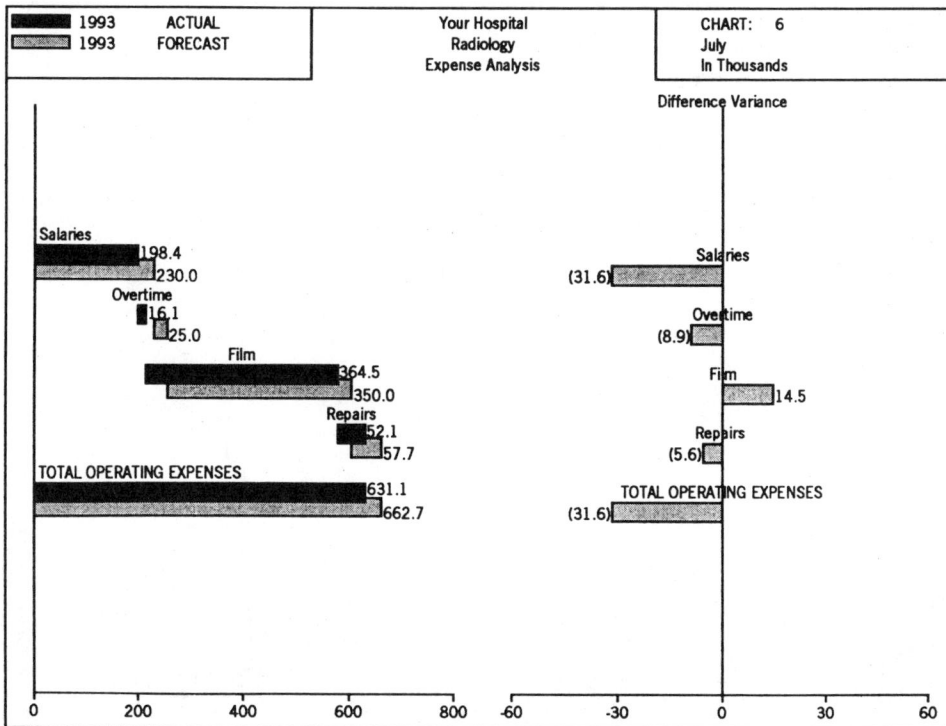

1993 ACTUAL	Your Hospital	CHART: 6
1993 FORECAST	Radiology	July
	Expense Analysis	In Thousands

Difference Variance

Salaries
198.4
230.0

Overtime
16.1
25.0

Film
364.5
350.0

Repairs
52.1
57.7

TOTAL OPERATING EXPENSES
631.1
662.7

Salaries
(31.6)

Overtime
(8.9)

Film
14.5

Repairs
(5.6)

TOTAL OPERATING EXPENSES
(31.6)

0   200   400   600   800   -60   -30   0   30   60

EXHIBIT 9.4A.16   Your Hospital—Radiology Expense Analysis

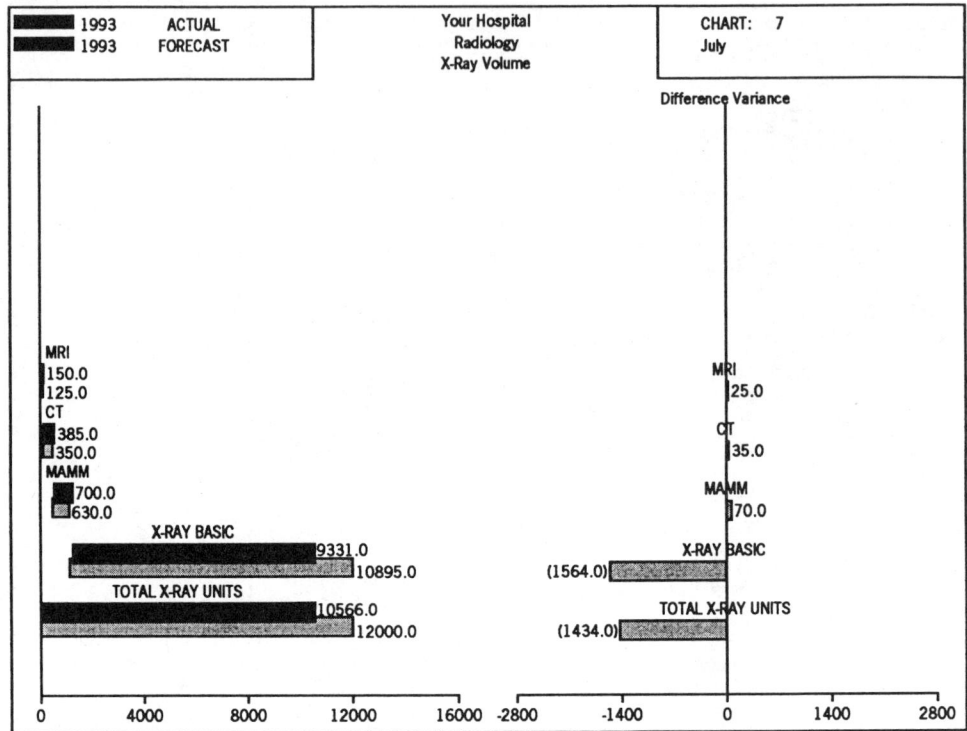

EXHIBIT 9.4A.17 Your Hospital—Radiology—X-Ray Volume

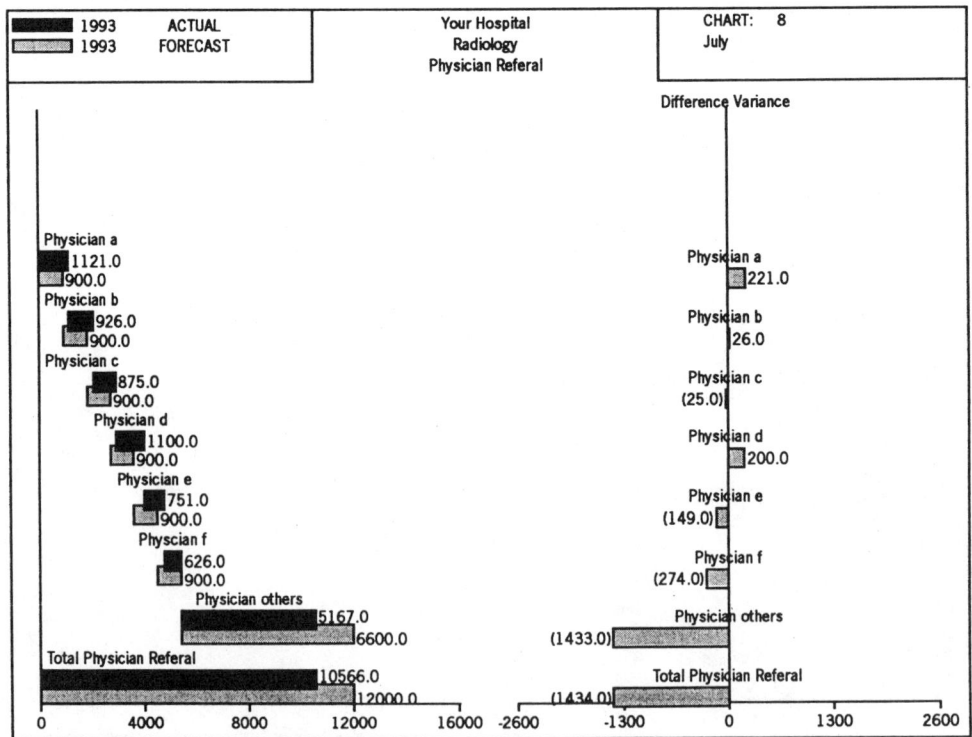

EXHIBIT 9.4A.18 Your Hospital—Radiology—Physician Referral

Section 3—Train the Health Care Professionals to Understand the Information

The training required to help the health care professional understand the new information and the new formats can be accomplished in a two-day seminar. Normally, a two-day seminar is designed to accomplish two goals:

1. Train the professionals how to see and understand the graphics. This part of the training will take about half a day.
2. Train the professionals to use the new information. Specific case studies are used to help secure the understanding necessary to operationalize the system.

Section 4—Help the Health Care Professionals Turn Their Understanding into Knowledge

Turning Understanding into knowledge requires the health care professional to internalize the new information formats and the new information. Once the internalization occurs, the professional can begin to blend the information with their own experiences. Each professional will complete the process at their own rate.

The *internalization* will occur through use of the system. Exhibit 9.4A.2 shows that at the PC level the graphics are divided into the three basic management levels. This is the first place where a human analyst gets involved. The first two steps are automated on the mainframe as the server sends the graphic results directly to the appropriate PCs that act as the clients engine.

The analyst reviews the graphics starting with the top level graphics for that department or division and then disaggregates the data until a clear picture of performance is identified. The charts presented last month (period) may not be relevant to the changing situations so the analysts must review all of the disaggregation paths to create a presentation that:

1. Supports the director information guidelines of the hospital or the hospital management system.
2. Serves as an early warning system for the three levels of governance: management and divisional and service line management;
3. Delineates the magnitude, chances, and exposure to potential losses. This last category deals with the management of uncertainty involved in situations that are often considered risk free.

Each level will receive approximately 30 graphs to define their performance and to identify action areas. The Board and CEO will concentrate on level 1 graphics with graphics displaying unusual differences or variances that need attention and should take about 30 minutes to show.

Top Level Managers concentrate on the level 2 series of graphics that are concerned with overviews of the functional areas they supervise. The division or service line managers are provided the three graphics (and lower level if needed) to point out detailed division or service line opportunities.

Section 5—Help the Health Care Professionals Turn Their Knowledge into Action

There will be little if any problem for the health care professional to turn their knowledge into action; they are trained to act.

Conclusion

The Paradigm shift Dr. Jarett discusses in the main body of this text has bypassed the administration of the health care system. There is an interesting dichotomy because the providers in the health care system are one of the primary users of computer graphics. The dichotomy is about to be closed with the invention of The Financial Graphic Alphabet.®

9.4B JASON PACKAGING GOES FINANCIAL GRAPHIC (New)

by
Greg Alton, President
Alton & Associates

Laurie DeBellis, Controller of the Chicago-area-based Jason Packaging, Inc., is working hard to cope with success. The privately held company has experienced double digit growth over the past four years and is working hard to maintain management control over the rapidly expanding business. Jason is a regional distributor of packaging and shipping systems and supplies throughout Illinois, Wisconsin, Indiana, and Michigan.

DeBellis installed the SBT Series 6.35 General Ledger, Accounts Receivable, Accounts Payable, and Inventory system about four years ago at the company's present location in Elk Grove Village, a Chicago suburb. Choosing SBT was simple. "We were running an accounting application written in C and we were practically tied to the hip of our programmer—especially during our most explosive growth phase. Customizing the system to our needs was a real headache. We needed better networking and more customizable reports. SBT's FoxPro environment gave us the flexibility we needed."

The privately held company started in 1972 as a one-person operation and today employs over 65 employees. The company maintains approximately 4,000 stock-keeping units (SKU) with high-volume sales orders each day. The company has utilized a *flat* organization structure to maximize employee productivity. A flat organization means that each manager is directly responsible for interpreting relevant operational and financial information.

Under the direction of the company's founder and CEO, Wayne J. Williams, Jason management takes pride in its "lean and mean" organizational structure. As Laurie DeBellis noted during a recent interview, "We don't have an excessive amount of support staff to filter the data. If management wants answers, they have to go out and get it. Thus, we need quick access to a wide variety of business information. We're definitely not spoon-fed."

As a result, DeBellis has been forced to demand more from the company's SBT Series 6.35 Accounting Information System. With the help of a dedicated local SBT reseller and the SBT/Fingraph Business Visualization module, a powerful new financial graphic integration, the system is delivering.

With a daily invoice volume sometimes approaching 200 per day and a 4,000 SKU inventory warehouse, Jason's management has the daunting task of gleaning information daily from the company's $12 million-a-year sales operation. This combination placed constraints on the ability of management to turn data into critical business information. Kathy Woolverton, Jason's Senior Business Administrator, has been with the company throughout its 19-year history. She also recognized the growing problem. "It seemed like it took too much involvement to get the answers to our critical management questions. Nobody really knew where to get the data to answer those questions."

After a careful analysis of their situation, DeBellis decided to install the SBT/Fingraph Business Visualization Module. "Basically we had a choice," said DeBellis. "We could hire more people to go through all this data or install a system capable of providing customized information quickly and automatically. The SBT/FinGraph Integration was the perfect solution."

The SBT/Fingraph GL integration installed on Jason's 15-workstation Novell LAN is easily accessible to DeBellis and other management, who use the graphs to help gauge daily, weekly, and monthly performances. She sees the graphic system becoming more and more integrated within other functions of the company. "We don't just use SBT for accounting. It's the primary information source for every function of our business. Every day, now, we run the automated sales, inventory, and cost of goods financial graphic analysis. Every person who has any responsibility for the purchasing, shipping, or selling of our merchandise uses the graphs."

What specific benefits do financial graphics provide Jason? "The graphs really help us ask the right questions," DeBellis commented. "Without integrated financial graphics some of our people would have no concept on where to look for the information. It's a big help, and it is automatic; all we have to do is look at the graphs. You don't have to go through the whole forest to get to the right tree—with graphics you can go straight to the information you need, and fast."

DeBellis likes to think of Jason Packaging as being on the cutting edge. "We're a young company. Nobody here is adverse to change—especially change that helps us do our jobs better. SBT and Fingraph do just that."

Here are a few of the automatic graphs that Jason management uses every day, week, or month. Exhibits 9.4B.1 through 9.4B.5 are normally shown together to provide a complete picture of sales and gross margin performance. The data has been adjusted from actual data.

Exhibit 9.4B.1—Top Seven Salesmen—Sales Contribution with % Variance. This automatically created component chart results from an analysis of the sales data base. The chart shows the total sales contributed by the top seven salesmen this year compared to their last year's sales and compared to the sales contributed by all the remaining salesmen. This pattern helps Jason manage their sales efforts.

Exhibit 9.4B.2—Top Seven Salesmen—Gross Margin Contribution with % Variance. This component chart is identical to Exhibit 9.4B.1 except it shows how much gross margin each of the seven top salesmen contributed to the total gross margin. It is easy to see that there is a difference in the two patterns. DeBellis noted, "The differences in the patterns help us pinpoint sales mix opportunities we may not have noticed before."

Exhibit 9.4B.3—Top Seven Salesmen as a % of Total Sales—Ratio Chart. This chart is always shown with Exhibit 9.4B.1 to highlight the top seven's sales performance.

Exhibit 9.4B.4—Top Seven Salesmen as a % of Gross Margin—Ratio Chart. This chart is always shown with Exhibit 9.4B.2 to highlight the top seven salesmen Gross Margin performance.

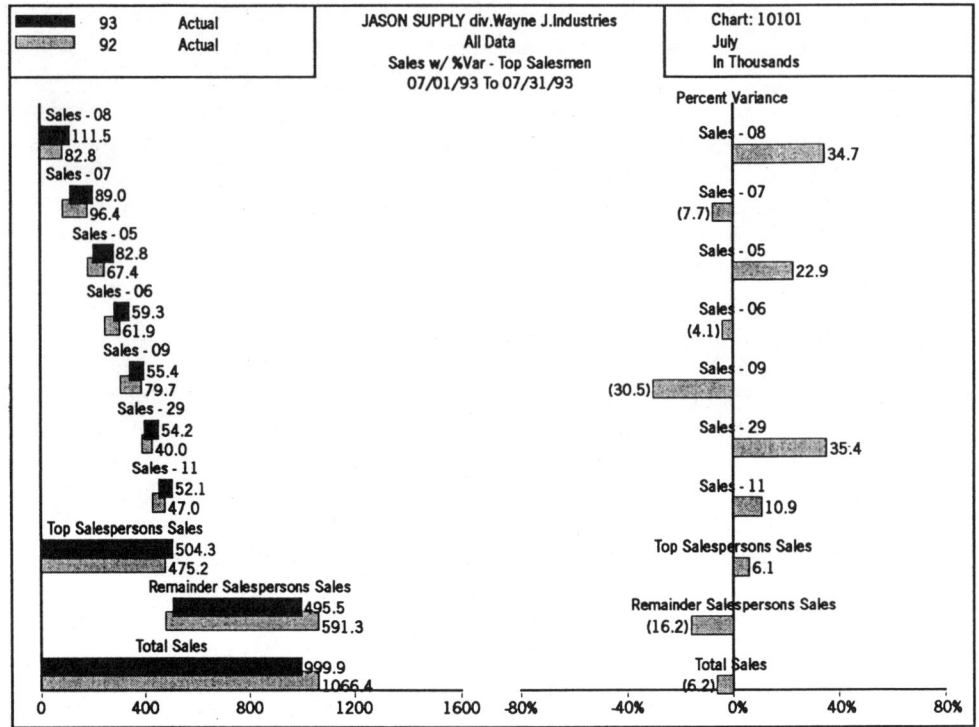

EXHIBIT 9.4B.1   Top Seven Salesmen—Sales Contribution with % Variance

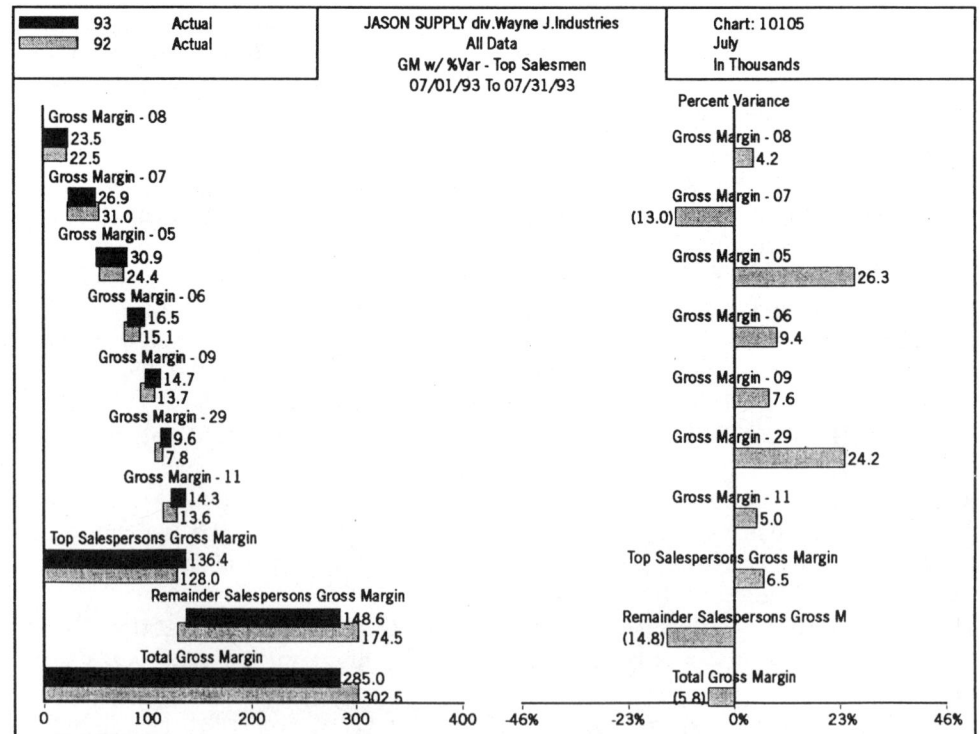

EXHIBIT 9.4B.2   Top Seven Salesmen—Gross Margin Contribution with % Variance

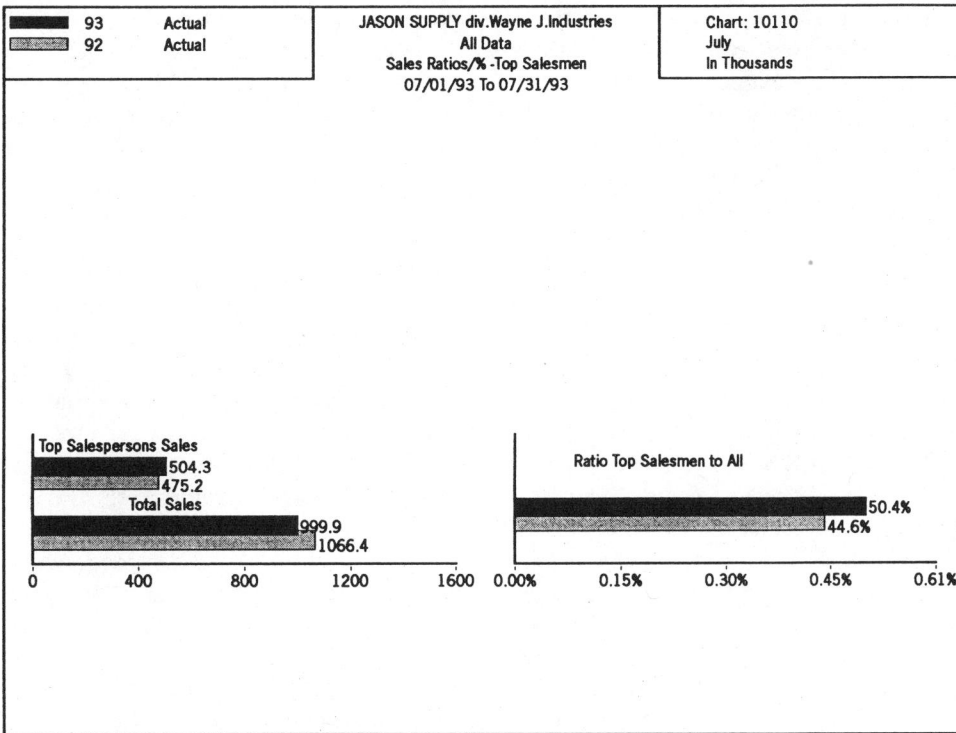

	93	Actual
	92	Actual

JASON SUPPLY div.Wayne J.Industries
All Data
Sales Ratios/% -Top Salesmen
07/01/93 To 07/31/93

Chart: 10110
July
In Thousands

Top Salespersons Sales
504.3
475.2
Total Sales
999.9
1066.4

0   400   800   1200   1600

Ratio Top Salesmen to All
50.4%
44.6%

0.00%   0.15%   0.30%   0.45%   0.61%

EXHIBIT 9.4B.3   Top Seven Salesmen as a % of Total Sales—Ratio Chart

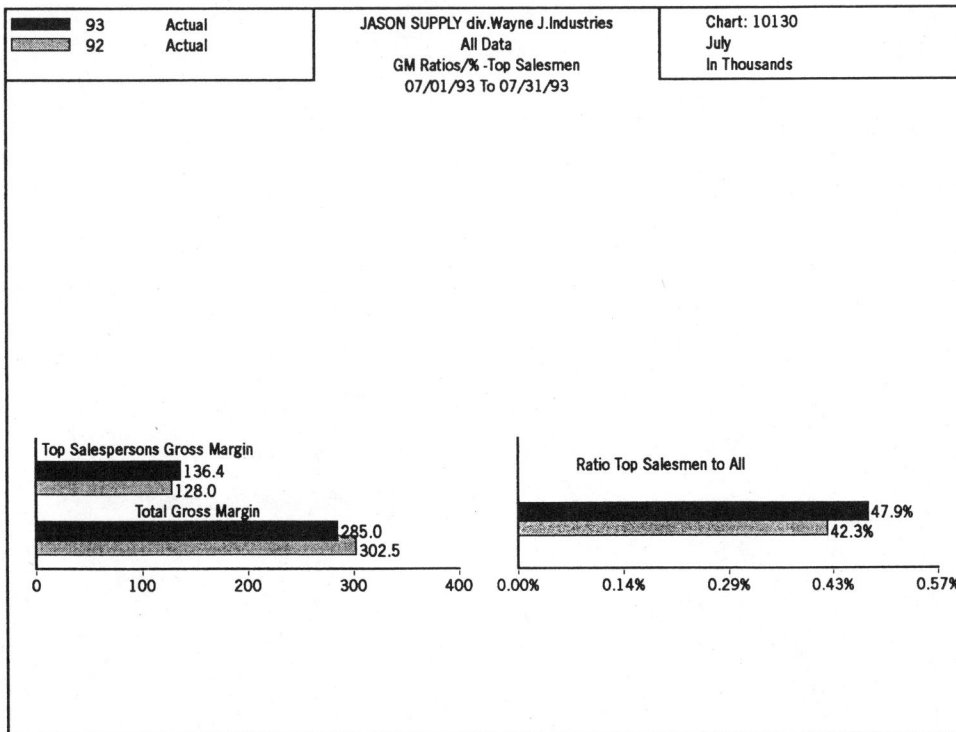

	93	Actual
	92	Actual

JASON SUPPLY div.Wayne J.Industries
All Data
GM Ratios/% -Top Salesmen
07/01/93 To 07/31/93

Chart: 10130
July
In Thousands

Top Salespersons Gross Margin
136.4
128.0
Total Gross Margin
285.0
302.5

0   100   200   300   400

Ratio Top Salesmen to All
47.9%
42.3%

0.00%   0.14%   0.29%   0.43%   0.57%

EXHIBIT 9.4B.4   Top Seven Salesmen as a % of Gross Margin—Ratio Chart

Exhibit 9.4B.5—Top Seven Items Sold Compared to Total Sales—Ratio Chart. This chart rounds out the sales performance pattern showing how the top seven items compared to the total sales. The first five charts provide a clear pattern of performance for the Jason sales team. "Our salesmen have always been interested in how they were performing compared to the other salesmen and to last year," DeBellis commented. "Now we can show them every day, and without a lot of effort!"

Exhibit 9.4B.6—Top Seven Salesmen—Receivable > 90 Days. This chart starts a second critical data series used at least weekly to monitor Accounts Receivable. Exhibits 9.4B.6 through 9.4B.9 were selected to show how Jason tracks the "over 90 days A/R" balances. (These figures were adjusted to make the point.) Study the charts to see how these patterns would help your company manage accounts receivable.

Exhibit 9.4B.7—Salesmen's A/R by Category—Ratio Chart. Shows that for Salesperson 01, the majority of the accounts receivable are seriously overdue.

Exhibit 9.4B.8—Top Seven Customers—Receivable > 90 Days. This automatically created chart presents a different pattern of accounts receivable over 90 days. It is fairly clear that the over 90 days A/R problem is concentrated in one customer.

Exhibit 9.4B.9—Sales Days A/R. This final chart in the Accounts Receivable series shows that there are 38.5 days of sales in Accounts Receivable. Imagine what the picture would look like if the one customer's late account was paid.

Exhibit 9.4B.10—Top Seven Selling Inventory Items. Exhibits 9.4B.10 and 9.4B.11 describe how one of Jason's largest assets, the inventory is performing. Exhibit 9.4B.10 shows that the Top Seven Selling Inventory Items account for a significant portion of total sales.

Exhibit 9.4B.11—Days of Inventory On Hand. The final chart shows how many days of inventory are on hand as of the date shown.

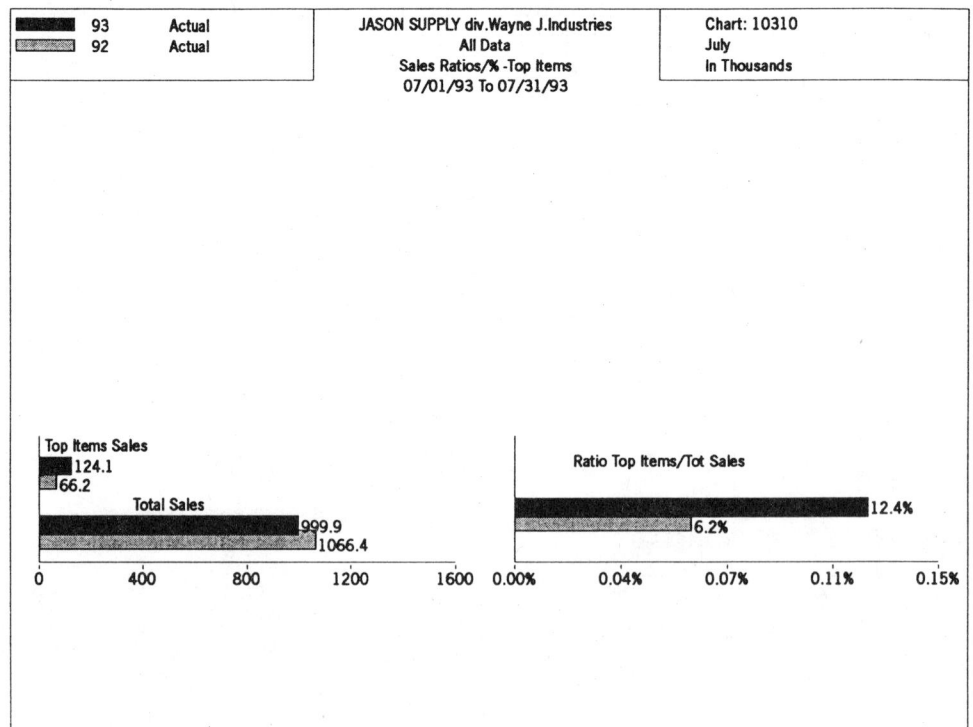

EXHIBIT 9.4B.5   Top Seven Items Sold Compared to Total Sales—Ratio Chart

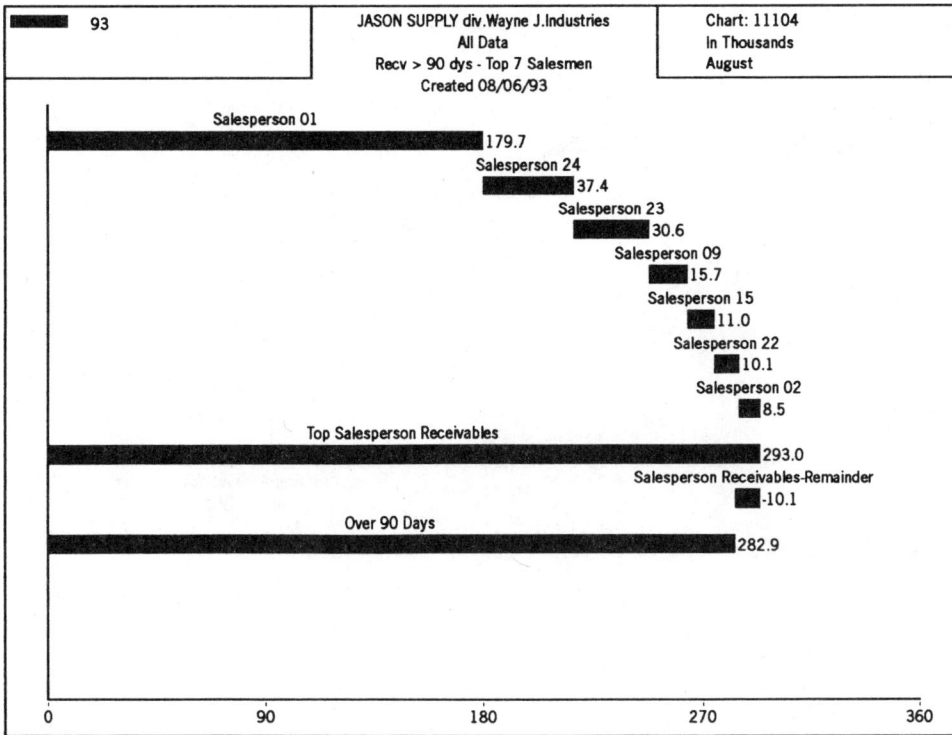

EXHIBIT 9.4B.6   Top Seven Salesmen—Receivable > 90 Days

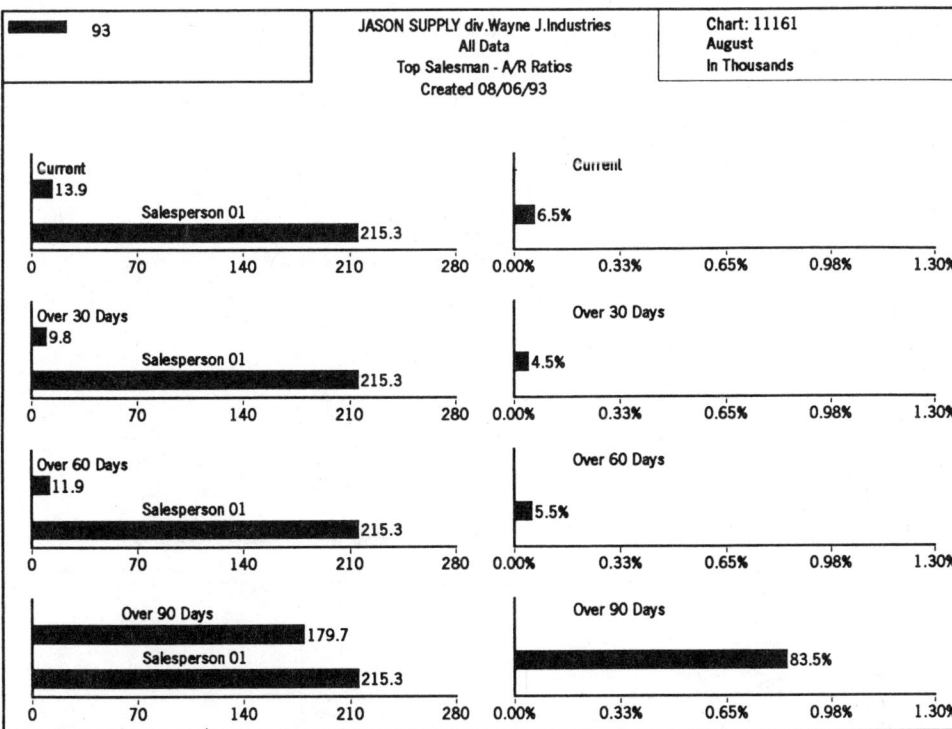

EXHIBIT 9.4B.7   Salesmen's A/R by Category—Ratio Chart

■ 93	JASON SUPPLY div.Wayne J.Industries All Data Recv > 90 dys - Top 7 Customer 07/01/93 To 07/31/93	Chart: 11204 August In Thousands

Customer A13 — 156.7
Customer E22 — 36.6
Customer C12 — 31.6
Customer D01 — 20.7
Customer J19 — 19.7
Customer C27 — 14.0
Customer N45 — 10.8
Top Customer Receivables — 290.0
Customer Receivables-Remainder — -7.1
Over 90 Days — 282.9

0   90   180   270   360

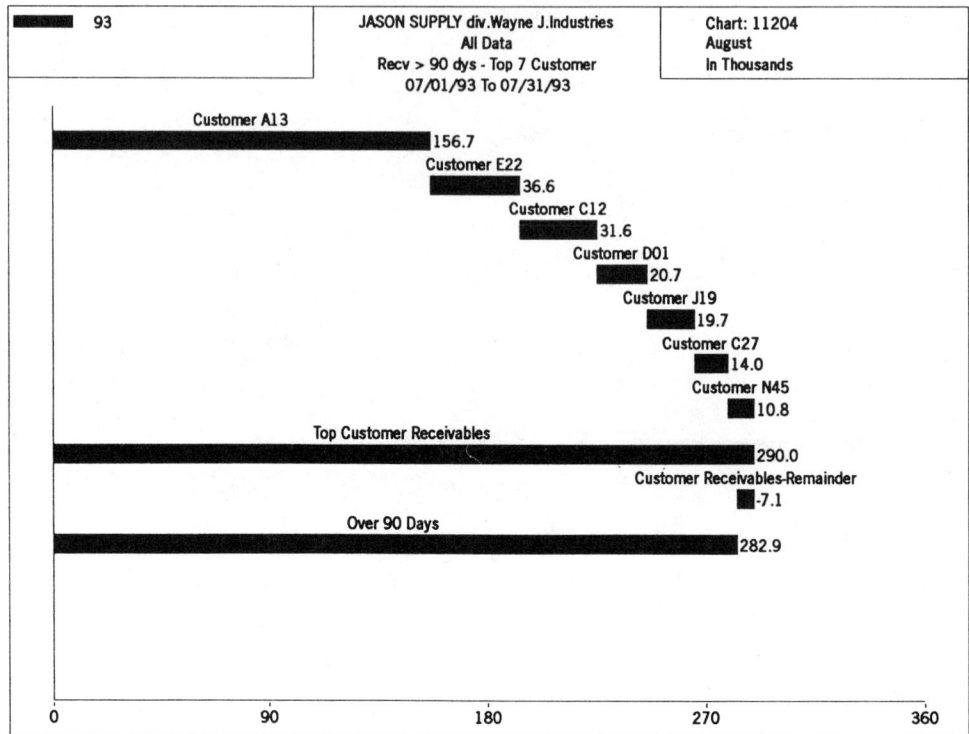

EXHIBIT 9.4B.8   Top Seven Customers—Receivable > 90 Days

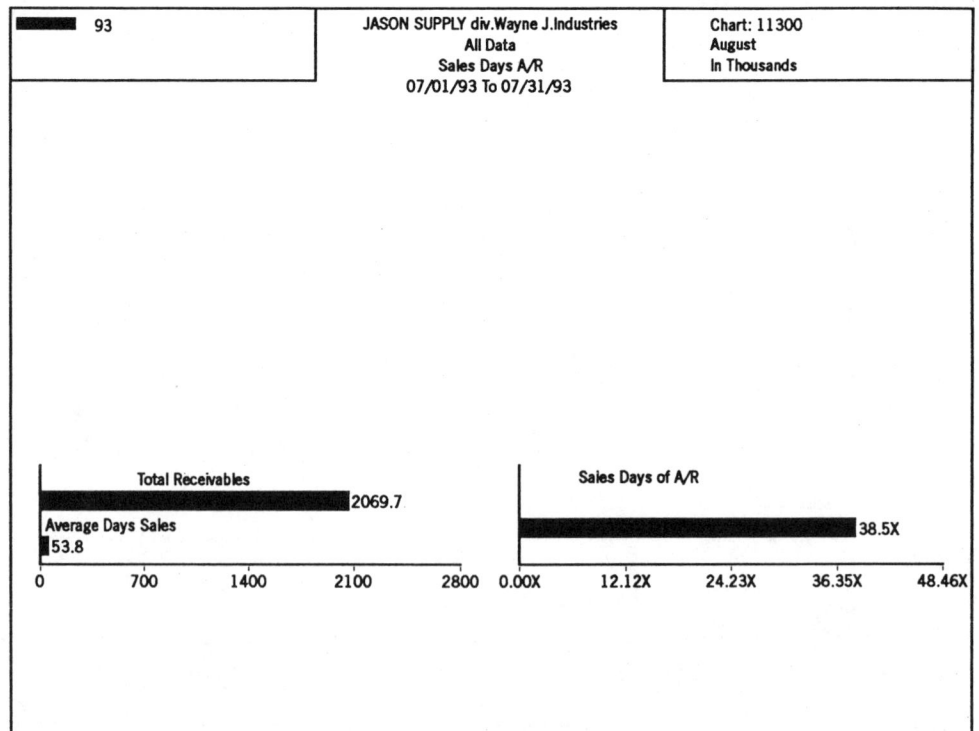

■ 93	JASON SUPPLY div.Wayne J.Industries All Data Sales Days A/R 07/01/93 To 07/31/93	Chart: 11300 August In Thousands

Total Receivables — 2069.7
Average Days Sales — 53.8
Sales Days of A/R — 38.5X

0   700   1400   2100   2800   0.00X   12.12X   24.23X   36.35X   48.46X

EXHIBIT 9.4B.9   Sales Days A/R

▬▬▬ 93	JASON SUPPLY div.Wayne J.Industries Inventory - Top 7 Items/Sales Created 08/06/93	Chart: 12101 August In Millions

Inventory Item A132-89
0.4
Inventory Item XZ87-96
0.2
Inventory Item FX23-958
0.1
Inventory Item ZZ21-980
0.1
Inventory Item PZ9-452
0.1
Inventory Item PX76-263
0.1
Inventory Item KX87-538
0.1
Top Inventory Item Sales
1.2
Inventory Item Sales-Remainder
10.5
Total Sales of Inventory - YTD
11.7

0   4   8   12   16

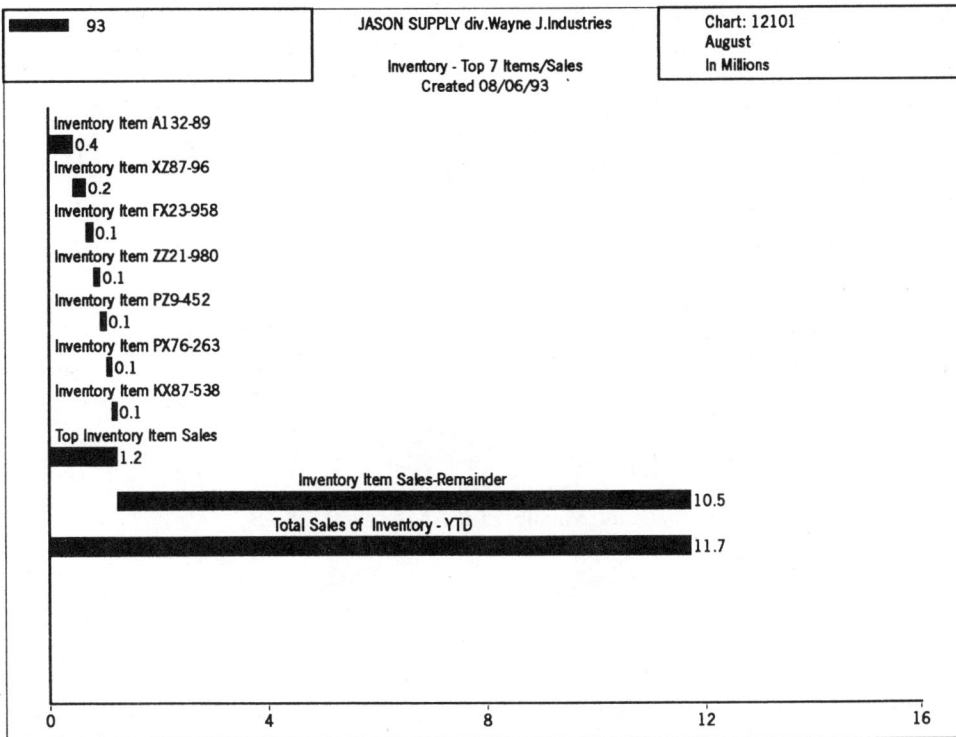

EXHIBIT 9.4B.10   Top Seven Selling Inventory Items

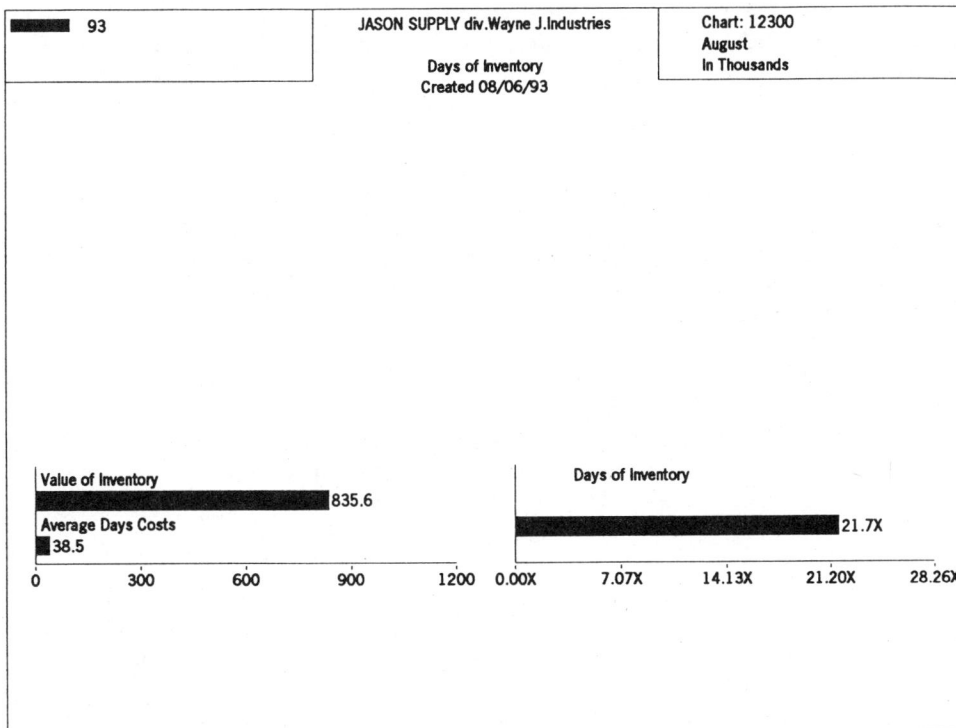

▬▬▬ 93	JASON SUPPLY div.Wayne J.Industries Days of Inventory Created 08/06/93	Chart: 12300 August In Thousands

Value of Inventory
835.6
Average Days Costs
38.5

0   300   600   900   1200

Days of Inventory
21.7X

0.00X   7.07X   14.13X   21.20X   28.26X

EXHIBIT 9.4B.11   Days of Inventory on Hand

We selected this set of charts because they typified the way management looks at the business each day. Sales, Accounts Receivable, and Inventory are the critical control points for a growing and constantly changing Jason. DeBellis concludes, "These few charts each day give us a picture of how we are doing. We know exactly where to put our management efforts. Management now depends on the information that was so recently hidden by the rows and columns of reports."

9.4C HOW SCS COMPUTE, INC. USES FINANCIAL GRAPHICS AS AN INTEGRAL PART OF THEIR SOFTWARE STRATEGY

by
Chris Bennett
Accounting Product Manager
Linda Peterson
Product Line Manager for AMI Tax Machine
Lou Ann Vandermore
Product Line Manager for LMS

SCS Compute, Inc. produces one of the oldest and most respected line of tax and write-up software for the accounting profession. As all successful software companies must, SCS responds to the perceived needs of their customers, the practicing accountant. Accountants, on the other hand, must respond to the needs of their customers, and the accountants' clients want graphics as an integral part of their financial reporting.

In early 1992, we were given the challenge of finding exactly what our customers, the practicing accountant, needed and expected in a modern line of tax and accounting software packages. We ran a series of interviews, focus groups, and personal conversations with a number of our key customers, sales managers, and salespeople. The answer was a resounding "Graphics"!

But there was more to the findings. Here are some of the findings summarized by what the accountants did and did not want from graphics:

1. Accountants did not want "fluff" or just pretty graphics. It was clear that the practicing accountants were fully aware of the colorful presentation graphic software systems with advanced font and graphic capabilities and the clip art used to highlight word charts used in client presentations. In fact, many of those interviewed said they made considerable use of such software in their practice and would continue to use them, but it did not meet their specific financial data needs.

2. What they did need were accurate and consistent representations of the financial and accounting numbers available from our versatile AMI Data Write™ report writer, AMI Tax Machine and LMS tax system.

3. Accountants did not want to take time from their busy work day to create the charts.

4. Accountants want graphics that are fully integrated with the report writer and the Tax Systems; fully automatic; and, provide a full range of graphic presentations. They wanted to choose from the available graphics to build a client presentation that clearly reflects the client's most critical business and tax patterns in the current data.

5. Accountants want graphics that meet their reporting responsibilities plus help them explain planning and profit opportunities to their clients.

Taken as a whole, we were not confident that such a complete solution was available in the marketplace. During one of our planning sessions, our lead programmer remembered that several years ago he heard someone speak about financial graphics that met at least some of the accountants' needs. After a quick search of his records, he found Dr. Jarett's name and within a short period of time we were in contact.

We met with Dr. Jarett and went through a rapid learning curve to understand The Financial Graphic Alphabet and how it would work in tax and write-up software. The result was a detailed design for a "smart" system that would analyze the structure of the reports and the tax returns to automatically create a set of charts that accurately and consistently present the information produced by the report writer and the tax systems.

A final consideration of our marketing research was to determine if The Financial Graphic Alphabet would work with both a write-up package and a tax package. We knew intuitively that the graphics would work directly with the write-up package. But it was not clear that the same financial graphic principles would fit with the highly structured requirements of the Federal and State tax returns. In fact, we found that the addition of graphics to the tax returns offers the accountant an extremely powerful communication process to explain to their clients the impact of the constantly changing tax laws.

We included a few of the charts that represent some of the more important graphic representations of the complete investigation. The charts reflected here are a direct result of the information contained in the reports or the tax forms. The critical design issue is that when a balance sheet is reported, the graphics are smart enough to create a comparative component chart; where ratios are appropriate, the system is smart enough to create the ratio charts; where data over time is available, the system is smart enough to prepare a time series chart. In short, all the accountant needs to do is create a good tabular report; the graphic integration module creates the appropriate financial graphic representation.

We included one example of a balance sheet tabular report produced by Data Write. All of the supporting graphics shown were automatically created by the visualization module. Note the wide range of charts from which the accountant can choose for the client presentation.

Exhibits 9.4C.1 through 9.4C.39 were produced directly from a Tax Machine and/or LMS produced 1040 return. Note the significant amount of information available for the accountant to explain why the taxes are different this year from last year and how the forecast data could affect their financial *lives*.

9.4D INTEGRATING FINANCIAL GRAPHICS WITH AUTOMATED CLIENT ENGAGEMENT (ACE™)

by
Ken Thygesen
McGladrey Pullen

Over the past few years, I was on the speakers' panel or exhibiting at a number of accounting and computer shows where Dr. Jarett was also speaking. As a result, I have heard him speak on several occasions and we held a number of conversations about using The Financial Graphic Alphabet to support the accountant during the audit engagement. Based on these conversations, we considered how graphics would improve the performance of the firms who use our Automated Client Engagement (ACE™) software.

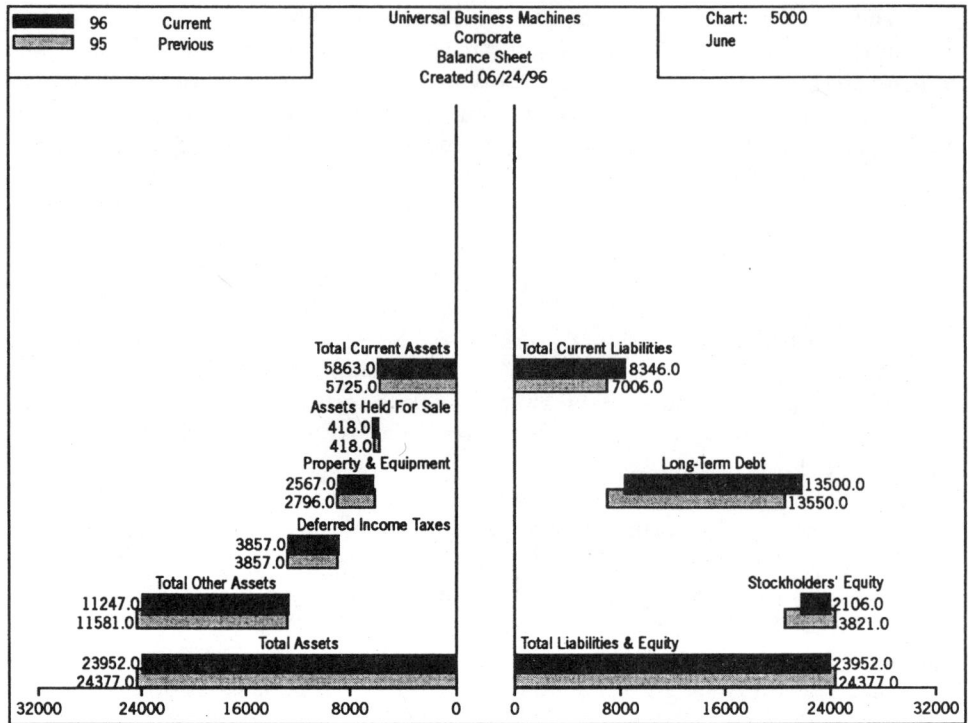

EXHIBIT 9.4C.1   Universal Business Machines—Corporate—Balance Sheet Created 06/24/96

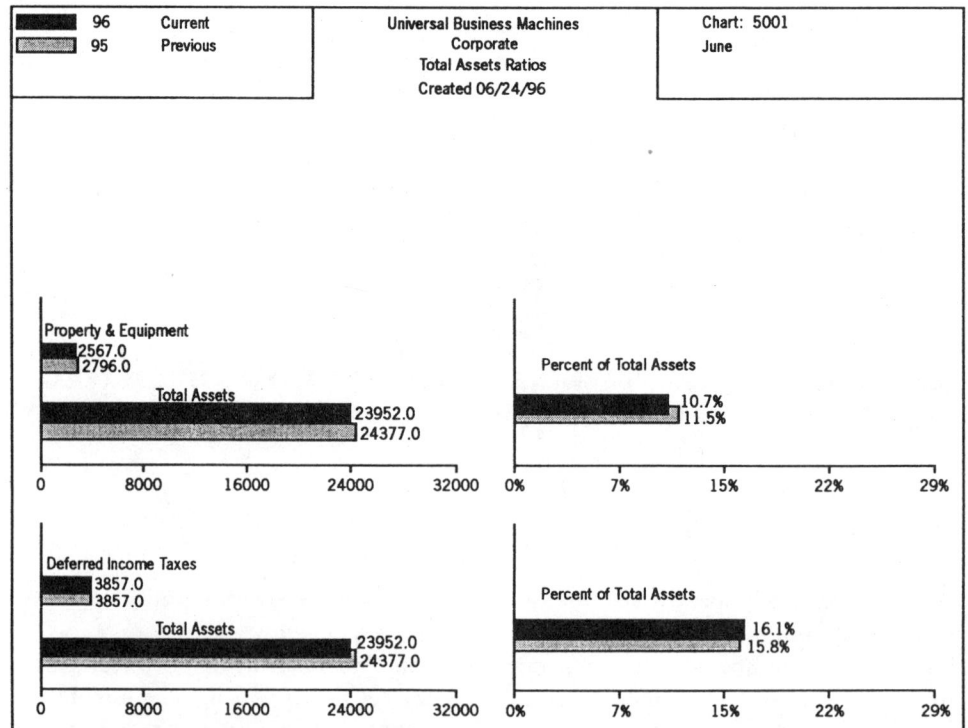

EXHIBIT 9.4C.2   Universal Business Machines—Corporate—Total Assets Ratios Created 06/24/96

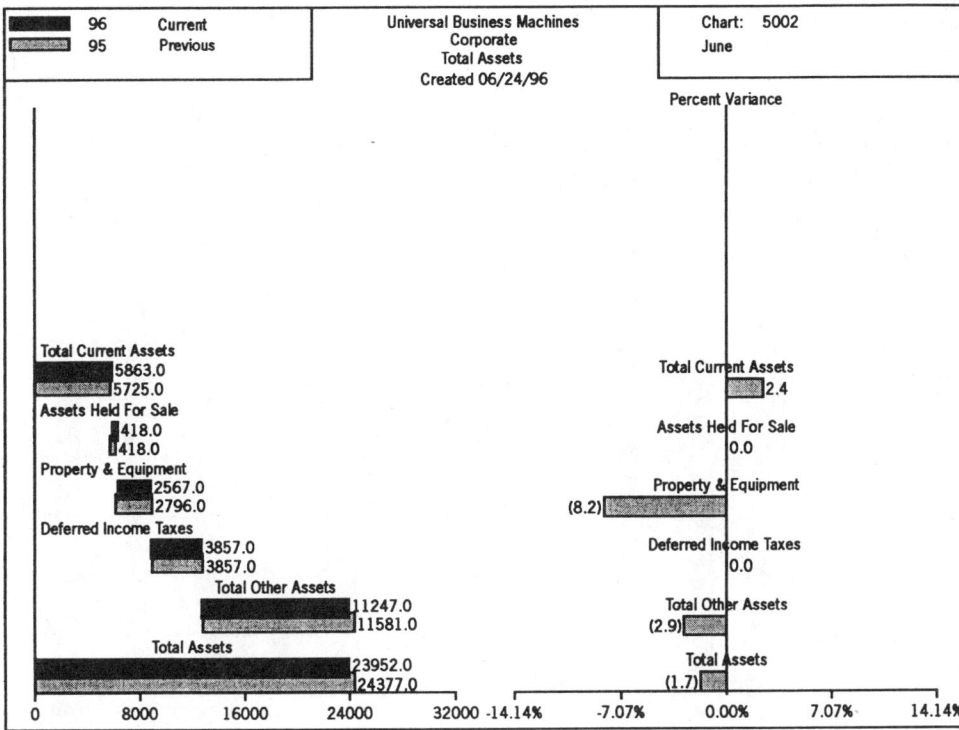

EXHIBIT 9.4C.3 Universal Business Machines—Corporate—Total Assets Created 06/24/96

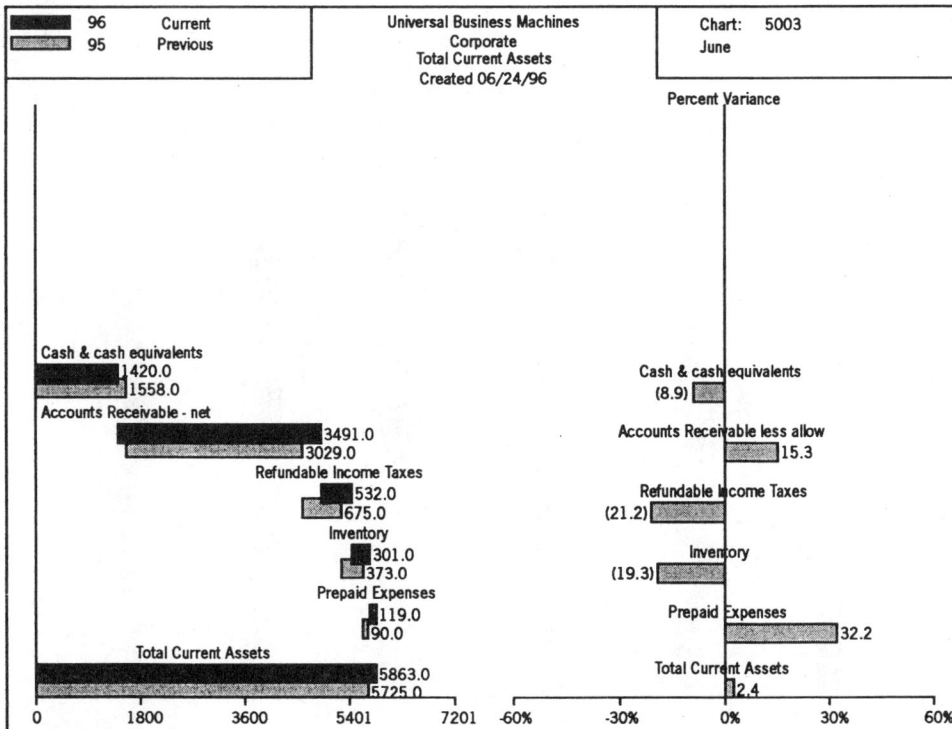

EXHIBIT 9.4C.4 Universal Business Machines—Corporate—Total Current Assets Created 06/24/96

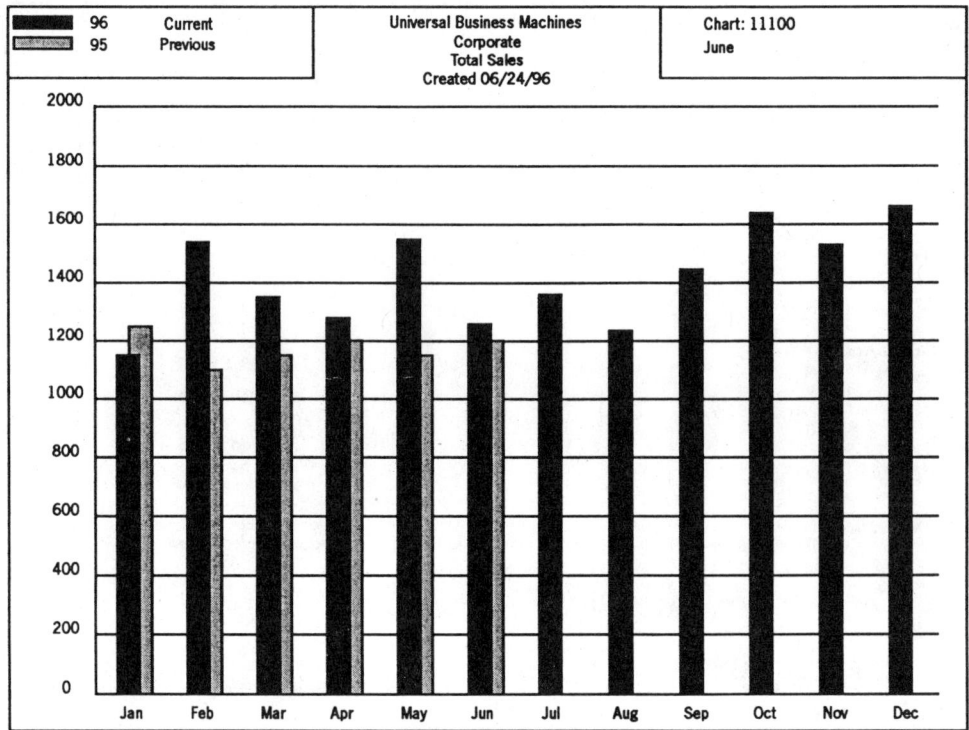

EXHIBIT 9.4C.5 Universal Business Machines—Corporate—Total Sales Created 06/24/96

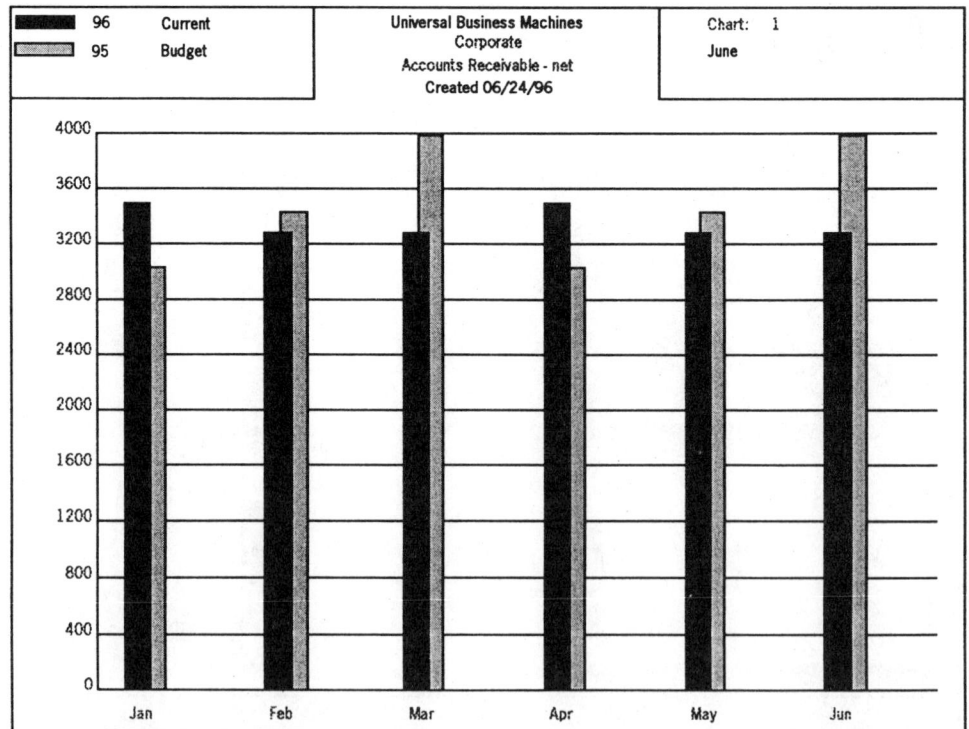

EXHIBIT 9.4C.6 Universal Business Machines—Corporate—Accounts Receivable—Net Created 06/24/96

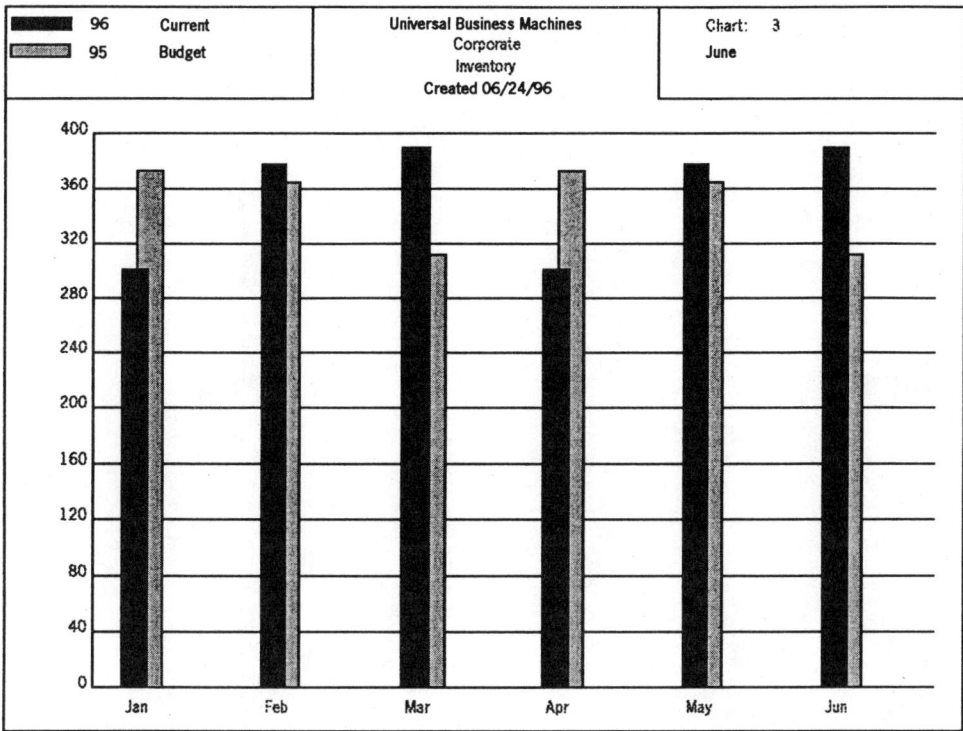

EXHIBIT 9.4C.7   Universal Business Machines—Corporate—Inventory Created 06/24/96

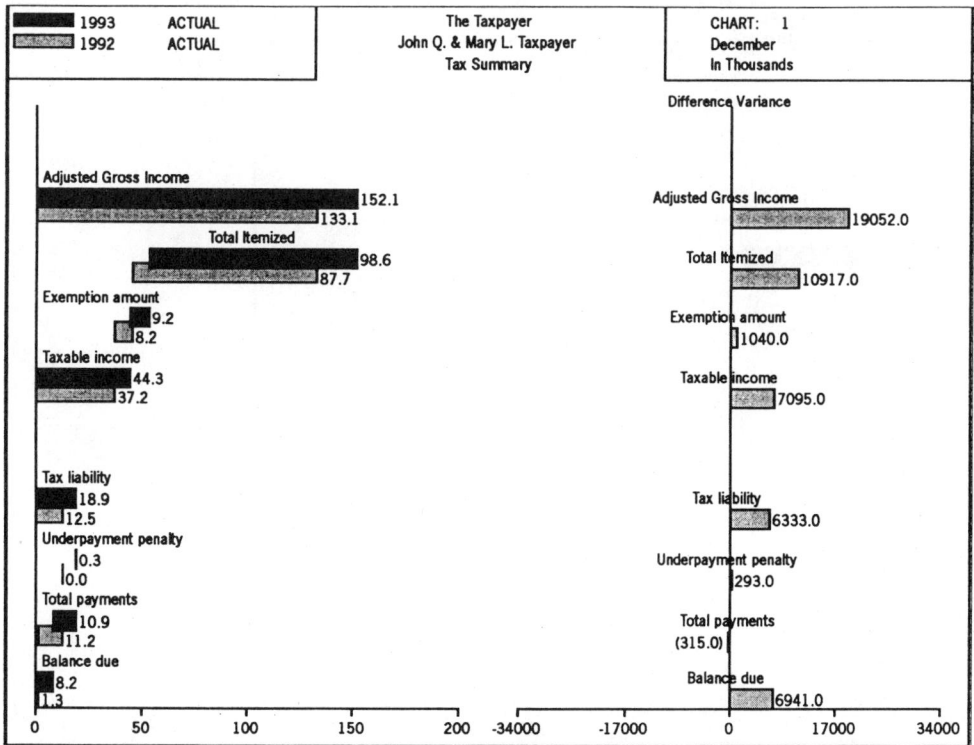

EXHIBIT 9.4C.8   The Taxpayer—John Q. & Mary L. Taxpayer—Tax Summary

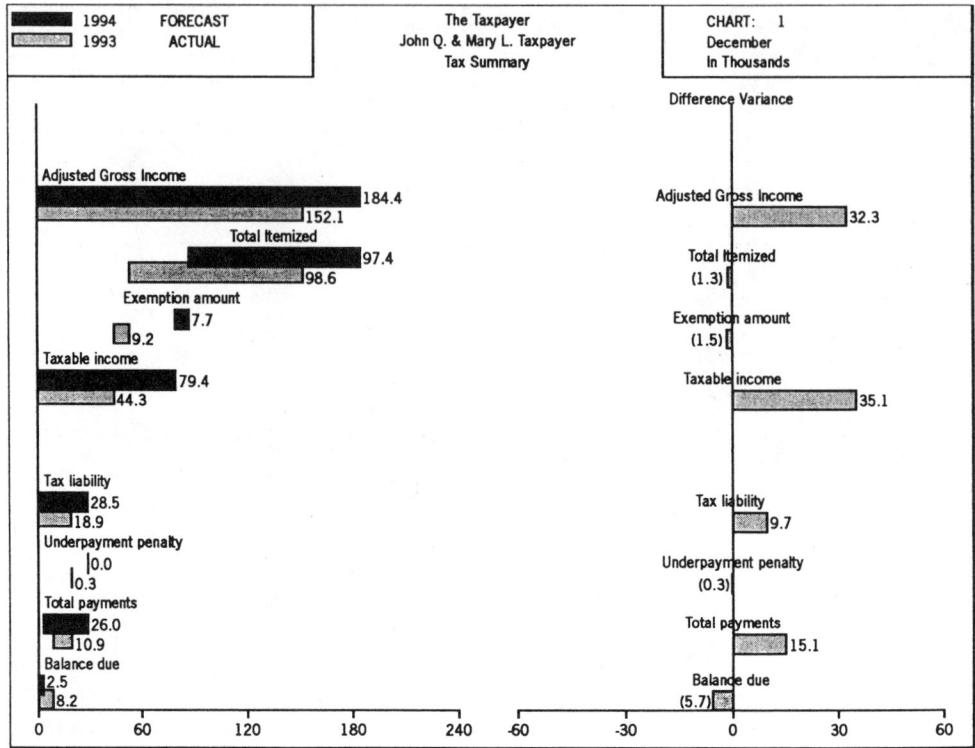

EXHIBIT 9.4C.9   The Taxpayer—John Q. & Mary L. Taxpayer—Tax Summary

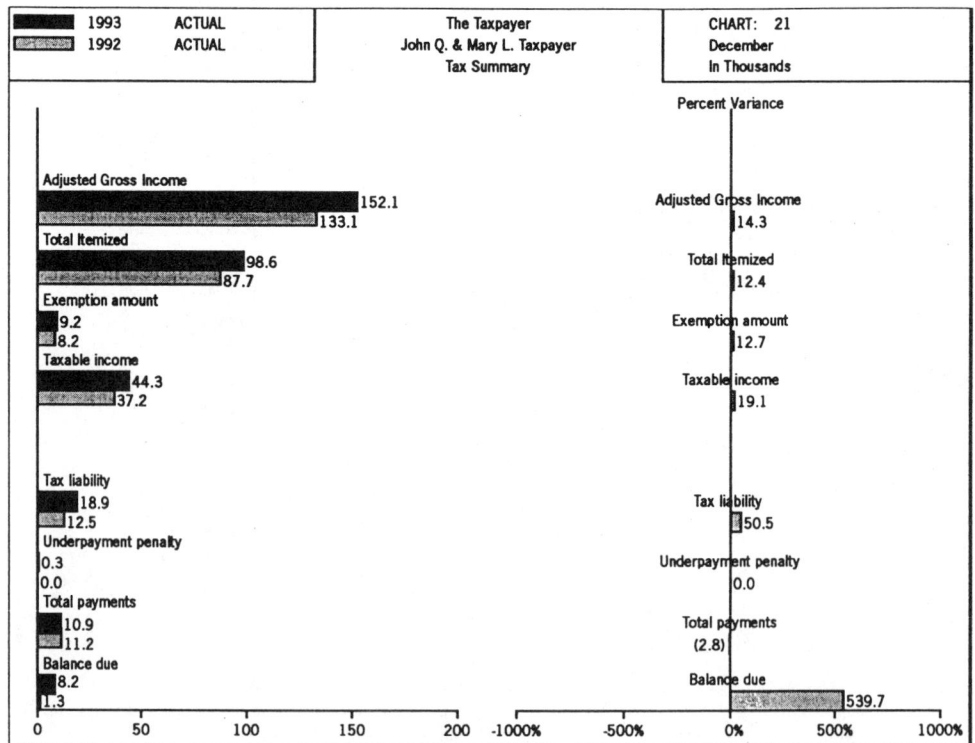

EXHIBIT 9.4C.10   The Taxpayer—John Q. & Mary L. Taxpayer—Tax Summary

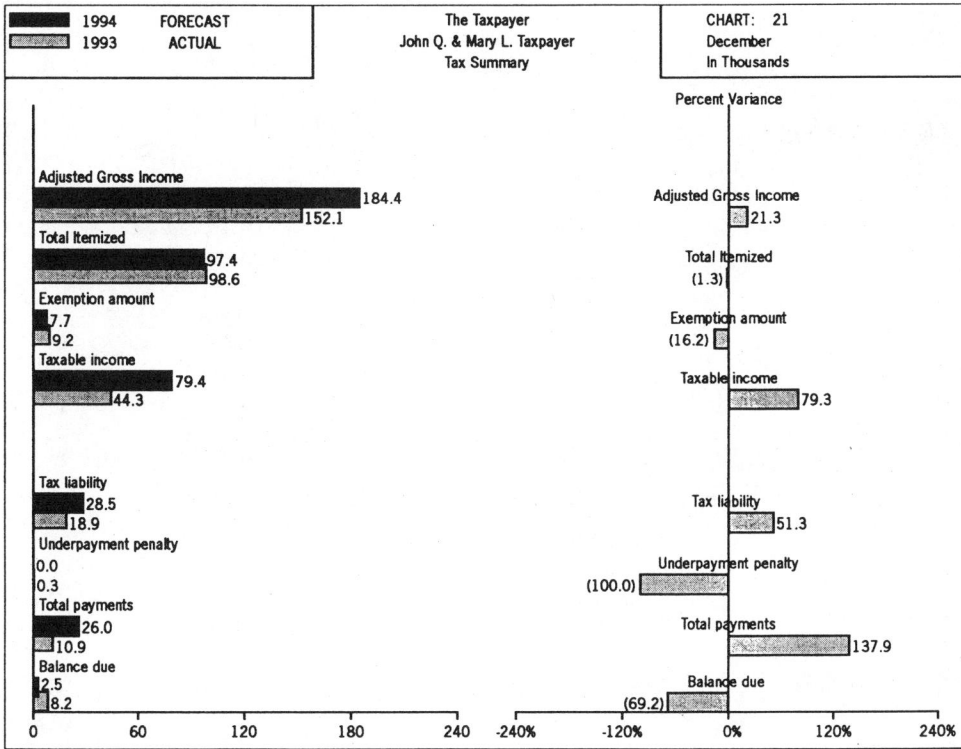

EXHIBIT 9.4C.11   The Taxpayer—John Q. & Mary L. Taxpayer—Tax Summary

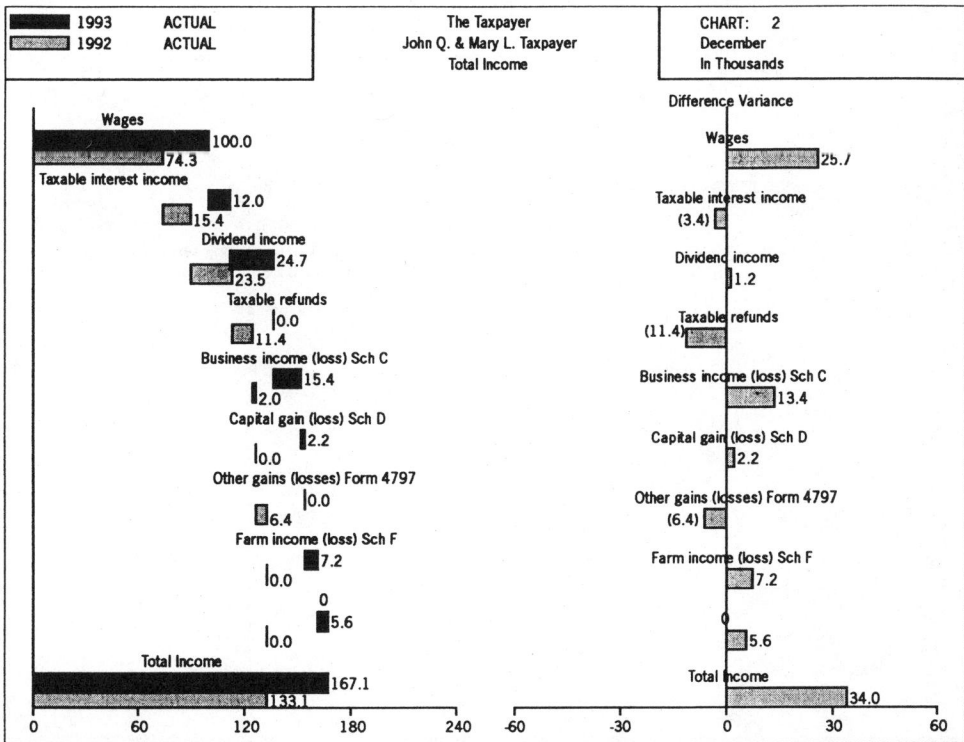

EXHIBIT 9.4C.12   The Taxpayer—John Q. & Mary L. Taxpayer—Total Income

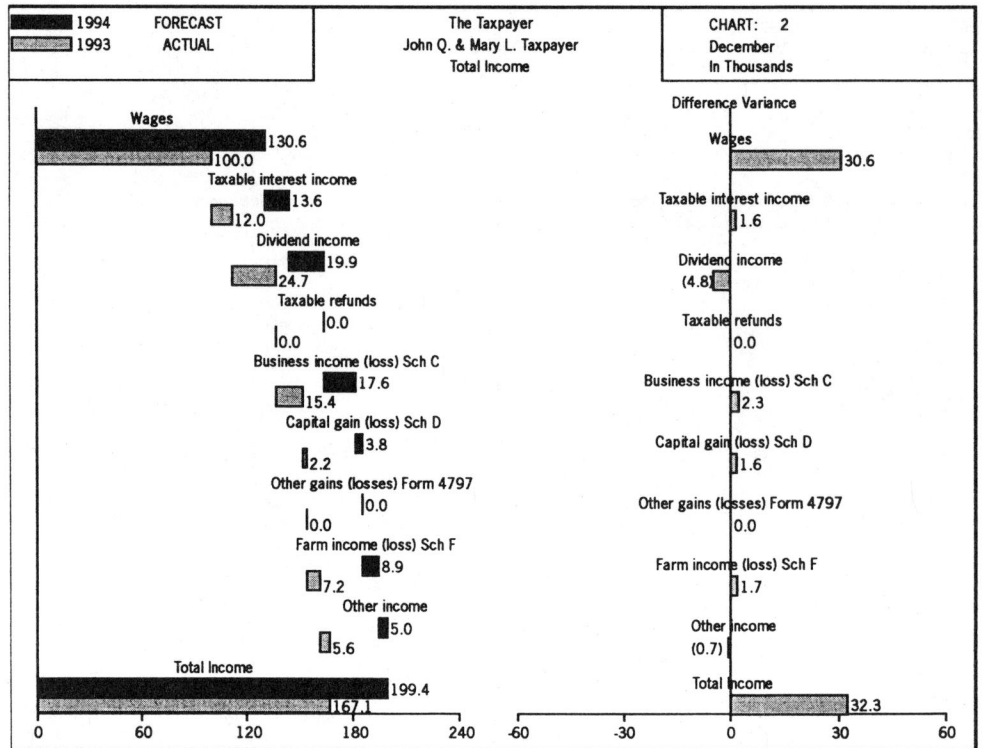

EXHIBIT 9.4C.13 The Taxpayer—John Q. & Mary L. Taxpayer—Total Income

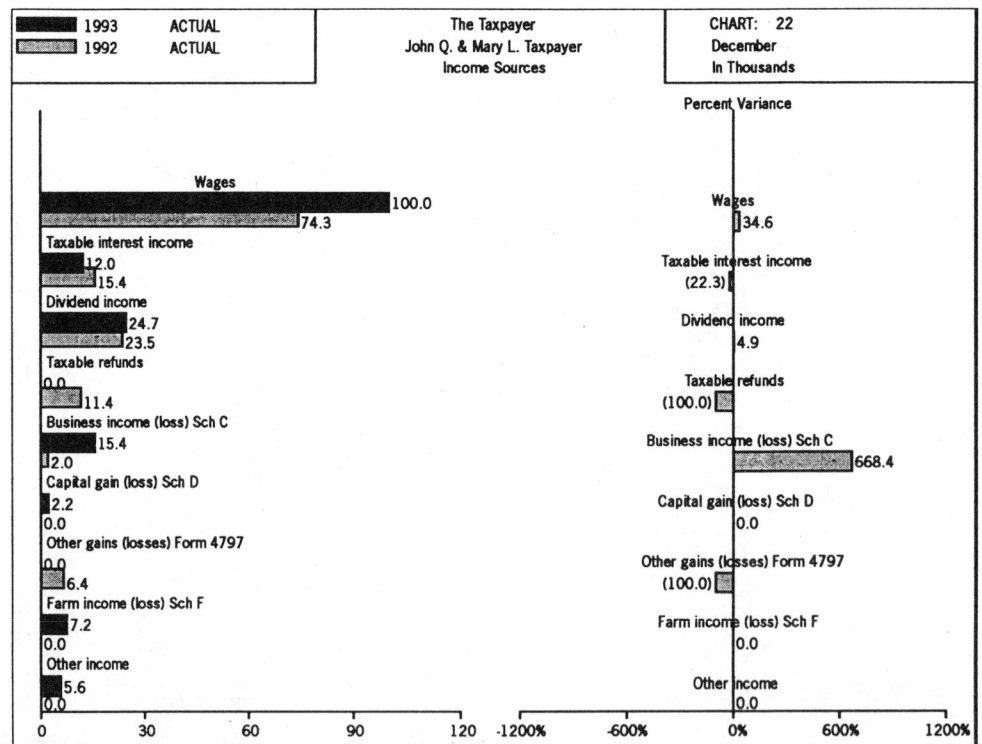

EXHIBIT 9.4C.14 The Taxpayer—John Q. & Mary L. Taxpayer—Income Sources

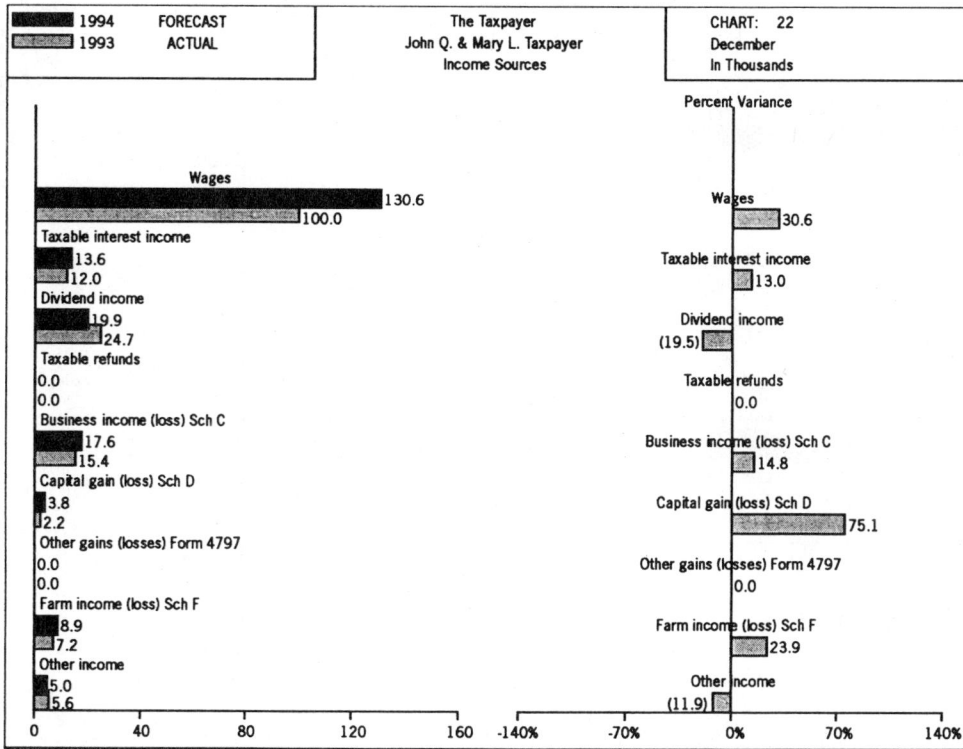

EXHIBIT 9.4C.15   The Taxpayer—John Q. & Mary L. Taxpayer—Income Sources

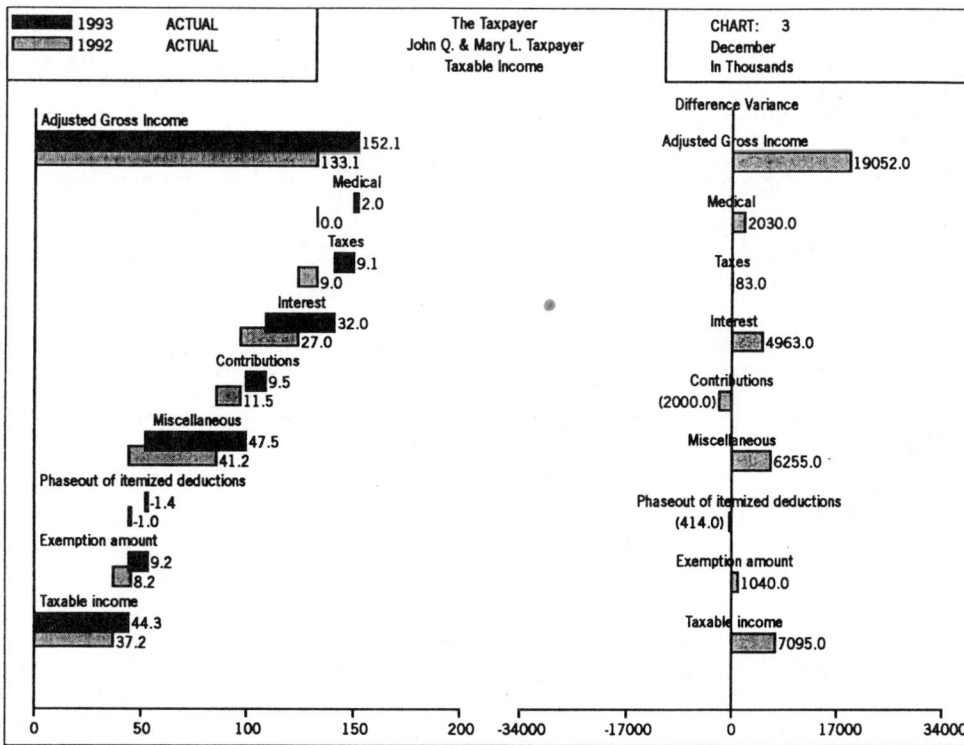

EXHIBIT 9.4C.16   The Taxpayer—John Q. & Mary L. Taxpayer—Taxable Income

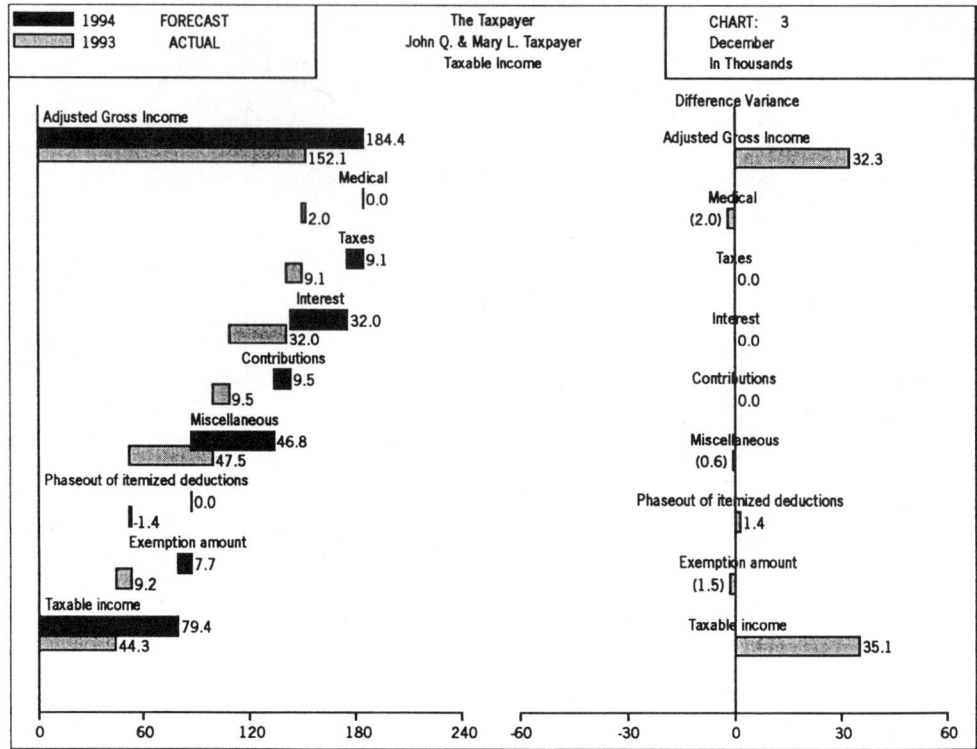

EXHIBIT 9.4C.17   The Taxpayer—John Q. & Mary L. Taxpayer—Taxable Income

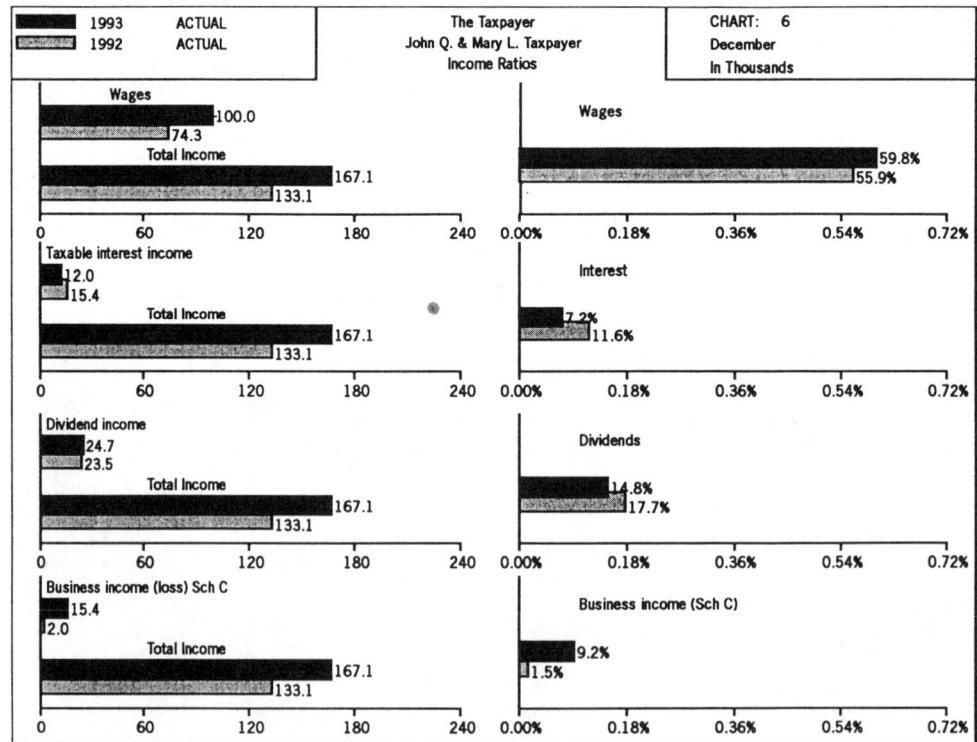

EXHIBIT 9.4C.18   The Taxpayer—John Q. & Mary L. Taxpayer—Income Ratios

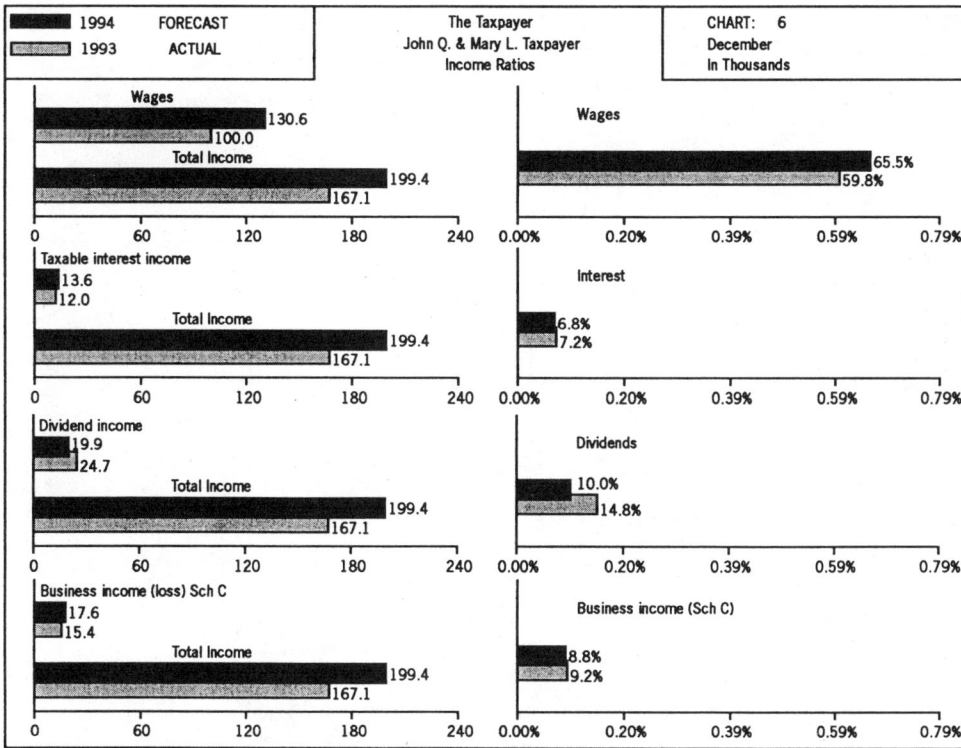

EXHIBIT 9.4C.19   The Taxpayer—John Q. & Mary L. Taxpayer—Income Ratios

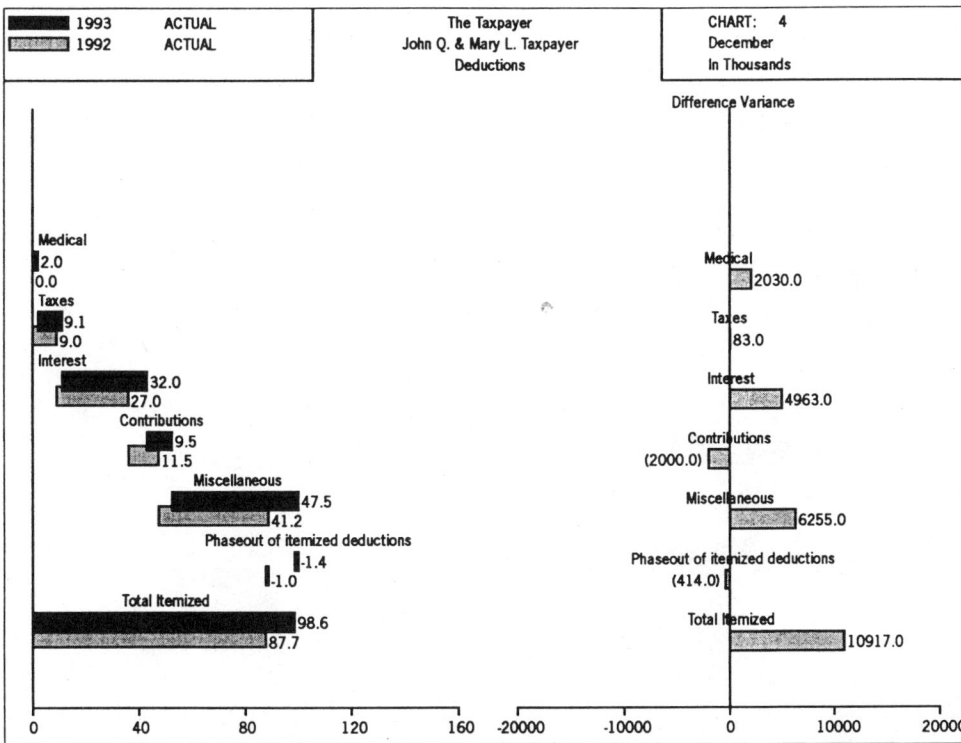

EXHIBIT 9.4C.20   The Taxpayer—John Q. & Mary L. Taxpayer—Deductions

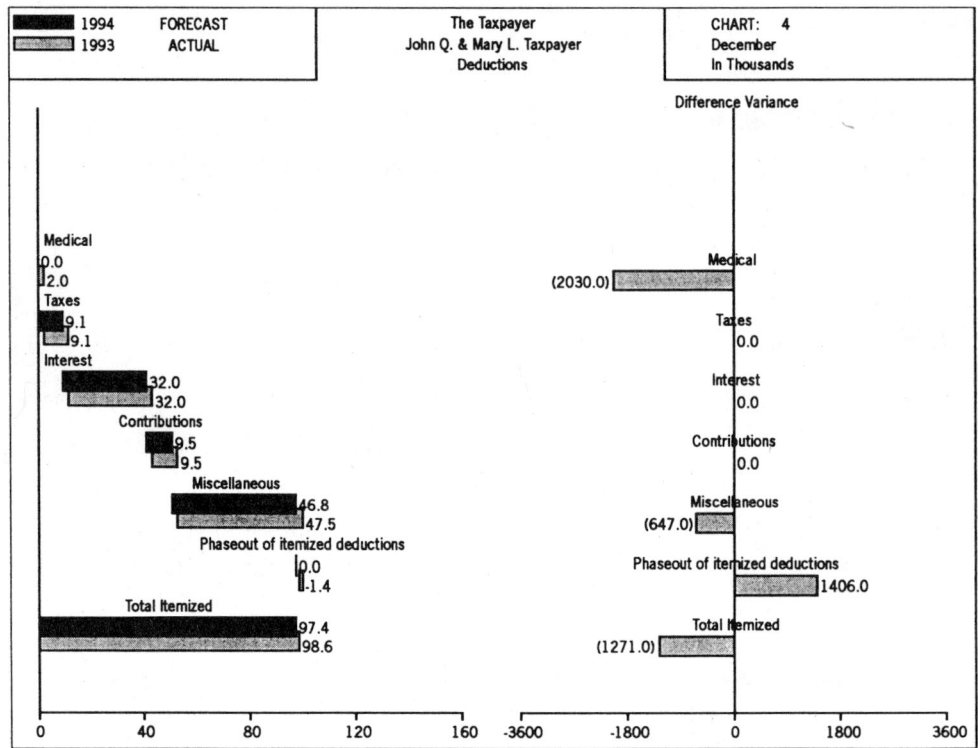

EXHIBIT 9.4C.21   The Taxpayer—John Q. & Mary L. Taxpayer—Deductions

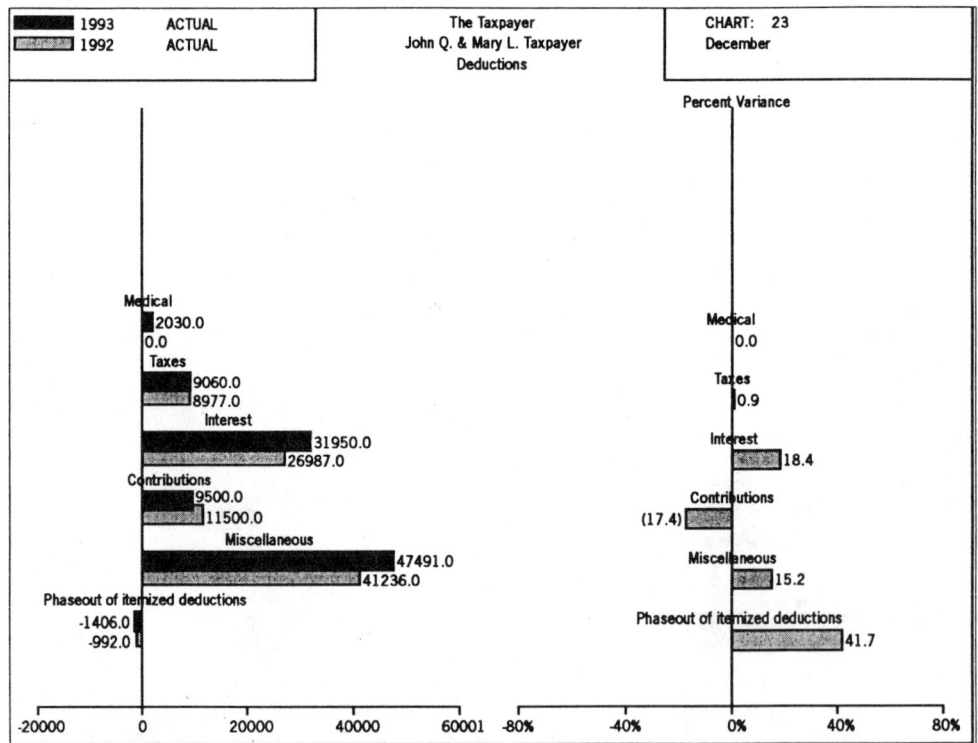

EXHIBIT 9.4C.22   The Taxpayer—John Q. & Mary L. Taxpayer—Deductions

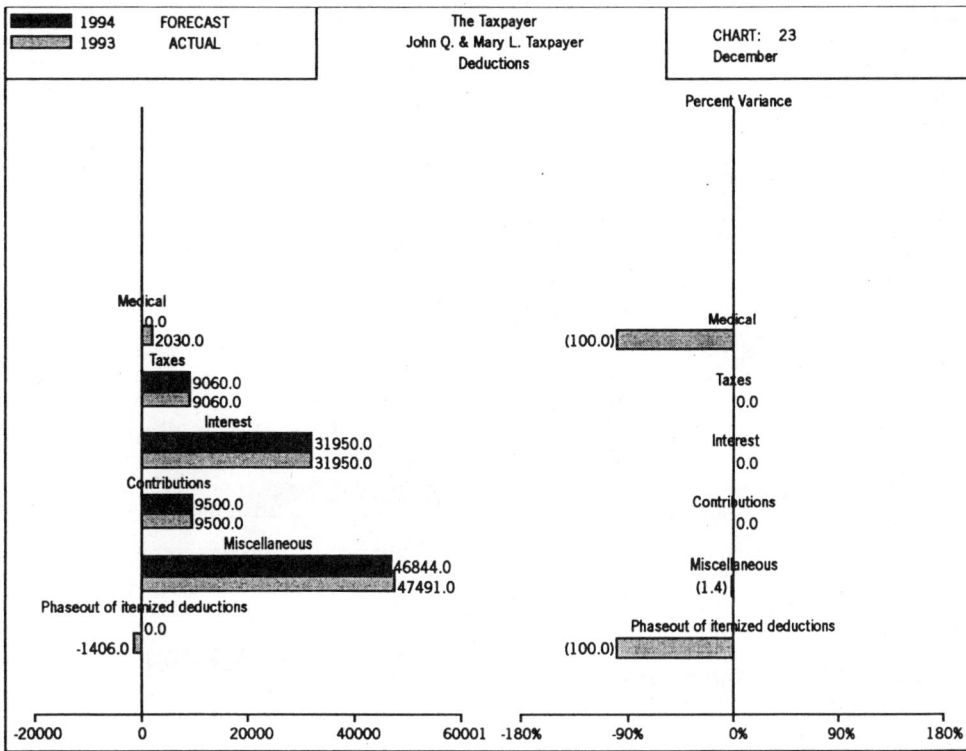

EXHIBIT 9.4C.23   The Taxpayer—John Q. & Mary L. Taxpayer—Deductions

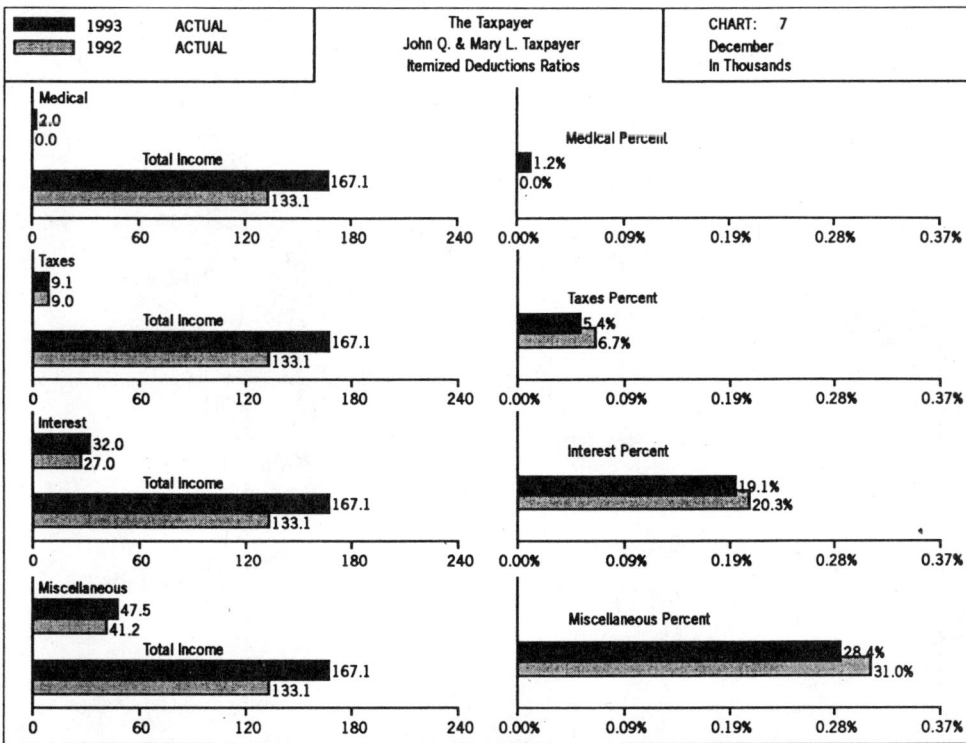

EXHIBIT 9.4C.24   The Taxpayer—John Q. & Mary L. Taxpayer—Itemized
Deductions Ratios

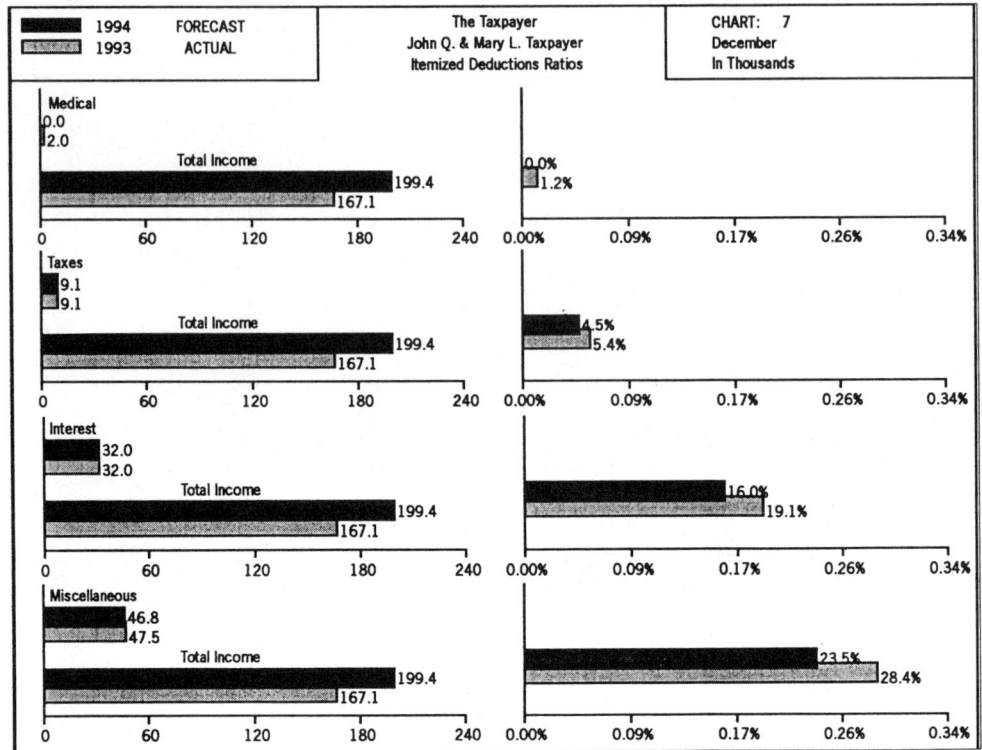

EXHIBIT 9.4C.25 The Taxpayer—John Q. & Mary L. Taxpayer—Itemized Deductions Ratios

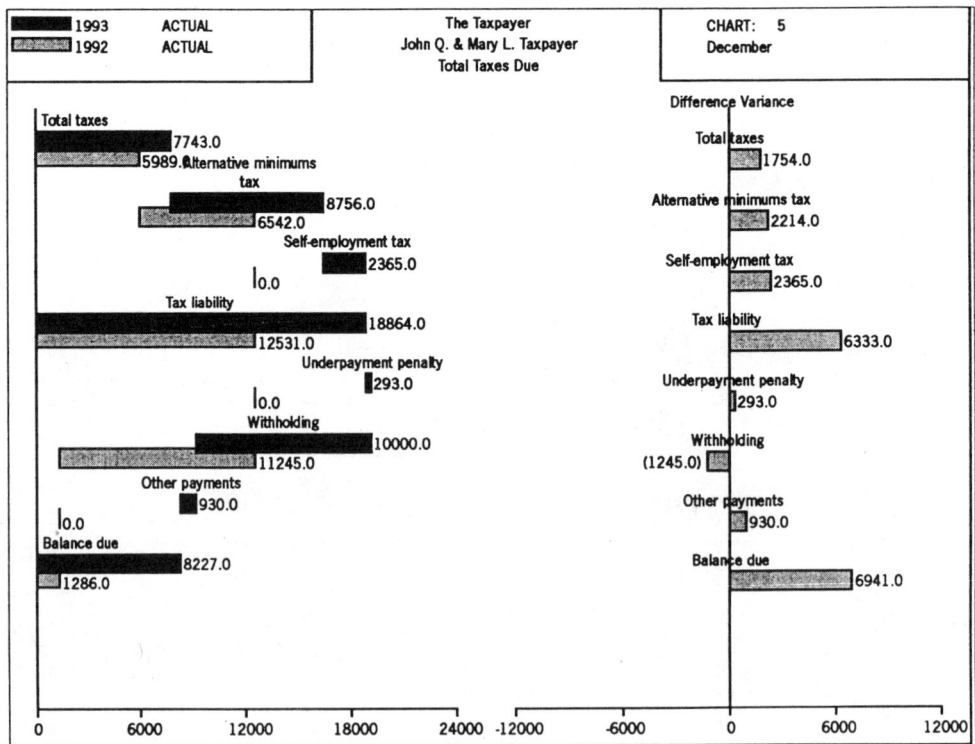

EXHIBIT 9.4C.26 The Taxpayer—John Q. & Mary L. Taxpayer—Total Taxes Due

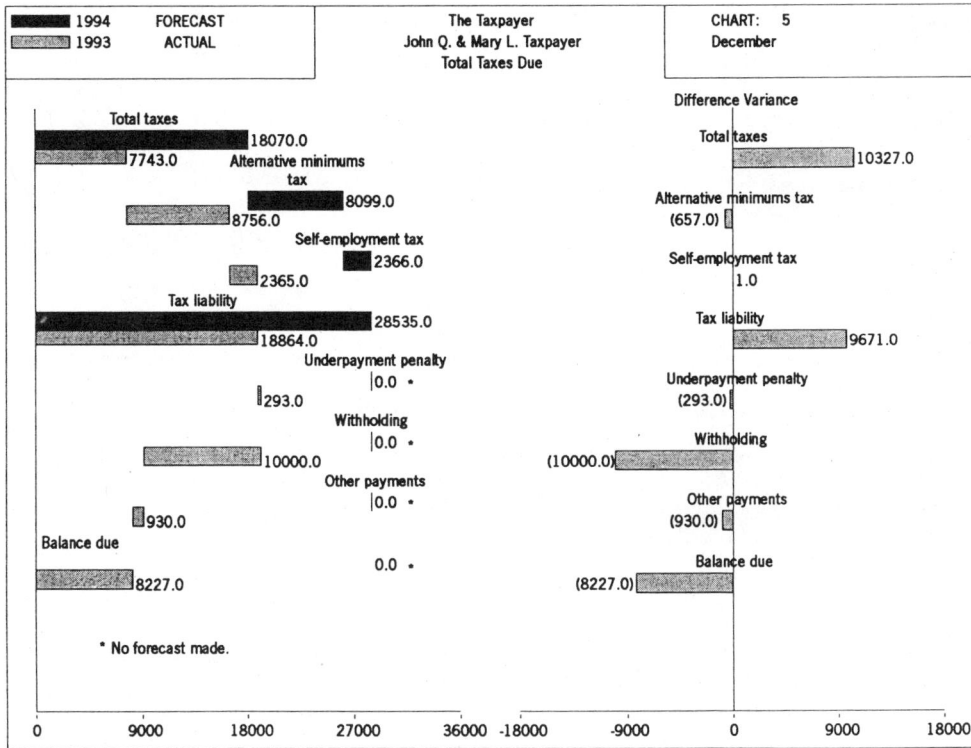

EXHIBIT 9.4C.27   The Taxpayer—John Q. & Mary L. Taxpayer—Total Taxes Due

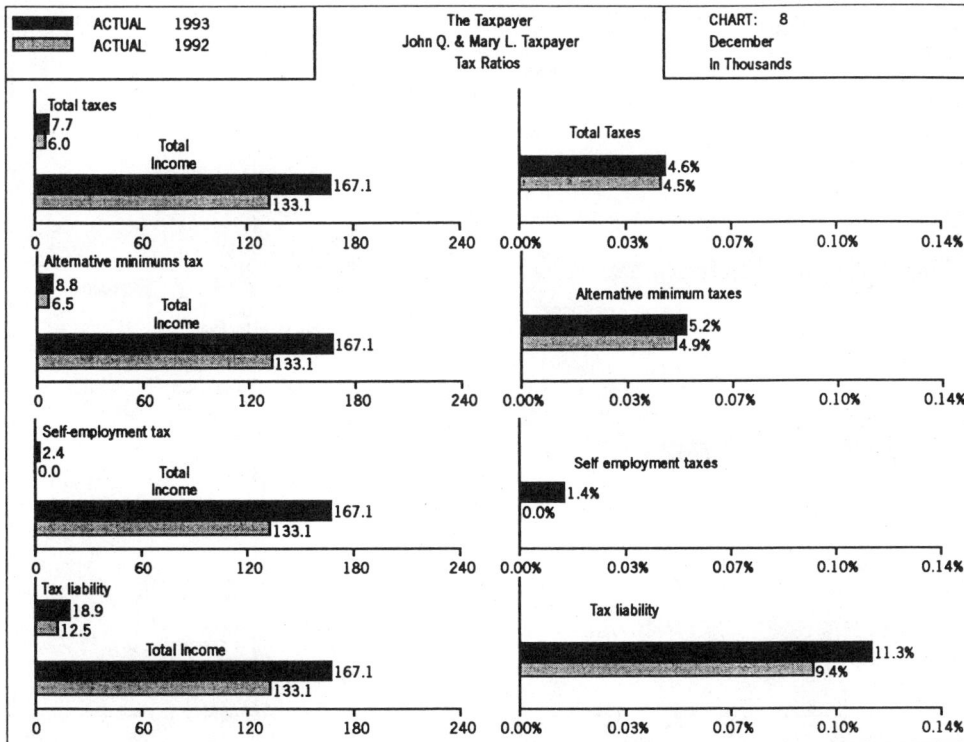

EXHIBIT 9.4C.28   The Taxpayer—John Q. & Mary L. Taxpayer—Tax Ratios

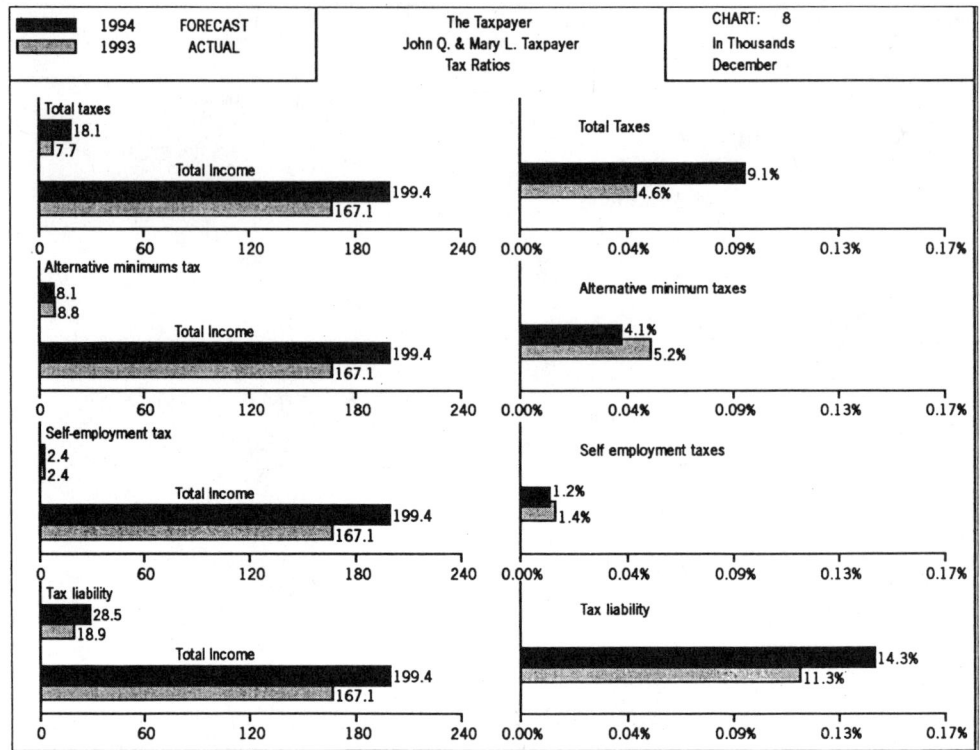

EXHIBIT 9.4C.29   The Taxpayer—John Q. & Mary L. Taxpayer—Tax Ratios

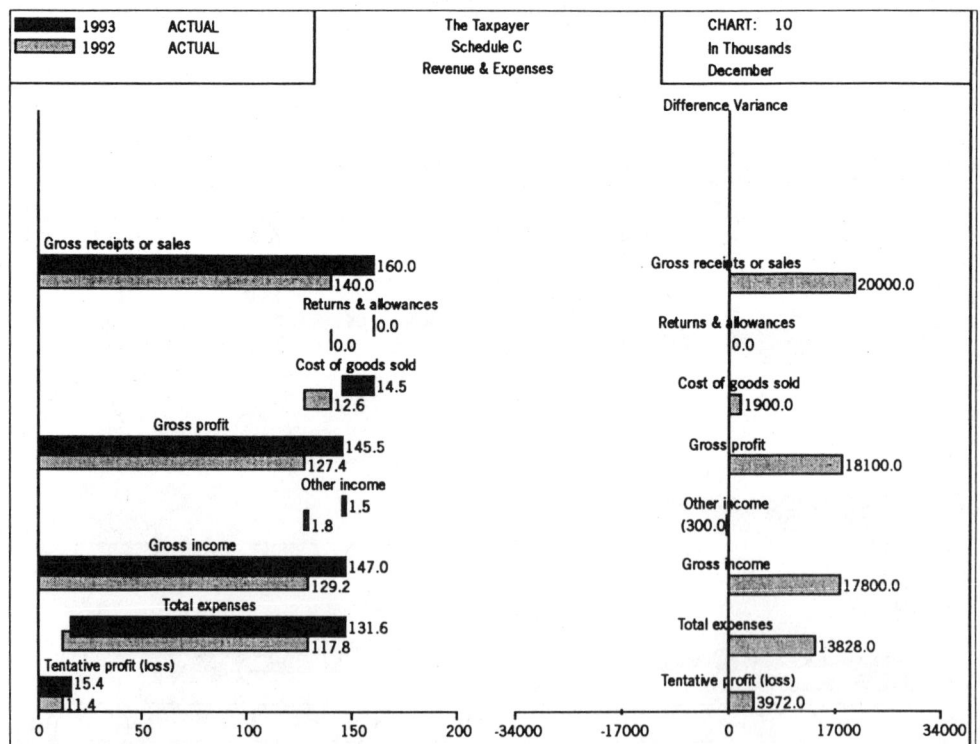

EXHIBIT 9.4C.30   The Taxpayer—Schedule C—Revenue & Expenses

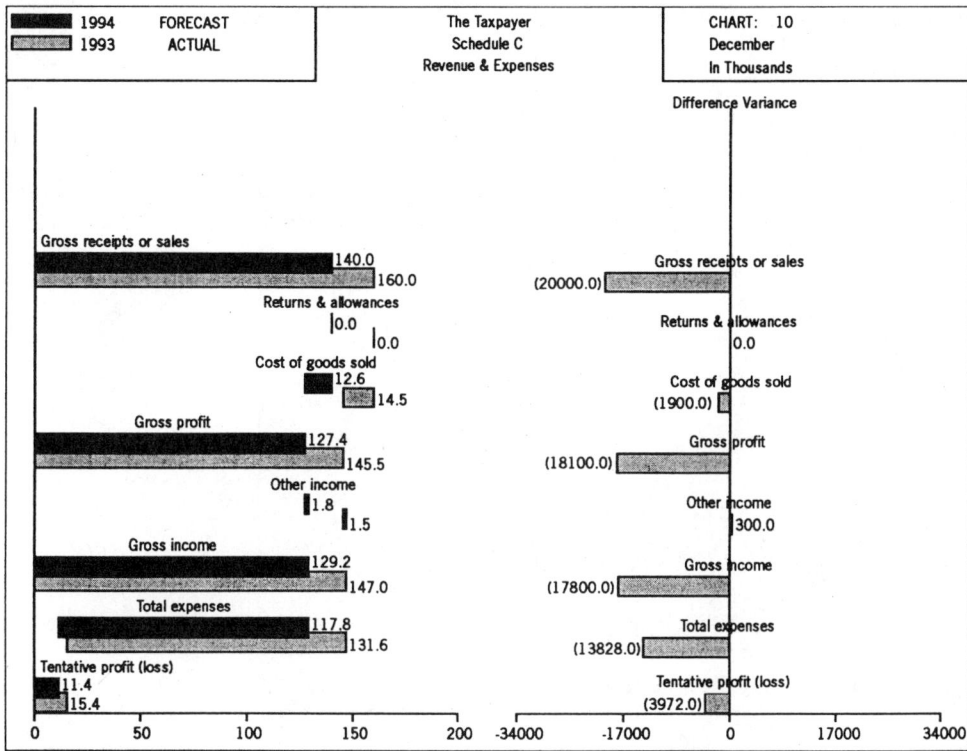

EXHIBIT 9.4C.31 The Taxpayer—Schedule C—Revenue & Expenses

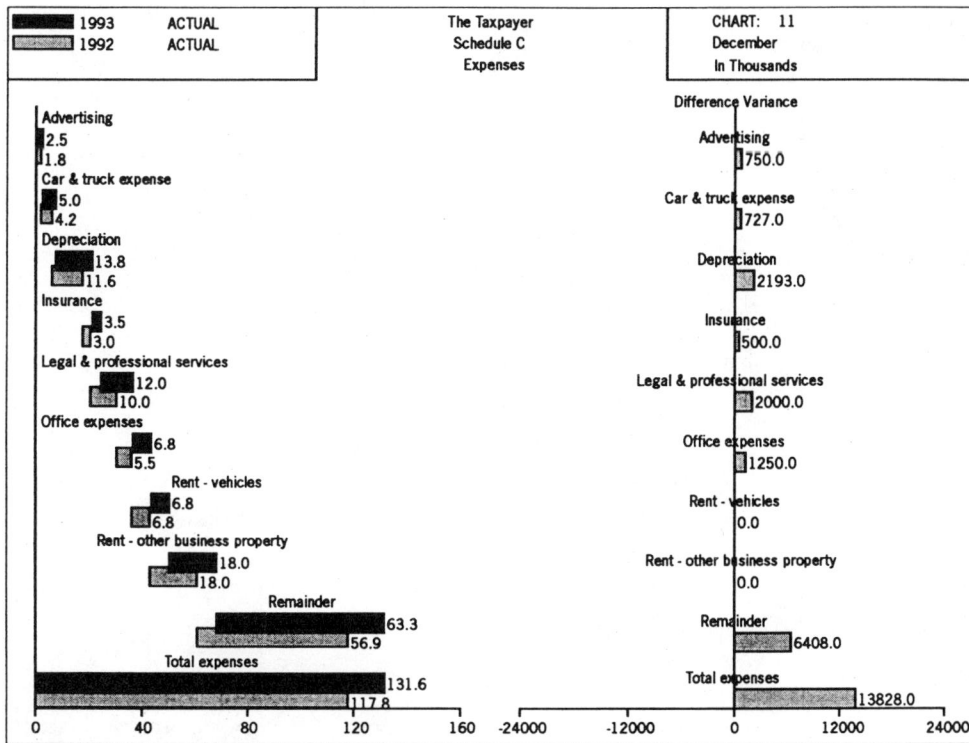

EXHIBIT 9.4C.32 The Taxpayer—Schedule C—Expenses

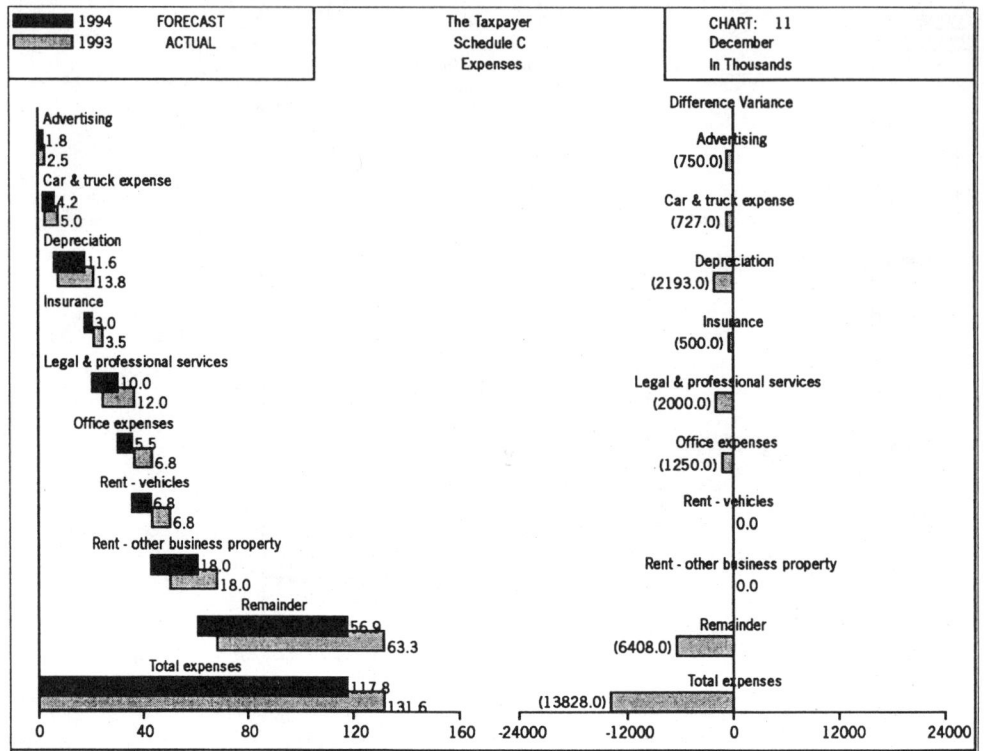

EXHIBIT 9.4C.33   The Taxpayer—Schedule C—Expenses

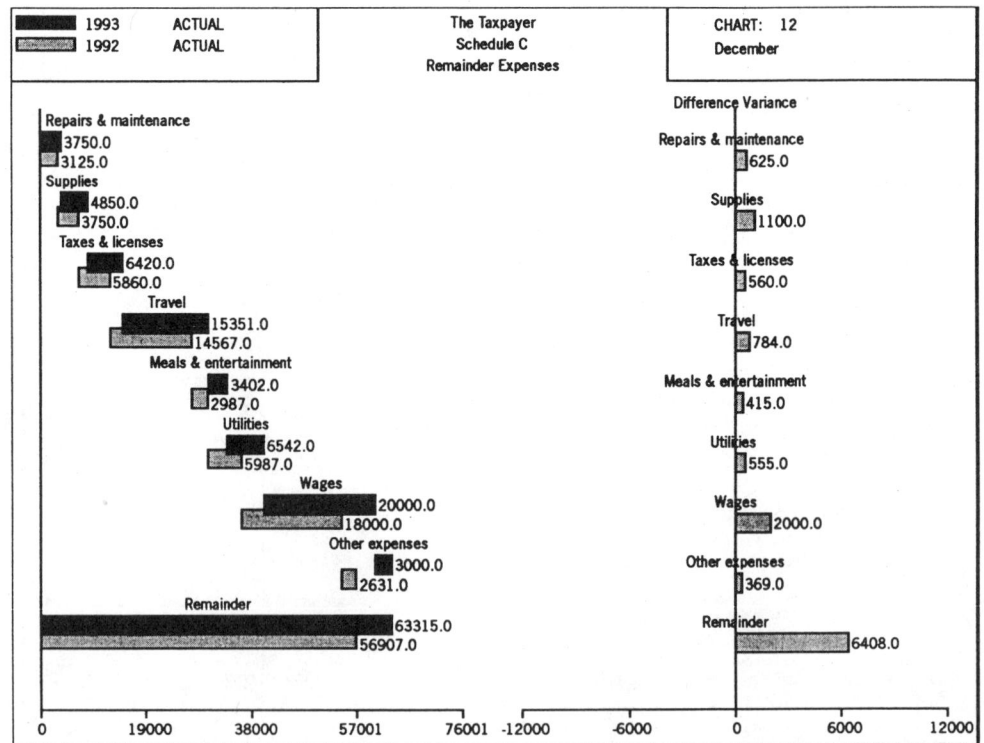

EXHIBIT 9.4C.34   The Taxpayer—Schedule C—Remainder Expenses

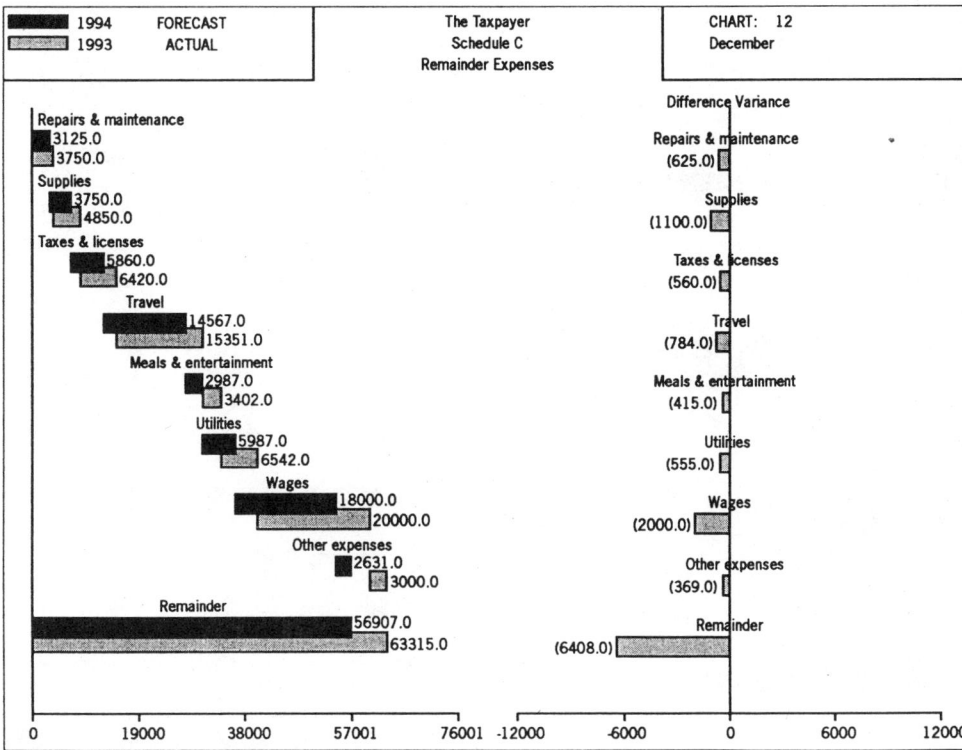

EXHIBIT 9.4C.35 The Taxpayer—Schedule C—Remainder Expenses

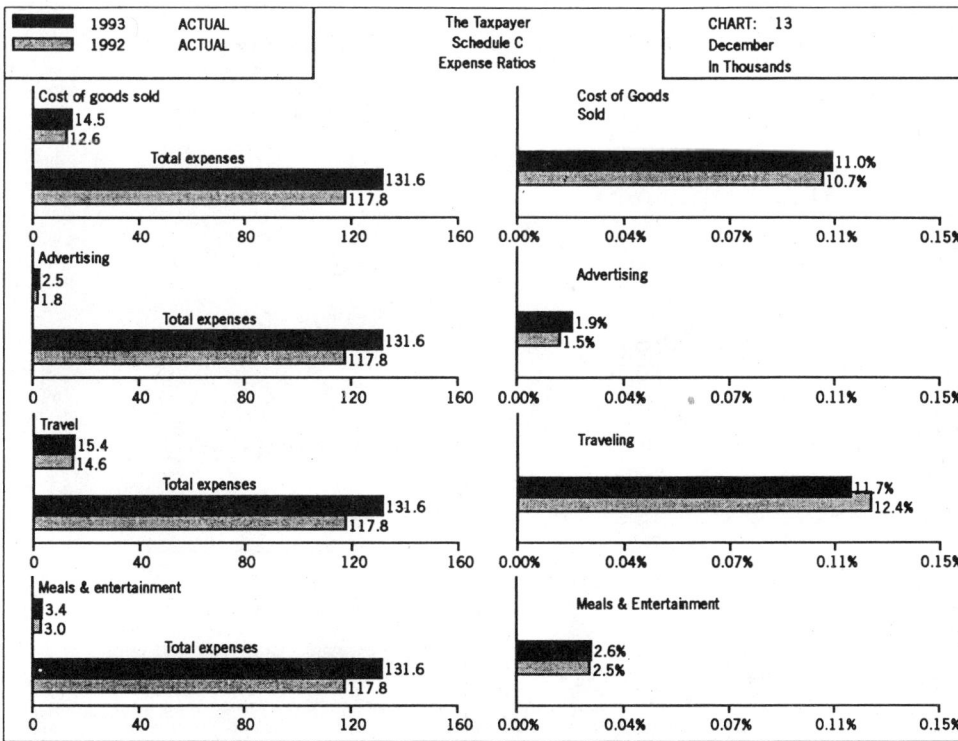

EXHIBIT 9.4C.36 The Taxpayer—Schedule C—Expense Ratios

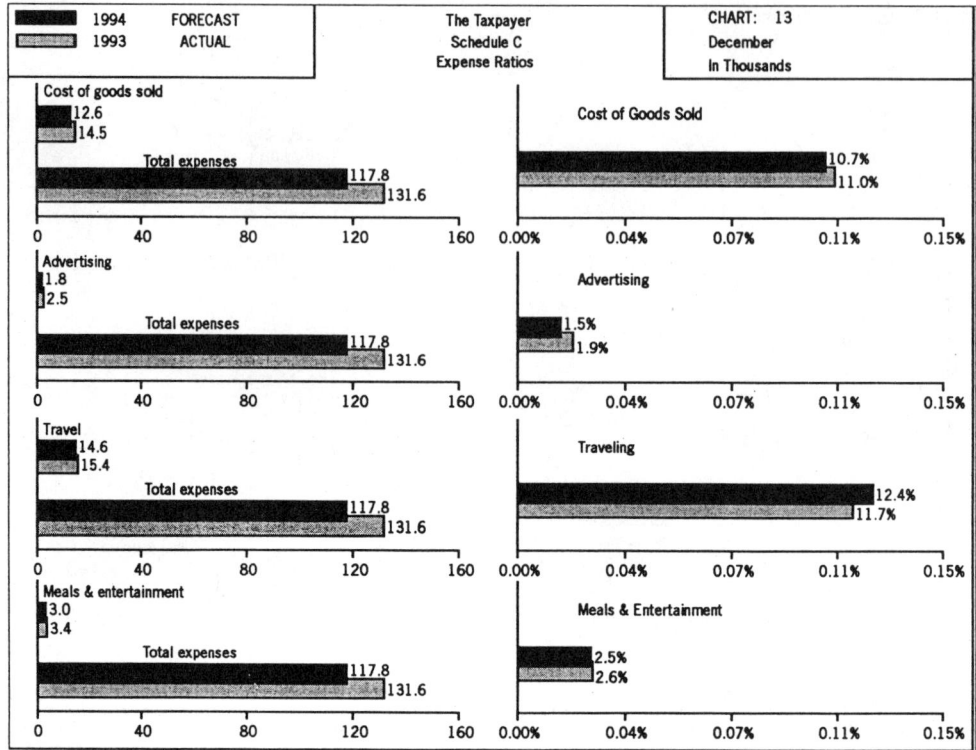

EXHIBIT 9.4C.37   The Taxpayer—Schedule C—Expense Ratios

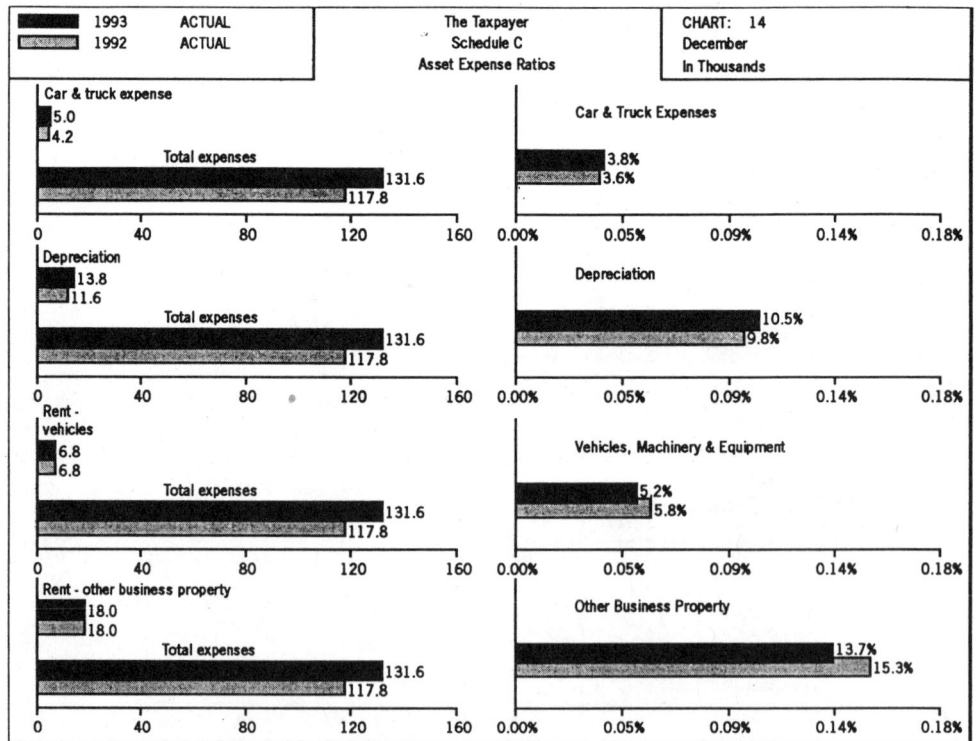

EXHIBIT 9.4C.38   The Taxpayer—Schedule C—Assets Expense Ratios

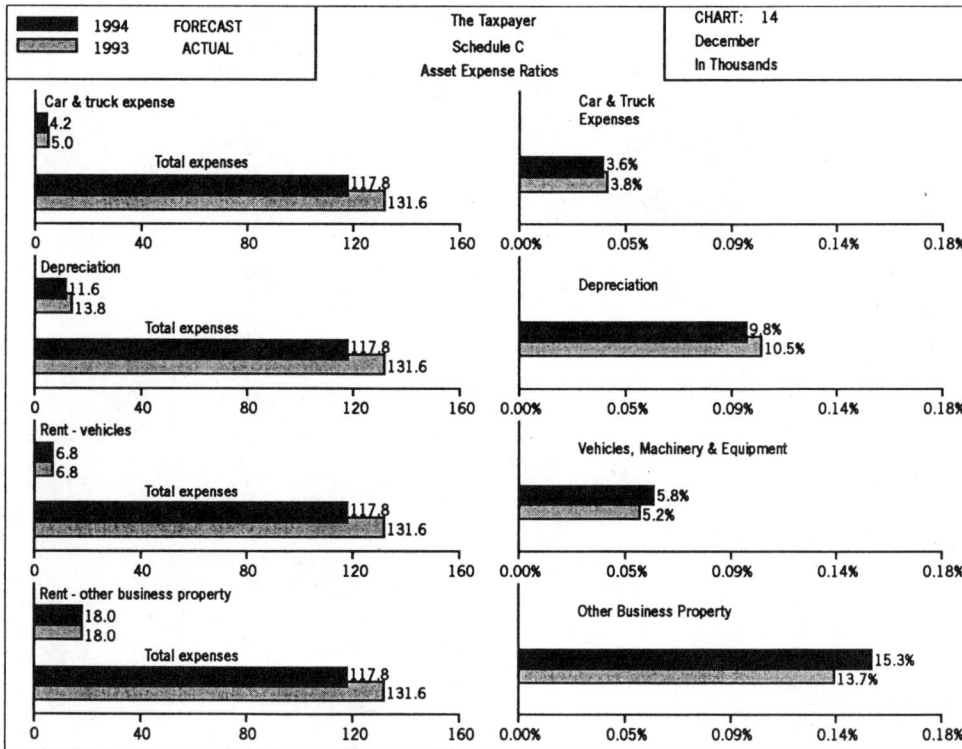

EXHIBIT 9.4C.39   The Taxpayer—Schedule C—Assets Expense Ratios

We know that one of the auditors' primary goals is to perform an efficient and appropriate audit that follows an appropriate scope and is completed on budget. We also know that helping the audit firm get a clear picture of the client's performance is essential for the audit partner to define the appropriate scope and testing procedures properly. Finally, we know that any process that will help the staff more efficiently understand the client's operations, and relate that understanding to the audit design, will enhance the staff's audit capabilities and result in a more consistent audit over the years. It would also build a more competent audit staff to move through the ranks, thus building a more profitable and constantly growing audit firm.

After a number of meetings, we concluded that highly structured financial graphics would help the auditors meet their audit goals. We also were able to assure ourselves that such an integration would be smart enough to automate the graph creation process and thus, the graphics would be available with no additional input from the auditor. Even more important, the graphs would be consistent over time providing a clear performance pattern over time to support the audit partner's selection of audit scope and testing requirements.

One of the most powerful features of ACE are the financial ratios that are produced with each audit. The presentation of the audit ratios in graphic formats provides a clear disaggregation path for the auditor to follow if the ratios do not meet expectations. We believe this feature will provide considerable benefits for the auditor as the expected patterns become part of their audit skills. Exhibits 9.4D.1 through 9.4D.12 are charts created automatically as part of the visualization module.

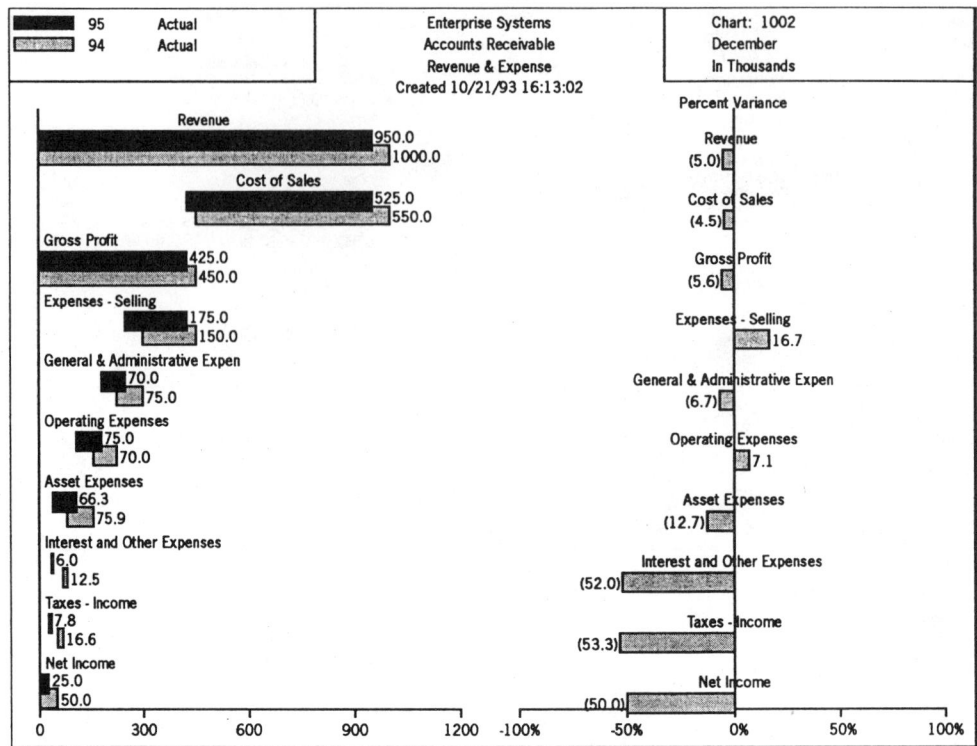

EXHIBIT 9.4D.1 Accounts Receivable—Revenue & Expense Statement—Enterprise Systems Corporate

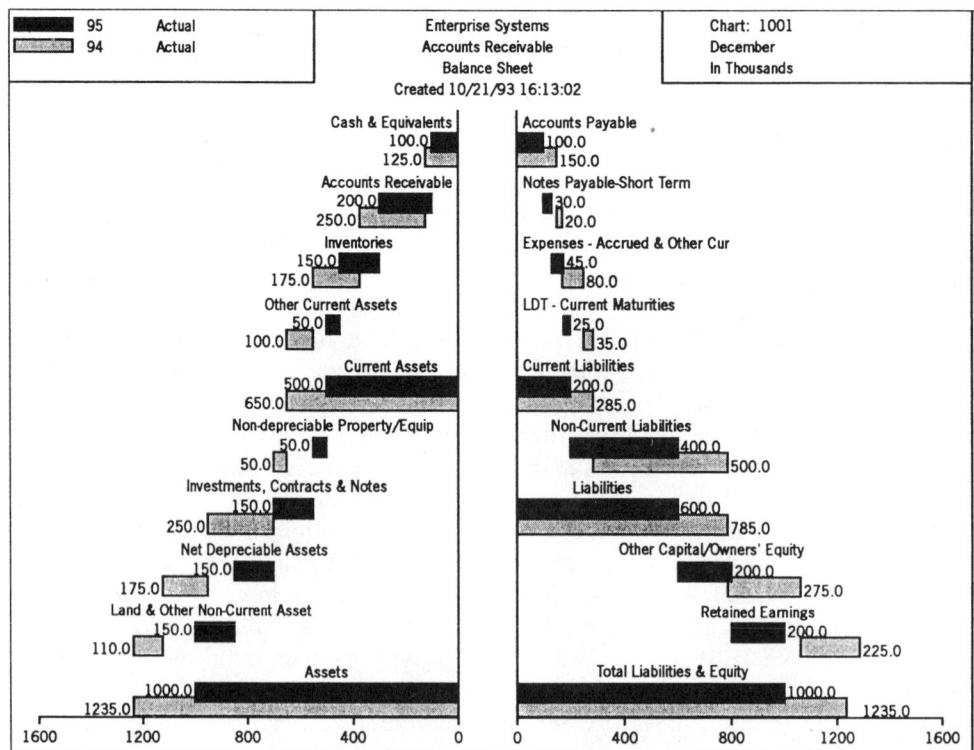

EXHIBIT 9.4D.2 Accounts Receivable—Balance Sheet—Enterprise Systems Corporate

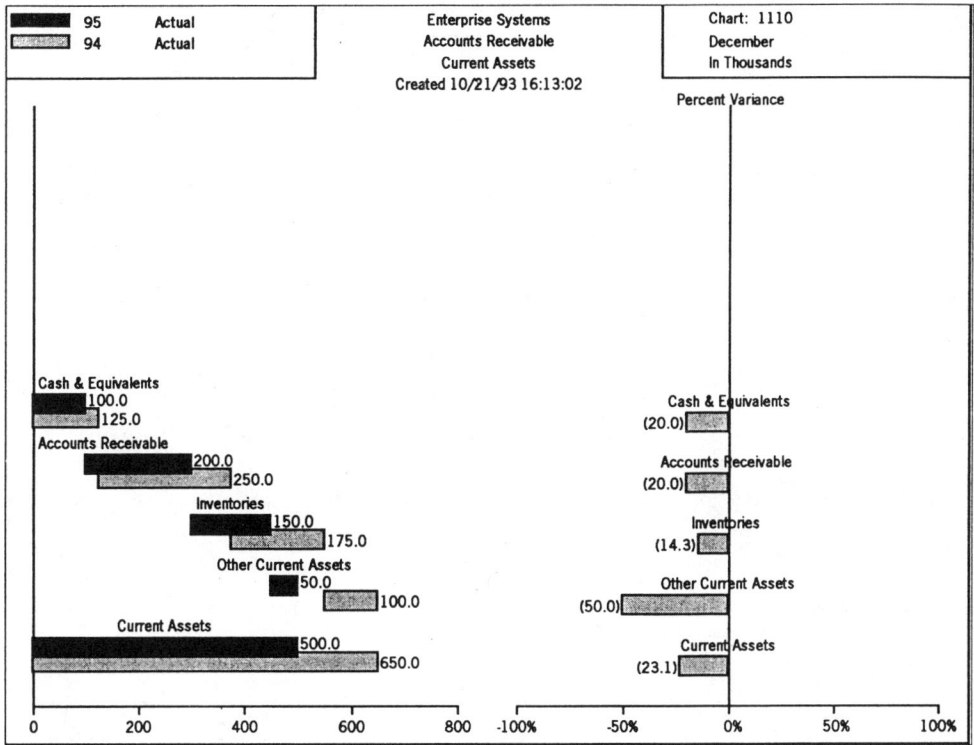

EXHIBIT 9.4D.3   Accounts Receivable—Current Assets—Enterprise Systems Corporate

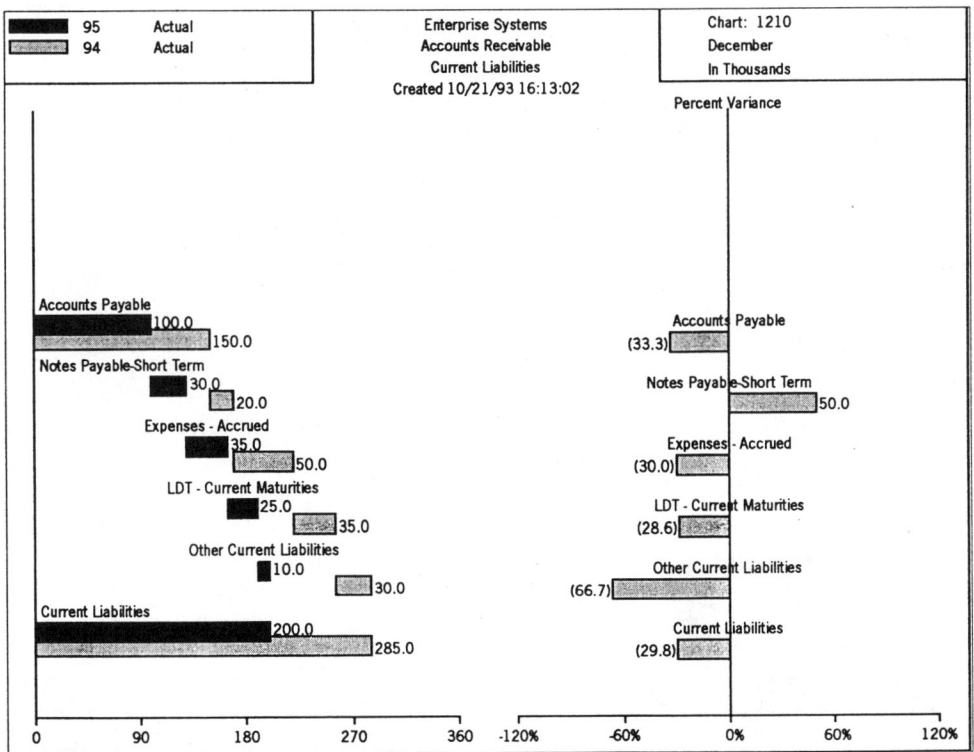

EXHIBIT 9.4D.4   Accounts Receivable—Current Liabilities—Enterprise Systems Corporate

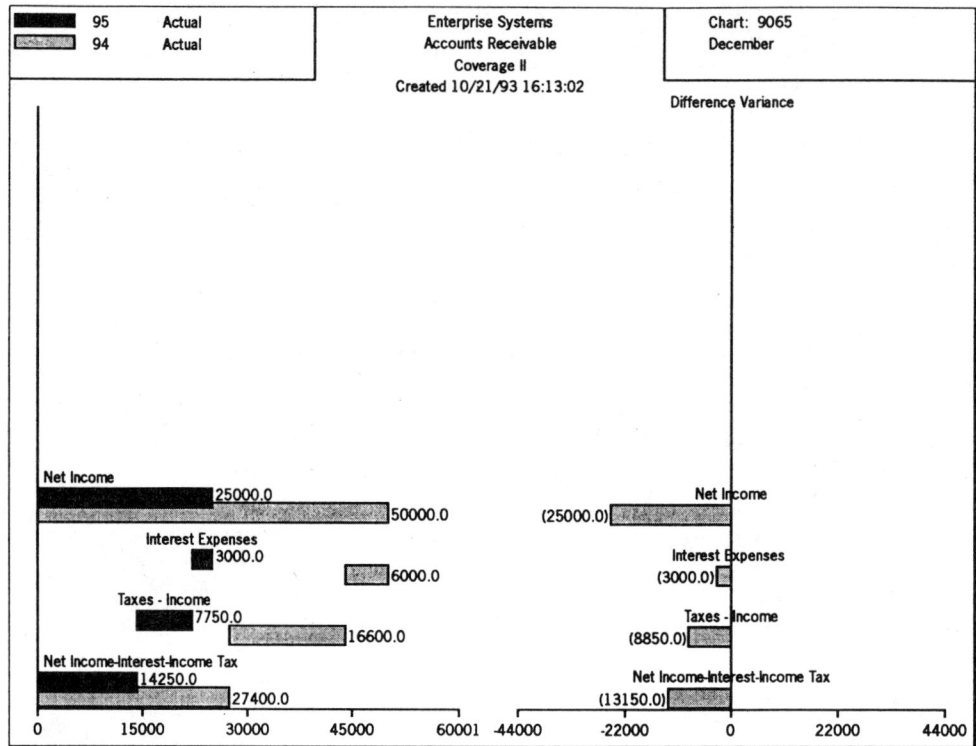

EXHIBIT 9.4D.5   Accounts Receivable—Coverage II—Enterprise Systems Corporate

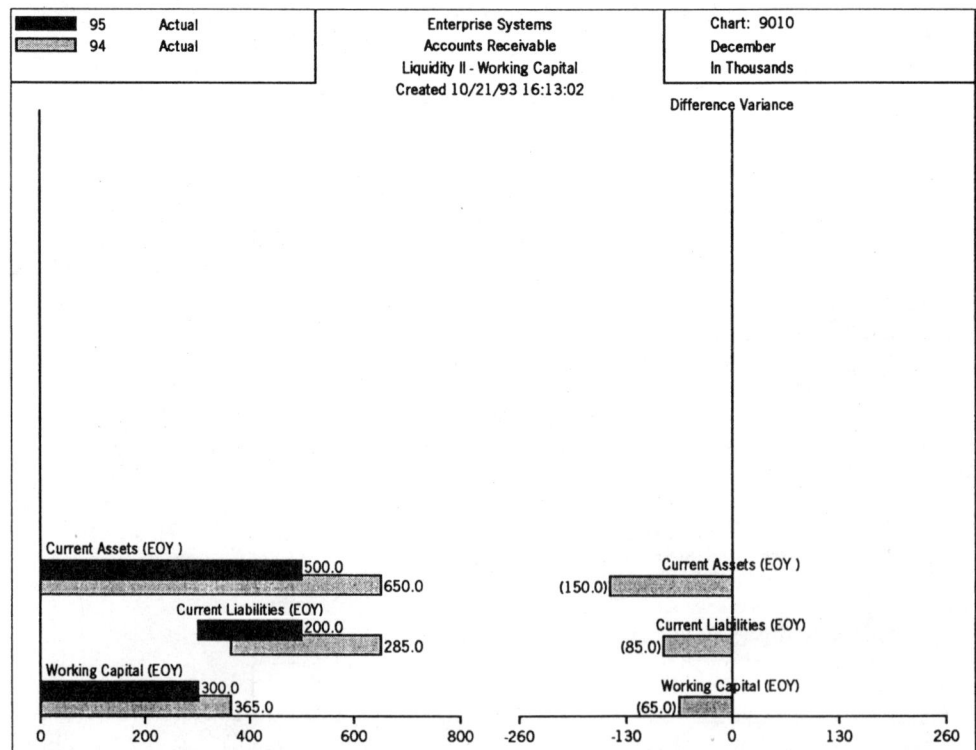

EXHIBIT 9.4D.6   Accounts Receivable—Liquidity II—Working Capital—Enterprise Systems Corporate

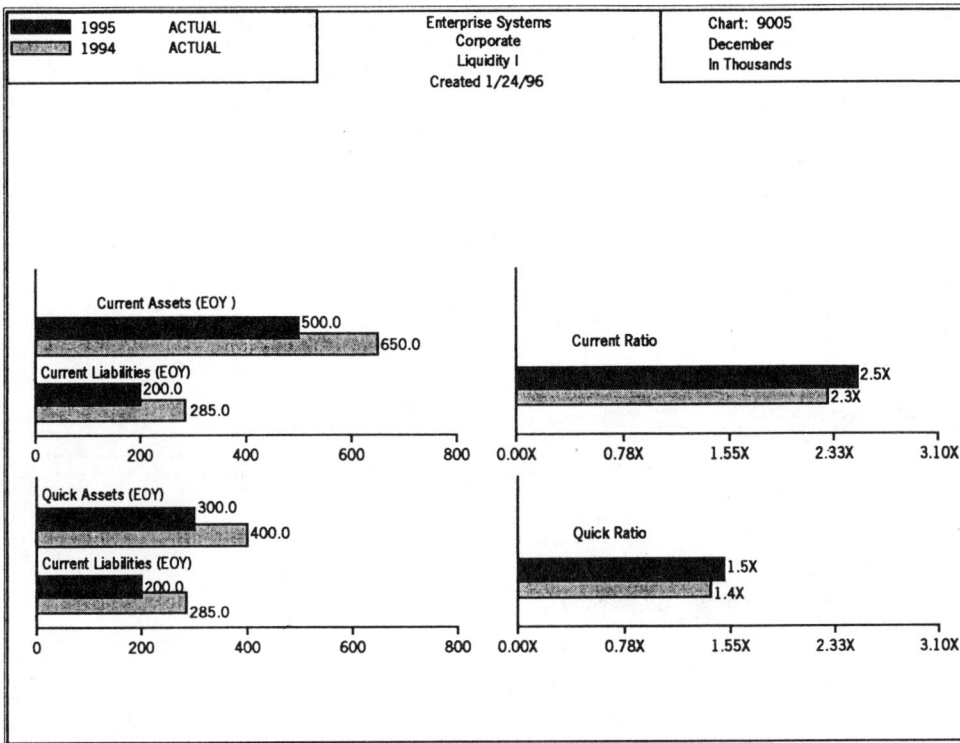

EXHIBIT 9.4D.7   Liquidity I—Working Capital—Enterprise Systems Corporate

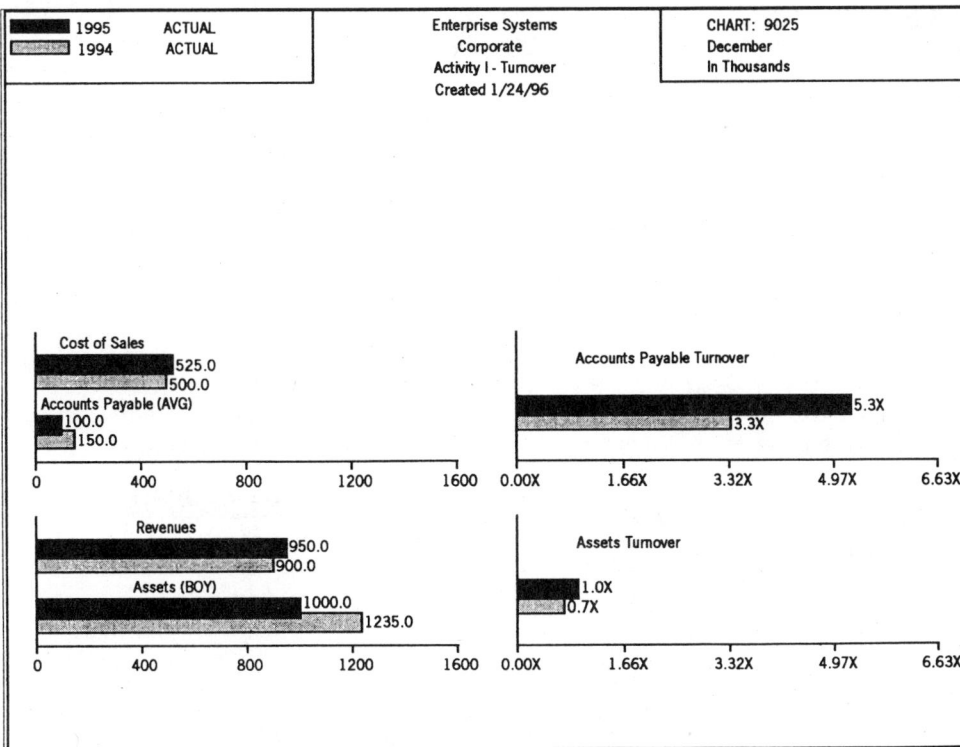

EXHIBIT 9.4D.8   Activity I—Turnover—Enterprise Systems Corporate

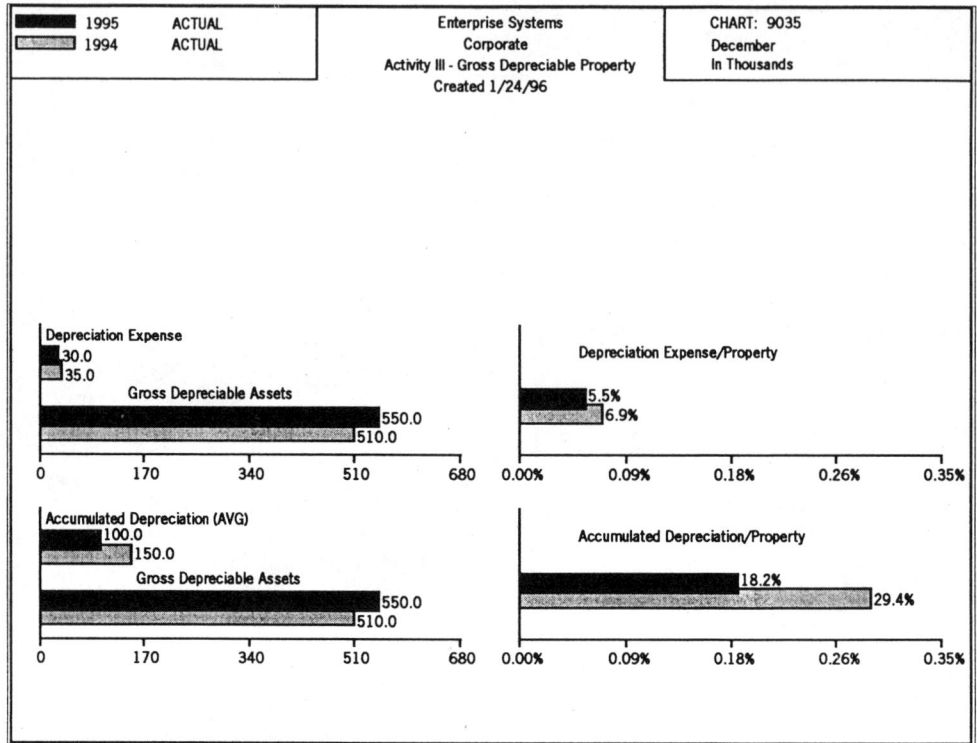

EXHIBIT 9.4D.9   Activity III—Gross Depreciable Property—Enterprise Systems Corporate

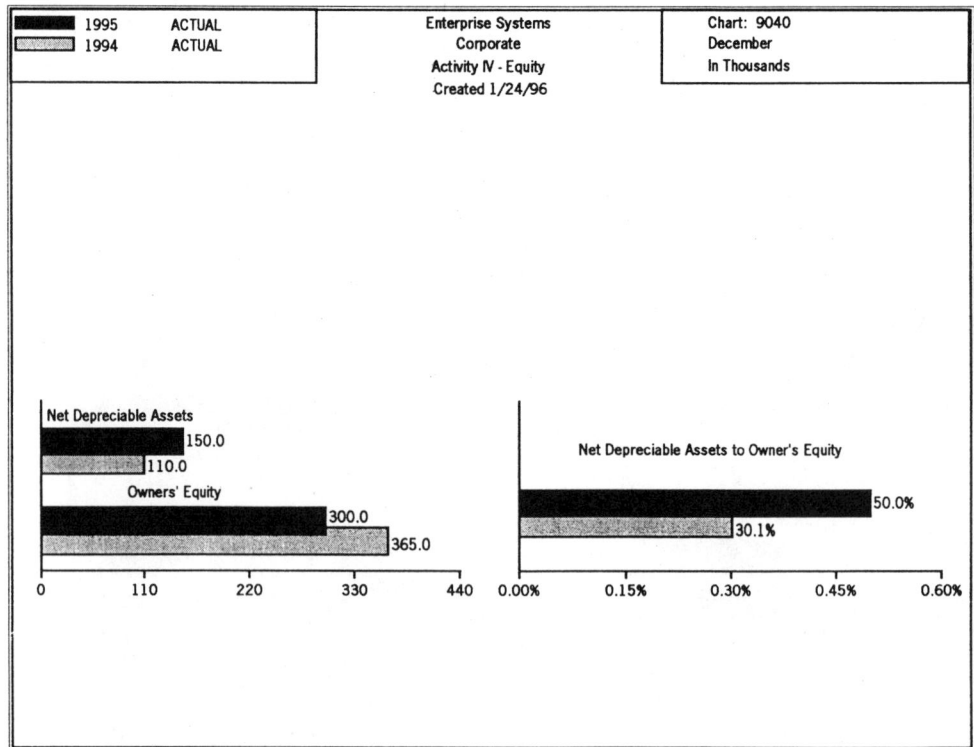

EXHIBIT 9.4D.10   Activity IV—Equity—Enterprise Systems Corporate

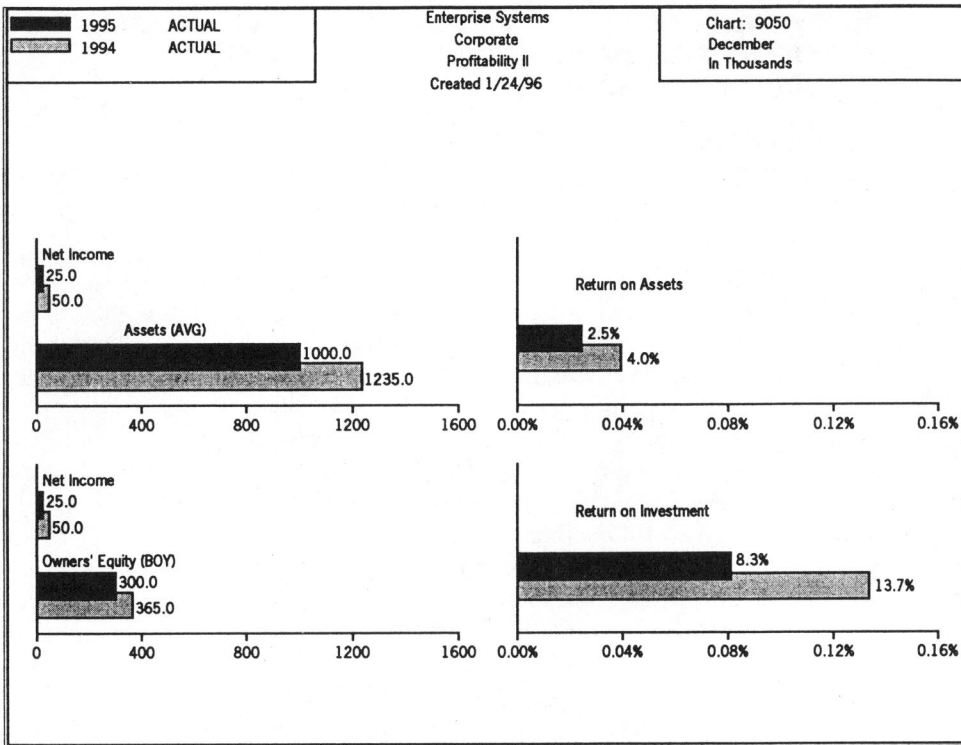

EXHIBIT 9.4D.11 Profitability II—Enterprise System Corporate

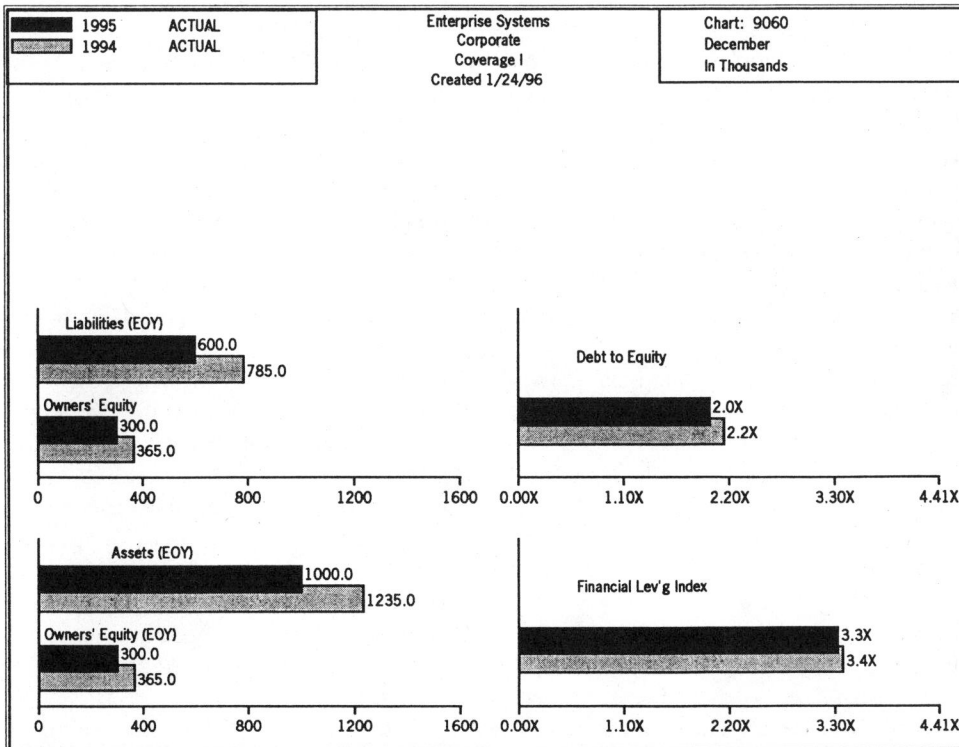

EXHIBIT 9.4D.12 Coverage I—Enterprise System Corporate

9.4E HOW FINANCIAL GRAPHICS ENHANCED THE ANNUAL FINANCIAL STATISTICS REPORT FOR TRADE ASSOCIATIONS (NEW)

by
Rodney S. Brutlag

One of the most valuable services a not-for-profit trade association can offer to its members is financial statistics reflecting conditions in the industry. There are several problems in providing such a service. One of the most significant challenges for many trade associations is presenting the information in a manner that all the members will understand. The owners of many small businesses are not necessarily educated sufficiently regarding financial reports and related data.

In designing a new industry financial data report product for trade associations, we recognized several challenges. First, there was the need to design a survey form that was user friendly to complete, even where the business person may not be able to produce some of their financial data. A form that requested very basic revenue & expense and balance sheet information, but also contained space requesting more detail, was the solution. The second challenge was screening the surveys that were returned to locate those that were obviously erroneous and also to determine if it was possible to back into the numbers needed where the data was incomplete. A system was designed to complete this step in an efficient manner. Finally, the largest challenge was to generate a report that was sophisticated enough to be meaningful to an accountant, but also understood by those who have trouble grasping the information in financial reports.

The first client to use our product represented an industry where 40% of their members had sales of $500,000 or less but 15% of their members had sales of $2.5 million or more. Many of the smaller owners started their business as a result of their mechanical skills rather than their knowledge of running a business, and they lacked financial skills. The association had been conducting their "cost of doing business" survey for a number of years but during the most recent five, the number of members participating had been declining. It was obvious that part of the reason for the decline was the old-fashioned presentation of the data, which needed upgrading to be more meaningful for all levels of owners. The solution was to put together a more helpful and exciting presentation of the survey results.

Recognizing that a transitional change over several years would be better accepted than a one-time radical change, the overall format of the report was reviewed and a set of changes scheduled. With the exception of two pie charts, two bar charts, and one graph, all the data in the old report was presented in tabular columns. One pie chart presented sources of revenue and the other expenses by major expense categories. The bar charts depicted the ratio of operating profit to gross operating profit by revenue category and the ratio of operating profit to gross operating profit by source of revenue and different types of businesses in the industry. The graph charted return on investment by size of firm for five years. One set of tabular data showed eleven different financial ratios, which are presented in columns representing the four most recent years. The remainder was made up of presentations of revenue and expense data and balance sheet data broken out by size, type of operation, and other categories.

The first step to redesign the report was to evaluate the usefulness of each type of financial data and the manner in which it was presented. Some data was judged to be of less value and was put on the list to be dropped while other new data was added. The format for presenting each type of data was evaluated, and it was decided that using more charts would make it more relevant. That was particularly true of the ratios. We decided that the ratios required charts, but they also required explanations of how the ratios are used, with interpretations of current data compared to the prior year. Several formats were tried but none of the charts lent themselves well to providing the data with new meaning. Then a chance meeting with a colleague not seen for over 20 years produced a dramatic new opportunity to produce the new meaning.

In bringing each other up to data on our lives, Dr. Jarett described to me his extensive research on how to present financial data in an easier to understand format. A sample of this new computerized financial graphics solved the whole problem of how to bring new meaning to our cost of doing business report. By the time the new industry data was collected and keyed into a computer, a new format for the report had been completed.

One page at the beginning of the report was devoted to explaining and illustrating the financial graphics used for addition, subtraction, and division—or ratios. Then, for transitional purposes, the sources of revenue and the breakout of major expense categories were presented in both the old pie chart and the new financial graphics format. The ease of both understanding the data and recognizing what was significant in the new format compared to the old was dramatic (see Exhibits 9.4E.1 through 9.4E.4). Next, all the financial ratios were presented in the computer graphics format, with an explanation of what they meant appearing on the side of each one (see Exhibits 9.4E.5 through 9.4E.7). Finally, the consolidated balance sheet, revenue & expense statement and expenses by percent of gross operating profit were presented in the new format (see Exhibits 9.4E.8 through 9.4E.10). Other changes were made in how the remaining data was presented to give the report a whole new appearance and meaning.

Plans were made to provide a new product from the data allowing members of the industry to compare their data to that of the industry on a computer. Members can order a floppy disk of the industry data, presented in the new computer graphics format. They can load the information into their computer and then key in their own data to allow comparisons in a new variety of ways. Armed with our novel approach to gathering data, calculating the information, and presenting the results utilizing financial graphics, we look forward to providing an exciting new alternative to the traditional trade association approach to publishing industry financial data.

Sources of Revenue and Major Expense Categories

Sources of Revenue

The Pie chart, "Sources of Revenue" and the Addition chart, "Sources of Revenue," Exhibits 9.4E.1 and 9.4E.2, are placed on the same page, and they both present the sources of revenue. The Pie Chart shows the revenue components for 1992 data.

The Addition chart, however, shows how the three components of Rental Income, Merchandise & Equipment Sales, and Other Operating Income add to make 100% of the Total Income for both 1991 and 1992. Furthermore, Exhibit 9.4E.2 visually presents at a glance the numbers describing the percent change from 1991 to 1992: Rental Income for 1992 and 1991 were approximately the same percent of Total Income; Merchandise and Equipment Sales for 1992 were slightly greater than 1991, a 1.7% increase; Other Operating Income for 1992 was

Sources of Revenue

385 Respondents, 1992

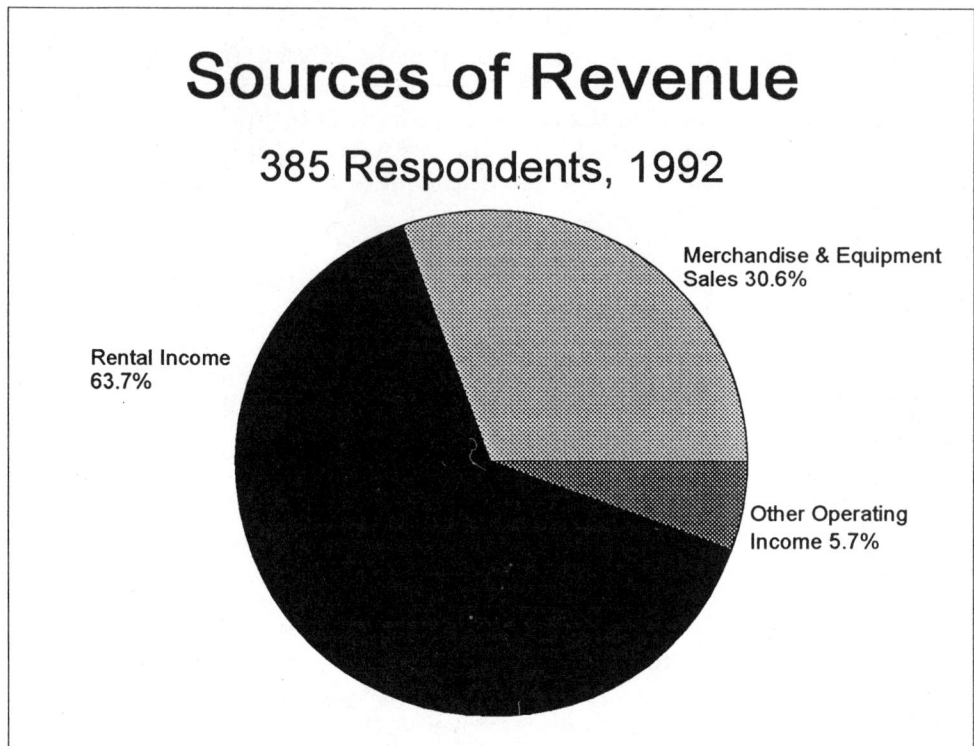

Merchandise & Equipment Sales 30.6%

Rental Income 63.7%

Other Operating Income 5.7%

EXHIBIT 9.4E.1   Sources of Revenue, 385 Respondents, 1992

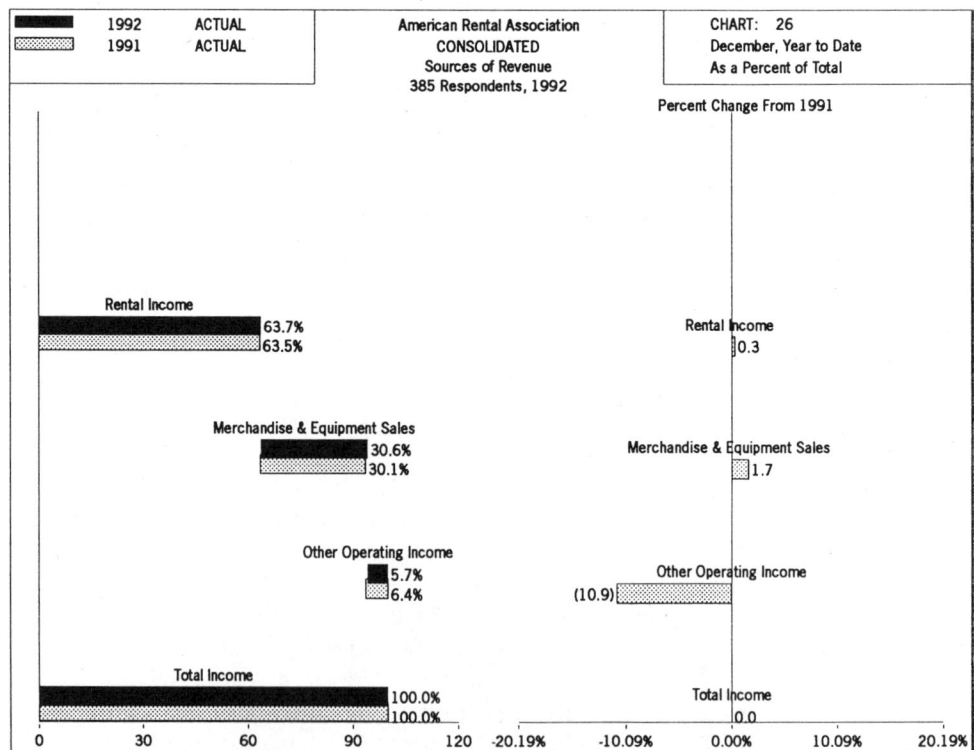

■ 1992 ACTUAL	American Rental Association	CHART: 26
▨ 1991 ACTUAL	CONSOLIDATED	December, Year to Date
	Sources of Revenue	As a Percent of Total
	385 Respondents, 1992	

Percent Change From 1991

Rental Income 63.7% / 63.5%   Rental Income 0.3

Merchandise & Equipment Sales 30.6% / 30.1%   Merchandise & Equipment Sales 1.7

Other Operating Income 5.7% / 6.4%   Other Operating Income (10.9)

Total Income 100.0% / 100.0%   Total Income 0.0

0   30   60   90   120   -20.19% -10.09% 0.00% 10.09% 20.19%

EXHIBIT 9.4E.2   Consolidated Sources of Revenue, 385 Respondents, 1992—American Rental Association

almost 11% less than 1991. Calculate the percent of your Revenue components for 1992 and draw the bars on top of the relevant bars to see how your company performed.

Major Expense Categories

The Pie Chart, "Major Expense Categories," and the Addition Chart, "Major Expense Categories," Exhibit 9.4E.4, are placed on the same page and they both present the major expense categories. The Pie Chart shows the Major Expense Categories for 1992 data.

The Addition Chart, however, shows how the nine major Expense Categories add to make 100% of the Total Expenses for both 1991 and 1992. Furthermore, Exhibit 9.4E.2 visually presents at a glance the numbers describing the percent change from 1991 to 1992. Advertising Expenses for 1992 and 1991 were approximately the same and All Other Expenses for 1992 were 5.8% less than 1991. Two of the largest expense categories showed significant increases: Salaries and Wages for 1992 were 4.5% greater than 1991; and Cost Of Sales for 1992 were 10.2% over 1991. Depreciation on Rental Equipment was significantly lower, (21.6%) in 1992, and was slightly less than one third of the Cost of Sales in 1992 and almost half in 1991. Occupancy costs were 10.3% higher in 1992, Equipment, Maintenance and Repair costs were 1.9% higher in 1992, and Employee Benefits were the same percent in 1992. Interest costs for 1992 showed a significant drop of 23.1% from 1991 and the reason for the drop is clearly shown in the ratio charts that follow. Calculate the percent of your Major Expense Categories for 1992 and draw the bars on top of the relevant bars to see how your company performed.

Exhibits 9.4E.3 and 9.4E.4 are based on the average data. To see how your company compares to the average, simply draw your bars on top of the relevant bars to see how your company compares to the average.

Financial Ratios #1

Current Ratio—Shows a significant increase from 1991 (1.4X) to 1992 (1.7X) due to Total Current Assets increasing at the same time Total Current Liabilities declined.

Acid Test Ratio—Shows a good increase from 1991 (0.8X) to 1992 (.09) due to Cash, Receivables and Securities increasing at the same time Total Current Liabilities declined.

Total Debt to Net Worth—Shows a good decrease from 1991 (1.4X) to 1992 (1.3X). Both components increased, Net Worth increased at a faster rate than Total Debt, lower interest resulted.

Average Collection Period—Shows a good decrease in Average Collection Period from 1991 to 1992 as a result of higher average daily sales.

Financial Ratios #2

Return on Investment—Shows a significant increase from 1991 (6.1%) to 1992 (9.4%). Income Before Income Taxes increased at a faster rate than Net Worth.

Return on Total Assets—Shows a good increase from 1991 (2.6%) to 1992 (4.1%) because Income Before Income Taxes increased at a faster rate than Total Assets.

Return on Revenues—Shows a good increase from 1991 (2.0%) to 1992 (3.1%) because Income Before Income Taxes increased at a faster rate than Total Operating Income.

Major Expense Categories

385 Respondents, 1992

Rental Equipment Depr. 8.7%

Equip. Maintenance & Repair 5.3%

Occupancy Cost 6.4%

All Other Expenses 16.3%

Advertising 2.1%

Salaries & Wages 27.9%

Cost of Sales 25.9%

Employee Benefits 4.4%

Interest 3%

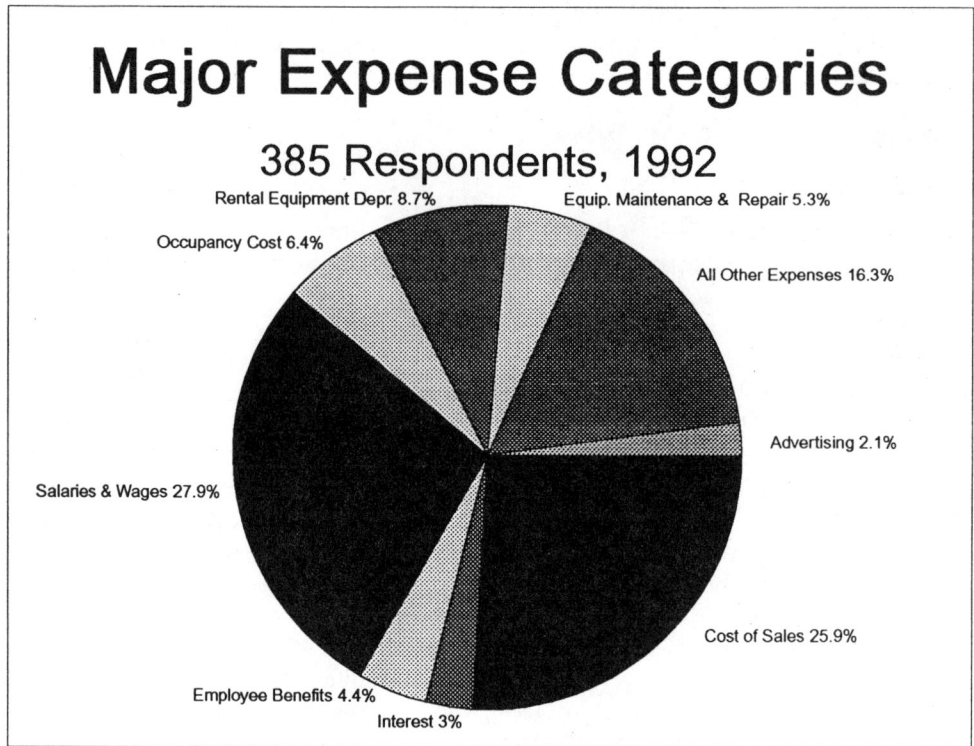

EXHIBIT 9.4E.3   Major Expense Categories, 385 Respondents, 1992

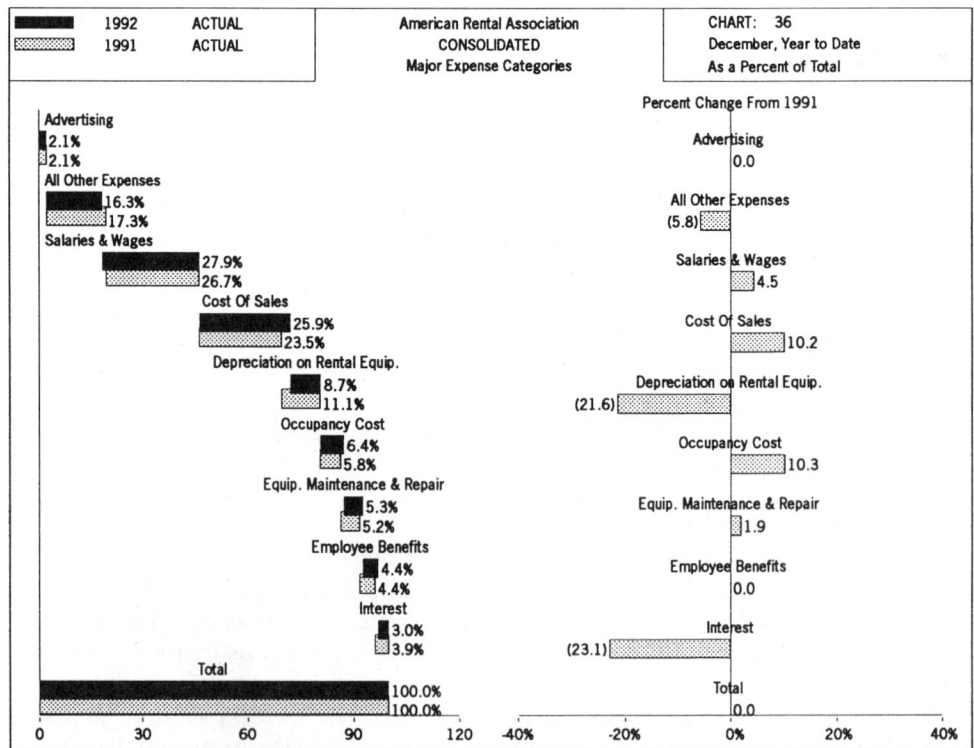

	1992	ACTUAL	American Rental Association	CHART: 36
	1991	ACTUAL	CONSOLIDATED	December, Year to Date
			Major Expense Categories	As a Percent of Total

Percent Change From 1991

Advertising
2.1%
2.1%

Advertising
0.0

All Other Expenses
16.3%
17.3%

All Other Expenses
(5.8)

Salaries & Wages
27.9%
26.7%

Salaries & Wages
4.5

Cost Of Sales
25.9%
23.5%

Cost Of Sales
10.2

Depreciation on Rental Equip.
8.7%
11.1%

Depreciation on Rental Equip.
(21.6)

Occupancy Cost
6.4%
5.8%

Occupancy Cost
10.3

Equip. Maintenance & Repair
5.3%
5.2%

Equip. Maintenance & Repair
1.9

Employee Benefits
4.4%
4.4%

Employee Benefits
0.0

Interest
3.0%
3.9%

Interest
(23.1)

Total
100.0%
100.0%

Total
0.0

0   30   60   90   120   -40%   -20%   0%   20%   40%

EXHIBIT 9.4E.4   Consolidated Major Expense Categories, 385 Respondents, 1992—
American Rental Association

■ 1992 ACTUAL	American Rental Association	CHART: 10000
▨ 1991 ACTUAL	CONSOLIDATED	December
	Financial Ratios #1	In Thousands

Total Current Assets
418.7
380.5

Current Ratio
1.7X
1.4X

0 — 130 — 260 — 390 — 520

0.00X — 0.55X — 1.10X — 1.65X — 2.20X

Cash, Receivables, Securities
226.9
221.7

Acid Test Ratio
0.9X
0.8X

Total Current Liabilities
247.4
265.4

0 — 80 — 160 — 240 — 320

0.00X — 0.33X — 0.66X — 0.98X — 1.31X

Total Liabilities
658.4
620.8

Total Debt To Net Worth
1.3X
1.4X

Net Worth
504.1
447.7

0 — 200 — 400 — 600 — 800

0.00X — 0.44X — 0.88X — 1.32X — 1.77X

Accounts Receivable
158.8
158.4

Average Collection Period (Days)
37.4X
41.8X

Average Daily Revenues
4.2
3.8

0 — 50 — 100 — 150 — 200

0.00X — 13.13X — 26.25X — 39.38X — 52.50X

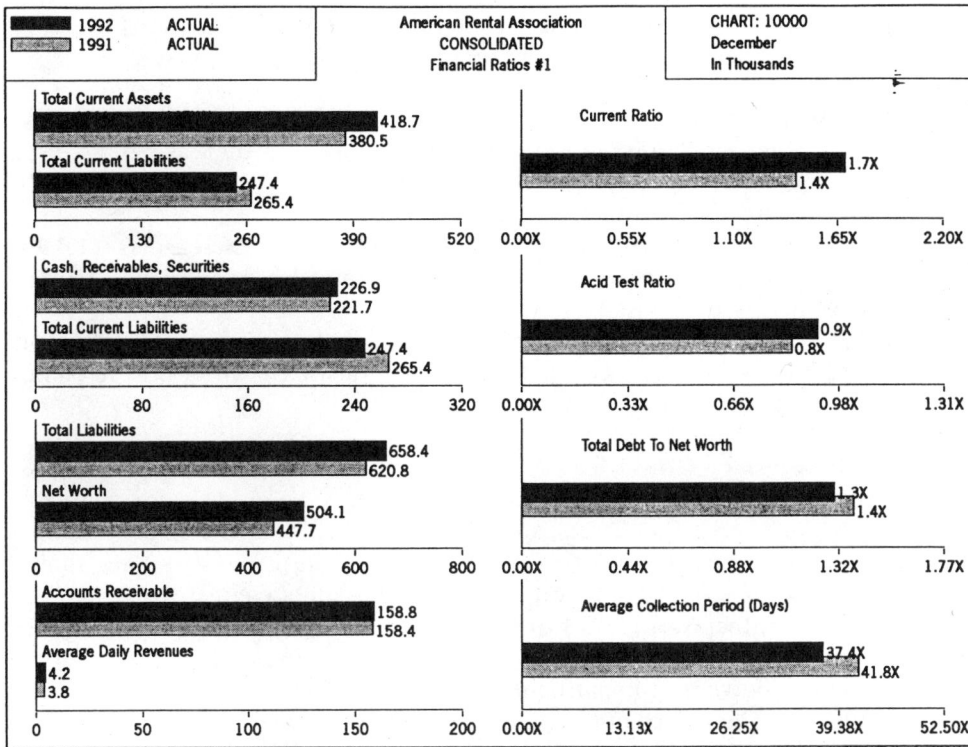

EXHIBIT 9.4E.5   Consolidated Balance Sheet—American Rental Association—
Financial Ratios #1

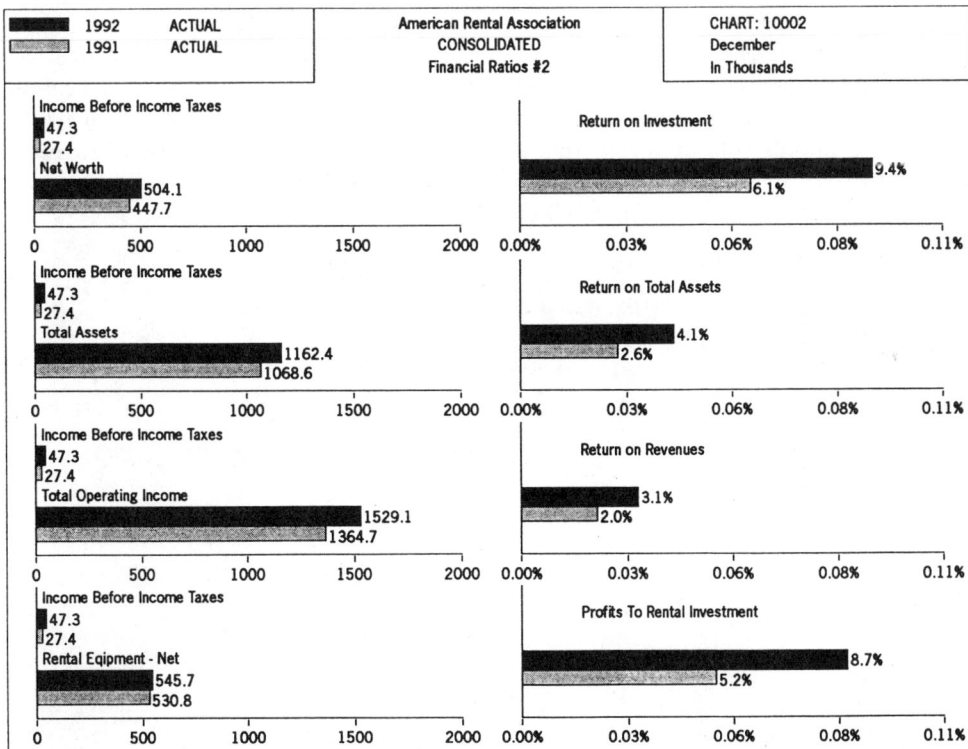

■ 1992 ACTUAL	American Rental Association	CHART: 10002
▨ 1991 ACTUAL	CONSOLIDATED	December
	Financial Ratios #2	In Thousands

Income Before Income Taxes
47.3
27.4

Return on Investment
9.4%
6.1%

Net Worth
504.1
447.7

0 — 500 — 1000 — 1500 — 2000

0.00% — 0.03% — 0.06% — 0.08% — 0.11%

Income Before Income Taxes
47.3
27.4

Return on Total Assets
4.1%
2.6%

Total Assets
1162.4
1068.6

0 — 500 — 1000 — 1500 — 2000

0.00% — 0.03% — 0.06% — 0.08% — 0.11%

Income Before Income Taxes
47.3
27.4

Return on Revenues
3.1%
2.0%

Total Operating Income
1529.1
1364.7

0 — 500 — 1000 — 1500 — 2000

0.00% — 0.03% — 0.06% — 0.08% — 0.11%

Income Before Income Taxes
47.3
27.4

Profits To Rental Investment
8.7%
5.2%

Rental Eqipment - Net
545.7
530.8

0 — 500 — 1000 — 1500 — 2000

0.00% — 0.03% — 0.06% — 0.08% — 0.11%

EXHIBIT 9.4E.6   Consolidated Revenues & Expenses—American Rental
Association—Financial Ratios #2

Profits to Rental Income—Shows a sound increase from 1991 (5.2%) to 1992 (8.7%) due to increased growth rate of Income Before Income Taxes.

Financial Ratios #3

Total Revenues to Rental Investment—Shows a solid increase from 1991 (2.6X) to 1992 (2.8X) because Total Operating Income had a good increase while Rental Investment was almost even.

Rental Revenues to Rental Investment—Shows a solid increase from 1991 (1.6X) to 1992 (1.8X) because Rental Income showed a good increase while Rental Investment was almost even.

Rental Revenues to Equipment Cost—Shows a good gain from 1991 (0.5X) to 1992 (0.6X) because Rental Income showed a good increase while Cost of Rental Equipment stayed almost the same.

Balance Sheet—Chart 3999

This unique view of the Balance Sheet provides a good basis for analyzing company performance. The Assets, shown on the left plot of the chart, describes the average investment pattern for your members. The Liabilities and Equity, shown on the right plot of the chart, describes where the average firms get their money to support the assets. Most of the ratio components come from either the Balance Sheet or the Revenue & Expenses statement. For example, the Current Ratio is clearly shown by comparing the length of the Total Current Assets bar to the length of the Total Current Liabilities bar. The average company is fairly low leveraged for the Net Worth bar is a major part of the Total Liabilities & Net Worth bar. Lay your Balance Sheet on top of the relevant bars to compare your pattern to the average.

Revenue & Expenses—Chart 4025

This unique view of the Revenue & Expenses statement clearly defines the operating pattern of the average member firm. The Cost of Goods Sold is a small percent of Total Operating Revenue, leaving a considerable Gross Margin to cover Operating Costs. It is easy to see how Operating Expenses account for most of the firm's expenses. Depreciation on Rental Expense significantly influences the final Operating Profit. Lay your costs on top of the relevant bars to see what your pattern shows.

Percent of Gross Operating Profit—Chart 2001

The chart shows the components of Operating Expenses as a percent of Gross Operating Profit. It is obvious that Salaries & Wages plus Depreciation account for over half of the costs. Lay your percent of operating costs on top of the relevant bars to see what your pattern shows.

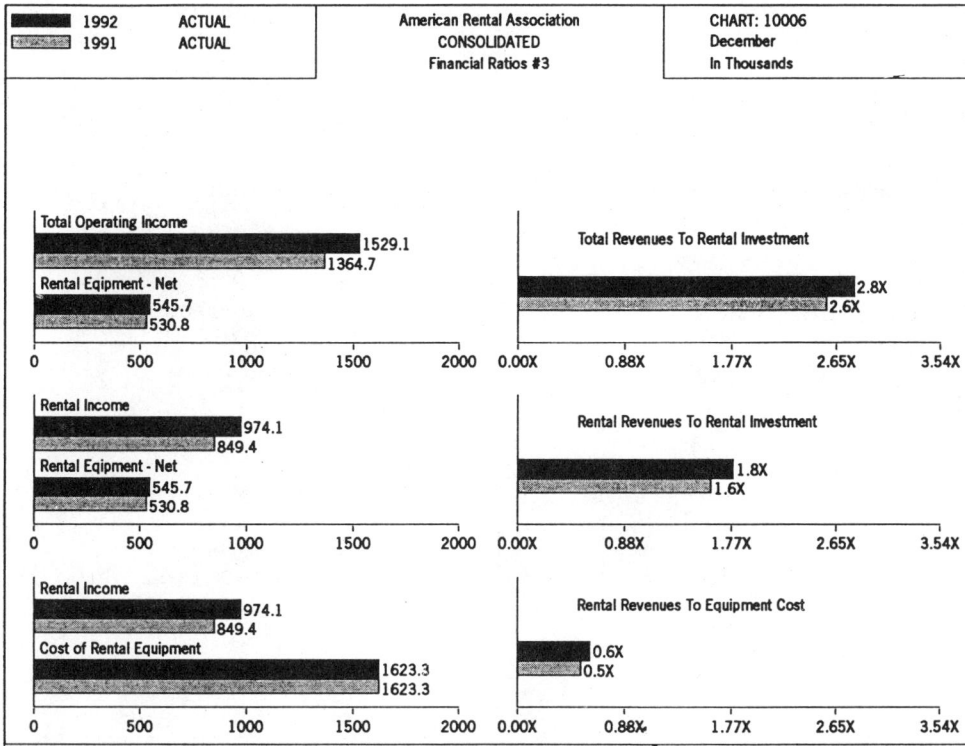

EXHIBIT 9.4E.7   Consolidated Percent of Gross Operating Profit—American Rental Association—Financial Ratios #3

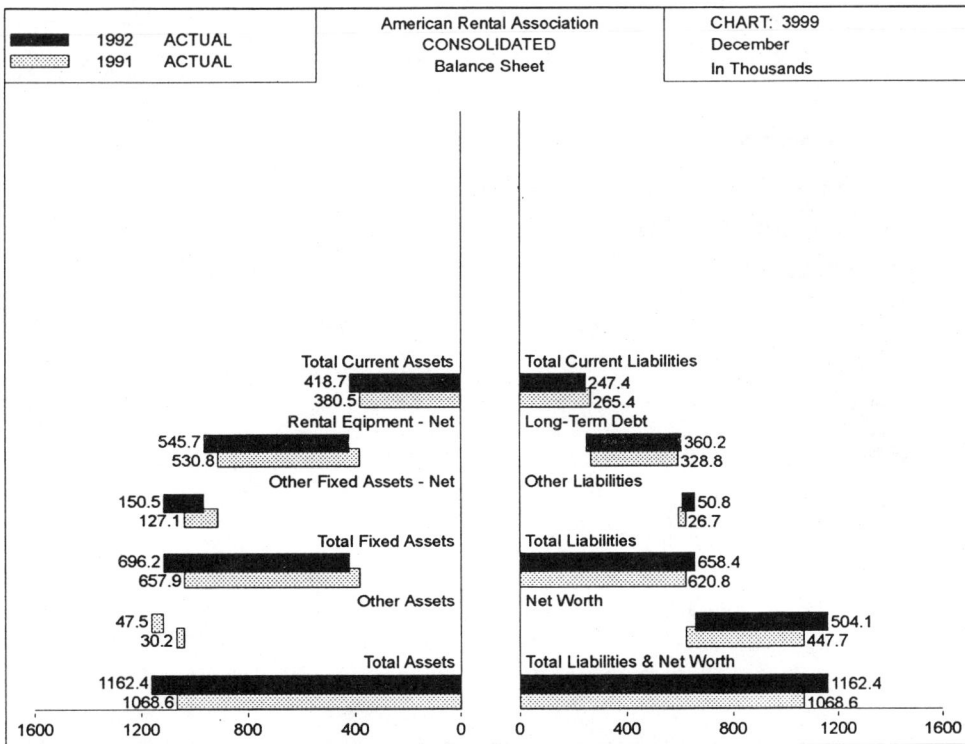

EXHIBIT 9.4E.8   Consolidated Balance Sheet—American Rental Association

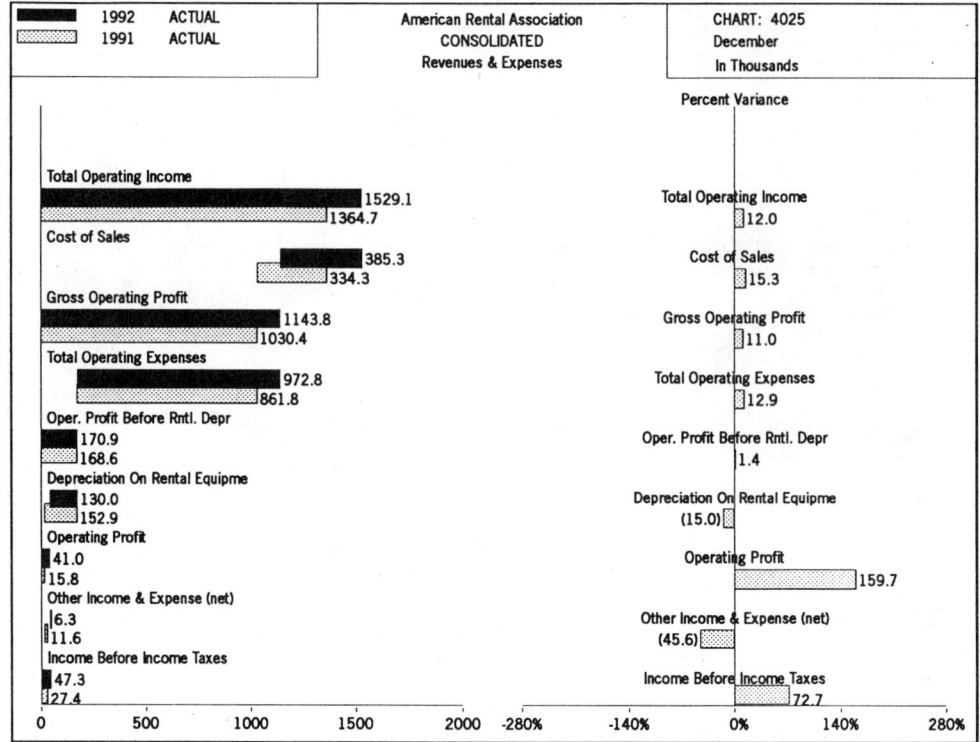

| 1992 | ACTUAL |
| 1991 | ACTUAL |

American Rental Association
CONSOLIDATED
Revenues & Expenses

CHART: 4025
December
In Thousands

Percent Variance

		Percent Variance
Total Operating Income	1529.1 / 1364.7	12.0
Cost of Sales	385.3 / 334.3	15.3
Gross Operating Profit	1143.8 / 1030.4	11.0
Total Operating Expenses	972.8 / 861.8	12.9
Oper. Profit Before Rntl. Depr	170.9 / 168.6	1.4
Depreciation On Rental Equipme	130.0 / 152.9	(15.0)
Operating Profit	41.0 / 15.8	159.7
Other Income & Expense (net)	6.3 / 11.6	(45.6)
Income Before Income Taxes	47.3 / 27.4	72.7

0   500   1000   1500   2000   -280%   -140%   0%   140%   280%

EXHIBIT 9.4E.9   Consolidated Revenue & Expenses—American Rental Association

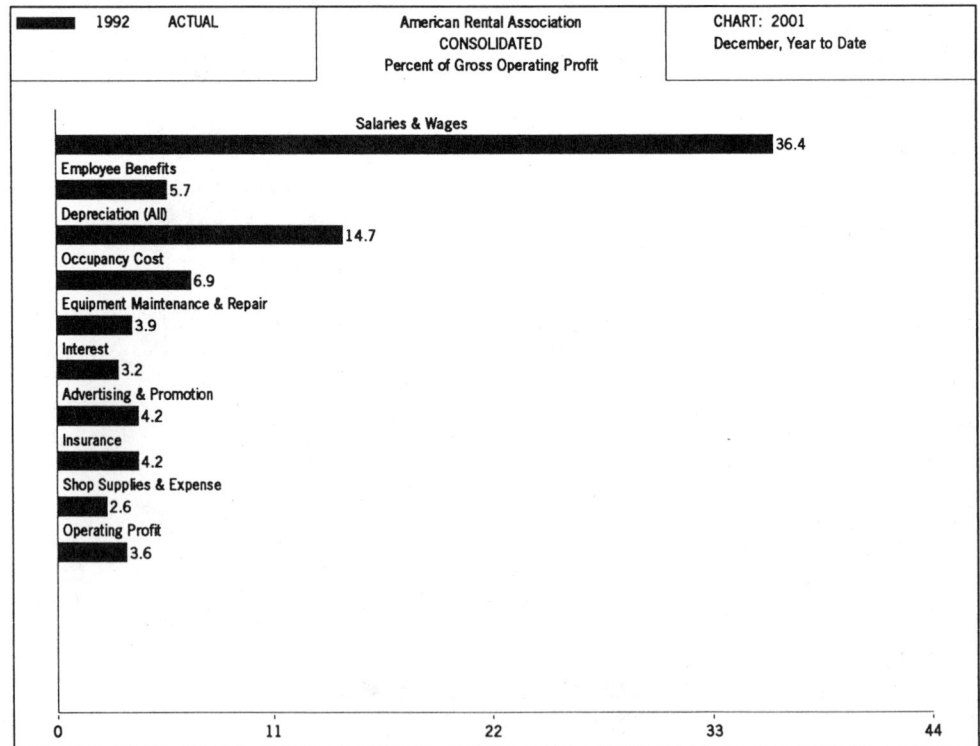

| 1992 | ACTUAL |

American Rental Association
CONSOLIDATED
Percent of Gross Operating Profit

CHART: 2001
December, Year to Date

Salaries & Wages	36.4
Employee Benefits	5.7
Depreciation (All)	14.7
Occupancy Cost	6.9
Equipment Maintenance & Repair	3.9
Interest	3.2
Advertising & Promotion	4.2
Insurance	4.2
Shop Supplies & Expense	2.6
Operating Profit	3.6

0   11   22   33   44

EXHIBIT 9.4E.10   Consolidated Percent of Gross Operating Profit—American
Rental Association

CHAPTER 23A (New)

USING GRAPHICS TO COMMUNICATE FINANCIAL RESULTS

23A.1 THE NEW OLD SAYING

There is a new "old saying," *if a picture is worth a thousand words, a chart is worth ten thousand numbers!* Like most old sayings, there is some truth and considerable hyperbole. Adding graphs to a badly composed set of financial statements is like putting a Band-Aid on an open wound. Not only does the bleeding continue, it looks foolish.

It is not easy to use graphics to present financial information. The biggest dilemma is that accountants are not trained to use graphics. We are, however, trained to use objective criteria for the presentation of financial information. Objectivity rather than subjectivity must be the basis for selecting the appropriate graphic form.

But, graphics invoke "subjectivity," or "taste." In response to the question Why did you use that chart, I often hear, "I like it." You use taste to buy the paintings you hang on the wall; if you don't like the picture, you don't buy it. If you present a balance sheet to your clients[1] and they "don't like it," will you change it to reflect what they like?

Both the tabular presentation and graphics must be appropriate, objective representations of the financial operations of a firm. There is no difference in the purpose of the presentation for they both represent the same financial information.

The fact is, all graphs are not created equal. Nor is finding the proper graphs to support various tabular reports intuitive. Finding the proper graphs for business reporting is straightforward if you understand and stick to a few basic ideas.

Adding graphics to a client presentation meets two business goals:

1. To help clients learn to interpret and use the financial statements to make business decisions.
2. To improve the communication of financial information to all levels of people in business organizations.

---

[1] "Clients" are defined as any person who will use the financial information to make business decisions.

23A.2 TASTE VS. ACCURACY

You must know *if* or *when* it is appropriate to let *taste* overcome *accuracy*. The "STOP" sign in Exhibit 23A.1 is "yellow." Is yellow the *accurate* color, or did taste prevail? Consider driving to work the morning after all the "red" STOP signs turn "yellow"!

Communicating financial or operating information dictates accuracy. This principle applies just as well to pictures, symbols, or number-based charts. Speaking of "taste," can you find the six fonts used to print "taste" in Exhibit 23A.1?

23A.3 TYPES OF GRAPHIC PACKAGES

There are three basic types of graphic packages in the market today: Spreadsheet Graphics, Financial Graphics, and Presentation Graphics.

A. Spreadsheet Graphics

Spreadsheet graphics use data from a range of rows and columns. Charts are totally dependent on the layout of the data in the spreadsheet range. While there are ways to build the charts faster and the charts can be saved and reused, each chart has to be built for each data range and separate ranges may have to be created to chart all of the information in the data sets. The leading use of spreadsheet graphics is to analyze the data being manipulated by the spreadsheet. Such use permits a rapid view of data relations that are not frequently or easily seen. The graphics included in spreadsheets have become more sophisticated with the introduction of the Windows versions. Graphics from Lotus, Excel, and QuatroPro are similar in form and process.

B. Financial Graphics

The graphics specifically designed to present financial information and financial statements. Financial graphics differ substantially from the spreadsheet graphics in three distinct ways:

1. *Financial graphics are "account" or "element" dependent.* The charts are defined by the relationships of the financial elements. Each element can be re-used to show an almost endless number of financial relationships. The Total Revenue element can be depicted as the first element in the Revenue and Expense statement. It can also be shown as the denominator or numerator for a large number of financial ratio charts. For example, the Inventory Turnover ratio defines the critical relationships between the Balance Sheet and the Revenue and Expense statement.

2. *Financial graphics are database dependent.* The data comes from live databases that are constantly changing. The most popular use of financial graphics is to integrate them with accounting, manufacturing, payroll, inventory, accounts payable, and all other accounting modules. The result is they pull the information directly from "the books of record." The integration with accounting systems takes three different forms:

   a. Template integration where the host system produces the same reports for all users. A specific set of financial graphics are designed for the reports, and they are always available.

Taste vs Accuracy

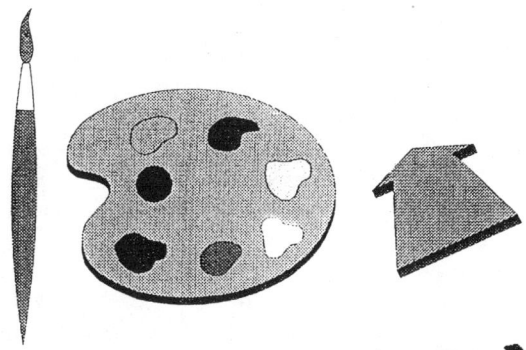

TASTE

TASTE

MAKE YOUR POINT!

TASTE

ΤΑΣΤΕ

TASTE

EXHIBIT 23A.1

b. Database dependent where the integration system is "smart" enough to query the database. The query result is used to build the graphs that correctly reflect the relevant information in the data base.

c. Report dependent where the integration is "smart" enough to analyze the report definitions and build the appropriate graphs to reflect the information in the reports.

The common thread in all three types of integration is that the user does not have to create the charts. All the user has to do is turn on the system and the charts automatically are created from the results of operations.

3. *Financial graphics show the arithmetic of the financial reports used to present the financial results of operations.* As opposed to analytical charting, the relationships shown by financial graphics are frequently seen and easily understood. Thus financial graphics reflect the same complex relationships in a chart, or a series of charts, as shown in the complete set of accounting and financial statements. Financial graphics are available in a growing number of accounting and other software including: ACE by Sequel/McGladrey; CaseWear by Wainright & Kidd Software; CAFRonMICRO by the Government Finance Officers Association; FinAlyzer by the National Association of College and University Business Officers; SBT Accounting Systems; SCS Compute Data Write and Tax Machine; as a Lotus 1-2-3 add in for Windows; and as part of CPAnalyst by Graphic M*I*S, LLC.

C. Presentation Graphics

The presentation graphic products are designed to help individuals (and corporations) make more sophisticated presentations. While they have the capacity to create charts from scratch, they are more often used to import and enhance charts created in other packages and integrate the charts into a complete presentation that can be shown from the computer and/or printed for handouts. The newer presentation packages include multimedia capability and utilize pictures, sound tracks, animation and film clips as a part of the finished presentation. These types of graphic packages are becoming more important to financial presentations but they are too complex to include in this chapter. Freelance for Windows by Lotus, Harvard Graphics by Software Publishers, Inc., Pro Draw by Gold Disk, Inc., Astound by Gold Disk, Inc., and Powerpoint by MicroSoft are a few of the most widely utilized presentation graphic titles.

Spreadsheet and Financial graphics each have their own strengths and weaknesses, some of which are noted in this chapter. Other types of graphic packages include Computer Aided Design (CAD), Desk Top Publishing, and advanced analytical packages designed specifically for a niche within an industry. Specific and true 3D packages discussed in the previous chapter have been designed for future and stock traders. Multimedia development and presentation tools are fast becoming a major force in the graphic industry, and accounting "games" are in development. Virtual reality programs are in the wings, and while a few specific applications are available, they are not yet useful for general purpose. Soon, we will walk through the valley of the cost of goods sold.

23A.4 COMMUNICATION

The single most important reason for using graphics is to help communicate the financial and operating information contained in the financial records of the company. Communication with and among humans consists of four major types of information inputs: tabular, written, pictorial (graphic), and verbal interpretations of the other three communication modalities. These four modalities are all the rage today because they are the foundation on which multimedia presentations are built.

A complete Interactive Multimedia information system must include all four types of presentations. The four modalities can be presented on a multimedia computer where the tabular reports are shown in one window, the graphics in a second window, the written analysis in a third window with a voice overlay to describe the information in the three windows. The most common multimedia presentation includes a hard copy report prepared with the same combination of tabular, graphic, and written presentations where the accountant presents the report to the client with a verbal explanation. The point is, you do not need to use a multimedia computer to make a multimedia presentation! See the last chapter in this supplement for a description of how the ultimate multimedia machine, YOU, can better communicate the financial results.

This chapter has a narrow focus: to describe with examples, the relationship between the tabular and graphic reports. Each presentation modality must support and/or enhance the accountants' ability to communicate complex financial information to their clients.

A.   Selecting the Charts that Support the Accounting Process

The new accounting systems report data almost any way you want. Real time posting simplifies daily reporting of operating or financial results. There is almost no limit to how the data can be sliced and diced. The problem is selecting the appropriate mix of data that produces useful information.

Certain types of information clearly benefit when supported by charts. Your company and your clients benefit as you learn how to integrate the tabular, graphic, and written analyses.

There are two primary categories of business reports: *Single-segment* reports and *Complex-component* reports. Single-segment reporting presents data tables about a single business element such as sales, costs, payroll expenses, or net income. Complex-component reporting presents a mixture of related data elements such as assets, liabilities and equities in a balance sheet. Revenue and expense statements mix revenues, costs, expenses and other operating related data elements. Here are a few simple and complex examples of how graphics can improve communications in both categories. Each example includes the logic used to select the specific graphic presentation.

B.   Single-Segment Data

1.   *Time Series*   Data has become the most common graphic form used to present single segment data. You see examples from daily reports with month-to-date results to formal annual reports with decade results.

Table 23A.1 shows the daily sales for Acme Sales & Service in December 1994 compared to 1993. The data in the 1994 column is bolded to help the eye connect to the 1994 data shown in the charts. Exhibit 23A.2 is a simple time series line chart of daily sales for December 1994 built in a spreadsheet system. The line chart is an appropriate metaphor to show analog figures. Daily figures qualify as analog in most sales environments. The results reported must reflect the business cycle. For example, minute-by-minute sales figures would find little value in most manufacturing companies, considerable use in commodities.

Exhibit 23A.3 is the same line chart with 1993 data added to the chart. It is obvious that the sales pattern for December 1994 and 1993 are almost identical. The result of the similar patterns is a vague chart. A clearer pattern results in Exhibit 23A.4 when vertical bars are used to present the information. Notice how the bold-type data in Table 23A.1 is much more intuitively related to the 1994 bars in Exhibit 23A.4. Exhibit 23A.4 was built by copying Exhibit 23A.3 and changing the chart type.

TABLE 23A.1   Acme Sales & Service Daily Sales

Week	Date	1994	1993	Variance
	1st	$110,235	$102,653	$7,582
	2nd	89,562	91,256	(1,694)
	3rd	125,687	118,659	7,028
	4th	185,962	172,912	13,050
	5th	219,395	198,736	20,659
	6th	325,868	298,527	27,341
Week one		$1,058,703	$984,736	$73,966
	8th	$122,361	$114,971	$7,389
	9th	99,414	102,207	(2,793)
	10th	139,513	132,898	6,614
	11th	206,418	193,661	12,756
	12th	243,528	222,584	20,944
	13th	361,713	334,350	27,363
Week two		$1,172,947	$1,100,672	$72,275
	15th	$137,044	$127,618	$9,426
	16th	111,343	113,449	(2,106)
	17th	156,254	147,517	8,737
	18th	231,188	214,964	16,224
	19th	272,752	247,069	25,683
	20th	405,119	371,129	33,990
Week three		$1,313,701	$1,221,746	$91,955
	22nd	154,860	145,485	9,375
	23rd	125,818	129,332	(3,514)
	24th	176,567	168,169	8,398
Christmas	25th	0	0	0
	26th	308,210	281,658	26,551
	27th	457,784	423,087	34,697
Week four		$1,223,239	$1,147,731	$75,507
	29th	140,923	138,211	2,712
	30th	114,494	122,866	(8,371)
	31st	160,676	159,761	915
Week five		$416,093	$420,837	($4,744)
Total December		$5,184,682	$4,875,723	$308,959

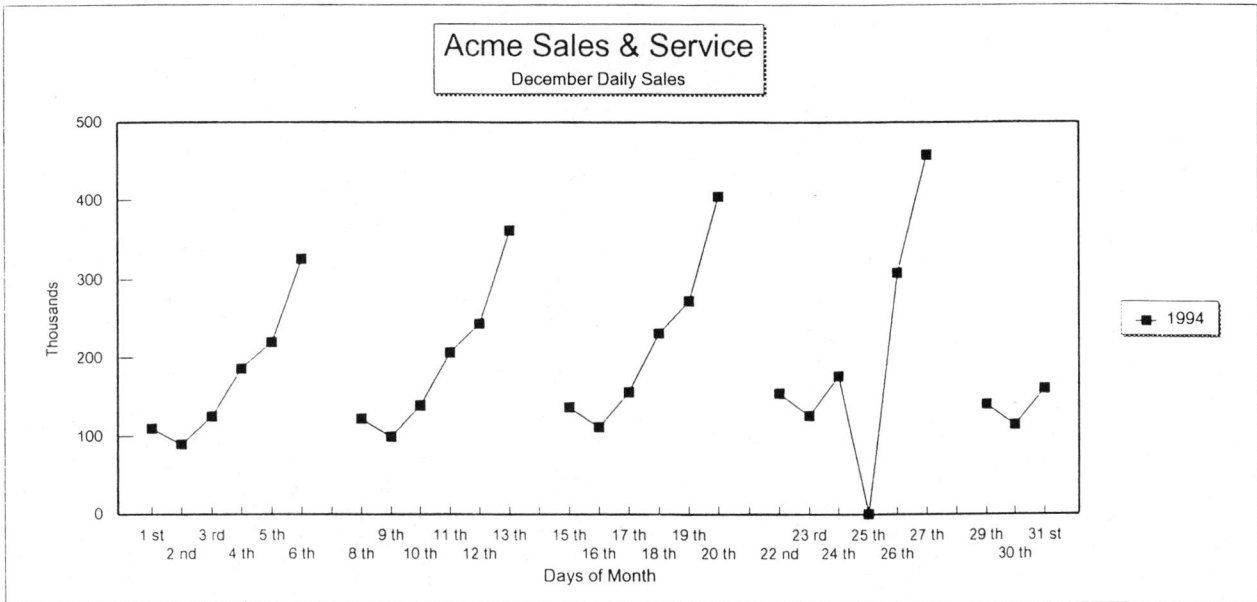

EXHIBIT 23A.2

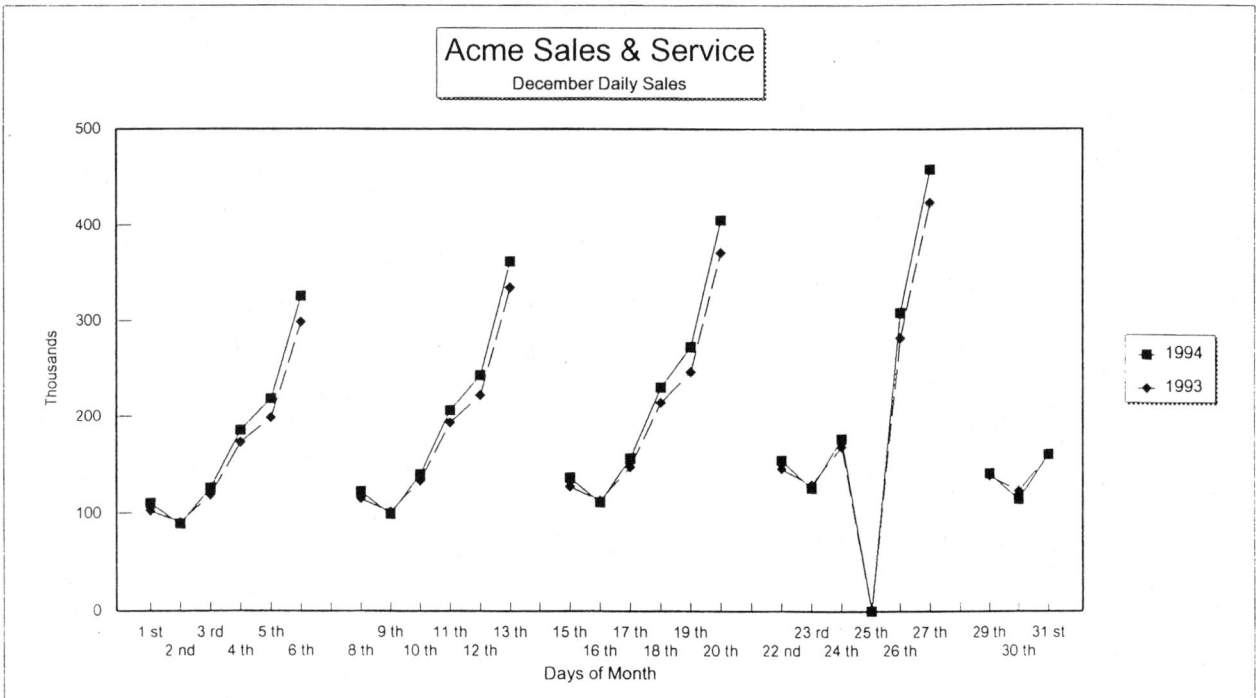

EXHIBIT 23A.3

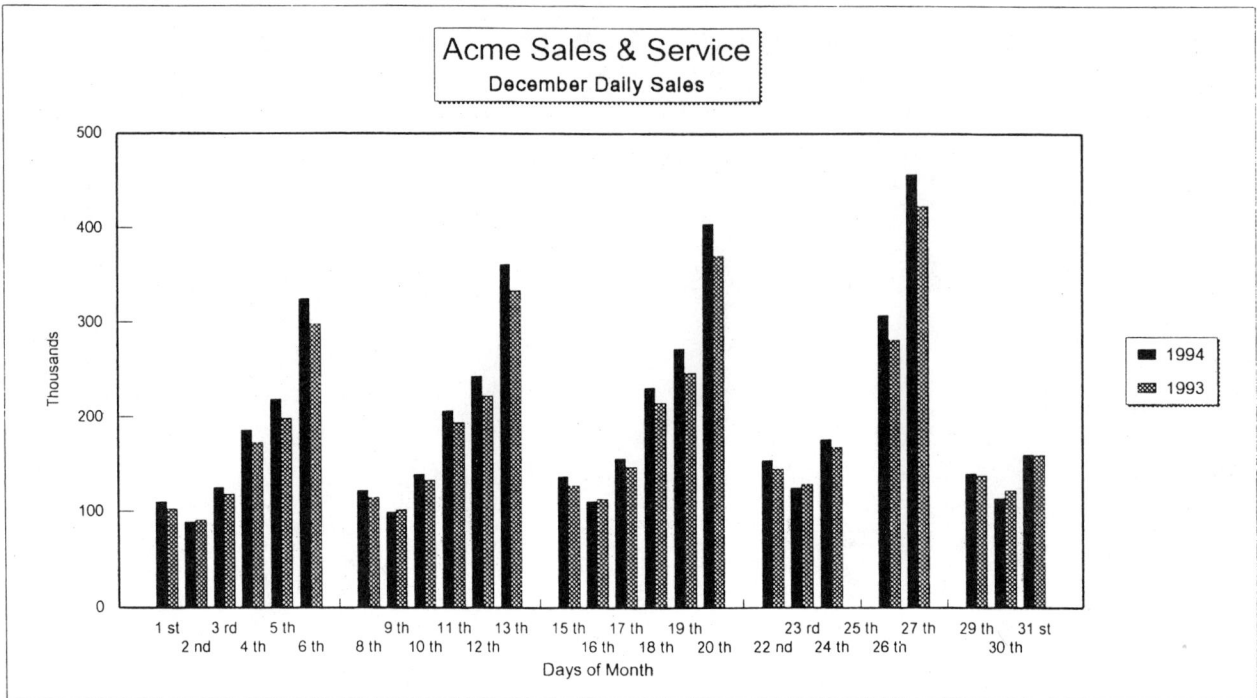

EXHIBIT 23A.4

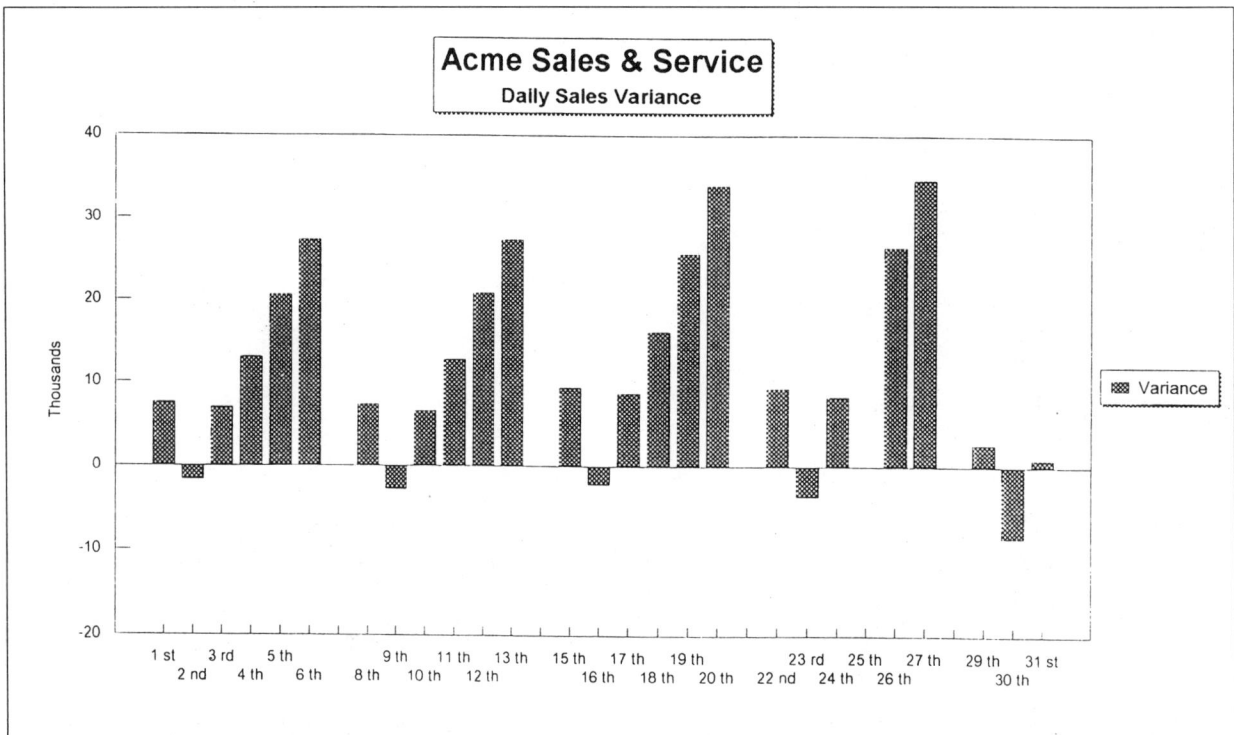

EXHIBIT 23A.5

Exhibit 23A.5 is a chart showing the variances from Table 23A.1. This chart was built in the spreadsheet by moving the Variance column next to the Date column and selecting those two columns as the operative range. When the chart feature was selected, the chart was placed below Exhibit 23A.4. It was sized, the name added, the name of the legend added, and the shading changed so that it would match the 1993 shading in Exhibit 23A.4. There is a significant problem when Exhibits 23A.4 & 23A.5 are shown together. The bars in Exhibit 23A.5 are twice as wide as those in Exhibit 23A.4, implying to the brain that the numbers are twice as large. The scales are properly shown, but the surface value is not readily comparable between the variances in Exhibit 23A.5 and the original data in Exhibit 23A.4.

Table 23A.2 is an annual sales report for Acme Sales & Service showing all 12 months with 1994 and 1993 results. Exhibits 23A.6 and 23A.7 show the same information in a vertical bar chart. Notice that viewing the tabular and graphic presentations together enhances the information transfer. The vertical bar chart is a more appropriate presentation of period data. Sales did not occur in a straight line from day 1 to the last day of December, see Exhibits 23A.2 through 23A.5. Monthly totals are not an analog presentation of how sales occurred each day. A vertical bar clearly reflects the value of each month's sales. The vertical bar chart, as opposed to the line chart, does not imply analog data.

TABLE 23A.2 Acme Sales & Service Monthly Sales

Month	1994	1993	Variance
Jan	$3,685,940	$3,822,800	($136,860)
Feb	3,069,813	3,392,735	(322,922)
Mar	2,699,871	2,987,563	(287,692)
Apr	3,998,232	3,569,821	428,411
May	3,987,526	3,625,919	361,607
Jun	4,242,365	3,985,261	257,104
Jul	4,511,275	4,023,659	487,616
Aug	4,456,892	4,212,334	244,558
Sep	4,951,487	4,365,821	585,666
Oct	4,983,259	4,485,692	497,567
Nov	5,023,651	4,439,665	583,986
Dec	5,184,682	4,875,723	308,959
Total	$50,793,000	$47,785,000	$3,008,000

A bigger problem emerges with the data presentation in Exhibits 23A.6 and 23A.7. The variance bars in Exhibit 23A.7 are much wider than the variance bars in Exhibit 23A.6. The width of the bars is totally dependent on the number of bars shown. As discussed throughout this text, different bar sizes present different data values to the brain. The use of a consistent bar size is a significant advantage of financial graphics over spreadsheet graphics. Notice that Exhibits 23A.8 and 23A.9 show the same data from Table 23A.2, but the bars are the same width. Different bar width is not a subtle difference to the brain. If the surface keeps changing, the right brain cannot recognize the pattern.

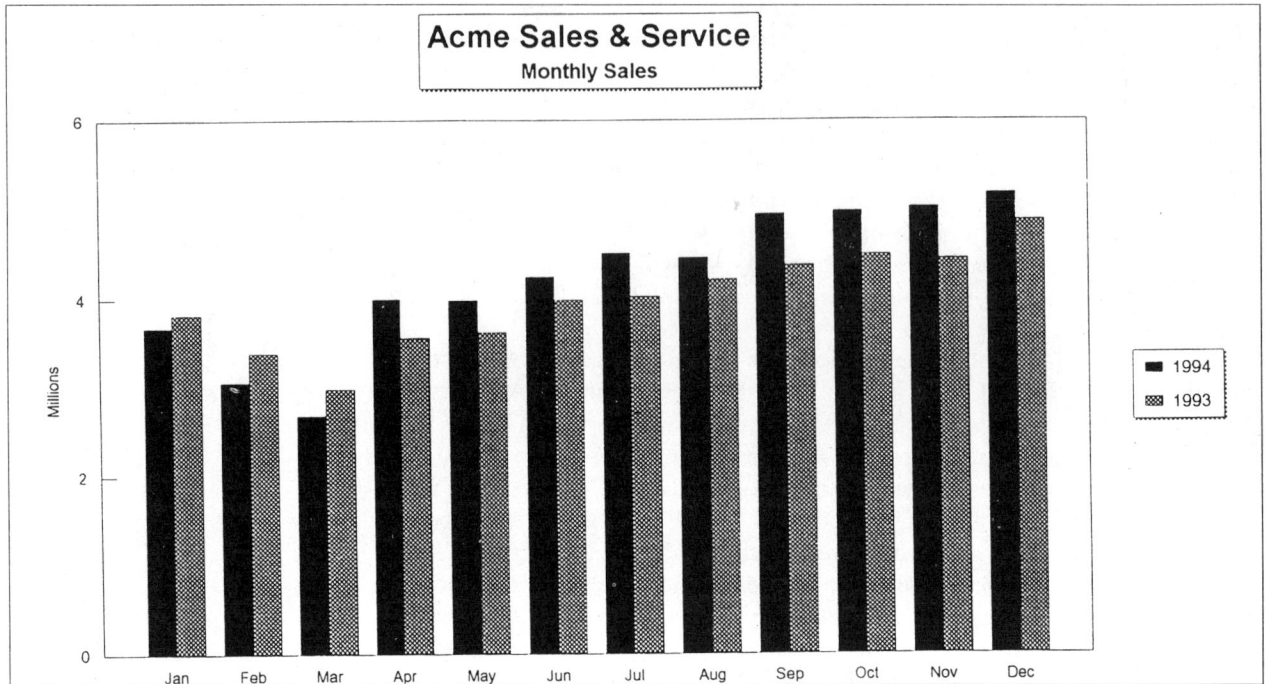

EXHIBIT 23A.6

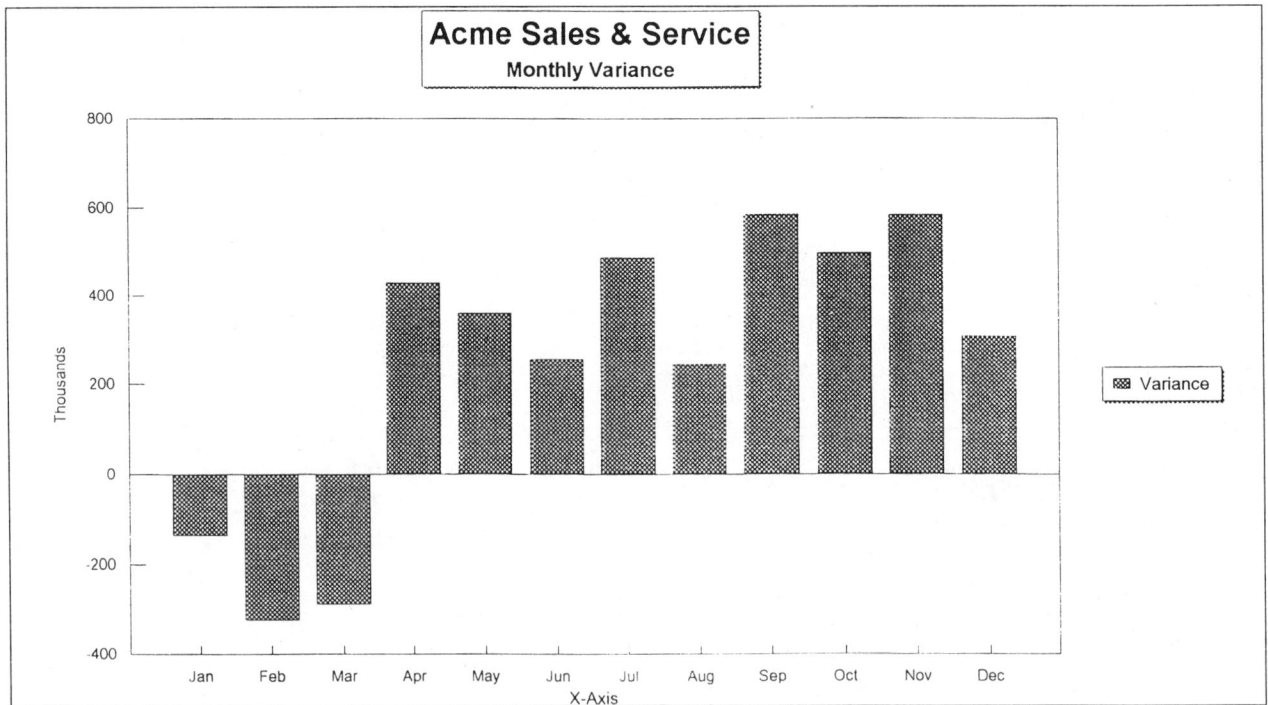

EXHIBIT 23A.7

2. *Comparative Data*   Managers compare results to evaluate performance. The comparative data can be: internal such as last year, budget, forecast; or internal such as people, product type, product, division. The comparative data can be external such as competitors, industry averages. Table 23A.3 contains 1994 sales data for nine salespeople who sell two products out of three divisions. Table 23A.3 is a simple data set, and a similar set can be found in most companies. Interestingly, this simple data set offers some serious charting obstacles. A good way to show the obstacles when using spreadsheet graphics is to show the charts that do and do not reflect the information in Table 23A.3. Section 1 shows the spreadsheet charts created from the simple data set. Section 2 shows a much more realistic and complex set of data shown in Table 23A.4.

TABLE 23A.3   Acme Sales & Services Sales by Sales Person

Name	Service '94	Product '94	Total '94	Division
Alfred	$1,000,000	$4,123,000	$5,123,000	N.Y.
Bertha	1,405,000	3,245,000	4,650,000	Chicago
Chester	2,341,000	1,234,000	3,575,000	L.A.
Dwight	3,451,000	4,322,000	7,773,000	N.Y.
Elmer	1,234,000	2,343,000	3,577,000	N.Y.
Fred	5,234,000	1,252,000	6,486,000	L.A.
Gerald	5,123,000	2,132,000	7,255,000	Chicago
Herbert	1,645,000	5,123,000	6,768,000	Chicago
Iggy	2,334,000	3,252,000	5,586,000	L.A.
Total	$23,767,000	$27,026,000	$50,793,000	

1.   Simple Data Set—The natural inclination of some apprentices (and unfortunately some veterans) using spreadsheet graphics is to go with the defaults, or the last chart used. The results as shown in this section can range from total distortion to OK. To properly display the information, you must know the data, know how the charts display the data, and match the data with the charts. There were well over 100 charts created with this simple data set. The ones shown in this section are considered representative.

The charts were all created using the spreadsheet defaults. The first chart in this section, Exhibit 23A.10, was created using a data range of the first four columns in Table 23A.3 down through the row named Iggy. The titles were added, and the words X-Axis and Y-Axis were deleted. Except as noted, the rest of the charts were created by copying Exhibit 23A.10 and then changing the chart type. Notes were added to the bottom of each chart so the reader can copy Table 23A.3 with the Exhibits as an office guide.

Exhibit 23A.10 shows what may be the single most common data-charting error. The data shown in Table 23A.3 is the total data for 1994, or point-in-time data. Using a vertical line chart indicates the data is time series data such as the data shown in Tables 23A.1 and 23A.2. The data between Alfred and Bertha has no causal relationship. Even though the chart is the wrong type, the following explanations use the same data to show additional data problems that could occur even with time series (analog) data. The chart type is an absolute data chart. Note that the lines cross four times. The rule of thumb is that if the lines cross more than three times, the viewer will not see the relationships among the data. In this case, the inclination is to use a chart where the lines do not cross.

Table 23A.4 Acme Sales & Service by Year

Service Sales

Name	Service '94	Service '93	Variance	Name	Variance
Alfred	$1,000,000	$1,250,000	($250,000)	Alfred	($250,000)
Dwight	3,451,000	2,999,000	452,000	Dwight	452,000
Elmer	1,234,000	1,012,000	222,000	Elmer	222,000
Tot N.Y.	$5,685,000	$5,261,000	$424,000	Tot N.Y.	$424,000
Chester	$2,341,000	$1,965,000	$376,000	Chester	$376,000
Fred	5,234,000	3,987,000	1,247,000	Fred	1,247,000
Iggy	2,334,000	3,564,000	(1,230,000)	Iggy	(1,230,000)
Tot L.A.	$9,909,000	$9,516,000	$393,000	Tot L.A.	$393,000
Bertha	$1,405,000	$989,000	$416,000	Bertha	$416,000
Gerald	5,123,000	4,789,000	334,000	Gerald	334,000
Herbert	1,645,000	1,111,000	534,000	Herbert	534,000
Tot Chi.	$8,173,000	$6,889,000	$1,284,000	Tot Chi.	$1,284,000
Total Service	$23,767,000	$21,666,000	$2,101,000	Total	$2,101,000

Product Sales

Name	Product '94	Product '93	Variance	Name	Variance
Alfred	$4,123,000	$3,659,000	$464,000	Alfred	$464,000
Dwight	4,322,000	4,721,000	(399,000)	Dwight	(399,000)
Elmer	2,343,000	2,012,000	331,000	Elmer	331,000
Tot N.Y.	$10,788,000	$10,392,000	$396,000	Tot N.Y.	$396,000

Table 23A.4 (Continued)

Name	Product '94	Product '93	Variance	Name	Variance
Chester	$1,234,000	$1,121,000	$113,000	Chester	$113,000
Fred	1,252,000	1,654,000	(402,000)	Fred	(402,000)
Iggy	3,252,000	2,568,000	684,000	Iggy	684,000
Tot L.A.	$5,738,000	$5,343,000	$395,000	Tot L.A.	$395,000
Bertha	$3,245,000	$2,987,000	$258,000	Bertha	$258,000
Gerald	2,132,000	1,765,000	367,000	Gerald	367,000
Herbert	5,123,000	5,632,000	(509,000)	Herbert	(509,000)
Tot Chi.	$10,500,000	$10,384,000	$116,000	Tot Chi.	$116,000
Total Service	$27,026,000	$26,119,000	$907,000	Total	$907,000

Total Sales

Name	Total '94	Total '93	Variance	Name	Variance
Alfred	$5,123,000	$4,909,000	$214,000	Alfred	$214,000
Dwight	7,773,000	7,720,000	53,000	Dwight	53,000
Elmer	3,577,000	3,024,000	553,000	Elmer	553,000
Tot N.Y.	$16,473,000	$15,653,000	$820,000	Tot N.Y.	$820,000
Chester	$3,575,000	$3,086,000	$489,000	Chester	$489,000
Fred	6,486,000	5,641,000	845,000	Fred	845,000
Iggy	5,586,000	6,132,000	(546,000)	Iggy	(546,000)
Tot L.A.	$15,647,000	$14,859,000	$788,000	Tot L.A.	$788,000
Bertha	$4,650,000	$3,976,000	$674,000	Bertha	$674,000
Gerald	7,255,000	6,554,000	701,000	Gerald	701,000
Herbert	6,768,000	6,743,000	25,000	Herbert	25,000
Tot Chi.	$18,673,000	$17,273,000	$1,400,000	Tot Chi.	$1,400,000
Total	$50,793,000	$47,785,000	$3,008,000	Total	$3,008,000

Exhibit 23A.11 shows the same data without the lines crossing. Separating the lines was accomplished by changing the chart type. Unfortunately, the chart type is a cumulative data chart and the lines add one to another. Note that the top of the scale on Exhibit 23A.10 is 10 million; on Exhibit 23A.11 it is 20 million. The Total 1994 data shown is twice the actual figure.

Exhibit 23A.12 shows a different data range that does not include the total column. It is always a consideration whether to include totals with the components. The total always shrinks the components and can significantly distort the pattern. Note that the scale is ok. But, another problem pops up. The legends have shifted! Exhibits 23A.10 and 23A.11 show Product as the first line and Service as the second line. The software made this change.

Exhibit 23A.13 is the same as Exhibit 23A.10, except there are no icons in the legend. Assuming this was a good representation of the data (and it is not), this presentation is more difficult to follow.

Exhibits 23A.14 and 23A.15 are the same as Exhibits 23A.10 and 23A.12, except they are horizontal. See notes on the charts.

Exhibit 23A.16 is the same as Exhibit 23A.15, except it is a cumulative surface chart. This chart type is totally useless for the point data in Table 23A.3. This chart type could be used to plot two closely related sets of analog data. The surface would then describe the volumes.

Exhibit 23A.17 is the same as Exhibit 23A.10, except vertical bar charts are used. This is a much better representation of the data, but still implies a time series. Also, comparing Alfred to Iggy is not immediate.

Exhibit 23A.18 is the same as Exhibit 23A.17, except the bars are horizontal. This is the best representation of the data in Table 23A.3 shown by the spreadsheet graphic system. Note how the bars are narrower again.

Exhibit 23A.19 is the same data, except a vertical stacked bar is used. Stacked bars are by definition, *cumulative* charts, so this is an erroneous representation of the data. Note that the scale jumped to 20 million, doubling the total data. That is because the cumulative chart added the total to the total of the other two.

Exhibit 23A.20 is the same as Exhibit 23A.15, except the horizontal stacked bar is connected with a line. If you must use stacked bars, use 100% stacked bars to show a common pattern. Stacked bars are difficult to compare and the lines seem to confuse.

Exhibit 23A.21 is the same as Exhibit 23A.17, except a pie chart is used. QUICK, compare Bertha to Gerald! What happened to the other data? Where is the other data? Pie charts are extremely limited. If more than four pieces are shown, the average user cannot see a pattern. If the pieces are less than 15°, the average user cannot see a pattern. If two or more pie charts are used, the average user cannot compare one to the other, especially if the radius of the pies are different. And if that does not convince you, how would you show a negative?

Exhibit 23A.22 is a horizontal bar with a total line added. The value of this presentation is that the components are clearly presented. The total is shown by the line. This is the second best presentation of the data in Table 23A.3.

Exhibit 23A.23 is a horizontal stacked bar with a total line. The total line is not needed with a stacked bar. The stacked bar is the total.

Exhibit 23A.24 is a horizontal bar chart with a surface for the total. This is a distortion of the information. As noted earlier, the surface is not indicative of the type data shown.

Exhibit 23A.25 is a truly bad chart. As noted in the first chapter of the supplement, this is a graphic artist's interpretation of a 3D line; it is not a 3D chart.

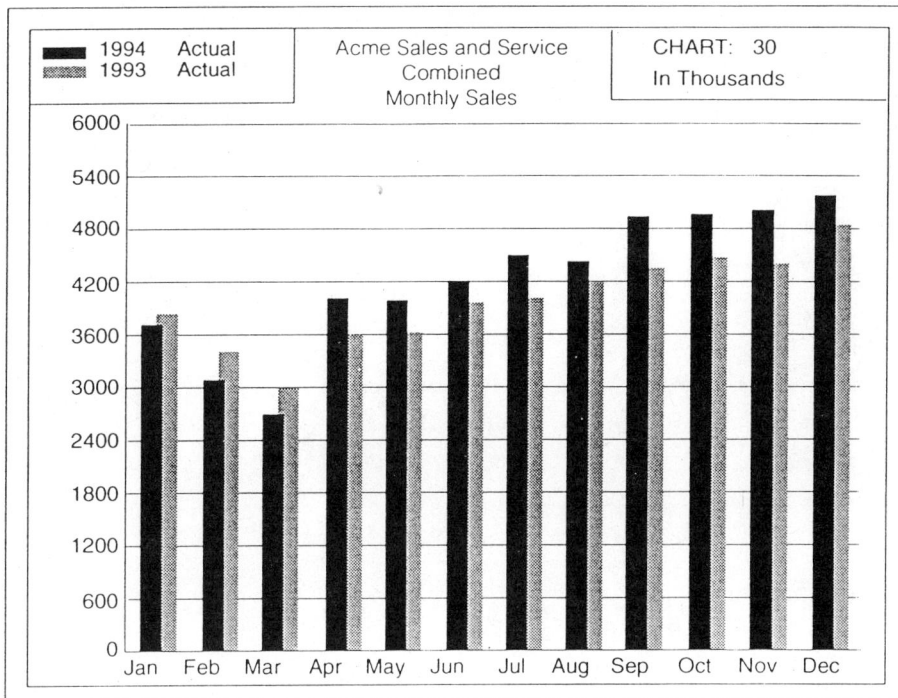

EXHIBIT 23A.8

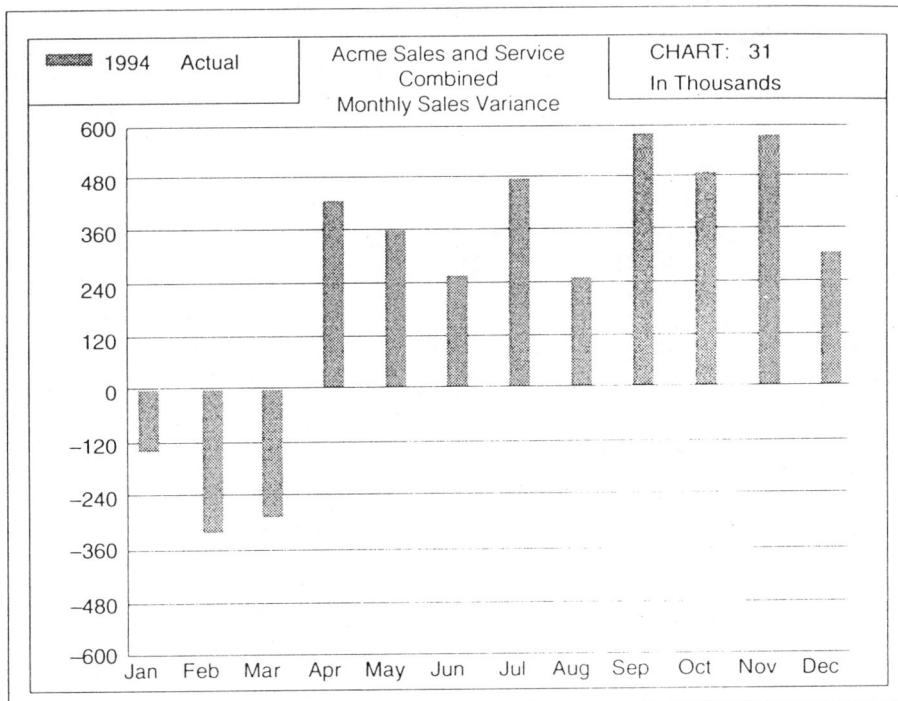

EXHIBIT 23A.9

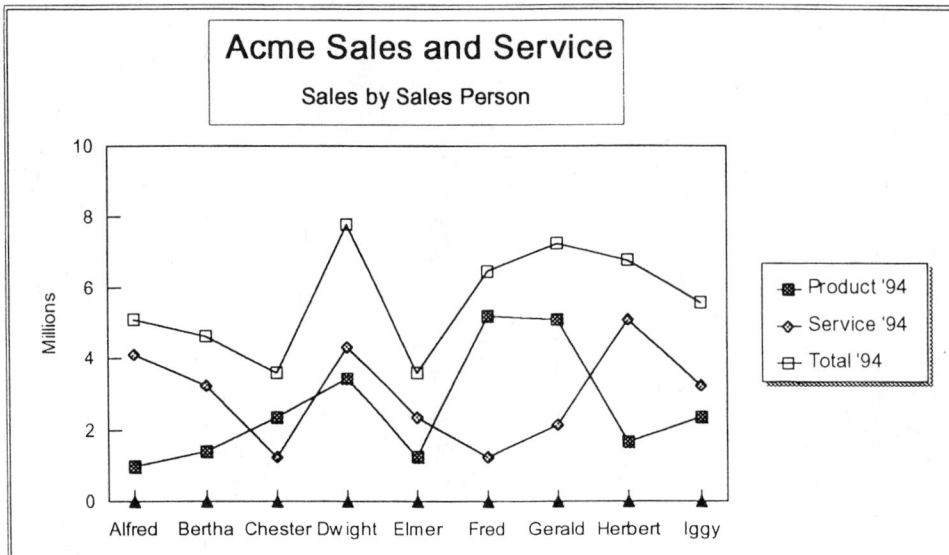

Acme Sales and Service
Sales by Sales Person

An "Absolute" data chart. Plots the absolute
data point. *Problem* with this chart: it implies a
time series. These are independent data point,
totally unrelated from point to point.

EXHIBIT 23A.10

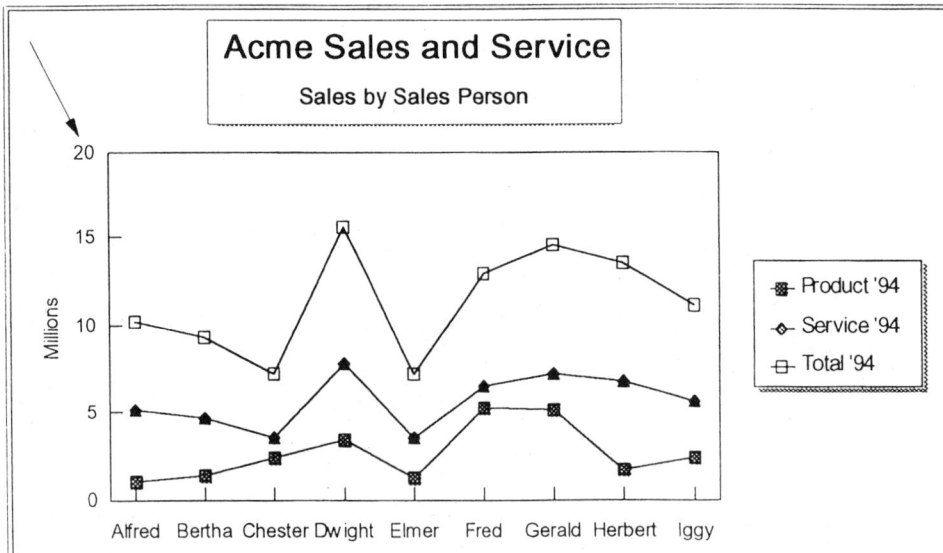

Acme Sales and Service
Sales by Sales Person

A "Cumulative" data chart. Plots the cumulative
data. *Problem* with this chart: it doubles the
data. The total is the cumulative result of adding
Product and Service.

EXHIBIT 23A.11

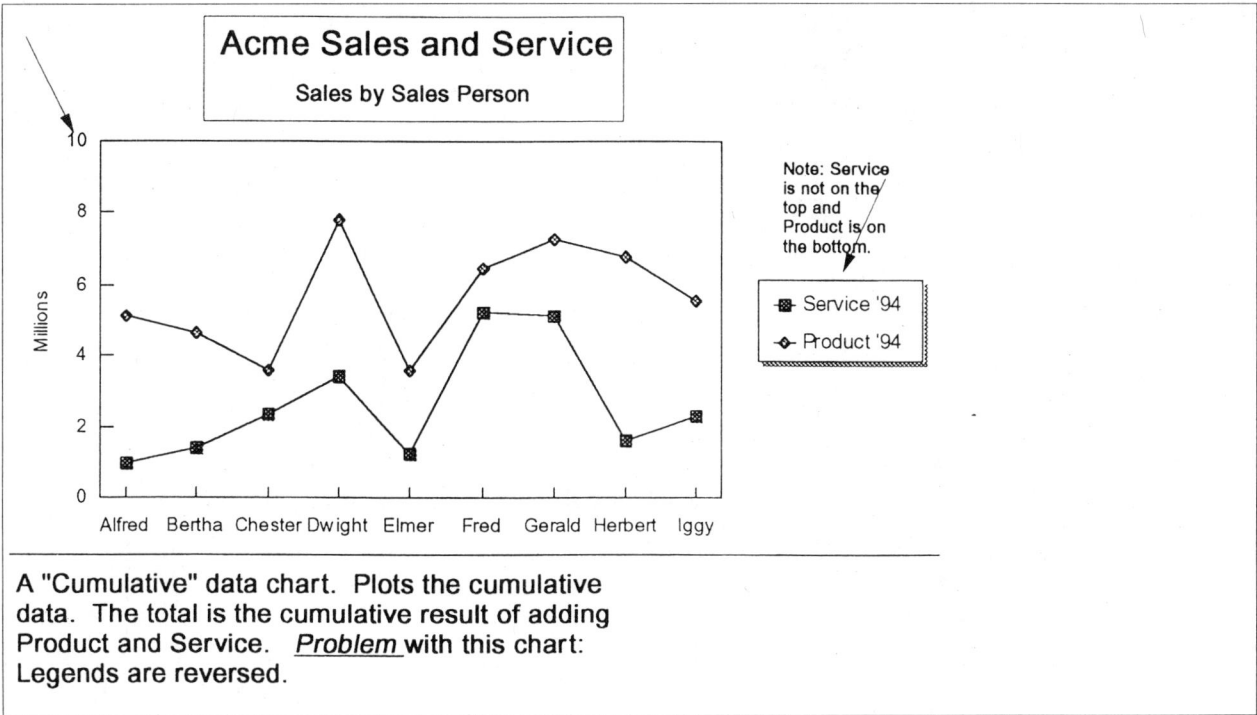

Acme Sales and Service
Sales by Sales Person

Note: Service is not on the top and Product is on the bottom.

- Service '94
- Product '94

(x-axis: Alfred, Bertha, Chester, Dwight, Elmer, Fred, Gerald, Herbert, Iggy)
(y-axis: Millions, 0 to 10)

A "Cumulative" data chart. Plots the cumulative data. The total is the cumulative result of adding Product and Service. *Problem* with this chart: Legends are reversed.

EXHIBIT 23A.12

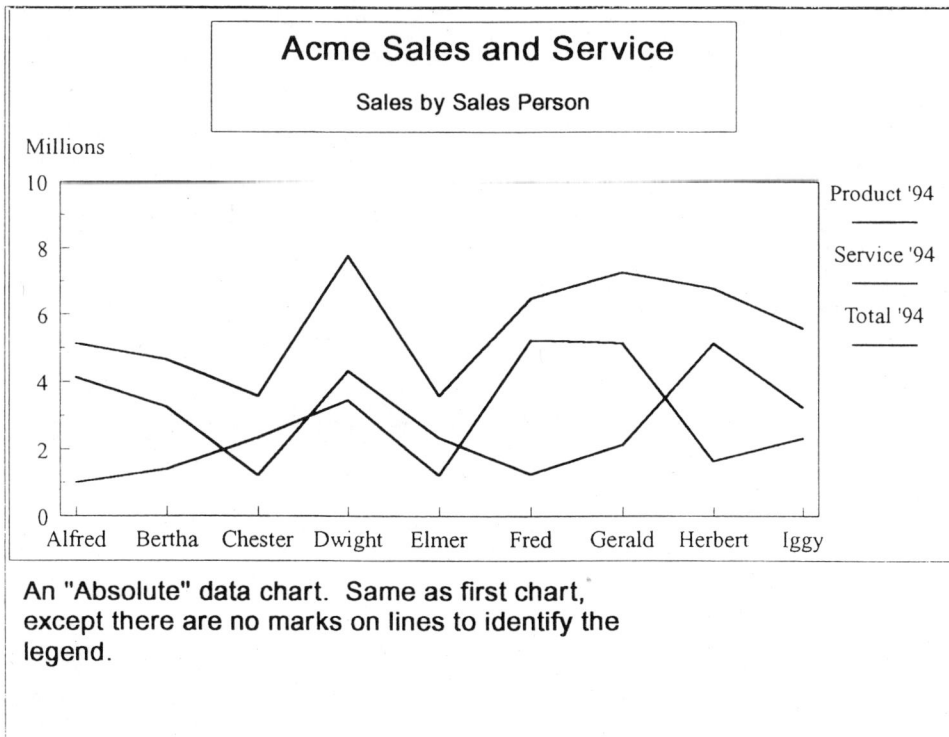

Acme Sales and Service
Sales by Sales Person

Millions

Product '94

Service '94

Total '94

(x-axis: Alfred, Bertha, Chester, Dwight, Elmer, Fred, Gerald, Herbert, Iggy)
(y-axis: 0 to 10)

An "Absolute" data chart. Same as first chart, except there are no marks on lines to identify the legend.

EXHIBIT 23A.13

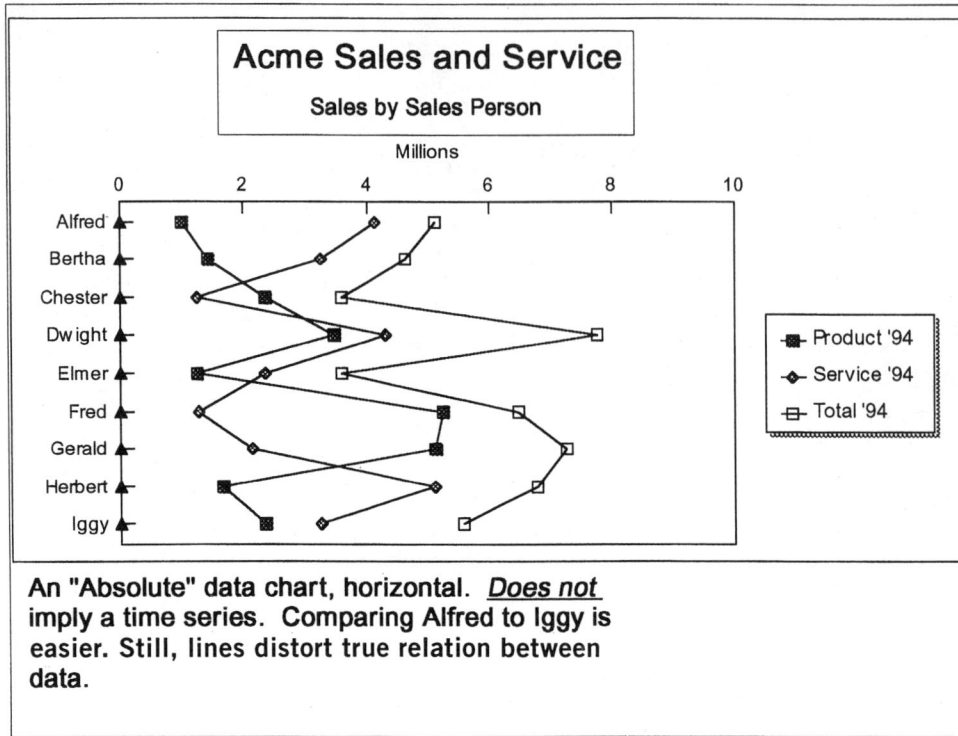

An "Absolute" data chart, horizontal. _Does not_ imply a time series. Comparing Alfred to Iggy is easier. Still, lines distort true relation between data.

EXHIBIT 23A.14

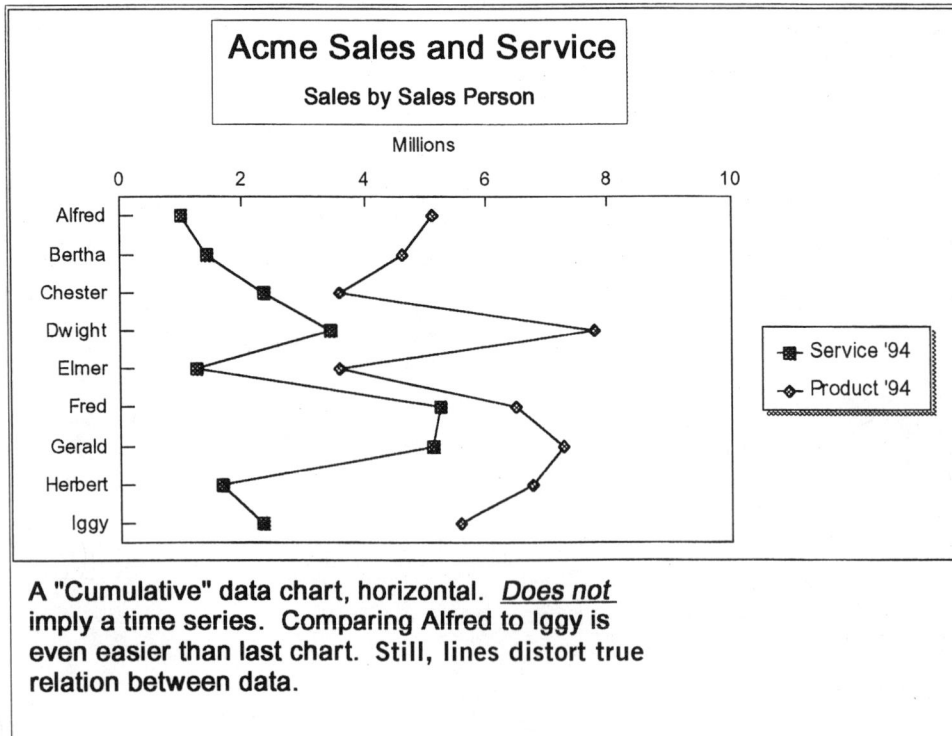

A "Cumulative" data chart, horizontal. _Does not_ imply a time series. Comparing Alfred to Iggy is even easier than last chart. Still, lines distort true relation between data.

EXHIBIT 23A.15

Acme Sales and Service

Sales by Sales Person

Millions

Notice that legend colors change!

- Service '94
- Product '94

A "Cumulative Surface" chart, horizontal. Problem with this chart is surface makes it impossible to compare the sales people. Brain uses surface to imply value. No way to compare value of Alfred's sales to Iggy's.

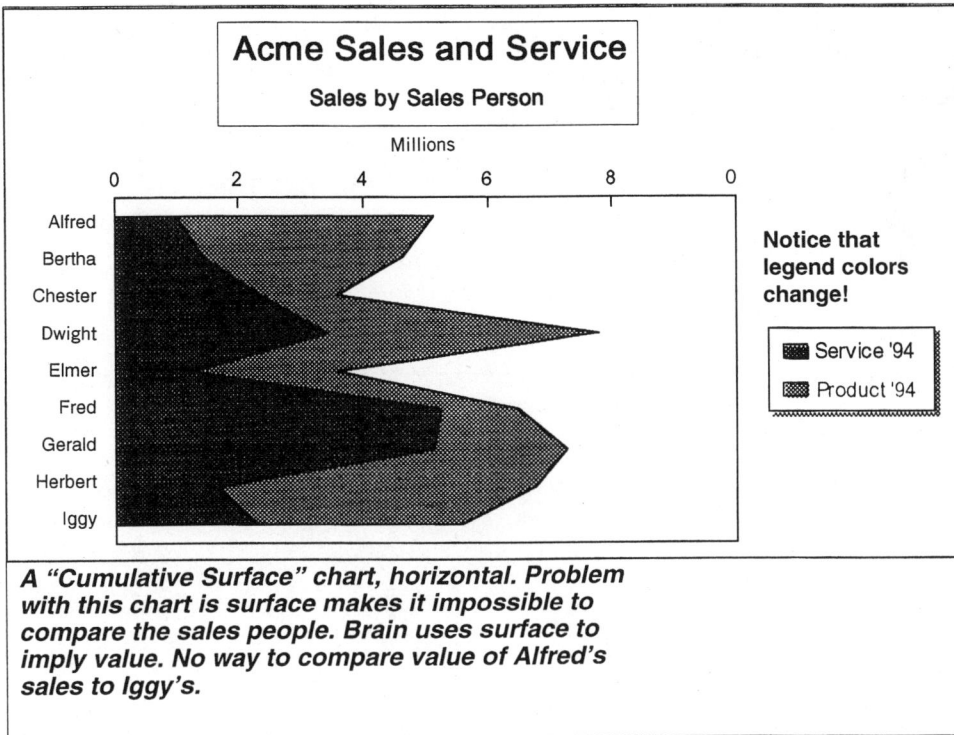

EXHIBIT 23A.16

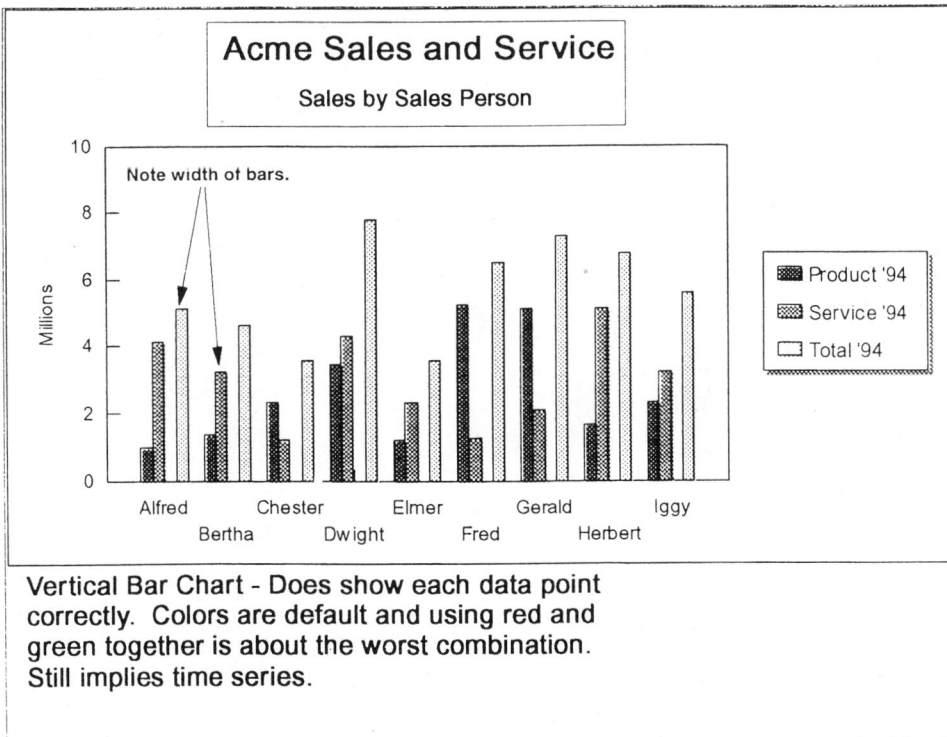

Acme Sales and Service

Sales by Sales Person

Note width of bars.

- Product '94
- Service '94
- Total '94

Vertical Bar Chart - Does show each data point correctly. Colors are default and using red and green together is about the worst combination. Still implies time series.

EXHIBIT 23A.17

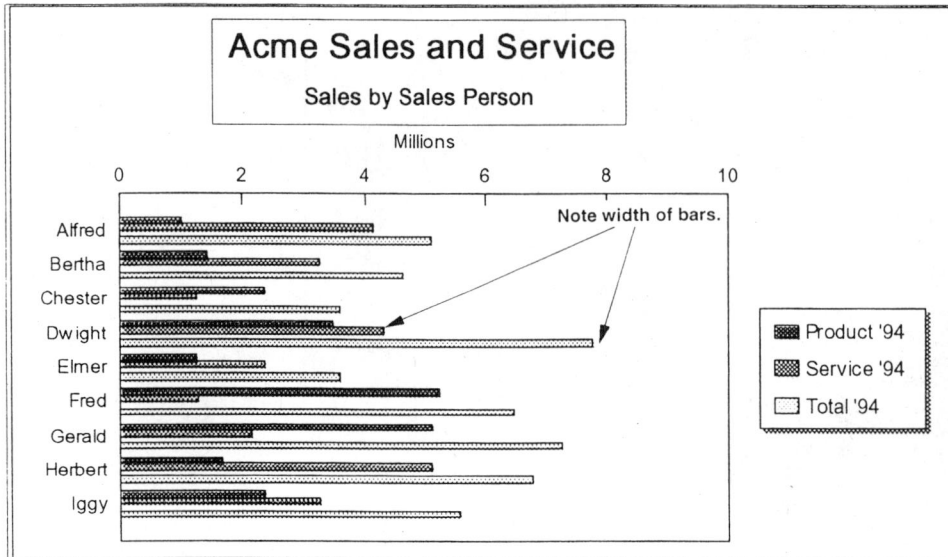

Horizontal Bar Chart - The best representation of
the data. Easiest to compare Alfred to Iggy.
Colors bad. Note how width of bars change from
one type to next. Confusing!

EXHIBIT 23A.18

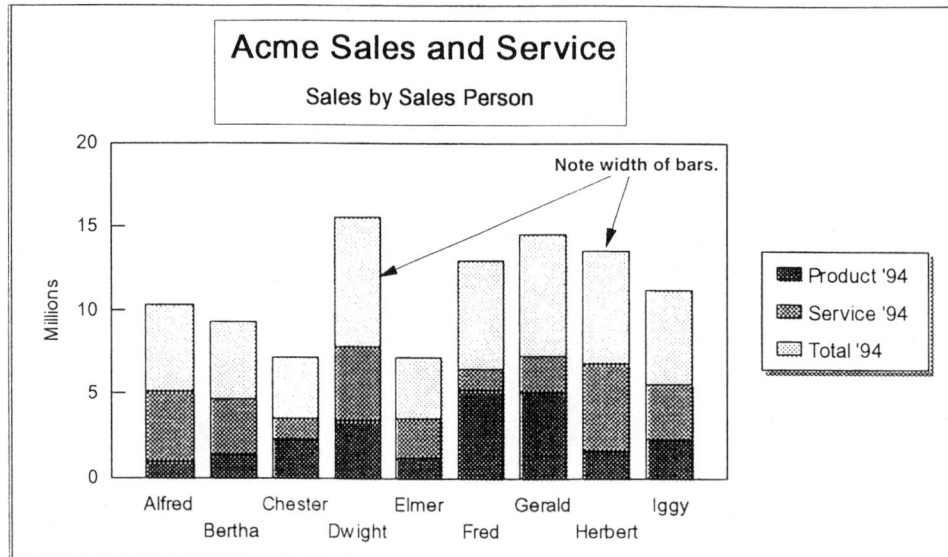

Stacked Bar Chart - Always a cumulative chart.
Should not show total, doubles the value. Never
possible to compare Services by sales person.

EXHIBIT 23A.19

Acme Sales and Service
Sales by Sales Person

Millions

Note width of bars.

Notice that legend colors change!

Service '94
Product '94

Alfred
Bertha
Chester
Dwight
Elmer
Fred
Gerald
Herbert
Iggy

Stacked Bar - Horizontal Shows total for each
sales person with lines for type of data. Difficult
to compare Product sales. Line confuses
picture. Colors bad.

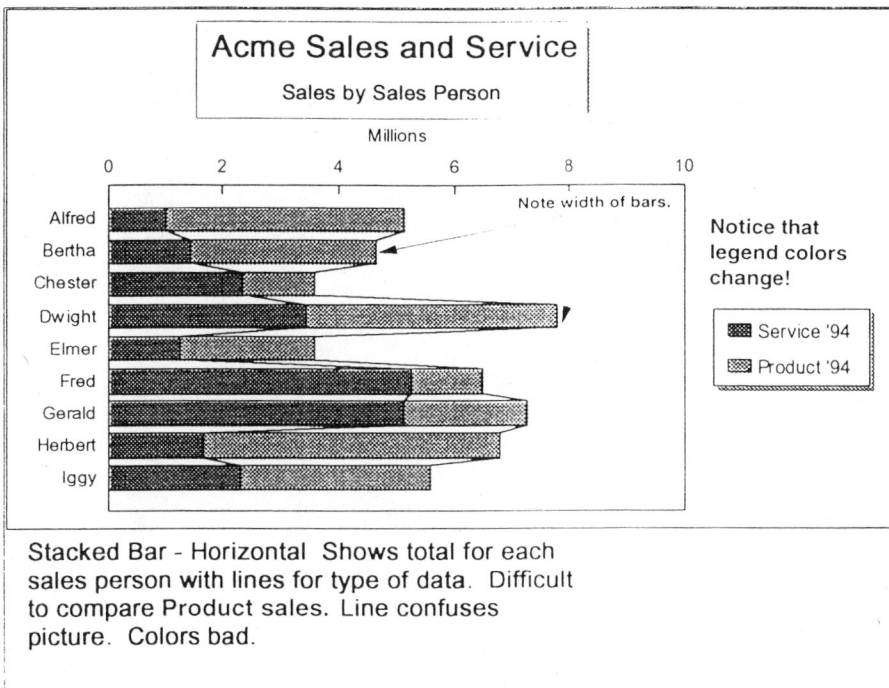

EXHIBIT 23A.20

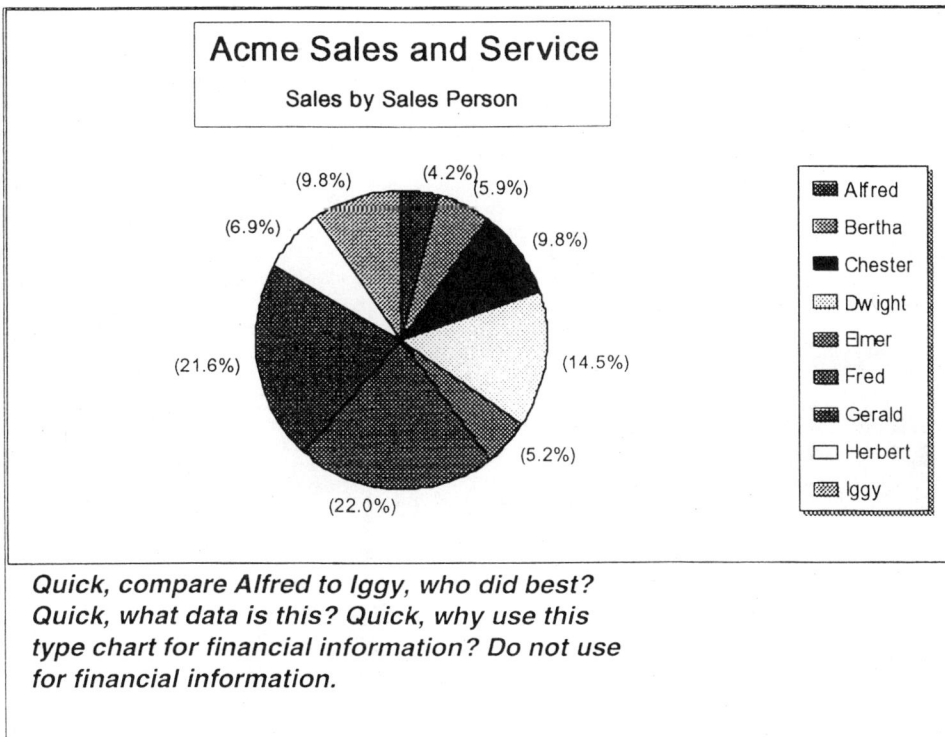

Acme Sales and Service
Sales by Sales Person

(9.8%) (4.2%) (5.9%)
(6.9%)   (9.8%)
(21.6%)   (14.5%)
(22.0%) (5.2%)

Alfred
Bertha
Chester
Dwight
Elmer
Fred
Gerald
Herbert
Iggy

*Quick, compare Alfred to Iggy, who did best?
Quick, what data is this? Quick, why use this
type chart for financial information? Do not use
for financial information.*

EXHIBIT 23A.21

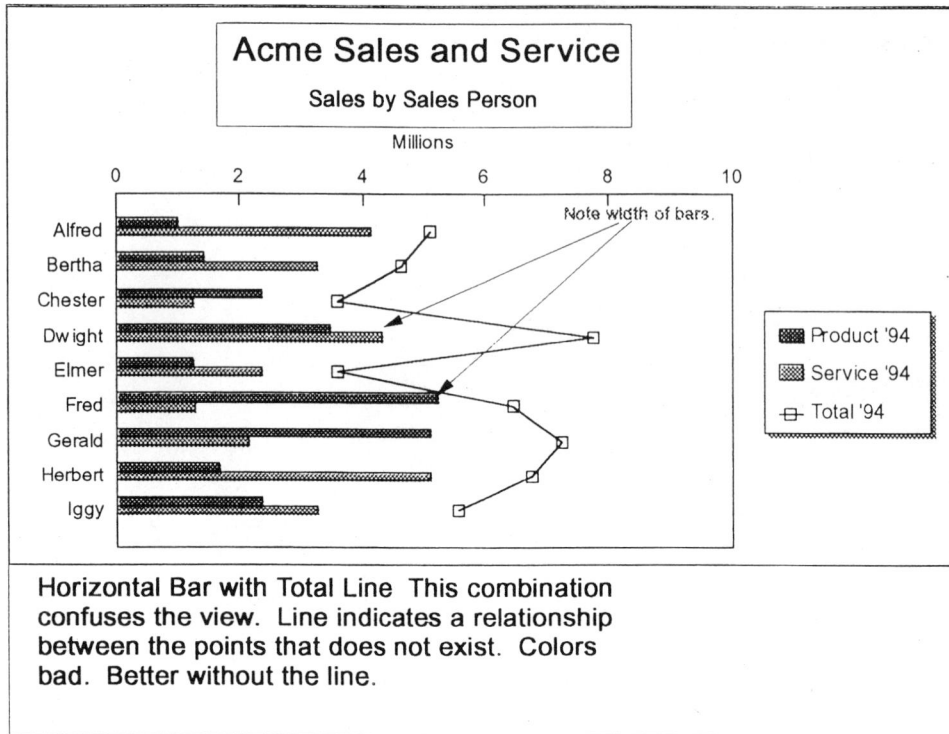

Horizontal Bar with Total Line This combination
confuses the view. Line indicates a relationship
between the points that does not exist. Colors
bad. Better without the line.

EXHIBIT 23A.22

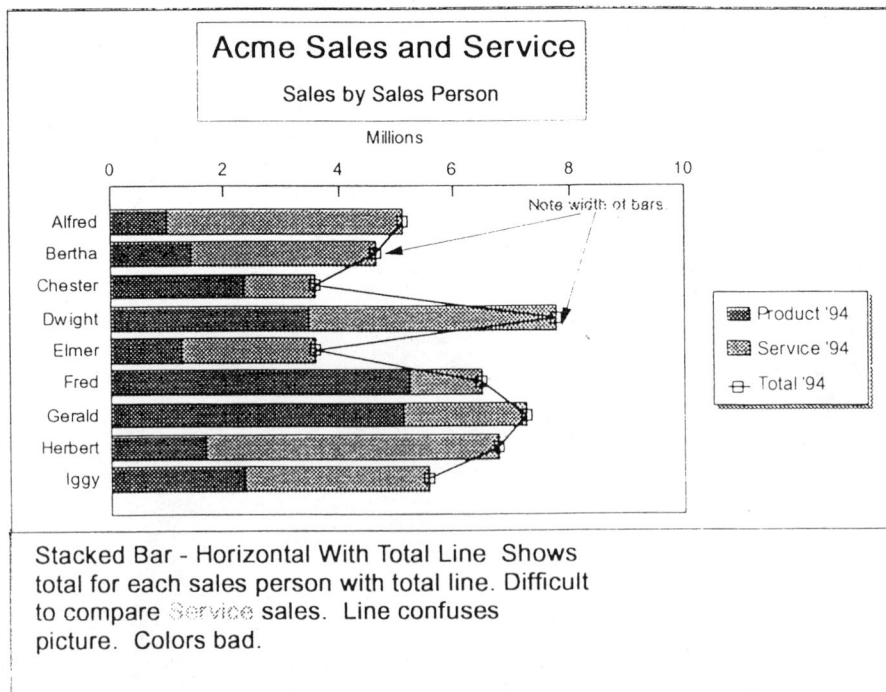

Stacked Bar - Horizontal With Total Line Shows
total for each sales person with total line. Difficult
to compare Service sales. Line confuses
picture. Colors bad.

EXHIBIT 23A.23

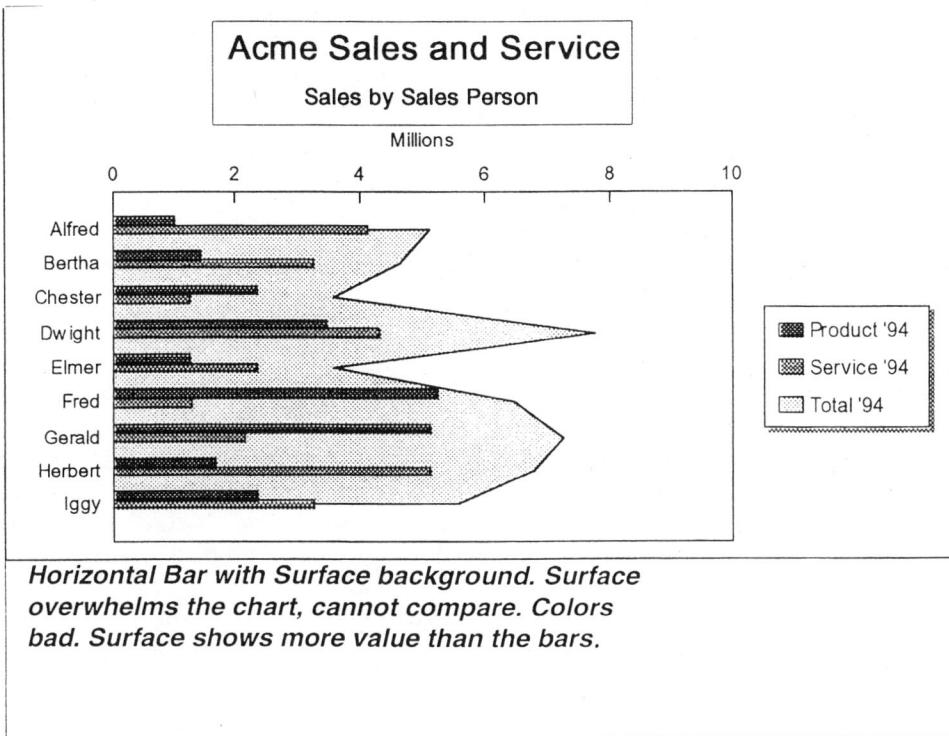

Acme Sales and Service
Sales by Sales Person

Horizontal Bar with Surface background. Surface overwhelms the chart, cannot compare. Colors bad. Surface shows more value than the bars.

EXHIBIT 23A.24

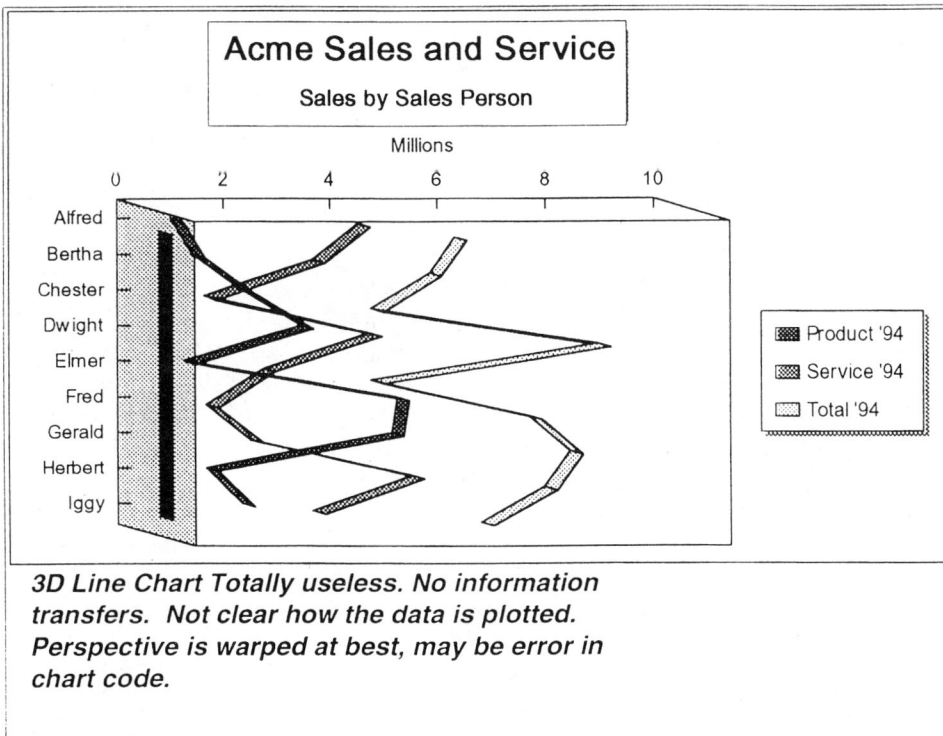

Acme Sales and Service
Sales by Sales Person

3D Line Chart Totally useless. No information transfers. Not clear how the data is plotted. Perspective is warped at best, may be error in chart code.

EXHIBIT 23A.25

There is no pattern that can be learned. In fact, there appears to be an error in the graphic presentation.

Exhibit 23A.26 is another in the series of fake 3D charts.

Exhibit 23A.27 takes a good horizontal bar chart and ruins it with the fake 3D presentation.

Exhibit 23A.28 is the worst possible display of bars. This fake 3D does nothing but confuse the issue. One has to question what positive reason would support the use of this chart in financial reporting.

Exhibit 23A.29 takes a chart that is not seeable at the best, Chart 20, tilts it for distortion, and then adds a fake dimension. Why?

Exhibit 23A.30 falls under the category of "Can't get anything from it anyway, might as well take out a piece."

2.   Table 23A.4 is a more realistic set of data that would be used to describe the sales by person, by product type, and within a division. The last two columns were necessary to add to the table to get the variance data into a range that would plot in the spreadsheet package. The financial graphic, element-based graphics package, computes the variance as the charts are created. The charts selected for this presentation show the total sales by person, by year, by product, and by division. As indicated earlier, the best representation of the data is the horizontal bar charts. The spreadsheet graphs show the element portion of the Item chart described in the body of this book. If the variance is shown, it must be shown in a separate chart. Thus two charts are required to show the data and the variances. The element-based graphics that follow show how the salespeople, the components, add to the total figures. The same patterns are used to show the divisional information in both the spreadsheet charts and the element-based charts.

Exhibits 23A.31 and 23A.32 are the graphic representations of the salespersons' Total Sales performance described in Table 4 for 1994 versus 1993. The totals were left out so that the individual elements would not be distorted.

Exhibits 23A.33 and 23A.34, and Exhibits 23A.35 and 23A.36 are the same graphic representations as Exhibits 23A.31 and 23A.32, except they are for Service and Product sales, respectively.

Exhibits 23A.37, 23A.38, and 23A.39 show how the total sales by salesperson adds to the total sales for the years 1994 and 1993 for Total sales, for Service sales, and for Product sales, respectively. The variances are shown on the same chart. The best image of the difference that can be seen in such a component presentation is shown when comparing Exhibits 23A.37 and 23A.38. Note that the data in Exhibit 23A.37 seems to imply that while there are some differences among the individual salespersons, they are all fairly close. When you look at Exhibit 23A.38, the *pattern* of addition for service sales is clearly different than the total. Exhibit 23A.39 shows that the *pattern* of individual differences for product sales are even more pronounced. The salespersons are displayed in alphabetical order.

Without significantly changing the layout of Table 23A.4, it is not possible to show how New York, Los Angeles, and Chicago sales add to Total Sales in the spreadsheet. Using the spreadsheet charts to consistently show the information in Table 23A.4 is difficult. Exhibits 23A.40, 23A.41, and 23A.42 are samples of the problem. The data cluster in each chart matches the data sets shown in Exhibit 23A.35 with the division totals added. Notice how Exhibits 23A.40, 23A.41, and 23A.42 indicate bigger data sets and more important information. They are neither bigger nor more important. This misperception is one of the most critical distinctions between range-based and element-based graphics.

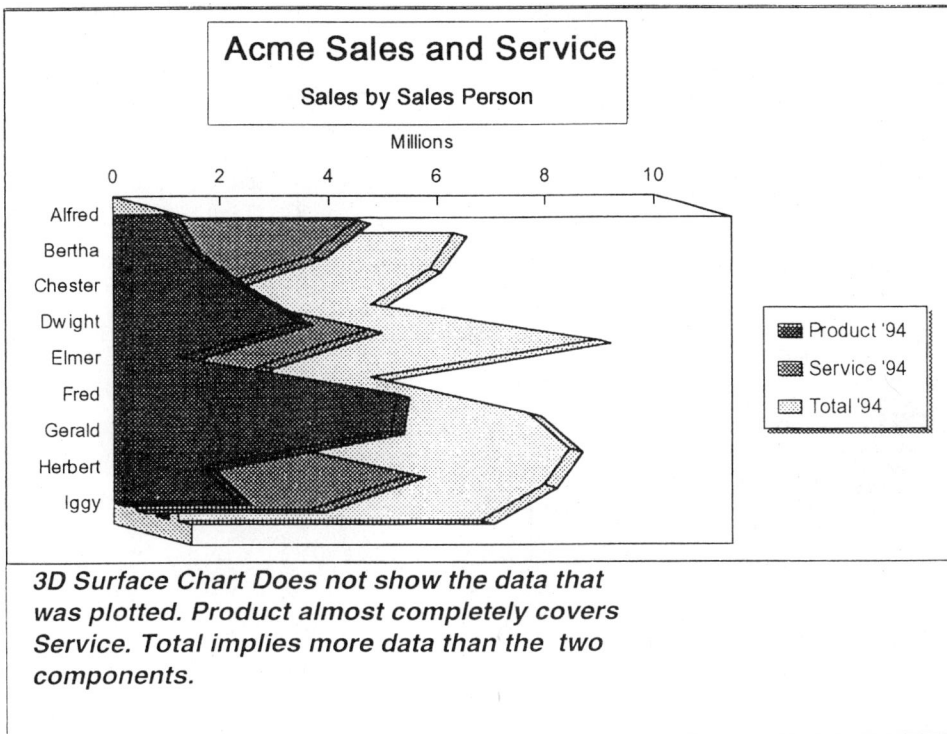

Acme Sales and Service
Sales by Sales Person

3D Surface Chart Does not show the data that was plotted. Product almost completely covers Service. Total implies more data than the two components.

EXHIBIT 23A.26

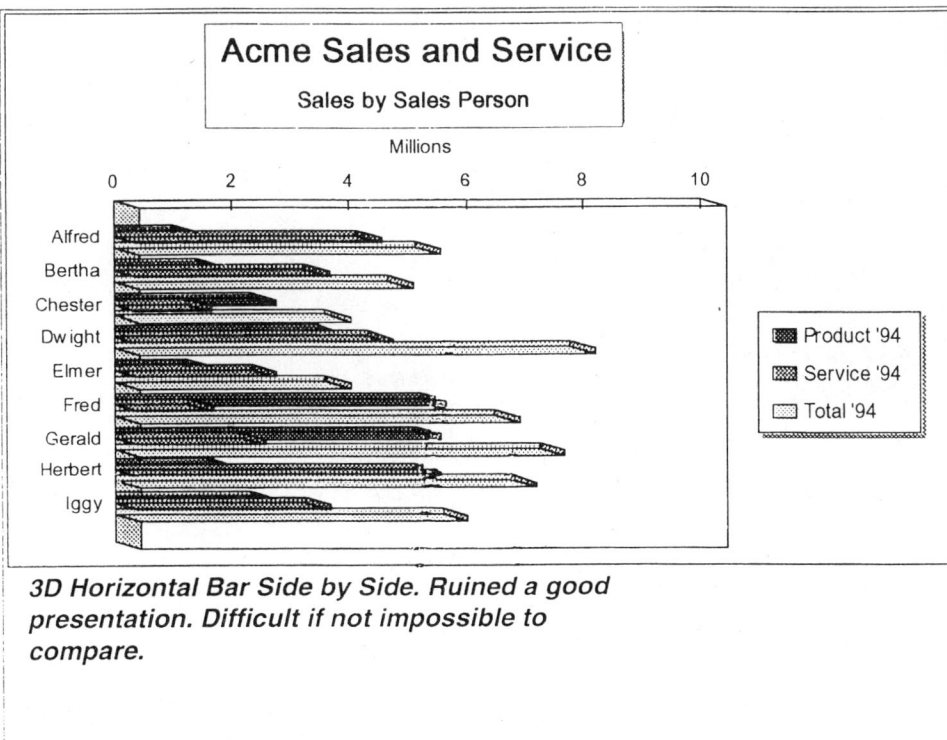

Acme Sales and Service
Sales by Sales Person

3D Horizontal Bar Side by Side. Ruined a good presentation. Difficult if not impossible to compare.

EXHIBIT 23A.27

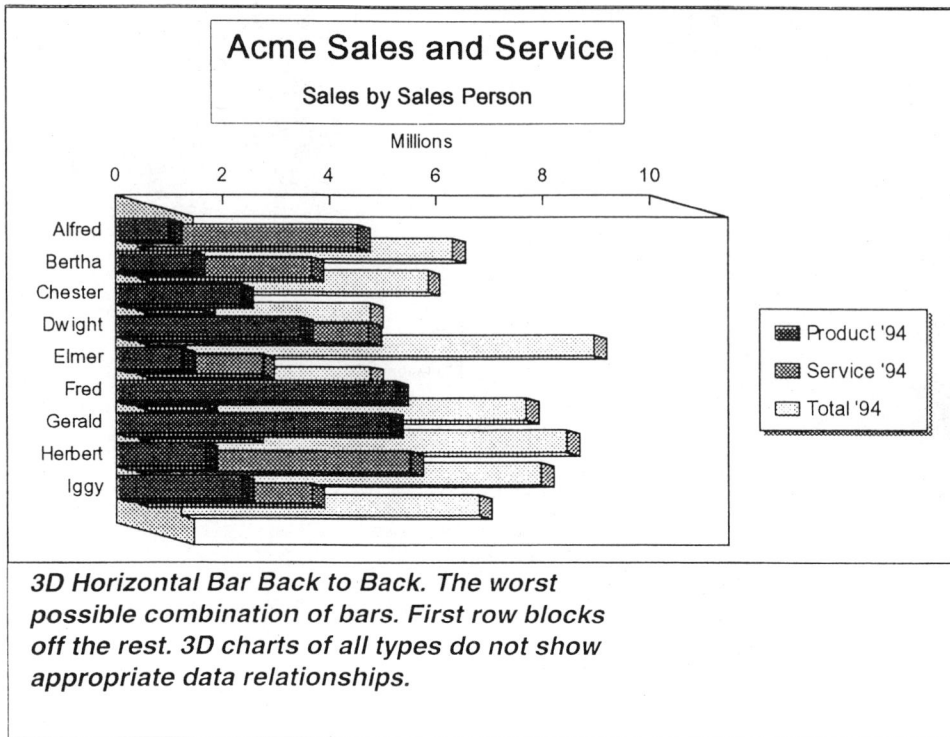

Acme Sales and Service

Sales by Sales Person

3D Horizontal Bar Back to Back. The worst possible combination of bars. First row blocks off the rest. 3D charts of all types do not show appropriate data relationships.

EXHIBIT 23A.28

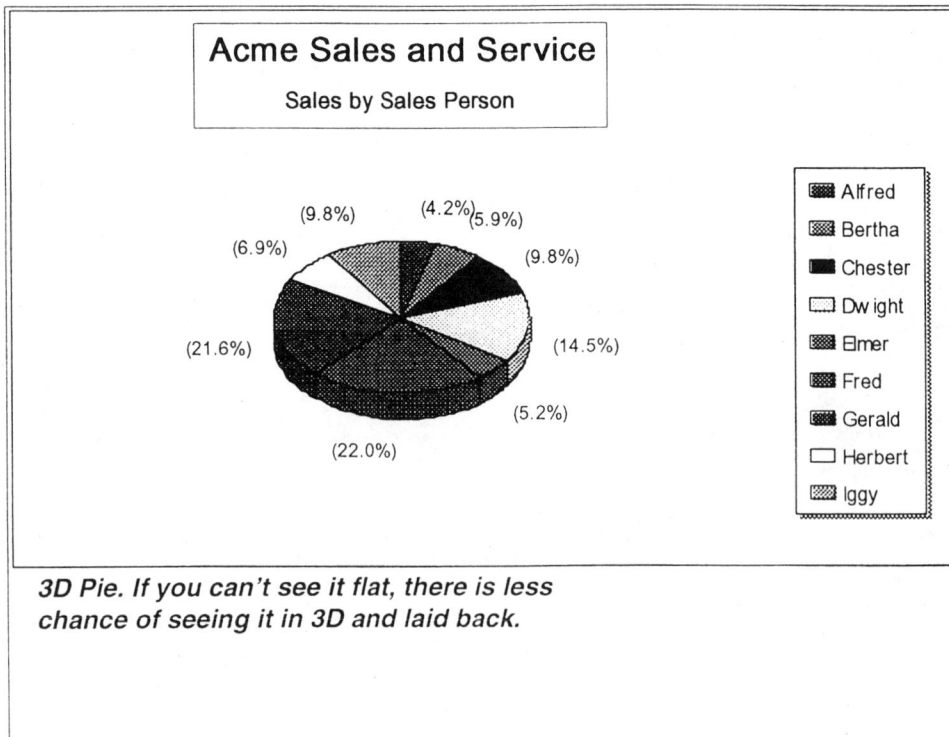

Acme Sales and Service

Sales by Sales Person

3D Pie. If you can't see it flat, there is less chance of seeing it in 3D and laid back.

EXHIBIT 23A.29

Acme Sales and Service

Sales by Sales Person

(9.8%)   (4.2%) (3.9%)
(6.9%)   (9.8%)
(21.6%)   (14.5%)
(5.2%)
(22.0%)

Legend:
- Alfred
- Bertha
- Chester
- Dwight
- Elmer
- Fred
- Gerald
- Herbert
- Iggy

3D Pie with Piece out. Make sure there is no way to compare, take the piece out.

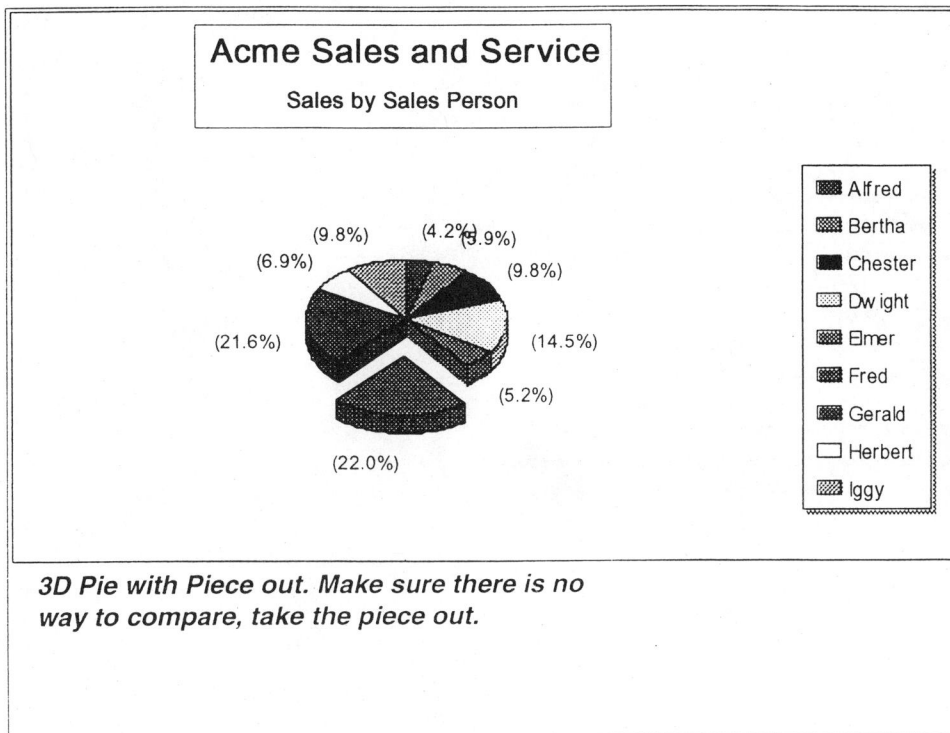

EXHIBIT 23A.30

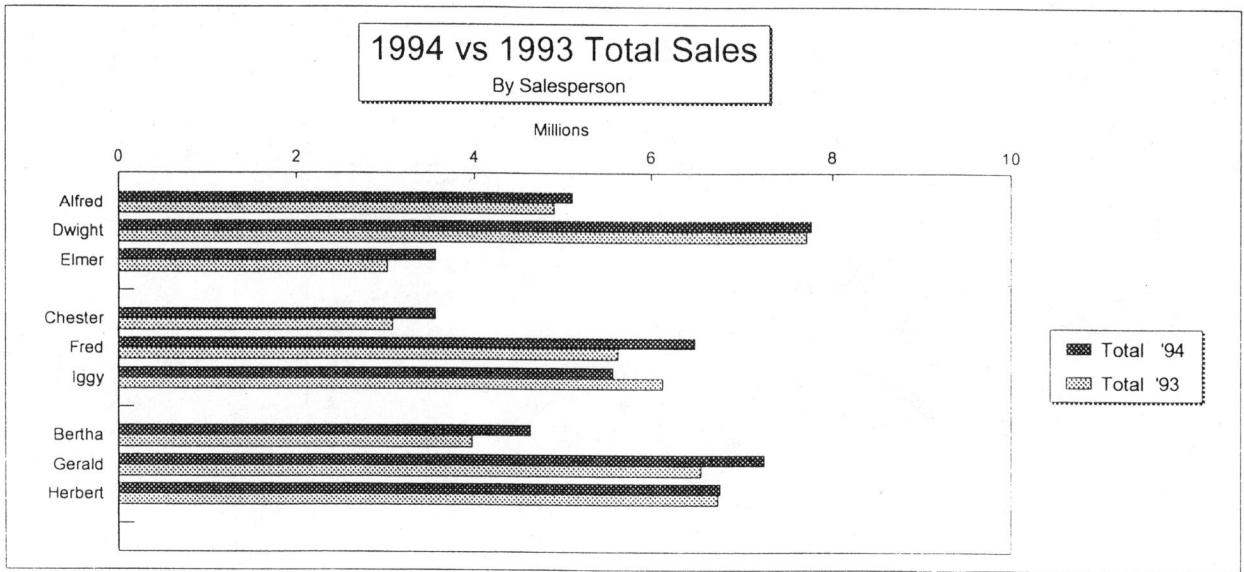

EXHIBIT 23A.31

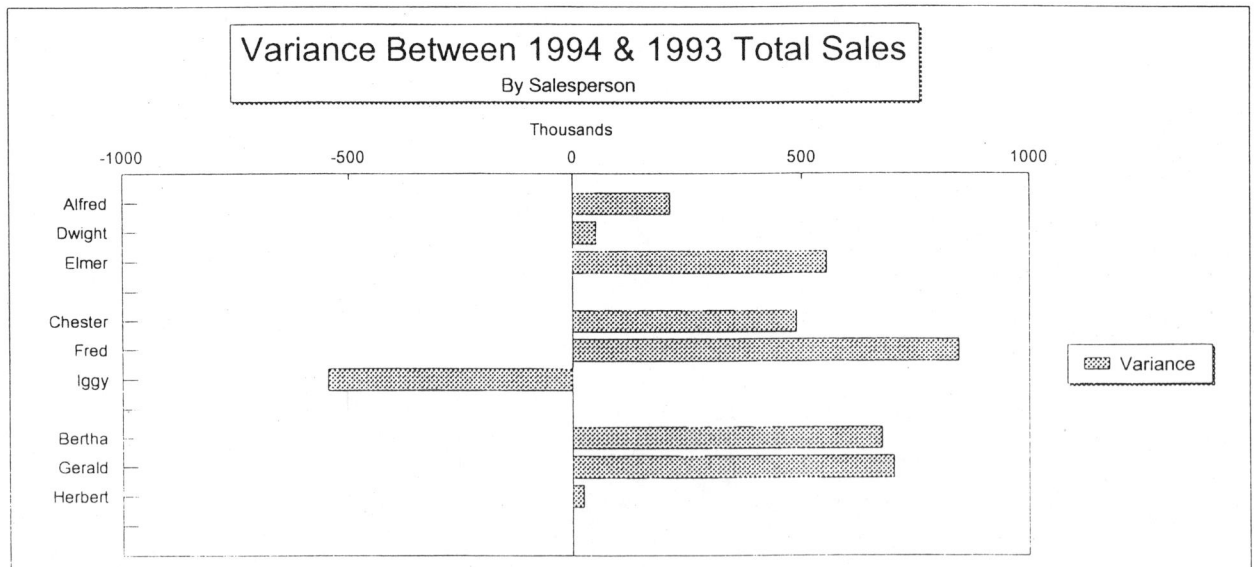

EXHIBIT 23A.32

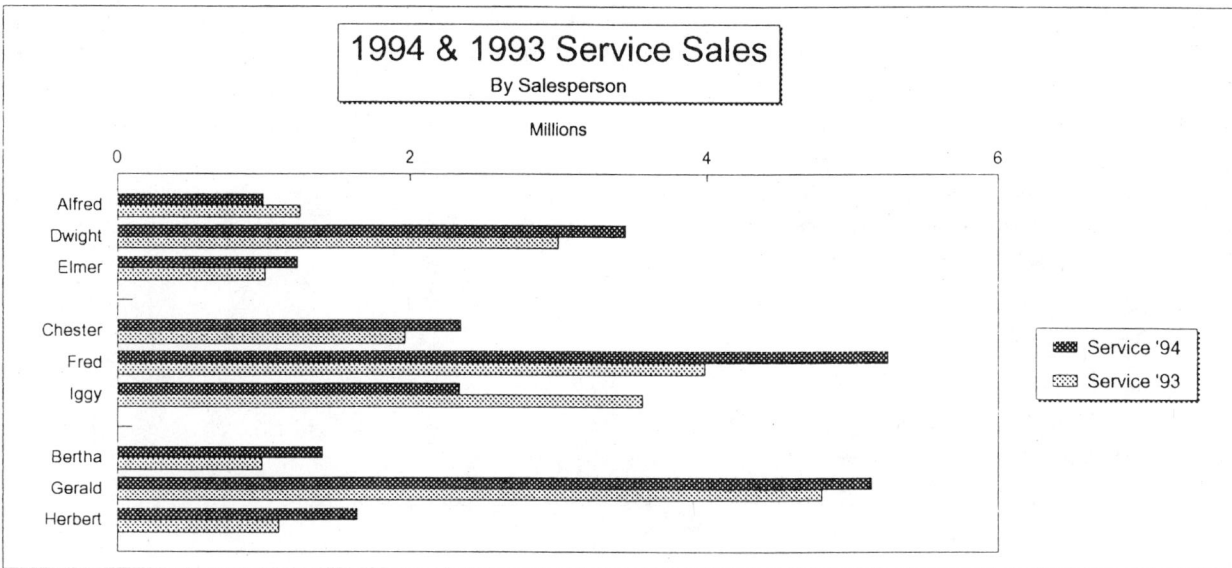

1994 & 1993 Service Sales
By Salesperson

EXHIBIT 23A.33

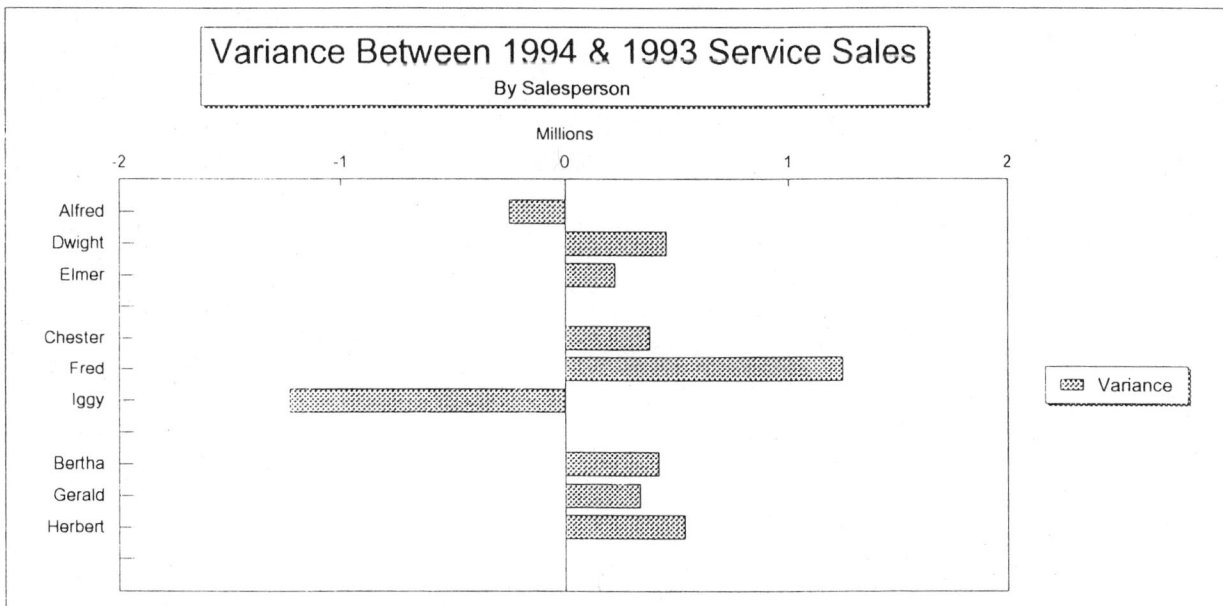

Variance Between 1994 & 1993 Service Sales
By Salesperson

EXHIBIT 23A.34

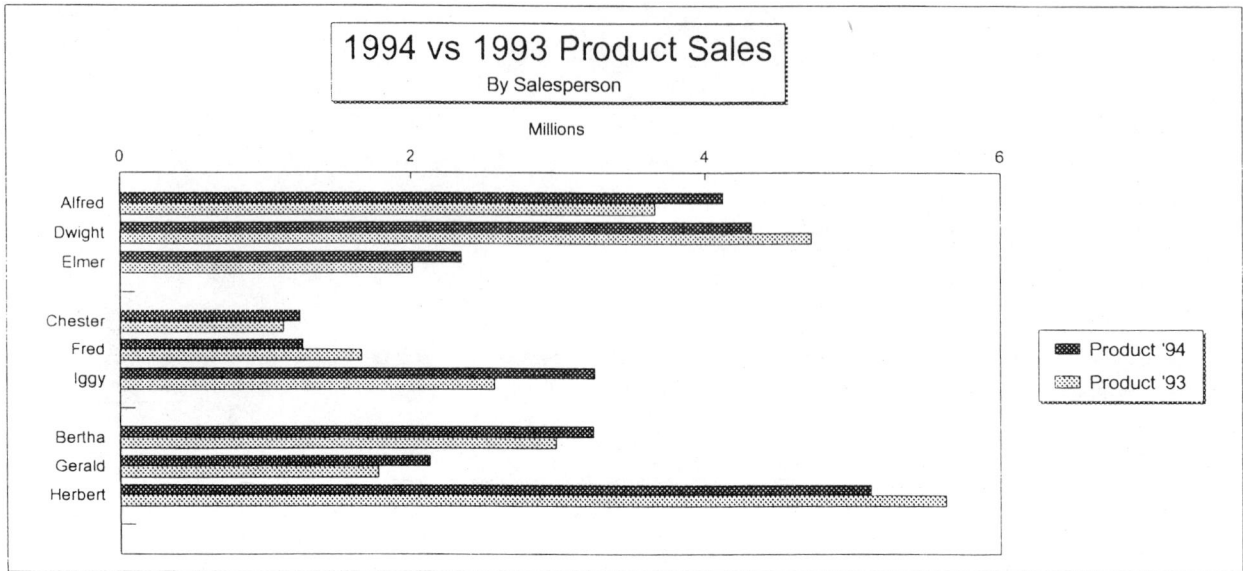

EXHIBIT 23A.35

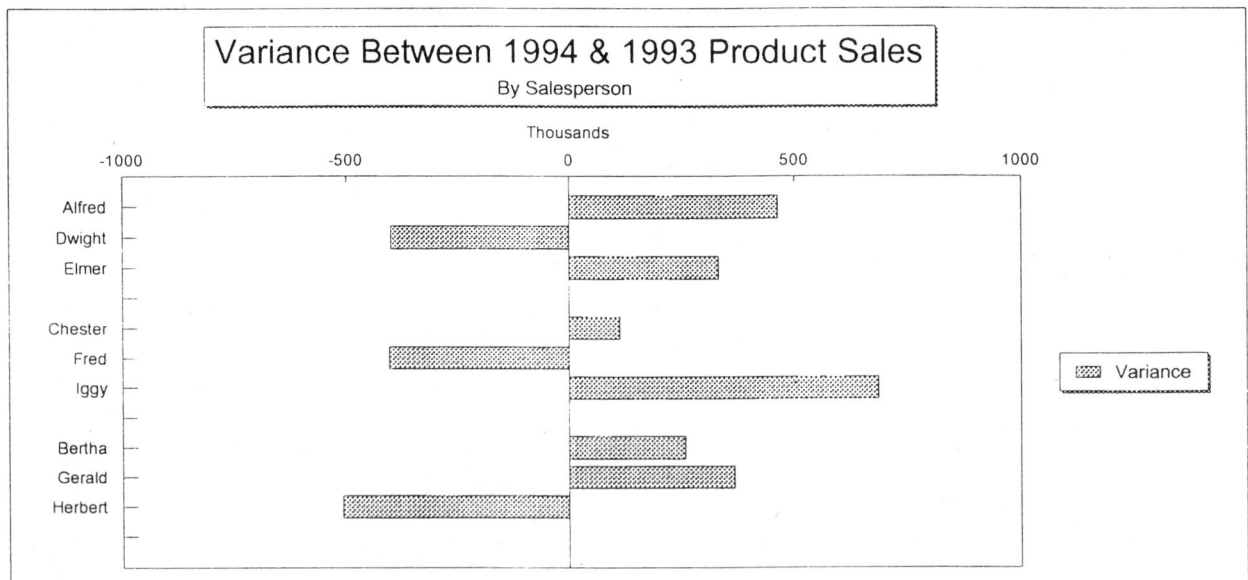

EXHIBIT 23A.36

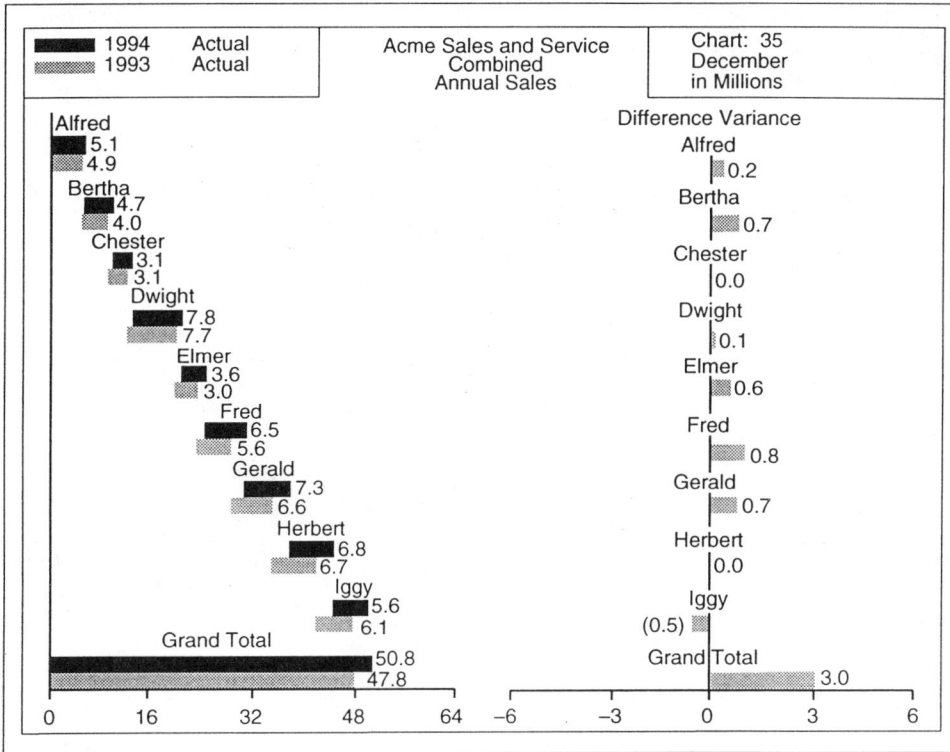

EXHIBIT 23A.37

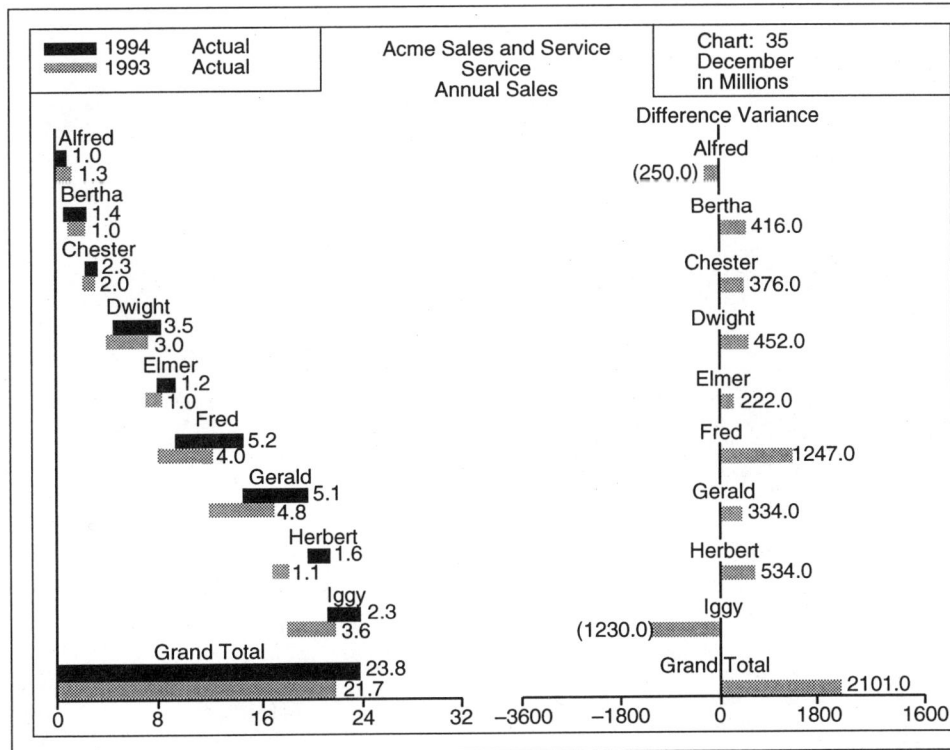

EXHIBIT 23A.38

■ 1984	Actual	Acme Sales and Service	Chart: 35
▦ 1993	Actual	Product	December
		Annual Sales	in Millions

Difference Variance

Alfred
4.1
3.7
Alfred   464.0

Bertha
3.2
3.0
Bertha   258.0

Chester
1.2
1.1
Chester   113.0

Dwight
4.3
4.7
Dwight
(399.0)

Elmer
2.3
2.0
Elmer   331.0

Fred
1.3
1.7
Fred
(402.0)

Gerald
2.1
1.8
Gerald   367.0

Herbert
5.1
5.6
Herbert
(509.0)

Iggy
3.3
2.6
Iggy   684.0

Grand Total
27.0
26.1
Grand Total   907.0

0   9   18   27   36   −1600   −800   0   800   1600

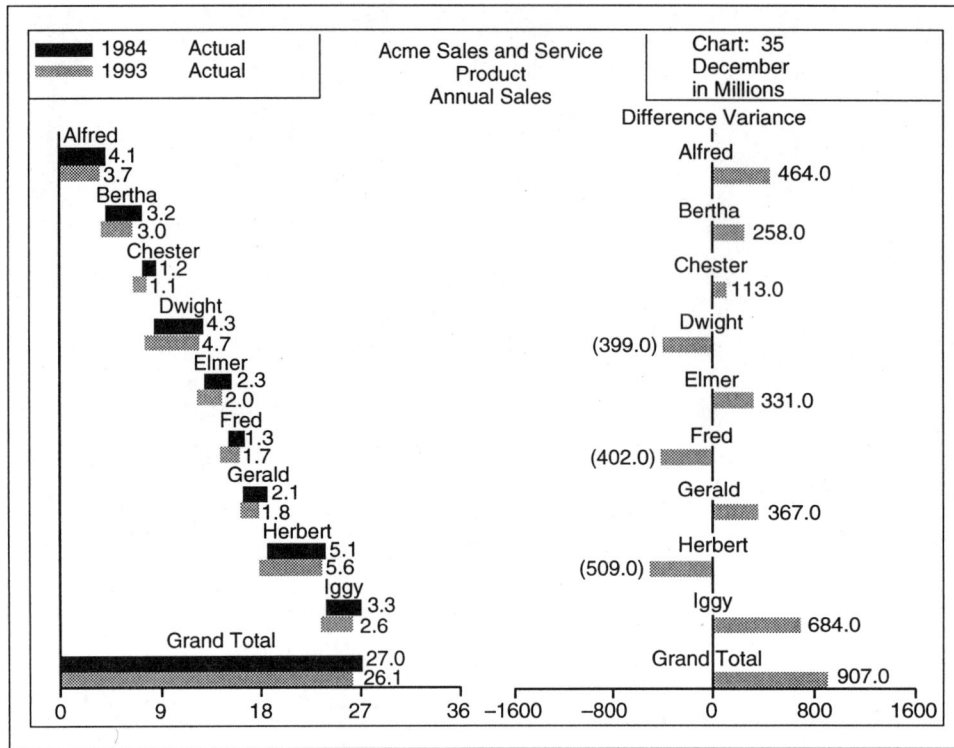

EXHIBIT 23A.39

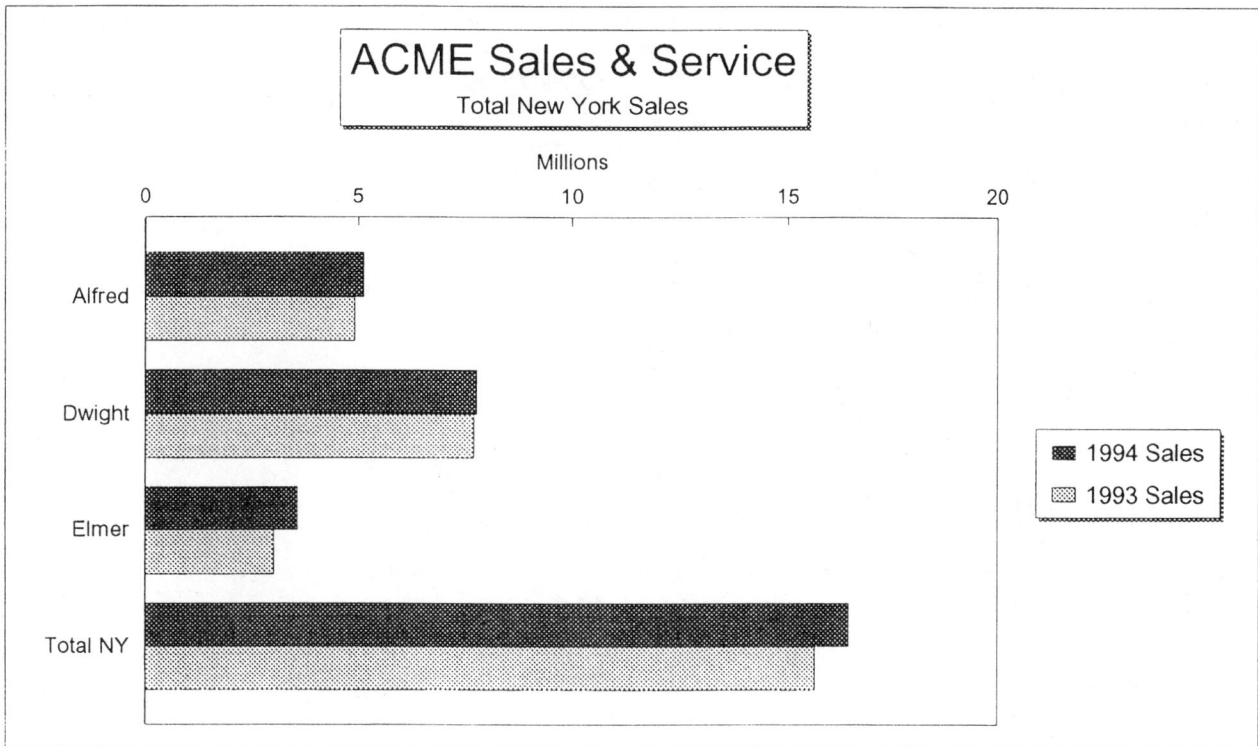

EXHIBIT 23A.40

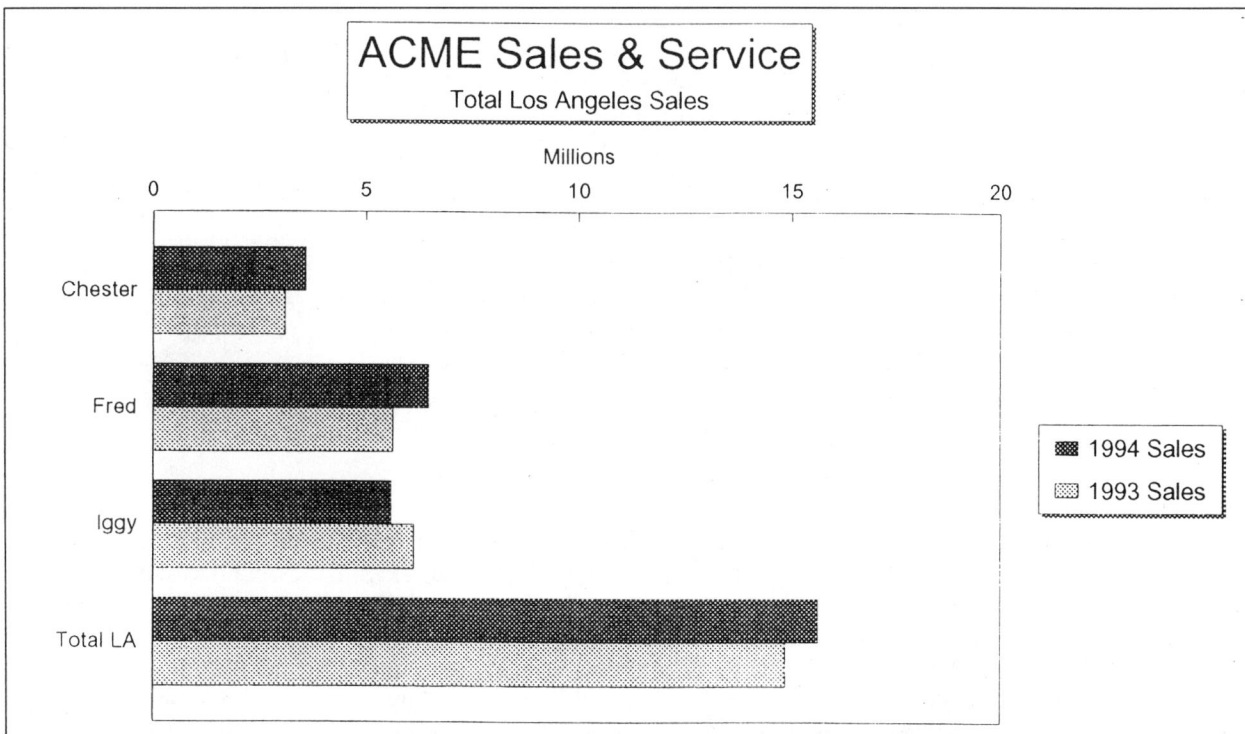

EXHIBIT 23A.41

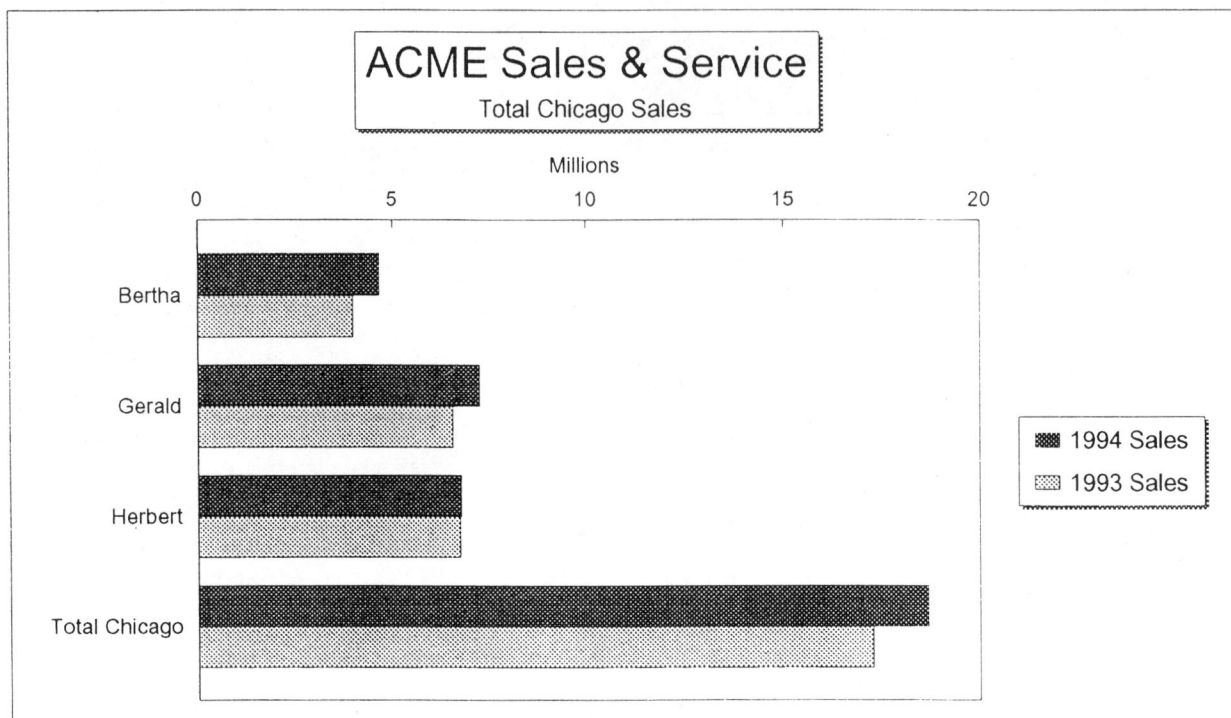

EXHIBIT 23A.42

Exhibits 23A.43, 23A.44, and 23A.45 show how New York, Los Angeles, and Chicago add to Total sales for Combined sales, Service sales, and Product sales, respectively. The remaining exhibits disaggregate the information for each of the divisions by describing the respective salesperson's performance.

A critical definition is that Exhibits 23A.43 through 23A.54 use different graphic words to present the same information in Table 23A.4. Each word adds meaning to the previous words to describe the relationships in the tabular data. Not all of the relationships need to be shown, nor would they all be useful. First you should decide which *relationships* (not results) you want to highlight. Then select the charts that most appropriately reflect the relationships in the data set. You may choose not to use all of the words available to you. Select the charts that best characterize the information. Your client will learn to depend on the combination of tabular data supported by the graphic words and enhanced by the written analysis.

C.   Complex Component Reporting

The financial statements including the balance sheet, the revenue and expense statement, the change in working capital statement, the retained earnings statement, and the cash flow statement are arguably the most important and complex accounting statements. They are also the most difficult to present in graphic form. The main body of the text shows how to create these financial graphic statements. The final chapter in this supplement shows how the financial statements can be integrated with the tabular and written analysis to form an accounting "Page."

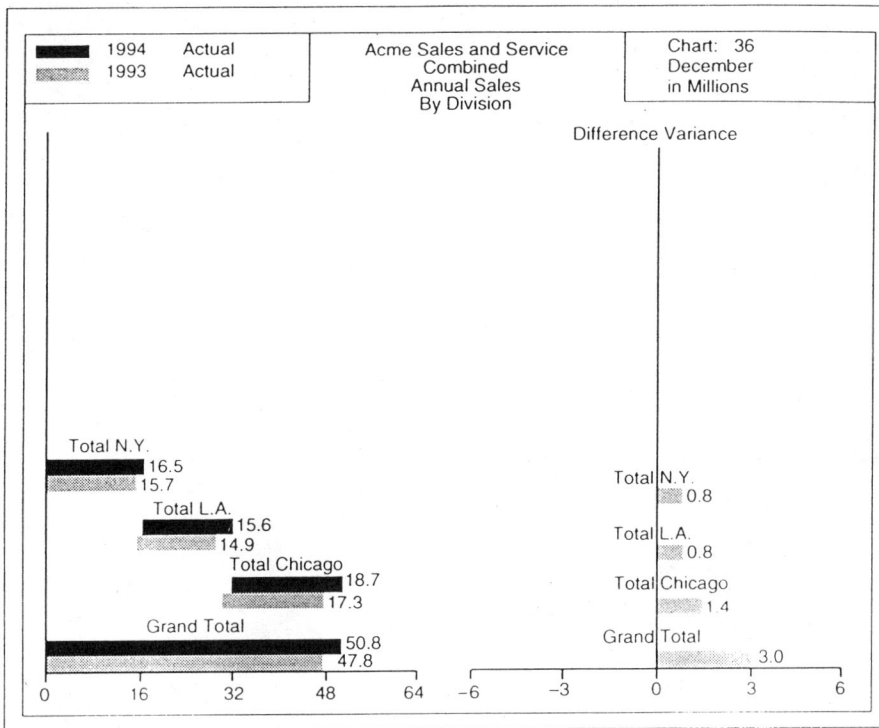

EXHIBIT 23A.43

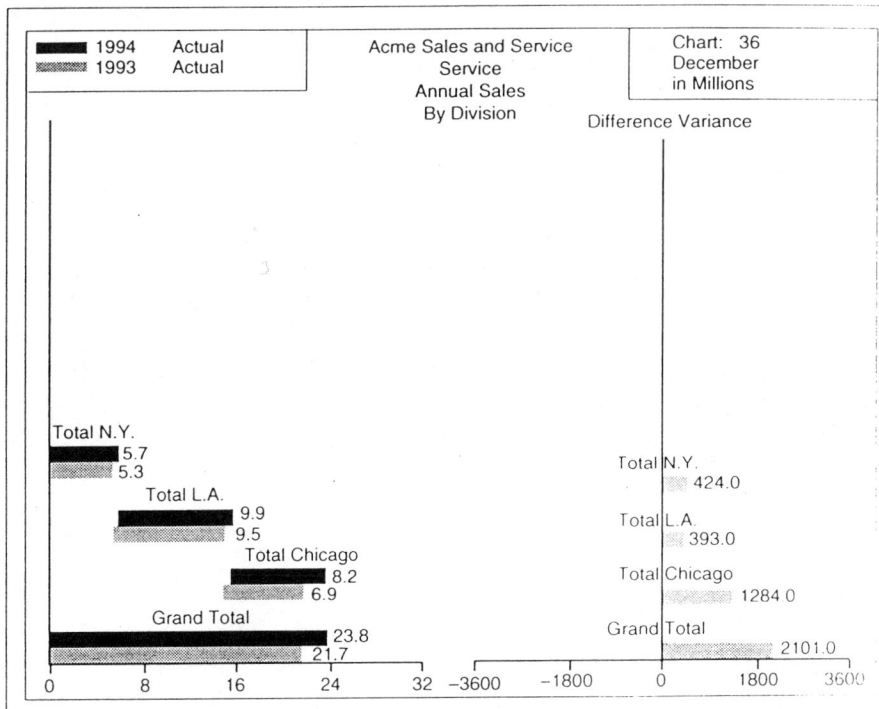

EXHIBIT 23A.44

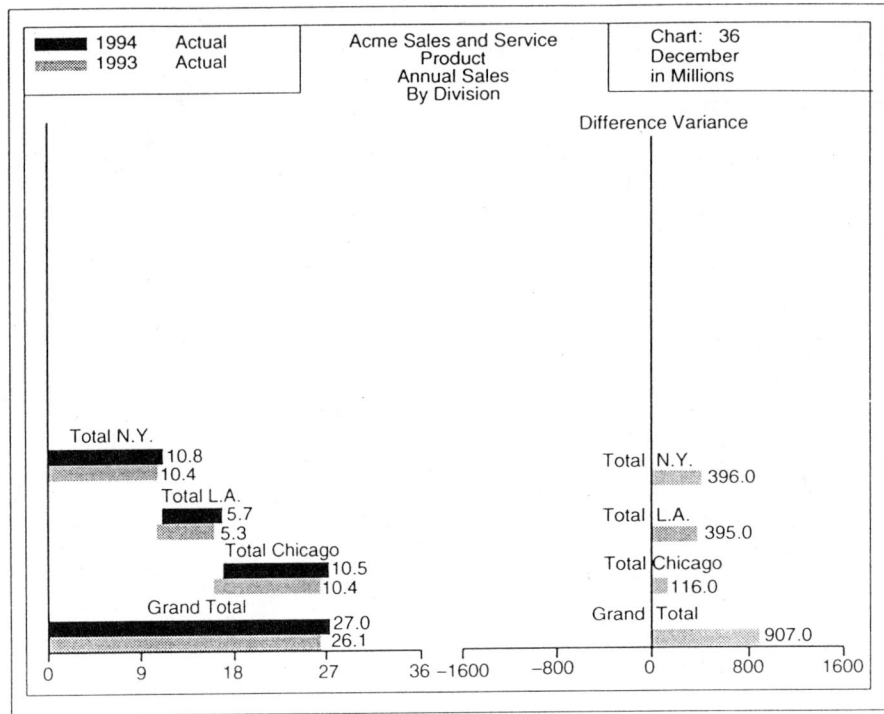

EXHIBIT 23A.45

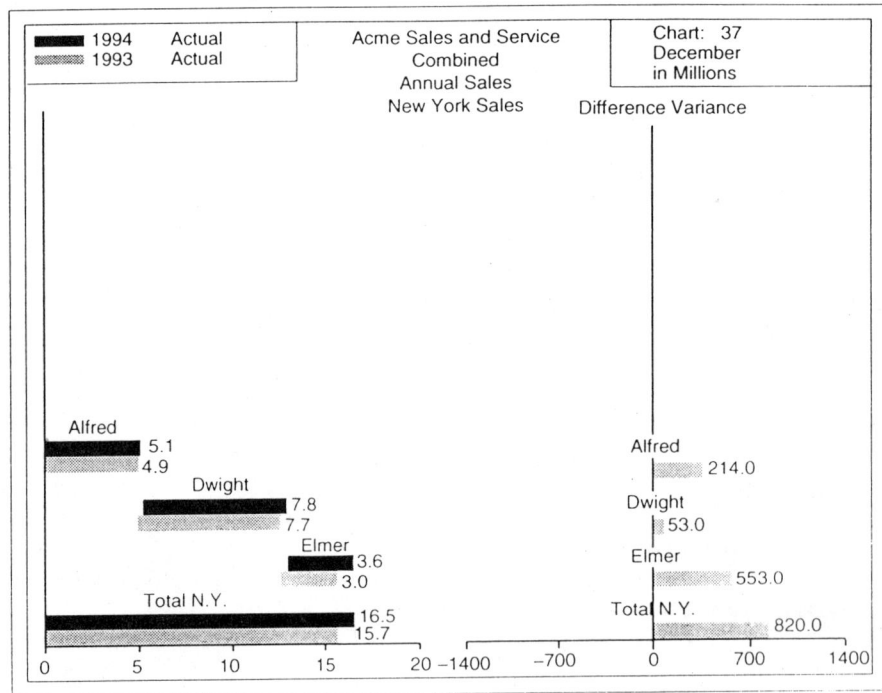

EXHIBIT 23A.46

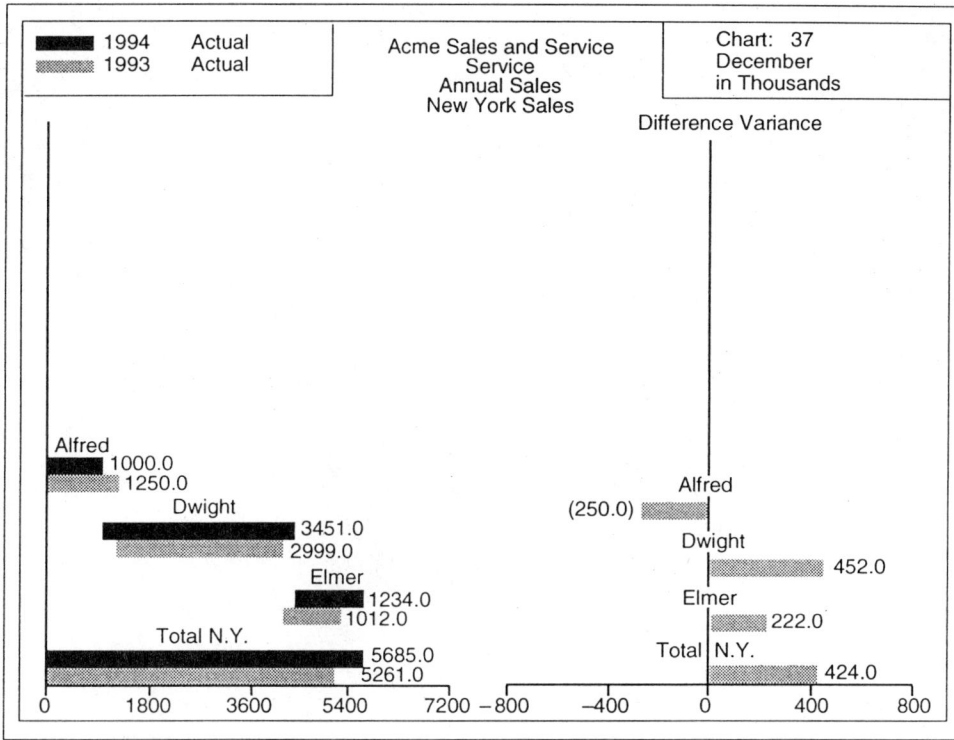

EXHIBIT 23A.47

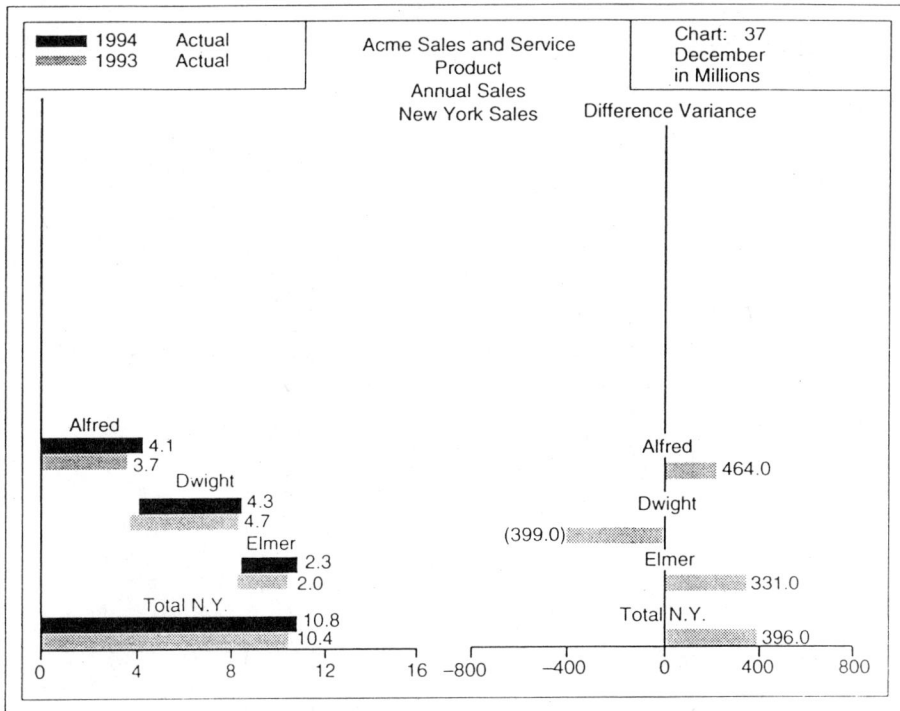

EXHIBIT 23A.48

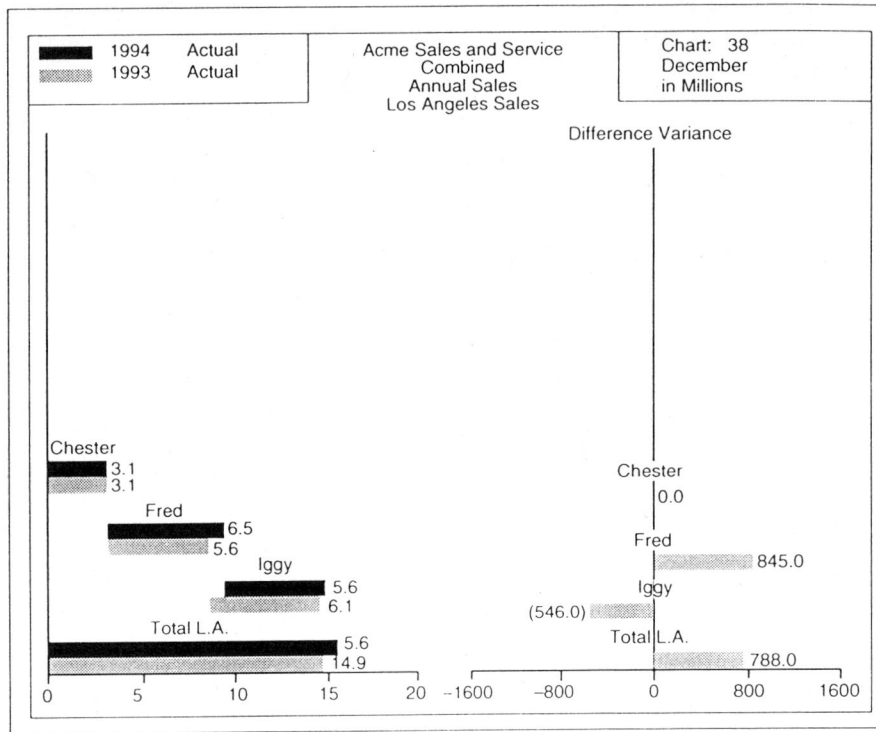

EXHIBIT 23A.49

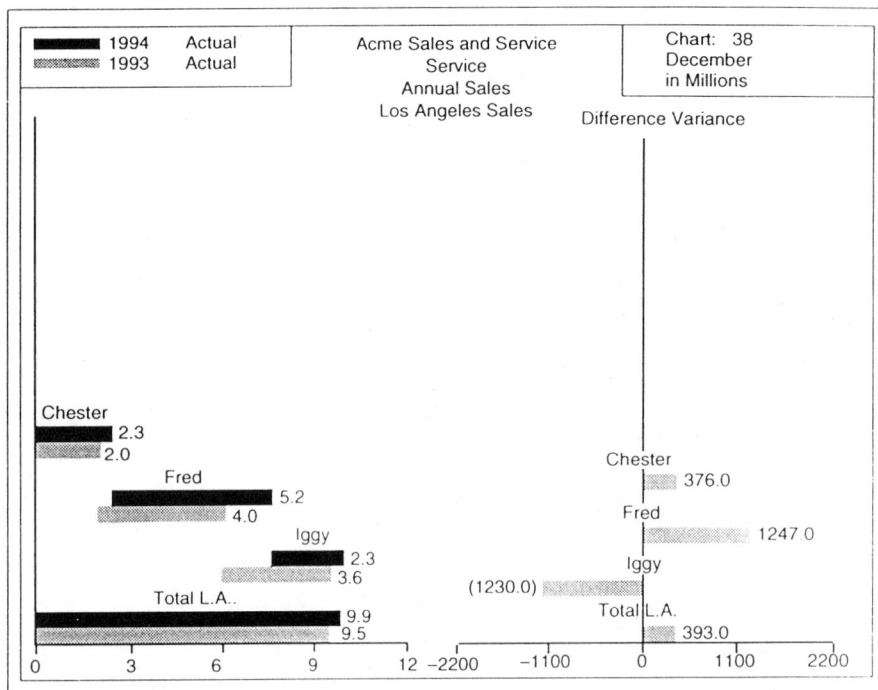

EXHIBIT 23A.50

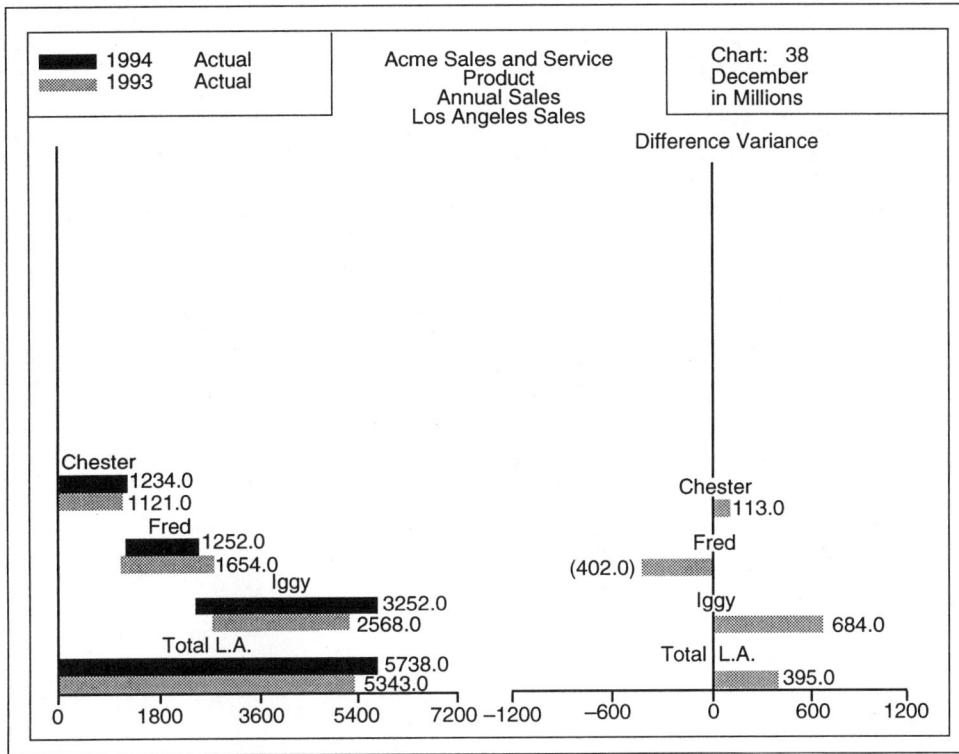

EXHIBIT 23A.51

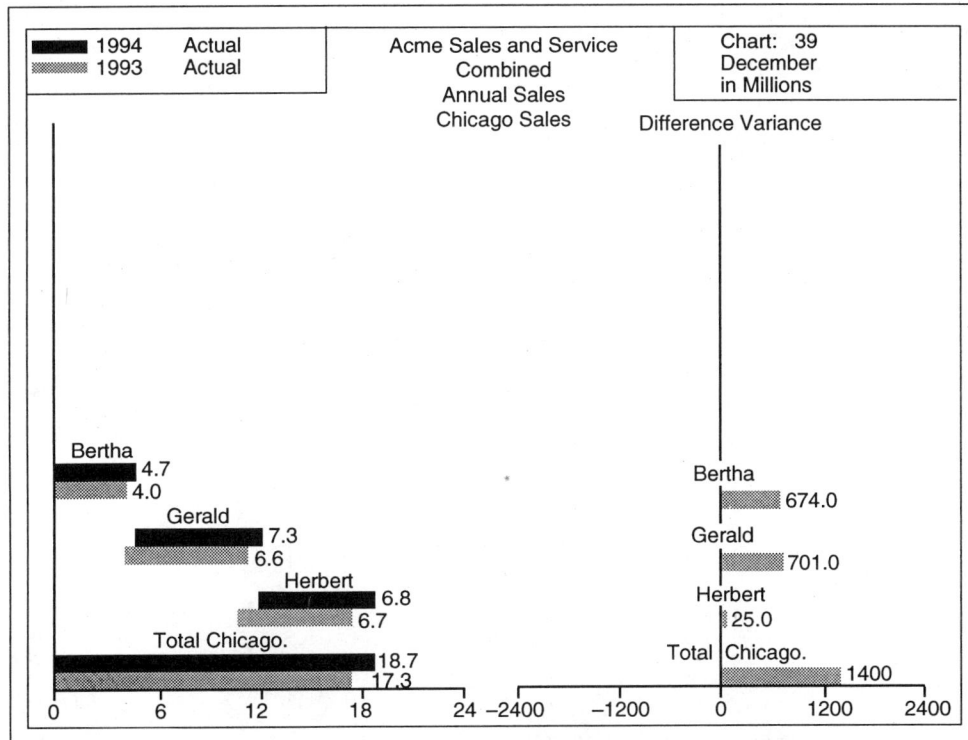

EXHIBIT 23A.52

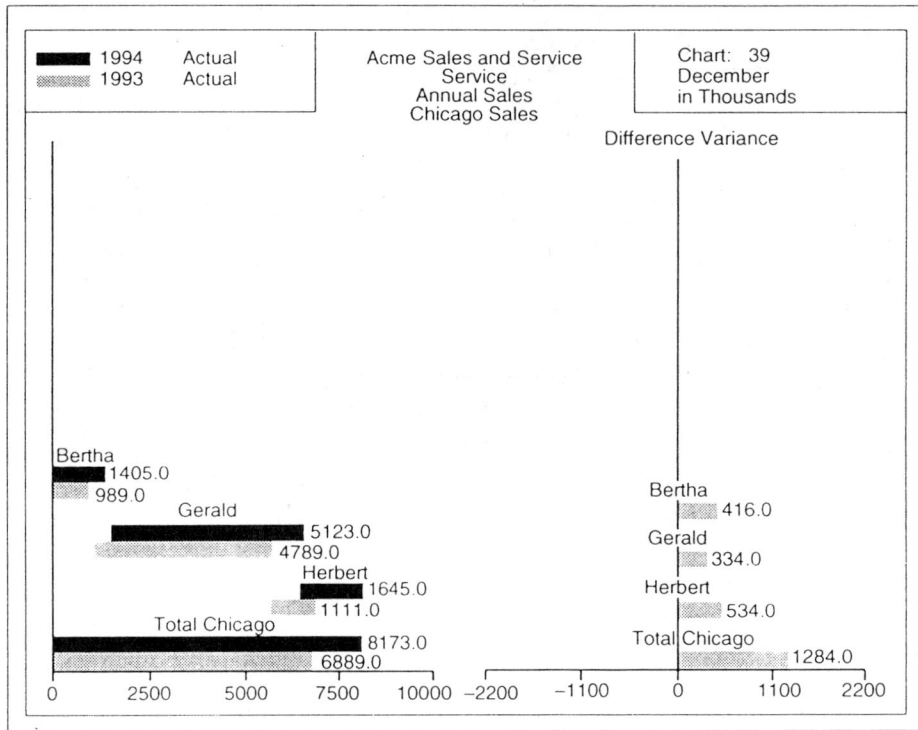

EXHIBIT 23A.53

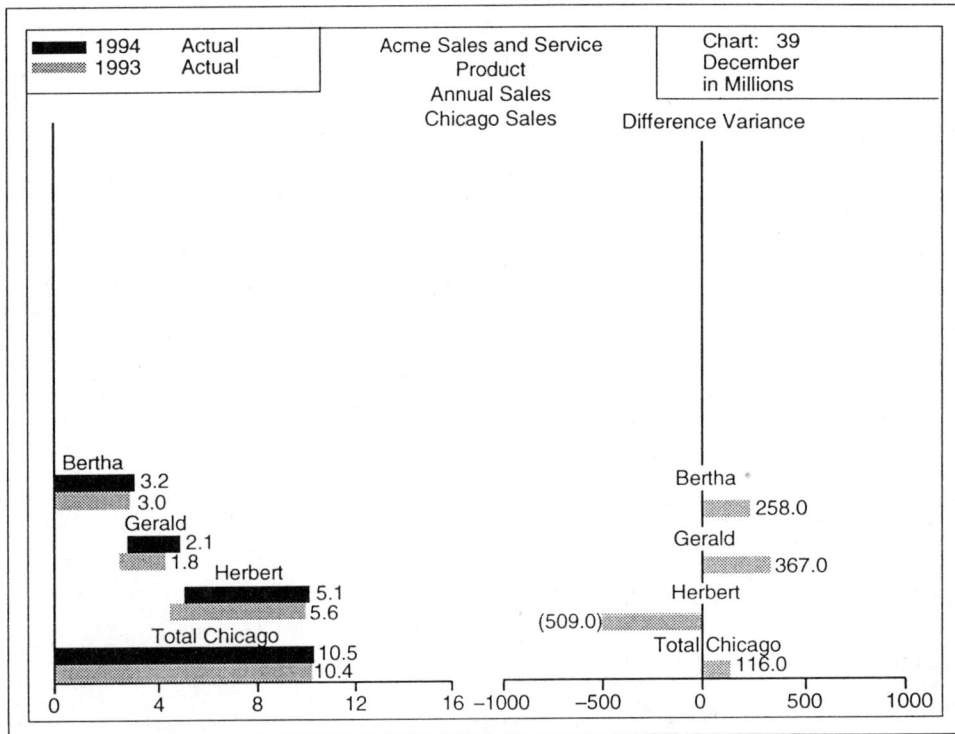

EXHIBIT 23A.54

D. Conclusion

Exhibits 23A.23 through 23A.30 present the fake 3D charts readily available in all of the spreadsheets and presentation graphic packages I have reviewed. Unfortunately, corporate America thinks these charts are flashy. The result is that taste prevails over accuracy, but not without jeopardy. It is very easy to create these fake 3D graphics. Fake 3D graphics distort the data, and the average person cannot see the information. Note that litigators equate such distortion to a purposeful misstatement. The same communication potency that graphics add to the information process can be used to distort or obscure the information. As noted earlier, communicating financial or operating information dictates accuracy. Be sure the charts you use accurately display the information.

This chapter has a narrow focus: to describe with examples, how the relationships described by tabular reports can be distorted or enhanced by charts. Graphics are one of four reporting mediums the accountant must master in today's multimedia environment. You must be just as comfortable with graphic representations of financial information as you are with tabular; just as comfortable with formal presentations as you are with the written word; just as comfortable with multimedia as you are with the spreadsheet.

In short, you must learn to use all of the mediums without distinction. You should *never* say: "Here are your financial statements. Oh, by the way, I threw in some graphics to spice up the presentation." Graphs are just as integral to the presentation of accounting information as tabular statements, written reports, and verbal presentations.

CHAPTER 23B (New)

HOW 16 MAJOR COMPANIES USE/MISUSE GRAPHICS TO DISPLAY FINANCIAL INFORMATION IN THEIR ANNUAL REPORTS

23B.1 INTRODUCTION

> The accounting profession is the only significant number based profession that does not have a formal graphical or physical representation of the information contained in the numbers we work with.[1]

In today's litigious society there is no way that the auditor, the CFO, and the company can escape their responsibilities to accurately reflect the corporate results. Because accountants have no foundation in graphic skills, they are unaware of the powerful potential for information transfer that is available with properly designed and presented financial graphics. The lack of knowledge will not protect the accountant when the unsophisticated investor depends on the charts as a performance indicator. Even the most sophisticated investor has trouble gleaning the information hidden by the rows and columns of numbers and the myriad words included in the annual reports; and they glance at the charts as indicators.

The graphic problem is so bad that the dean of a prestigious business school indicated at a recent public meeting that he did not see a problem when the graphics showed "Profits in Red!" Such nescience will only prove the point in a court of law.

23B.2 ANNUAL REPORTS

The impact of graphics on the reporting of financial information is obvious in the annual reports of major companies. These "slick" marketing products are issued to the stockholders and the public. The purpose of the report is to describe to the stockholders the prominence of their company and how efficiently (or badly) the company performed.

---

[1] Irwin M. Jarett, *Financial Reporting Using Computer Graphics,* 1994, John Wiley & Sons, New York, NY, vii.

To the lay stockholder it is difficult, if not impossible, to distinguish between the accountant's report and the management's report. They see charts in the report that depict financial information. The document contains an auditor's opinion. The charts appear to be direct representations of financial information and seem to be easier to see and understand. It is not illogical for the stockholder (or lay reader) to assume that the accountants approved, if not created, the charts. Thus it would not be illogical for the lay reader to use the charts to make or confirm investment decisions. Seeing their company in the red could surely influence their decision.

The material collected in the study contains significantly more information than can be reported in this chapter. The data is organized in this chapter to meet three goals:

A.   To summarize how the use of financial graphics in annual reports is changing, using the ICPA[2] and the CICA[3] reports as a baseline.

B.   To show how color, format, and presentation styles are inconsistent:

   1.   Between companies;

   2.   Between years in the same company, and even in the same year.

C.   To show several of the most obvious examples of graphs that are presented to conform to the taste of the preparer rather than to present information in a more useful format.

23B.3   FINANCIAL GRAPHICS AND ANNUAL REPORTS

The use of financial graphics in the annual report is growing each year (see Table 23B.1, Comparison of Chart Usage in Annual Reports). In 1988 the ICPA published their landmark study on the use of graphics in annual reports. Out of the 499 annual reports reviewed for the study, 255 (51%) included graphic presentations of financial information. In 1993 the CICA published their discriminating study on the use of graphics in annual reports. Out of the 200 annual reports reviewed, 166 (83%) included graphic presentations of financial information.

In preparation for this chapter, four file drawers of annual reports were selected from the annual report collection at Chicago's Harold Washington Public Library. The selection process was carefully followed but was not statistically sound. Several of the thickest annual reports were selected to review from each file drawer. A total of 17 major companies was selected including both U.S. and foreign companies. A letter was mailed to each company asking for copies of their 1991 and 1992 annual reports. All but one sent both reports, and the other company sent one report, for a total of 33 annual reports.

Each report was reviewed page-by-page and all charts containing financial information were recorded in the database. The final results were reviewed by two other competent financial graphic professionals to ensure an objective description of the charts recorded in the database. Thirty of the 33 reports contained financial graphs, 91% of the reports examined. One set of reports used a

---

[2] Illinois CPA Society, *Financial Graphics - Communications for the 1990's, The Need for Financial Graphic Standards,* 1988, Chicago, IL.

[3] The Canadian Institute of Chartered Accountants, *Using Ratios and Graphics in Financial Reporting,* 1993, Toronto, Canada.

number of charts, but the charts did not contain financial data. Many of the reports included nonfinancial charts, which were not included in the study.

Table 23B.1   Comparison of Chart Usage In Annual Reports (*Reported by The Illinois CPA Society (ICPA) and The Canadian Institute of Chartered Accountants (CICA)*) and Reports Used for This Chapter

	ICPA		CICA		Chapter	
Number of annual reports reviewed	499		200		33	
Number of annual reports with financial graphics	255		166		30	
Percent with financial graphics	51%		83%		91%	
Total number of charts shown—financial only	3921		1683		248	
Average number of charts per report with charts	15.38		10.14		8.27	
Types of charts used						
Vertical bar—simple	2664	68%	727	43%	122	49%
Vertical bar—stacked	710	18%	185	11%	26	10%
Surface	0		54	3%	32	13%
Horizontal bar	0		112	7%	11	4%
Pie	143	4%	182	11%	55	22%
Other	404	10%	423	25%	2	1%
Total charts	3921	100%	1683	100%	248	100%
Location of charts						
Financial review (MD&A)	NA		753	45%	86	35%
Highlights	NA		283	17%	46	19%
Review of operations	NA		471	28%	44	18%
Letter to shareholders	NA		77	5%	22	9%
Supplementary info	NA		59	4%	12	5%
Historical summary	NA		19	1%		0%
Financial statements	NA		21	1%	38	15%
			1683	100%	248	100%

Table 23B.1 summarizes the findings of this study compared to the 1988 ICPA study where 51% of the annual reports had financial graphics; and the 1993 CICA study showed that 83% of the annual reports had financial graphics. With the paradigm shift from tabular to graphic well under way, it is not surprising to see such a rapid movement to financial graphics.

The companies were coded and each financial chart was recorded with the following information:

A. Section of report where charts were shown.
B. Page number.
C. Chart title.
D. Chart type.
E. Is this the same chart as last year? for 1992 reports only where 1991 was available. Same chart meant same type and same data. Not same color.
F. Number of years shown, where applicable.
G. Were the numbers shown on the chart?
H. Was a scale shown?

I. Same scale as last year? for 1992 reports only where 1991 was available and the charts were the same.

J. Color legend—colors used and to what purpose, when apparent.

K. Does the color used distort the information?

L. Does the chart have borders?

M. Are the other charts on the same page clearly separated from each other?

N. Are special effects used in the chart? Special effects would be any type of combined chart (line and bar, data overlays, etc.), 3D effects, etc.

O. Did the special effects distort the information in the chart?

The detailed entries were re-sorted and summarized to provide comparisons between the ICPA and the CICA reports as shown in Table 23B.2. The fact that this study was more limited in scope and the reports were not randomly selected means that the numbers are not directly comparable in all respects.

In my opinion the most important finding is where the charts were found. Many of the reports used different colored paper for the financial statements, and some used the different paper to show both the financial statements and other analyses. When charts were included on the same color paper, the charts were considered to be part of the financial report. The percent of charts found in the financial statements moved *from 1% in the CICA study to 15% in the current study.*

The mix of charts in Table 23B.1 shows a dramatic pattern of change. Vertical bar charts showing data over time dropped from 68% of the charts reviewed in the ICPA study, to 43% in the CICA study and back to 49% in the current study. Vertical bars are still the most popular form of chart.

The pie and surface charts were found much more often in this study. The comparison between the ICPA study and the CICA study shows a major increase in the Other charts shown. The difference in Other charts between the CICA and the current study is that all the charts in the current study were codified in detail (Table 23B.2) and then summarized by major type for Table 23B.1. Only two charts were listed in the Other category.

The range of charts found in the current study are recorded in Table 23B.2. Comparative data from the other studies were not available. The number of so-called 3D charts total over 7% of the charts included in this study. These so-called 3D charts are not 3D. A three-dimensional chart results only when a third variable is added to the normal Cartesian coordinates. The *only way* to build a 3D chart is to add a third variable.

Table 23B.2 Comparison of Chart Usage In Annual Reports (*Reported by The Illinois CPA Society (ICPA) and The Canadian Institute of Chartered Accountants (CICA)*) and Reports Used for This Chapter

Detailed Type of Charts Used	Numbers	Percent
Vertical bar-simple	82	33%
Vertical bar-stacked	12	5%
Vertical bar-partial stacked	13	5%
Vertical bar-cluster	8	3%
Vertical bar-w number overlay	2	1%
Vertical bar-w percent overlay	18	7%
3DVBar-cluster	2	1%
3DVBar	8	3%
3DVBar - w single year stack	1	0%

Table 23B.2   *(Continued)*

3DVBar-raised with shadow	2	1%
Surface-with years separated	24	10%
Two surfaces, years separated	6	2%
Six surfaces, years separated	1	0%
Seven surfaces, years separated	1	0%
Horizontal bar	11	4%
Pie	39	16%
3D pie	2	1%
3D pie rotated	3	1%
Pie drawn as hexagon	1	0%
Pie drawn with symbol and concurrent circles	1	0%
2 pie cluster	1	0%
3 pie cluster	8	3%
Line and VBar-stacked, 2 scales	1	0%
Line with 2 scales	1	0%
Other		
Total charts	248	100%

True 3D charts are used to show line frameworks of objects or the same framework covered with a "surface." They are used in Computer Aided Design systems to help engineers design and produce new products with new forms. Medical graphics allow doctors to use 3D graphics to show the human body and the physical construction of medicine and diseases. Architects use 3D graphics to show how new buildings fit the landscape and blend with other buildings. Advanced financial graphic presentations use 3D graphics to describe the complex relationships of puts and calls by representing as a surface the interactions between value at a point in time (Y), the spot price (X), and the volatility (Y).[4] Exhibit 23B.1 is a simple example of a 3D object shown with the values Y, X, and Z. A true 3D representation can be rotated so that the viewer can see all sides of the object.

In most cases the so-called 3D charts in the drawing and spreadsheet packages simply add a perspective to the lines or bars. They do not allow you to add a third variable. The picture you see is an object that appears to have volume. Such graphic "artistry" adds distortion; it does not add a third dimension.

If all of the other "complex" charts such as surface, overlays, double-scale, special pie, and others are included, they account for over a third of the 248 charts shown in the annual reports. As shown below, most of these charts are difficult to view, and in many cases distort the information unless the viewer stops to analyze the data presented. In such cases, there is no benefit showing a chart rather than the tabular information. In fact, there is the highly likely potential of misinterpretation.

[4] Steven Feiner and Clifford Beshers, "World within Worlds, Metaphors for Exploring n-Dimensional Virtual Worlds," 1990 ACM 089791-410-4/90/00 10/10076.

A Simple 3D Plot

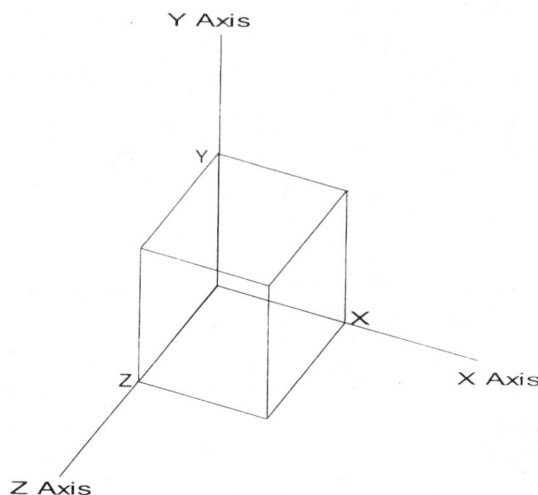

EXHIBIT 23B.1

23B.4 CONSISTENCY

This section reviews how color, format, and presentation style are inconsistent between companies, and within companies, between years and even within a year. The real issue here is whether the consistent transfer of information is the primary decision factor for chart selection, or if some computerized artistic taste is the determining factor. If one compares the way the charts are presented to the financial graphic standards summarized in the body of the book, it is easy to see that the financial graphs shown in the 33 reports were based on artistic taste. Artistic taste is not an appropriate basis for describing the financial results of operations.

A. **Color as the most volatile characteristic.** The most notable misuse of color was the color red. One of the most common business phrases used to describe how a company performed is to say: "They are in the black!" meaning they were profitable; or "They are in the red!" meaning they were not profitable. Yet companies consistently used red to show all forms of financial data, from revenue to profit. Red was used 63 times, or in 25% of the charts reviewed for this study. If the 19 times pink, purple, and plum were added to the charts, a third of the charts had a red or red hue in the mix.

   The CICA study showed that 28% of the 166 companies used red in their presentations. The current study showed that 10 of the 16 companies (63%) used red in one or more of their financial charts.

B. **Use of colors and other graphic combinations.** In addition to the extensive use of red, other difficult-to-see color and graphic combinations were utilized. Here are a few of the most obscure combinations. A sample of these or similar charts are shown in the next section. No attempt is made in this chapter to show how the companies could have used TFGA to more accurately and consistently transfer financial information to the viewer.

   1. One company used a shading pattern from dark green to a light yellow shown on bright white paper. The light yellow was used to display the

latest information, and it was almost impossible to see on the white background.

2. In 1992 a graphing system must have added a 3D triangle option with the point of the triangle facing down. Two companies moved from a simple vertical bar chart to show five years of data to the 3D triangle. In addition the bars were quite thin and there was shading on one face of the triangle. The last year showed a semistacked bar format by changing the shading of the last vertical element.

3. Rotated 3D pies had a considerable presence in 1992. In all cases they were not able to transfer the information to the viewer. The supporting data tables were much more useful.

4. Another company went from a simple vertical bar series to a complex 3D presentation where the bottom of the bar was folded under and toward the rear.

5. Pies were drawn as a silver dollar, a hexagon, concentric circles with a red star in the middle, and various other taste-based presentations.

6. Others used a number of vertical stacked bar charts with conflicting color segments to show long-range divisional performance. There was no way the user could follow a division across the time line.

7. One company went from a simple vertical bar with a slightly exaggerated number overlay to a 3D vertical Bar, raised from the axis so the shadow distorted the volume and used red for the last year, indicating bad, when in fact the year was good. The overlays were even more distracting and made viewing for information nearly impossible.

8. Another company that consistently used charts from year to year inserted a broken scale in 1992 so the full value was not visible.

9. One company used two different formats to show the same type of data. First they used a vertical bar with an actual or percent overlay of the comparative data using gray on top of red one year and red on gray the next. The actual or percent figure was laid inside the vertical bar disrupting the values. Next, they used a three-cluster pie chart to show the value of three different ratios using gray on red one year and red on gray the next. In the same year they used the same cluster and color format to show how three different divisions performed. If they had used a color different than red, and if they had used a different color combination to show the divisions, the information would have had more internal consistency.

10. One company used stacked vertical bars with two lines on top of the stacked bars. Two different scales were used as well as the color red. This presentation was not useful.

C. **Same chart as last year.**   Only four of the companies consistently used charts between 1992 and 1993. The remaining companies changed their graphics from year to year.

D. **Same scale as last year.**   Of the 95 charts where the scales could have been the same, 63 (66%) were different. Half of the differences were due to a change in the numbers, but a full third of the opportunities to be consistent were not consistent. Note that some of the charts that were different from last year could have used the same scale. For example a simple vertical bar chart could have the same scale as a 3D triangle-shaped vertical bar.

E.   **Charts clearly separated.**   Out of the 248 charts reviewed, only 54 (22%) had borders (lines or background) to distinguish one chart from another. Borders are the simplest and easiest way to make sure each chart stands on its own.

23B.5   A LOOK AT SOME CHARTS

The following charts were selected for a single reason: to show how the use of color and form can mask the information contained in the financial statements.

A.   **Turnover and trading cash flow, single year.** (Exhibit 23B.2)

   1.   Use of red is inappropriate.
   2.   Overlay is actually a percent of the trading cash flow attributed to the total turnover. This presentation is difficult at best to internalize.
   3.   The placement of numbers in the bar distorts the view and confuses the viewer.
   4.   Scale is not relevant to both numbers shown, using two different scales prevents chart from accurate viewing.

B.   **Proportion of group (2)—turnover, net trading income, trading assets employed, single year.** (Exhibit 23B.3)

   1.   Use of red is inappropriate.
   2.   Unique presentation with no clear legends. Numbers and percents are not shown together. Most difficult to internalize comparisons.
   3.   No way to compare group performance to company total.

C.   **Sales proceeds—beer and net turnover.**   Two years compared showing same colors, but second year has a different scale with a split scale.

   1.   Movement from green to yellow on a white background distorts the last few bars shown. Difficult to differentiate between the light yellow fading out and the white background. (Exhibit 23B.4)
   2.   The scale increase from year to year is due to rising sales and would be expected. Using a split scale is inappropriate and negates the ability of a viewer to "see" the values. (Exhibit 23B.5)

D.   **Costs and profit excluding extraordinary income,** *as a percentage of the net turnover.*   Two years compared. (Exhibits 23B.6 and 23B.7)

   1.   Both charts use similar colors, but the legends are different each year. Too many colors, not possible to compare the value of the pieces.
   2.   Both charts use too many small pieces, not possible to make any comparisons between the pieces.
   3.   The 1992 chart is distorted to the point of being "art" rather than information. The red star draws the eye and prohibits any comparison of the parts.
   4.   The 1992 chart—the concentric rings prevent a comparison of the parts of the "pie."

E.   Income per Share from Continuing Operations Assuming Full Dilution.   Two years compared. The first year is a horizontal chart, and the second year is a 3D vertical triangular solid with the point down and the right side has a different scale to indicate a Restructuring Effect. (Exhibits 23B.8 and 23B.9)

   1.   The 1991 chart is simple, well laid out, and clearly shows the values during the five years. The bars are thin, but they are consistent throughout the report. The only anomaly is the very light shade of gray extending from 87 to indicate a Nonrecurring gain on sale of subsidiary stock and a provision for restructure.

   2.   The 1992 chart is a complex 3D vertical triangular solid and difficult at best to establish value. The addition of the different shading on the right side compounds the viewing difficulty. The pointed solids push the eyes to the bottom in this case.

F.   Sales.   Two years compared. In both years a vertical bar chart was used to compare five years' worth of sales. (Exhibits 23B.10 and 23B.11)

   1.   The 1991 chart uses a solid red vertical bar laid directly onto a tan, vertical page with no border. The chart is located on the same page as four other charts, one on top of the other. Each chart has a separate scale. The height of the various charts is limited to stack four charts on the page. There are no borders, and the charts appear to be part of a single presentation. A second chart on the same page, Dividends Per Share, uses the same red and represents a different financial function, and scale. The numbers representing the years are placed horizontally inside the bars rather than at the bottom of the plot, disrupting the bar. Red is not an appropriate color to show financial information.

   2.   The 1992 chart uses a thinner (about one third the first year), solid black, and vertical bar on a rectangular green background drawn on the white landscape page. The width of the chart is about one fourth the width of the first year and approximately three times the height. The same four data are shown, this time placed side-by-side. Each chart uses a different color background. The color acts as a border separating the four charts. There is no scale for any of the charts. The numbers are placed vertically inside the bars so the viewer has to turn the page (or their head) to see the numbers. The numbers representing the years are placed vertically inside the bars rather than at the bottom of the plot, further disrupting the bar. The charts appear to be showing totally different ranges of data when in fact the only difference is the last year.

G.   The 1991 Sales By Product.   A single year. This chart is a 3D, rotated pie chart attached to a data table. (Exhibit 23B.12)

   1.   The pie is a light sand color with light reflecting on the surface. The shading gives the appearance of different heights.

   2.   The lines separating the pieces of the pie are difficult to see.

   3.   It is not possible to compare the pieces of the pie.

H.   Operating Earnings, *Dollars per Common Share.*   Two years compared. Both years use identical charts except for color and placement. (Exhibits 23B.13 and 23B.14)

1. The 1991 Operating Earnings is prominently placed just below the middle of the page on the left side with another similar-sized chart, Net Income, placed toward the bottom on the right. The page is in portrait mode and is titled Highlights. Neither chart has a border. There is no other information on the page. The charts and the title are bright red. The chart headings and the scales are black. The charts are certainly easy to view and show the five-year fluctuations. Red is not an appropriate color to show financial information.

2. The 1992 Operating Earnings chart is placed on the bottom of a landscape page with four other charts and a table. This chart is placed at the far right of the four chart set. There are no borders. All the charts have a scale, and they are all in black. The 1992 Operating Earnings chart shows a scale using the same numbers for 88, 89, 90, and 91. The year 1992 was a loss so a negative scale is added to the bottom. The distance between each step in the 1992 scale is smaller, resulting in a shorter set of bars that does not imply as much change between the years and makes the loss look smaller than it would on the 1991 scale. Comparing the two years is not possible.

I. **Sales, a single year.**   The 1992 chart is a complex 3D vertical triangular solid and difficult to establish value. The pointed solids push the eyes to the bottom in this case. This is the only example of the same chart used by two different companies. (Exhibit 23B.15)

J. **_____'s international revenues.**   Two years compared. Both charts are identical stacked bar charts on similar quality paper; 1991 is a lighter color than the 1992 paper. The color selections for the stacked portions are completely different even though the names of the portions are identical. The color placement in both years makes it almost impossible to follow the changing proportions of any of the stacked pieces. Red is not an appropriate color to show financial information. (Exhibits 23B.16 and 23B.17)

K. **Gross Revenue, *fully taxable equivalent basis,* a single year.**   The 1992 chart is a stacked bar with six different pieces and six different colors. The chart has a border, the title is on top, the scales are well laid out, the years are clearly placed on the below the bars and the horizontal axis. The color placement combined with the number of pieces stacked turns this chart into an artistic creation, not a data transfer vehicle. Red is not an appropriate color to show financial information. (Exhibit 23B.18)

L. **Noninterest Expenses and Income, a single year.**   A five-year vertical, stacked bar chart combined with a line chart laid on top of the vertical bars. The chart has a border, the title is on top, the scales are well laid out, the years are clearly placed below the bars and the horizontal axis. The vertical stacks use red and green colors, two of the colors that conflict the most. In addition the two lines are drawn to a percent scale that is set so that the 900 (million) appears to be directly related to the 90 (percent). The two ratios are directly related because of the common denominator. Any other relationships require a detailed review of the data, which defeats the purpose of a chart. Red is not an appropriate color to show financial information. (Exhibit 23B.19)

Omset en
bedryfskontantvloei
(R miljoen)

■ Omset

▨ Bedryfskontantvloei

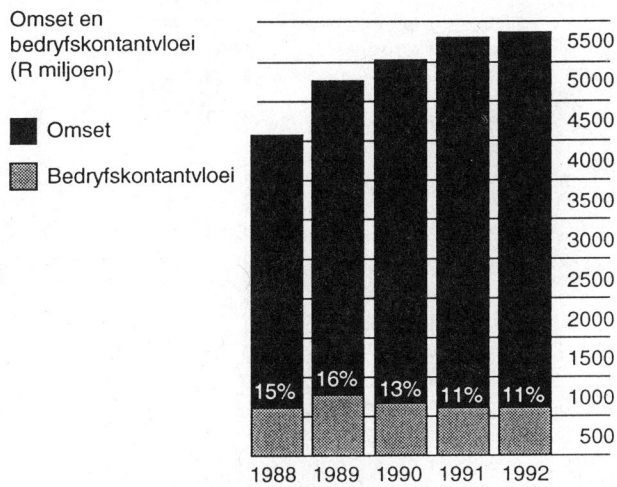

EXHIBIT 23B.2

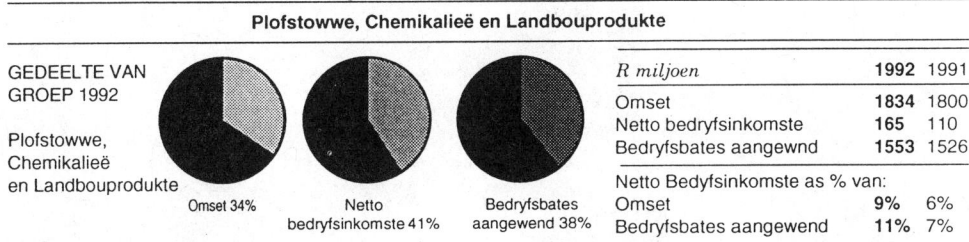

Plofstowwe, Chemikalieë en Landbouprodukte

GEDEELTE VAN
GROEP 1992

Plofstowwe,
Chemikalieë
en Landbouprodukte

Omset 34%

Netto
bedryfsinkomste 41%

Bedryfsbates
aangewend 38%

R miljoen	1992	1991
Omset	1834	1800
Netto bedryfsinkomste	165	110
Bedryfsbates aangewend	1553	1526
Netto Bedyfsinkomste as % van:		
Omset	9%	6%
Bedryfsbates aangewend	11%	7%

EXHIBIT 23B.3

**Sales proceeds beer
and net turnover**
in milliards of guilders

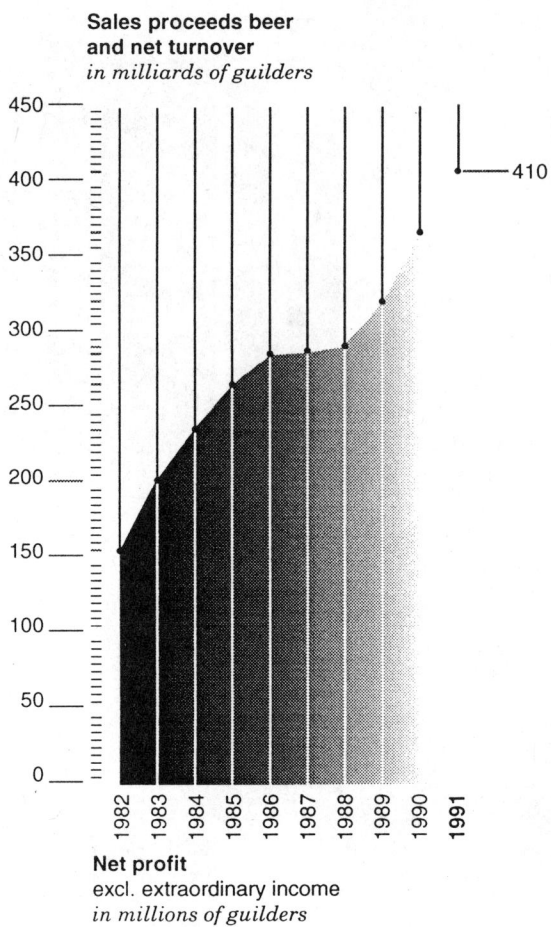

Net profit
excl. extraordinary income
in millions of guilders

EXHIBIT 23B.4

**Sales proceeds beer
and net turnover**
in billions of guilders

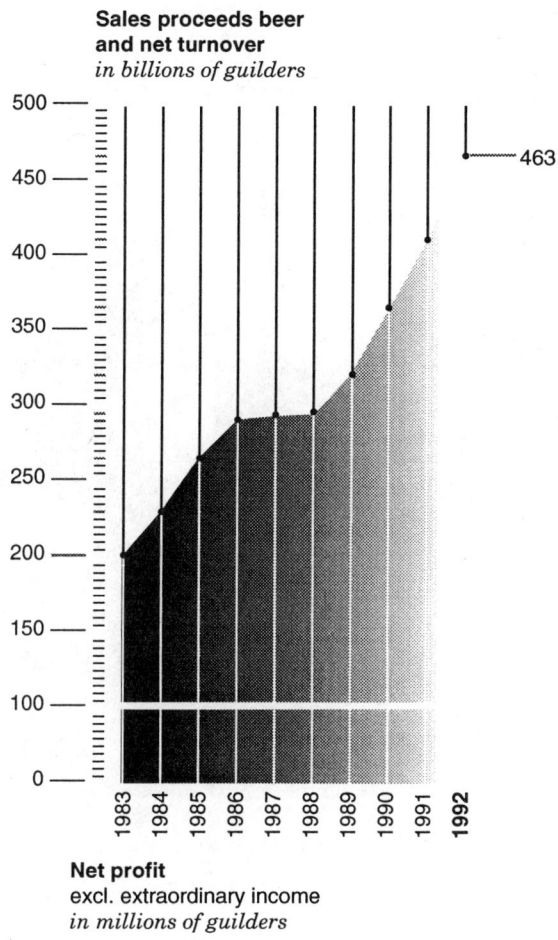

Net profit
excl. extraordinary income
in millions of guilders

EXHIBIT 23B.5

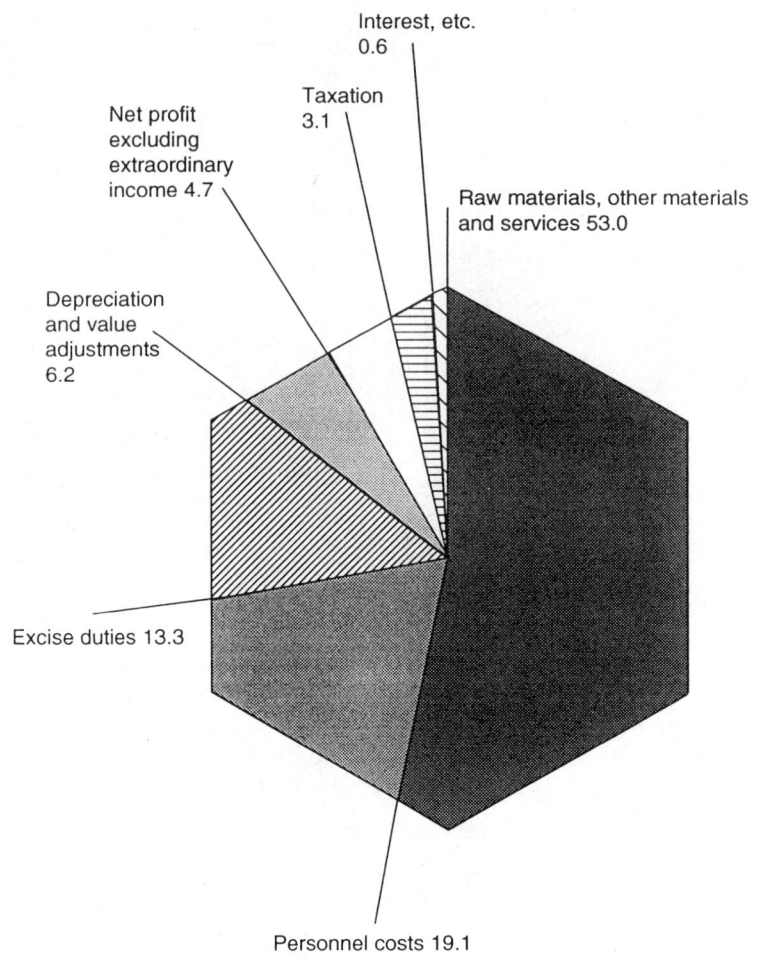

Costs and profit excluding extraordinary income
as a percentage of the net turnover

EXHIBIT 23B.6

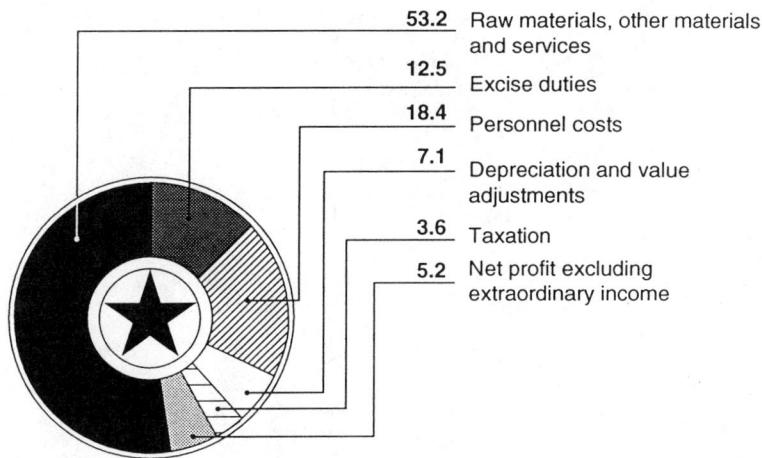

53.2	Raw materials, other materials and services
12.5	Excise duties
18.4	Personnel costs
7.1	Depreciation and value adjustments
3.6	Taxation
5.2	Net profit excluding extraordinary income

Costs and profit excluding extraordinary income
as a percentage of the net turnover

EXHIBIT 23B.7

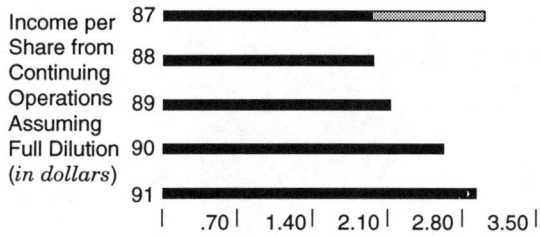

Income per
Share from
Continuing
Operations
Assuming
Full Dilution
(*in dollars*)

87
88
89
90
91

| .70 | 1.40 | 2.10 | 2.80 | 3.50 |

▨ *Nonrecurring gain on sale of subsidiary stock and a provision for restructure.*

EXHIBIT 23B.8

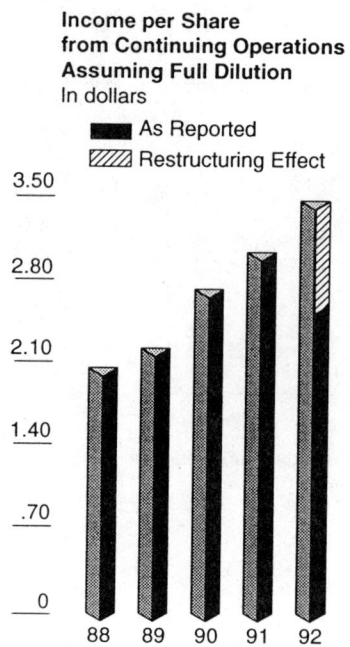

**Income per Share
from Continuing Operations
Assuming Full Dilution**
In dollars

■ As Reported
▨ Restructuring Effect

EXHIBIT 23B.9

Five Year Highlights

Sales*
(in millions of dollars)

Income*
(in millions of dollars)

Stockholders' Equity
(in millions of dollars)

Dividends per share**
(in dollars)

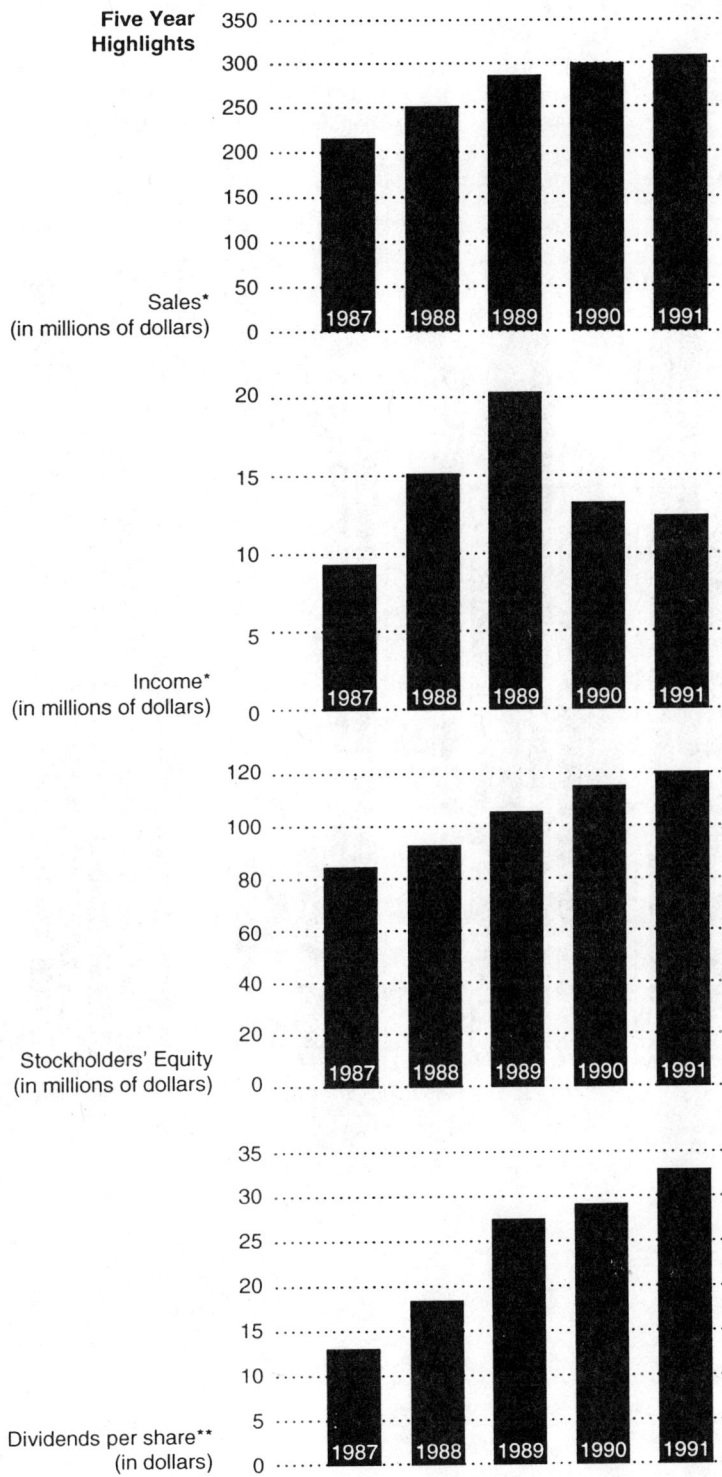

 * From continuing operations
** Dividends per share for years prior to 1989 are
   restated for the 1989 three for two stock split

EXHIBIT 23B.10

FIVE YEAR HIGHLIGHTS

SALES (in thousands of dollars)	NET INCOME (in thousands of dollars)	STOCKHOLDERS' EQUITY (in thousands of dollars)	DIVIDEND PER SHARE* (in dollars)

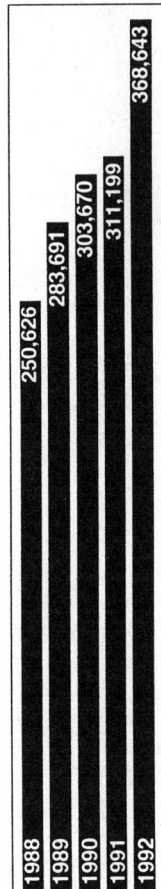

*Dividends per share for 1988 are restated for the 1989 three for two stock split.

EXHIBIT 23B.11

1991 SALES BY PRODUCT
(in millions of $)

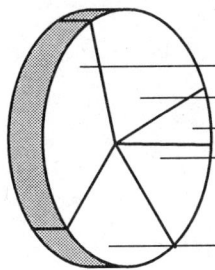

		1991	1990	1989	1988	1987
38%	Flat-rolled products	**2,776**	3,368	3,406	3,152	2,821
17%	Extruded, rolled, drawn products	**1,293**	1,516	1,640	1,578	1,166
11%	Other fabricated products	**835**	827	781	666	470
17%	Ingot products					
	—own primary ingot	**592**	749	402	549	566
	—other	**636**	690	1,135	1,297	616
17%	Non-aluminum products	**1,237**	1,303	1,215	1,033	908
100%	Total sales	**7,369**	8,453	8,579	8,275	6,547
	Operating revenues and other income	**461**	466	468	351	331
	Total	**7,830**	8,919	9,047	8,626	6,878

EXHIBIT 23B.12

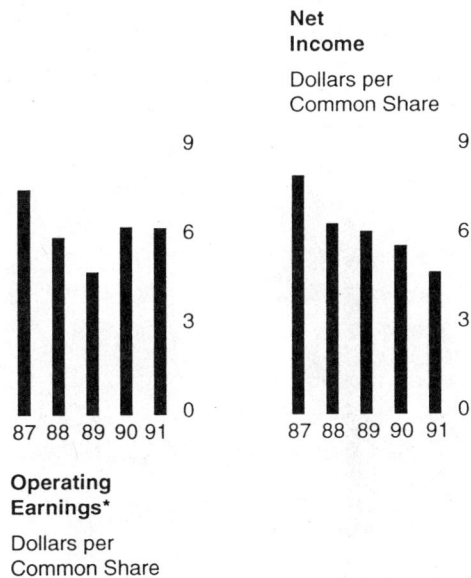

Net Income

Dollars per Common Share

Operating Earnings*

Dollars per Common Share

EXHIBIT 23B.13

Shareholders' Equity
Dollars per common share

Net Income
Dollars per common share

Dividends Declared
Dollars per common share

Operating Earnings*
Dollars per common share

*Net income before extraordinary items, discontinued operations, cumulative effect adjustments and net realized capital gains (losses), net of tax.

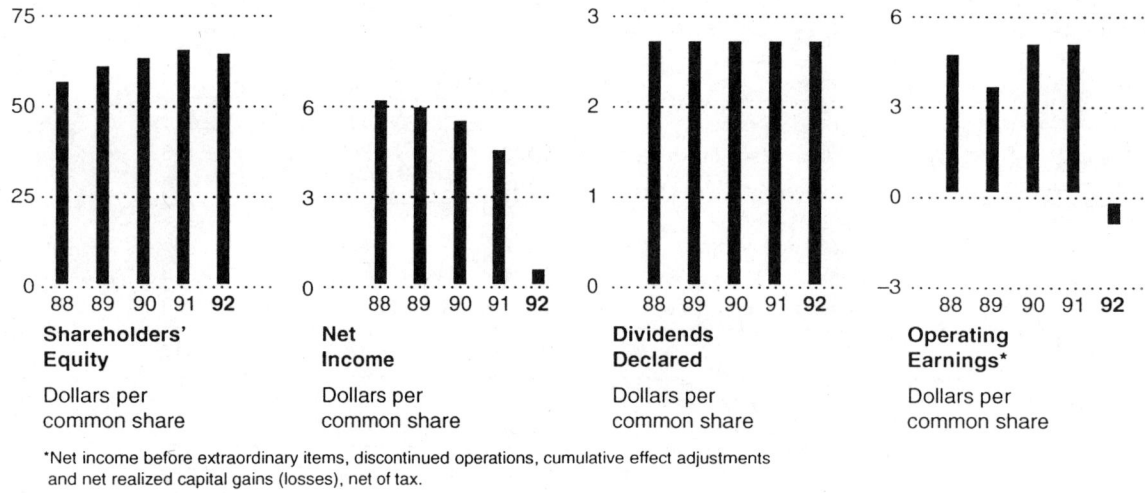

EXHIBIT 23B.14

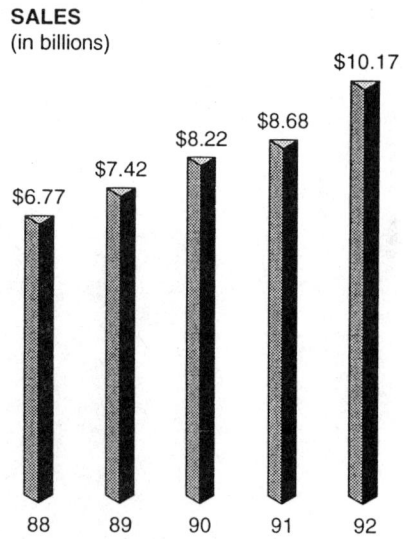

SALES
(in billions)

$6.77 $7.42 $8.22 $8.68 $10.17

88 89 90 91 92

EXHIBIT 23B.15

revenues
(In billions) $50

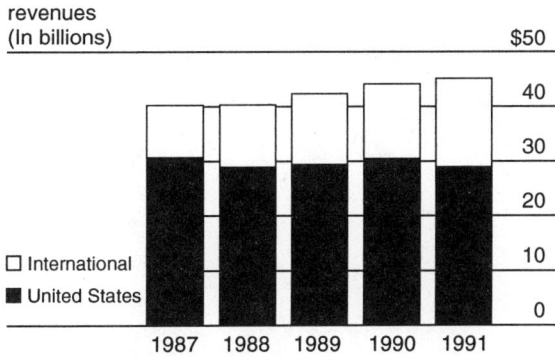

□ International
■ United States

      1987 1988 1989 1990 1991

EXHIBIT 23B.16

international revenues
(In billions) $18.0

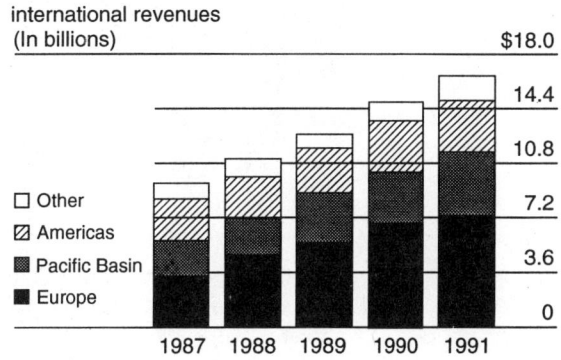

□ Other
▨ Americas
■ Pacific Basin
■ Europe

      1987 1988 1989 1990 1991

revenues from continuing operations
(In billions) $42.0

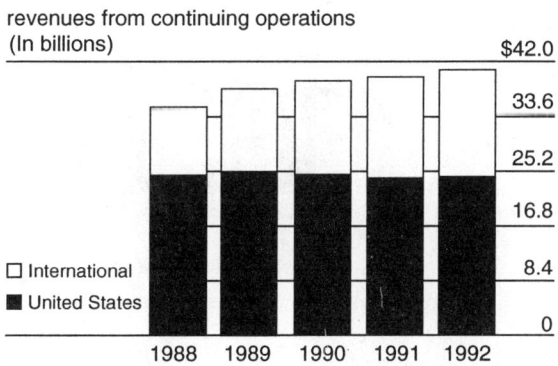

□ International
■ United States

      1988 1989 1990 1991 1992

EXHIBIT 23B.17

international revenues from continuing operations
(In billions) $16.0

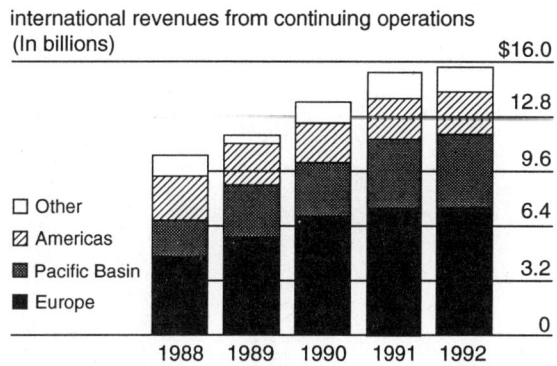

□ Other
▨ Americas
■ Pacific Basin
■ Europe

      1988 1989 1990 1991 1992

Gross Revenue fully taxable equivalent basis

in millions of dollars

	1988	1989	1990	1991	1992
900					
800					
700					
600					
500					
400					
300					
200					
100					

Net interest income   ●

Trust and investment management fees   ◎

Trading account and foreign exchange   ○

Charge card   ◎

Service fees and charges   ⊘

Other operating income   ◕

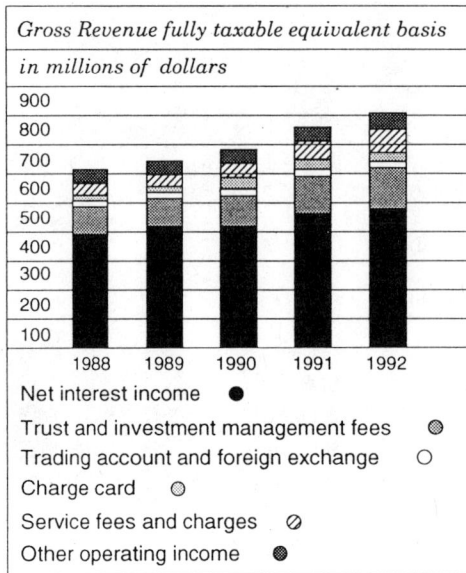

EXHIBIT 23B.18

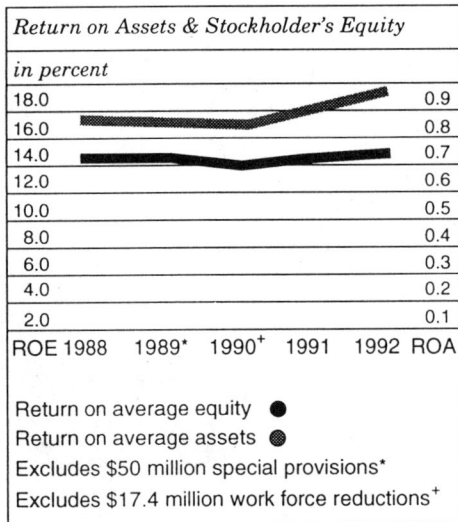

Return on Assets & Stockholder's Equity

in percent

		ROA
18.0		0.9
16.0		0.8
14.0		0.7
12.0		0.6
10.0		0.5
8.0		0.4
6.0		0.3
4.0		0.2
2.0		0.1

ROE 1988   1989*   1990+   1991   1992 ROA

Return on average equity   ●

Return on average assets   ◕

Excludes $50 million special provisions*

Excludes $17.4 million work force reductions+

Noninterest Expenses and Income

in millions of dollars					*in percent*
900					90
800					80
700					70
600					60
500					50
400					40
300					30
200					20
100					10

    1988   1989   1990   1991   1992

Noninterest expenses to gross revenues ○

Noninterest income to gross revenues ◕

Net interest income ●

Noninterest income ○

EXHIBIT 23B.19

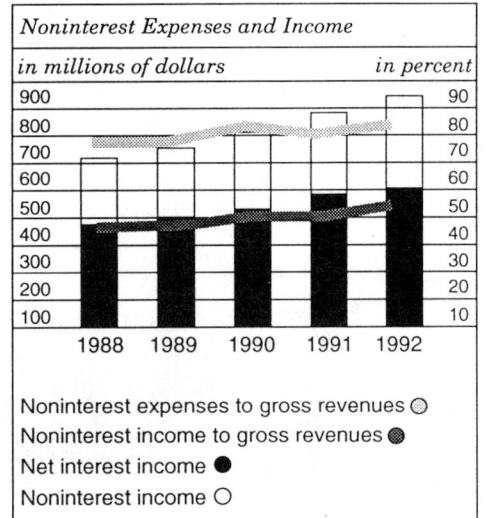

23B.6 CONCLUSION—INFORMATION TRANSFER OR ARTISTIC TASTE

It is difficult to see how the pervasive inconsistency, use of inappropriate graphic formats, and the inappropriate use of color could be anything other than a case of artistic taste overriding the need for information transfer. The move from simple to complex and from plain to excessive is startling. There are several charts where the line between inappropriate taste and deceit is thinner than the lines shown in the charts.

After their studies were complete, the Illinois CPA Society research committee and the Canadian Institute of Chartered Accountants research committee were both convinced of the need for financial graphic standards.[5,6,7] This study is even more convincing when the rapid rate of change is considered.

---

[5] Further discussion of the need for general standards on graphics is set out in the following materials: P. J. Steinbart, "The Auditor's Responsibility for the Accuracy of Graphs in Annual Reports: Some Evidence of the Need for Additional Guidance," *Accounting Horizons* (September 1989) pp. 60–70; Illinois CPA Society, *Financial Graphics - Communications for the 1990's: The Need For Financial Graphic Standards* (1988); I. M. Jarett and Y. Babad, "Guidelines and Standards for Accounting Graphics," *Journal of Accounting and EDP* (Summer 1988) pp. 4–14; B. J. Taylor and L. K. Anderson, "Misleading Graphs: Guidelines for the Accountant," *Journal of Accountancy* (October 1986) pp. 126–135; J. R. Johnson, R. R. Rice and R. A. Roemmich, "Pictures That Lie: The Abuse of Graphs in Annual Reports," *Management Accounting* (October 1980) pp. 50–56.

[6] Refer to V. A. Beattie and M. J. Jones, *The Communication of Information Using Graphs in Corporate Annual Reports,* Research Report 31 (London: Chartered Association of Certified Accountants, 1992). The survey findings are discussed in several articles including: "The Uses and Abuse of Graphics in Annual Reports: A Theoretical Framework and Empirical Study," *Accounting and Business Research* (Autumn 1992); "Graphic Accounts," Certified Accountant (UK) (September 1992) p. 101.

[7] The Canadian Institute of Chartered Accountants, *Using Ratios and Graphics in Financial Reporting,* Research Report (October, 1993) pp. 7–34.

[8] Calvin F. Schmid, *Handbook of Graphic Presentations,* 2nd edition, John Wiley & Sons, New York, 1979.

APPENDIX 23B.1

A SUMMARY OF THE FINANCIAL GRAPHIC STANDARDS AS DEFINED IN FINANCIAL REPORTING USING COMPUTER GRAPHICS

Table 3—Graphic Standards

The following graphic standards were adopted from Schmid's Handbook,[8] The American Standards ASA Y15.1—1959, *Illustrations for Publications and Projections* and my own research.

I.	Borders	Use clearly defined borders for each chart or graph. The shape of the borders, chart, or graph should not detract from the content.
II.	Background	Use unobtrusive background colors (i.e., light grey or off-white).
III.	Use of Color	Use to identify type (i.e., cost, sales, or financial data) or owner (i.e., function or division) of data; or to highlight areas for inspection. Use same color for same purpose, never mix colors. *Do not use color to communicate data values.*
IV.	Number of colors	Use a maximum of four colors that do not clash or confuse, each with a clear purpose and legend.
IV.	Dimensions	Never use three-dimensional forms where the reader is asked to infer the volume of the three-dimensional form.
V.	Width of bars and spacing	Use bars that are a uniform width and evenly spaced. The bars should not be either disproportionately long and narrow or short and wide.
VI.	Scale	Use a carefully planned scale in every chart. Scales: A. should always begin at zero, B. should never be broken, C. should be shown on the axes in even segments.
VII.	Title, legend, and chart identification	Place the title, legend, and chart identification in the same position for all charts.
VIII.	Negative numbers	Show negative numbers in opposite direction of positive numbers.

The material that is available indicates, however, that at some point there is an absolute limit to the amount of information that can be seen by the human visual system in any given moment. A graph that is cluttered with too much information and too much data will simply not be properly perceived by the untrained eye, as it requires too much effort. The criteria for the appropriate amount of data should be established according to the following guideline: *The information presented on the chart can be seen and assimilated without having to be read.*

Behind that guideline, however, are several important assumptions:

A. The individuals who see the data are familiar with the operations of the firm and have some experience in reading data about the firm in tabular form.

B. The viewer has been trained in graphic pattern recognition and is "graphic literate." This statement indicates that the viewer knows what is being shown, understands the graphic formats and graphic statements, and can see the graphic words. Such users can relate the information to their experience by seeing without having to think about it.

C. The data or information being presented is of concern to the viewer, and performance can be evaluated simply by viewing the data. This assumption is based on the fact that if the information is not perceived to be of value to the viewer, the charts can display as little or as much data as you want; the viewer will not use it.

D. Basis of organizational information: assumption that the results of operations reflect a system, that such results have a consistency, and that such consistency can be represented by the patterns of a well organized and well-thought-out graphic representation. Therefore, the charts must be constructed so that the data drive the format to create a pattern of operations that is more important than the data themselves. This requirement is built into all of the charts presented in this text. Thus the trained viewer should learn to *see* the patterns, not *read* the data.

Table 4—The Financial Graphic Standards

The following standards are proposed specifically for graphs that display financial data prepared by accountants for internal and/or external distribution. Financial graphics must accurately and consistently reflect the information contained in operating and financial statements. The proposed standards comply with the standards in the Illinois CPA Society report, the CICA report, and *Financial Reporting Using Computer Graphics* by John Wiley & Sons, Inc.

I. Data cluster

Show Financial/Operating data in a data cluster showing up to three data elements using horizontal clusters for replicating financial or operating results; vertical clusters for replicating time series data.

    A. The Primary bar, the most important data, is shown in the center of the data cluster.

    B. The Secondary bar, the second most important data, is shown below and partially covered by the primary bar.

    C. The Tertiary bar, the third most important data, is shown on top of and partially covered by the primary bar.

II. Data cluster—color

Use the same color for all data clusters on a chart and within a series.

    A. Primary bar—use a primary color with a solid pattern for the primary bar.

    B. Secondary bar—use the same color as the primary color but with a slightly lighter, nondirectional, shading pattern.

C. Tertiary bar—use the same color as the primary color but with a slightly lighter, nondirectional, shading pattern than the secondary bar.

D. Use colors with the same hue. It is acceptable to show variations in lightness or intensity for the secondary and tertiary bars. For example, black could be used for the primary bar, dark grey for the secondary bar, and light grey for the tertiary bar on a white or off-white background.

III. Chart structure—financial/operating data—date or period

A. Show financial or operating data as horizontal bars (elements).

B. Use graphics that mirror the math and/or the data relationships described in the tabular statements.

C. Use graphics that mirror the structure and purpose of the tabular statements.

D. Use font sizes that are proportional to the height of the elements.

E. Place numbers at the end of the elements farthest from the axis.

  1. Show numbers so they can be footed to the absolute totals.

  2. Show numbers at the end of the element bar and slightly separated from the element.

  3. Never place numbers over or inside the element bar.

F. Place element name above the element bar, justified to the axis or centered.

IV. Chart structure—financial/operating data—time series

A. Show time series data with vertical rather than horizontal data clusters.

B. Do not use numbers with vertical data clusters.

C. Use light horizontal dashed lines to indicate scale values across the chart.

V. Chart structure—background & border color(s)

Background:

A. Use unobtrusive background colors that enhance the contrast but do not clash with the color of the data clusters.

B. Use solid background colors with no patterns.

C. Use background colors that will provide contrast on black & white printers as well as color printers.

D. Use background colors to index charts by organization or function.

Border

E. Use border colors to further index charts by organization or function.

VI. Legend, title, and chart identification

Show the legend in the top-left-hand corner insert; the title in the top center; the chart identification, date, and scale in the top-right-hand corner insert. Such placement permits all reading (left brain activity) to be at the top of the chart moving from left to right and top to bottom, and all visualization (right brain activity) to take place in the body of the chart.

VII. Legend, title, and chart identification—color

Legend

A. Use same color as data clusters.

Title & Chart Identification

B. Use colors to further index charts by organization or function.

VIII. Amount of data

Humans can learn to see patterns of large, complex number sets when displayed in properly constructed graphics.

A. Show only one pattern per chart—do not mix type of patterns or type of information. It is most appropriate to show the actual or percentage variance of the data sets on the same chart.

B. Clearly separate data with different scales—use different charts for different size data. The single most common data presentation error is to show data that do not relate to a similar scale. Do not show prepaid expenses of $5,000 and fixed assets of $250,000,000, the $5,000 will round off to "$0." (It does not make sense in a tabular construct either and only adds to the confusion of the reader.)

C. Compare items that have clear relationships, and the same basic data structure (i.e., show the relationship between cost of goods sold by product type and revenue by product type; don't show cost of goods sold by product type and revenue by customer type within the same borders).

D. Use only the number of elements that fit gracefully within the standard presentation size and permit properly proportioned bars to be shown for the primary and both comparative bars.

E. If there is any doubt about the amount of data to be shown on a chart, use two charts. *In graphics, less is more.*

IX. Headings

All headings in the graphic financial statements should be centered and as close as practicable to the headings used in tabular financial reporting.

A. For public statements, use only those abbreviations that would normally be used in a tabular statement.

B. For internal reporting, common abbreviations are appropriate and, eventually, when the users are so familiar with the patterns that they know the elements by position and shading, certain graphic comparisons may be made without names or numbers.

C. Clearly distinguish between the heading of the chart and the names of the elements shown. There should be a clear separation between the headings and the body of the chart.

X. Fonts

A. Use easily recognized, business-appropriate fonts.

B. Use font sizes that are easily readable, but do not distract the eye from the data elements.

The word "Charts" in this table is limited to graphs that contain financial data

Year	Code	Chart #	Section of Report	Page	Chart Title	Same Chart Last Year	Chart Type	Years	Numbers Shown	Scale Shown	Same Scale as Last Year	Scale Range (%)
1991	btn1	1	Highlights	1	SALES	NA	VBar	5	Yes	No	NA	Billions
1991	btn1	2	Highlights	1	NET EARNINGS	NA	VBar	5	Yes	No	NA	Millions
1991	btn1	3	Highlights	1	RETURN ON AVERAGE ASSETS	NA	VBar	5	Yes	No	NA	Percent (%)
1991	btn1	4	Management's Discussion And Analysis Of Results of Operations And Financial Condition	18	SALES	NA	VBar	5	Yes	No	NA	Billions
1991	btn1	5	Management's Discussion And Analysis Of Results of Operations And Financial Condition	18	OPERATING PROFIT AS A PERCENT TO SALES	NA	VBar	5	Yes	No	NA	Percent (%)
1991	btn1	6	Management's Discussion And Analysis Of Results of Operations And Financial Condition	19	NET EARNINGS	NA	VBar	5	Yes	No	NA	Millions
1991	btn1	7	Management's Discussion And Analysis Of Results of Operations And Financial Condition	19	NET EARNINGS AS A PERCENT TO SALES	NA	VBar	5	Yes	No	NA	Percent (%)
1991	btn1	8	Management's Discussion And Analysis Of Results of Operations And Financial Condition	19	1991 SALES DOLLAR ANALYSIS	NA	Pie	NA	Yes	NA	NA	Cents
1991	btn1	9	Management's Discussion And Analysis Of Results of Operations And Financial Condition	20	RETURN ON AVERAGE STOCKHOLDERS' EQUITY	NA	VBar	5	Yes	No	NA	Percent (%)
1991	btn1	10	Management's Discussion And Analysis Of Results of Operations And Financial Condition	20	RETURN ON AVERAGE ASSETS	NA	VBar	5	Yes	No	NA	Percent (%)
1991	btn1	11	Management's Discussion And Analysis Of Results of Operations And Financial Condition	21	CAPITAL EXPENDITURES	NA	VBar	5	Yes	No	NA	Millions
1992	btn2	1	Highlights	1	SALES	No	3DVBar	5	Yes	No	No	Billions
1992	btn2	2	Highlights	1	NET EARNINGS	No	3DVBar	5	Yes	No	No	Millions
1992	btn2	3	Highlights	1	RETURN ON AVERAGE ASSETS	No	3DVBar	5	Yes	No	No	Percent (%)
1992	btn2	4	Financial Section	16	OPERATING PROFIT AS A PERCENT TO SALES	No	3DVBar	5	Yes	No	No	Percent (%)
1992	btn2	5	Financial Section	16	NET EARNINGS AS A PERCENT TO SALES	No	3DVBar	5	Yes	No	No	Percent (%)
1992	btn2	6	Financial Section	16	CAPITAL EXPENDITURES	No	3DVBar - W Single year stack	5	Yes	No	No	Millions
1992	btn2	7	Financial Section	16	1992 SALES DOLLAR ANALYSIS	No	Pie	NA	Yes	NA	No	Cents

There are other similar non-financial charts in these annual reports

EXHIBIT 23B.20

The word "Charts" in this table is limited to graphs that contain financial data

Year	Code	Color Legend	Does Color Distort	Borders Shown	Other Charts Separated	Special Effects	Special Effects Distortion
1991	btn1	Blue - Tan Background	No	Yes - Background	Yes	No	No
1991	btn1	Light Brown - Tan Background	No	Yes - Background	Yes	No	No
1991	btn1	Light Green - Tan Background	No	Yes - Background	Yes	No	No
1991	btn1	Blue - Tan Background	No	Yes - Background	Yes	No	No
1991	btn1	Green - Tan Background	No	Yes - Background	Yes	No	No
1991	btn1	Blue - Tan Background	No	Yes - Background	Yes	No	No
1991	btn1	Green - Tan Background	No	Yes - Background	Yes	No	No
1991	btn1	Silver (Dollar)	No	Yes - Background	Yes	Pie is in shape of silver dollar with exploding pieces	Yes - not able to compare exploded pieces
1991	btn1	Blue - Tan Background	No	Yes - Background	Yes	No	No
1991	btn1	Green - Tan Background	No	Yes - Background	Yes	No	No
1991	btn1	Green - Tan Background	No	Yes - Background	Yes	No	No
1992	btn2	Light & Dark Green sides w Black top	Slight	No	Yes	3D triangle with points down	Yes - difficult to judge volume, points move eyes down.
1992	btn2	Light & Dark Orange sides w Black top	Slight	No	Yes	3D triangle with points down	Yes - difficult to judge volume, points move eyes down.
1992	btn2	Light & Dark Blue sides w Black top	Slight	No	Yes	3D triangle with points down	Yes - difficult to judge volume, points move eyes down.
1992	btn2	Light & Dark Green sides w Black top	Slight	No	Yes	3D triangle with points down	Yes - difficult to judge volume, points move eyes down.
1992	btn2	Light & Dark Orange sides w Black top	Slight	No	Yes	3D triangle with points down	Yes - difficult to judge volume, points move eyes down.
1992	btn2	Light & Dark Blue sides w Black top plus orange stack	Slight	No	Yes	3D triangle with points down	Yes - difficult to judge volume, points move eyes down. Single year stack is see-able
1992	btn2	Orange, green, red, blue	Yes	No	Yes	Pie is shown in a reclining 3D position	Yes - not able to compare pieces

EXHIBIT 23B.20 (Continued)

The word "Charts" in this table is limited to graphs that contain financial data.

Year	Code	Chart #	Section of Report	Page	Chart Title	Same Chart Last Year	Chart Type	Years	Numbers Shown	Scale Shown	Same Scale as Last Year	Scale Range (%)
1991	nau1	1	Selected Financial Statistics	1	Earnings Per Share	NA	VBar	6	Yes	No	NA	Actual
1991	nau1	2	Selected Financial Statistics	1	Dividends Paid Per Share	NA	VBar	5	Yes	No	NA	Actual
1991	nau1	3	Selected Financial Statistics	1	Revenue	NA	VBar	6	Yes	No	NA	Billions
1991	nau1	4	Selected Financial Statistics	1	Return on Equity	NA	VBar	6	Yes	No	NA	Percent (%)
1991	nau1	5	Management's Discussion and Analysis of Financial Condition and Results of Operations	18	Cash Construction Expenditures	NA	VBar	6	Yes	No	NA	Millions
1992	nau2	1	Financial Summary	Inside Cover	Revenues	No	VBar	6	Yes	No	No	Billions
1992	nau2	2	Financial Summary	Inside Cover	Return on Equity	No	VBar	6	Yes	No	No	Percent(%)
1992	nau2	3	Presidents Report	3	Earnings Per Share	No	VBar	6	Yes	No	No	Actual
1992	nau2	4	Presidents Report	3	Dividend Growth	No	VBar	6	Yes	No	No	Actual
1992	nau2	5	Management's Discussion and Analysis of Financial Condition and Results of Operations	19	Cash Construction Expenditures	No	VBar	6	Yes	No	No	Millions

There are other similar non-financial charts in these annual reports

EXHIBIT 23B.20 (*Continued*)

The word "Charts" in this table is limited to graphs that contain financial data

Year	Code	Color Legend	Does Color Distort	Borders Shown	Other Charts Separated	Special Effects	Special Effects Distortion
1991	nau1	Red	Yes - red indicates "bad" in finance	No	Yes	No	No
1991	nau1	Dark Green	No	No	Yes	No	No
1991	nau1	Light Blue	No	No	Yes	No	No
1991	nau1	Dark Green	No	No	Yes	No	No
1991	nau1	Light Blue	No	No	Yes	No	No
1992	nau2	LtOrange	No	No	Yes	Yes - bottom of bars are folded under and go to rear	Yes - horizontal lines appear to be toward back making it difficult to judge relative heights
1992	nau2	Purple	No	No	Yes	Yes - bottom of bars are folded under and go to rear	Yes - horizontal lines appear to be toward back making it difficult to judge relative heights
1992	nau2	Purple	No	No	Yes	Yes - bottom of bars are folded under and go to rear	Yes - horizontal lines appear to be toward back making it difficult to judge relative heights
1992	nau2	Red	Yes - red indicates "bad" in finance	No	Yes	Yes - bottom of bars are folded under and go to rear	Yes - horizontal lines appear to be toward back making it difficult to judge relative heights
1992	nau2	Red	Yes - red indicates "bad" in finance	No	Yes	Yes - bottom of bars are folded under and go to rear	Yes - horizontal lines appear to be toward back making it difficult to judge relative heights

EXHIBIT 23B.20 (Continued)

The word "Charts" in this table is limited to graphs that contain financial data.

Year	Code	Chart #	Section of Report	Page	Chart Title	Same Chart Last Year	Chart Type	Years	Numbers Shown	Scale Shown	Same Scale as Last Year	Scale Range (%)
1991	nai1	1	Financial Highlights	2	Sales	NA	VBar	5	No	Yes	NA	Millions
1991	nai1	2	Financial Highlights	2	Income	NA	VBar	5	No	Yes	NA	Millions
1991	nai1	3	Financial Highlights	2	Stockholders' Equity	NA	VBar	5	No	Yes	NA	Millions
1991	nai1	4	Financial Highlights	2	Dividends per share	NA	VBar	5	No	Yes	NA	Actual
1991	nai1	5	Chairman and President's Letter	4 Insert	Percent Share of 1991 Sales - Products	NA	Pie	NA	Yes	NA	NA	Percent(%)
1991	nai1	6	Chairman and President's Letter	4 Insert	Percent Share of 1991 Sales Domestic vs International	NA	Pie	NA	Yes	NA	NA	Percent(%)
1991	nai1	7	Chairman and President's Letter	4 Insert	Percent Share of 1991 Sales Equipment vs Supplies	NA	Pie	NA	Yes	NA	NA	Percent(%)
1992	nai2	1	Financial Highlights	1	Sales	No	VBar	5	Yes	No	No	Thousands
1992	nai2	2	Financial Highlights	1	Net Income	No	VBar	5	Yes	No	No	Thousands
1992	nai2	3	Financial Highlights	1	Stockholders' Equity	No	VBar	5	Yes	No	No	Thousands
1992	nai2	4	Financial Highlights	1	Dividends per share	No	VBar	5	Yes	No	No	Actual
1992	nai2	5	Chairman and President's Letter	2	Percent Share of 1992 Sales By Products	No	Pie	NA	Yes	NA	No	Percent(%)
1992	nai2	6	Chairman and President's Letter	5	Percent Share of 1992 Sales Domestic Vs International	No	Pie	NA	Yes	NA	No	Percent(%)
1992	nai2	7	Chairman and President's Letter	8	Percent Share of 1992 Sales Equipment Vs. Supplies	No	Pie	NA	Yes	NA	No	Percent(%)
1991	vco1		No charts were present in the 1991 report.									
1992	vco2	1	Operations Review									

There were three charts utilized. Since they did not contain financial data, they are not included. If they were considered, the charts included one pie chart with 15 segments in large to very small pieces and 15 colors covering the spectrum. The second pie chart included 6 segments with fairly well defined pieces and 6 bright colors. The third chart was a 12 year stacked bar chart with 13 segments and 13 colors, little if any information could be determined.

EXHIBIT 23B.20 (Continued)

The word "Charts" in this table is limited to graphs that contain financial data.

Year	Code	Color Legend	Does Color Distort	Borders Shown	Other Charts Separated	Special Effects	Special Effects Distortion
1991	nai1	Red	Yes - red indicates "bad" in finance	No	Yes	No	No
1991	nai1	Black	No	No	Yes	No	No
1991	nai1	Purple	No	No	Yes	No	No
1991	nai1	Red	Yes - red indicates "bad" in finance.	No	Yes	No	No
1991	nai1	Red, Gray, Black, Lilac, Purple	Yes - red indicates "bad" in finance.	No	Yes	No	Slight, too many pieces
1991	nai1	Red, Black	Yes - red indicates "bad" in finance.	No	Yes	No	No
1991	nai1	Red, Purple	Yes - red indicates "bad" in finance.	No	Yes	No	No
1992	nai2	Black on Green	No	Yes - Color background	Yes	No	No
1992	nai2	Black on Yellow	No	Yes - Color background	Yes	No	No
1992	nai2	Black on Purple	No	Yes - Color background	Yes	No	No
1992	nai2	Black on lime	No	Yes - Color background	Yes	No	No
1992	nai2	Blue/Gray, LtLime, DkLime, Violet, Gold, all with shading effect	Yes, hard to tell pieces, shading distorts with so many colors.	No	Yes	No	Slight, too many pieces
1992	nai2	DkGreen, LtLime	Slight, shading distorts the sizes, even with two pieces	No	Yes	No	No
1992	nai2	Lilac, Yellow	Slight, shading distorts the sizes, even with two pieces	No	Yes	No	No
1991	vco1						
1992	vco2						

EXHIBIT 23B.20 (Continued)

The word "Charts" in this table is limited to graphs that contain financial data.

Year	Code	Chart #	Section of Report	Page	Chart Title	Same Chart Last Year	Chart Type	Years	Numbers Shown	Scale Shown	Same Scale as Last Year	Scale Range (%)
1991	cam1	1	Management Discussion And Analysis - Financial Performance	13	1991 ... Sales by Market	NA	3DPie, Rotated	NA	Yes	NA	NA	Percent(%)
1991	cam1	2	Management Discussion And Analysis - Financial Performance	14	1991 ... Sales by Product	NA	3DPie, Rotated	NA	Yes	NA	NA	Percent(%)
1991	cam1	3	Management Discussion And Analysis - Financial Performance	14	1991 ... Gross Profit by Product	NA	3DPie, Rotated	NA	Yes	NA	NA	Percent(%)
1991	cam1	4	Management Discussion And Analysis - Financial Performance	16	Capital Expenditures And Cash From Operations	NA	3DVBar Cluster	5 actual 1 estimated	No	Yes	NA	Millions
1991	cam1	5	Management Discussion And Analysis - Financial Performance	17	Total Borrowings And Equity	NA	3DVBar Cluster	5	No	Yes	NA	Millions
1992	cam2	1	Financial Review	17	Total Borrowings And Equity	Different Colors	VBar Cluster	5 actual	No	Yes	Yes	Millions
1992	cam2	2	Financial Review	18	Capital Expenditures And Cash From Operations	Different Colors	VBar Cluster	5 actual 1 estimated	No	Yes	No	Millions

There are other similar non-financial charts in these annual reports

EXHIBIT 23B.20 (*Continued*)

The word "Charts" in this table is limited to graphs that contain financial data.

Year	Code	Color Legend	Does Color Distort	Borders Shown	Other Charts Separated	Special Effects	Special Effects Distortion
1991	cam1	Gold shaded	Cannot distinguish pieces	No	Yes	Yes - Pie is rotated	Yes, the lines separating the pieces are too light and the rotated position makes it almost impossible to get an impression of the data.
1991	cam1	Gold shaded	Cannot distinguish pieces	No	Yes	Yes - Pie is rotated	Yes, the lines separating the pieces are too light and the rotated position makes it almost impossible to get an impression of the data.
1991	cam1	Gold shaded	Cannot distinguish pieces	No	Yes	Yes - Pie is rotated.	Yes, the lines separating the pieces are too light and the rotated position makes it almost impossible to get an impression of the data.
1991	cam1	Dark blue, Light blue on gold	No	Yes - Color Background	Yes	Yes - slight 3D	Slight, the bars are so thin, the 3D skews the foreground.
1991	cam1	Dark blue, Light blue on gold	No	Yes - Color Background	Yes	Yes - slight 3D	Slight, the bars are so thin, the 3D skews the foreground.
1992	cam2	Dark purple, Light green on white with shading.	Slight, shading makes it appear 3D	Yes	Yes	No	No
1992	cam2	Dark purple, Light green on white with shading	Slight, shading makes it appear 3D	Yes	Yes	No	No

EXHIBIT 23B.20 (*Continued*)

The word "Charts" in this table is limited to graphs that contain financial data

Year	Code	Chart #	Section of Report	Page	Chart Title	Same Chart Last Year	Chart Type	Years	Numbers Shown	Scale Shown	Same Scale as Last Year	Scale Range (%)
1991	tle1	1	Highlights	2	Operating Earnings, Dollars per Common Share	NA	VBar	5	No	Yes	NA	Dollars per Common Share
1991	tle1	2	Highlights	2	Net Income, Dollars per Common Share	NA	VBar	5	No	Yes	NA	Dollars per Common Share
1991	tle1	3	Highlights	3	Dividends Declared, Dollars per Common Share	NA	VBar	5	No	Yes	NA	Dollars per Common Share
1991	tle1	4	Highlights	3	Shareholders' Equity, Dollars per Common Share	NA	VBar	5	No	Yes	NA	Dollars per Common Share
1991	tle1	5 - 14	Financial Reports	42 +	Invested Assets	NA	Pie	NA	Yes	NA	NA	Percent(%)

There are 9 other identical Pie charts showing different data in this section of the report.

Year	Code	Chart #	Section of Report	Page	Chart Title	Same Chart Last Year	Chart Type	Years	Numbers Shown	Scale Shown	Same Scale as Last Year	Scale Range (%)
1992	tle2	1	Highlights	2	Shareholders' Equity, Dollars per Common Share	Different Colors	VBar	5	No	Yes	No	Dollars per Common Share
1992	tle2	2	Highlights	2	Net Income, Dollars per Common Share	Different Colors	VBar	5	No	Yes	No	Dollars per Common Share
1992	tle2	3	Highlights	3	Dividends Declared, Dollars per Common Share	Different Colors	VBar	5	No	Yes	Yes	Dollars per Common Share
1992	tle2	4	Highlights	3	Operating Earnings, Dollars per Common Share	Different Colors	VBar	5	No	Yes	No	Dollars per Common Share
1992	tle2	5 - 14	Financial Reports	28 +	Invested Assets	Yes	Pie	NA	Yes	NA	NA	Percent(%)

There are 9 other identical Pie charts showing different data in this section of the report.

EXHIBIT 23B.20 (Continued)

The word "Charts" in this table is limited to graphs that contain financial data

Year	Code	Color Legend	Does Color Distort	Borders Shown	Other Charts Separated	Special Effects	Special Effects Distortion
1991	tle1	Red	Yes - red indicates "bad" in finance	No	Yes	No	No
1991	tle1	Red	Yes - red indicates "bad" in finance	No	Yes	No	No
1991	tle1	Red	Yes - red indicates "bad" in finance	No	Yes	No	No
1991	tle1	Red	Yes - red indicates "bad" in finance	No	Yes	No	No
1991	tle1	Light gray with thin white lines separating pieces	Slight, the contrast between pieces and lines is difficult to see	No	Yes	No	Yes, difficult to identify the pieces
1992	tle2	Black	No	No	Yes	No	No
1992	tle2	Black	No	No	Yes	No	No
1992	tle2	Black	No	No	Yes	No	No
1992	tle2	Black	No	No	Yes	No	No
1992	tle2	Light gray with thin white lines separating pieces	Slight, the contrast between pieces and lines is difficult to see	No	Yes	No	No

EXHIBIT 23B.20 (*Continued*)

The word "Charts" in this table is limited to graphs that contain financial data

Year	Code	Chart #	Section of Report	Page	Chart Title	Same Chart Last Year	Chart Type	Years	Numbers Shown	Scale Shown	Same Scale as Last Year	Scale Range (%)
1991	nal1	1	Financial Section	25	Consolidated revenues	NA	VBar	5	No	Yes	NA	Billions
1991	nal1	2	Financial Section	25	Earnings per share	NA	VBar Cluster	5	No	Yes	NA	Actual
1991	nal1	3	Financial Section	25	Dividends per share	NA	VBar	5	No	Yes	NA	Actual
1991	nal1	4	Management's Discussion of Consolidated and 's Operations	32	Consolidated earnings	NA	VBar Cluster	5	No	Yes	NA	Billions
1991	nal1	5	Management's Discussion of Consolidated and 's Operations	33	/S&P dividends per share increase compared with 1986	NA	VBar Cluster	5	No	Yes	NA	Percent(%)
1991	nal1	6	Summary of Industry Segments	36	's revenues	NA	VBar-Stacked	5	No	Yes	NA	Billions
1991	nal1	7	Summary of Industry Segments	36	's international revenues	NA	VBar-Stacked	5	No	Yes	NA	Billions
1991	nal1	8	Management's Discussion of 's (subsidiary) Operations	37	's (subsidiary) revenues	NA	VBar	5	No	Yes	NA	Billions
1991	nal1	9	Management's Discussion of Financial Resources and Liquidity	39	Consolidated total assets	NA	VBar	5	No	Yes	NA	Billions
1991	nal1	10	Management's Discussion of Financial Resources and Liquidity	40	's property, plant and equipment expenditures	NA	VBar	5	No	Yes	NA	Billions
1991	nal1	11	Management's Discussion of Financial Resources and Liquidity	41	Total assets of 's (subsidiary)	NA	VBar	5	No	Yes	NA	Billions
1992	nal2	1	Financial Section	25	Revenues	No	VBar-Stacked	5	No	Yes	No	Billions
1992	nal2	2	Financial Section	25	Earnings per share before accounting change	No	VBar-Stacked	5	No	Yes	No	Actual
1992	nal2	3	Financial Section	25	Dividends per share	Different Colors	VBar	5	No	Yes	Yes	Actual
1992	nal2	4	Management's Discussion of Operations	32	Earnings before accounting change	No	VBar-Stacked	5	No	Yes	Yes	Billions
1992	nal2	5	Management's Discussion of Operations	33	/S&P dividends per share increase compared with 1987	Different Colors	VBar Cluster	5	No	Yes	Yes	Percent(%)
1992	nal2	6	Summary of Industry Segments	36	's revenues from continuing operations	Different Colors	VBar-Stacked	5	No	Yes	No	Billions
1992	nal2	7	Summary of Industry Segments	36	's international revenues from continuing operations	Different Colors	VBar-Stacked	5	No	Yes	No	Billions
1992	nal2	8	Summary of Industry Segments	37	's (subsidiary) revenues	No	VBar	5	No	Yes	NA	Billions
1992	nal2	9	Management's Discussion of Financial Resources and Liquidity	39	Consolidated total assets	Different Colors	VBar	5	No	Yes	No	Billions
1992	nal2	10	Management's Discussion of Financial Resources and Liquidity	40	's borrowings as a percent of total capital invested	No	VBar	5	No	Yes	No	Percent(%)
1992	nal2	11	Management's Discussion of Financial Resources and Liquidity	41	Total assets of 's (subsidiary)	No	VBar	5	No	Yes	No	Billions

There are other similar non-financial charts in these annual reports

EXHIBIT 23B.20 (Continued)

The word "Charts" in this table is limited to graphs that contain financial data

Year	Code	Color Legend	Does Color Distort	Borders Shown	Other Charts Separated	Special Effects	Special Effects Distortion
1991	nal1	Bright orange	No	No	Yes	No	No
1991	nal1	LtGreen Green - Unadjusted	No	No	Yes	No	No
1991	nal1	DkBlue Blue - Net					
1991	nal1	Red	Yes - red indicates "bad" in finance	No	Yes	No	No
1991	nal1	DkBlue - Unadjusted	Slight, - hue combo blurs	No	Yes	No	No
1991	nal1	Orange - Net					
1991	nal1	Orange -	Yes - red indicates "bad" in finance, red draws eye	No	Yes	No	Slight, the stacked bar format does not permit comparison of same segment from year to year but two segments can work
1991	nal1	Red - S&P 500	No	No	Yes	No	Yes, the stacked bar format does not permit comparison of same segment from year to year with four segments
1991	nal1	Gray - International					
1991	nal1	Blue - United States					
1991	nal1	Purple - Other	Yes - red indicates Red on bottom with green above is difficult to view	No	Yes	No	No
1991	nal1	Orange - Americas					
1991	nal1	Green - Pacific Basin					
1991	nal1	Red - Europe					
1991	nal1	Green	No	No	Yes	No	No
1991	nal1	Blue	No	No	Yes	No	No
1991	nal1	Red	Yes - red indicates "bad" in finance	No	Yes	No	No
1991	nal1	Aqua	No	No	Yes	No	No
1992	nal2	LtOrange - Discontinued Operations	No	No	Yes	No	Slight, the stacked bar format does not permit comparison of same segment from year to year but two segments can work
1992	nal2	Orange - Continuing operations	No	No	Yes	No	Slight, the stacked bar format does not permit comparison of same segment from year to year but two segments can work
1992	nal2	LtPurple - Discontinued Operations	No	No	Yes	No	Slight, the stacked bar format does not permit comparison of same segment from year to year but two segments can work
1992	nal2	Purple - Continuing operations					No
1992	nal2	Green	No	No	Yes	No	Slight, the stacked bar format does not permit comparison of same segment from year to year but two segments can work
1992	nal2	LtPlum - Discontinued Operations	No	No	Yes	No	Slight, the stacked bar format does not permit comparison of same segment from year to year but two segments can work
1992	nal2	Plum - Continuing operations					No
1992	nal2	Green - 's	No	No	Yes	No	Slight, the stacked bar format does not permit comparison of same segment from year to year but two segments can work
1992	nal2	Blue - S&P 500	No	No	Yes	No	Yes, the stacked bar format does not permit comparison of same segment from year to year with four segments
1992	nal2	LtOrange - Discontinued Operations	Yes - red indicates Red on finance top draws eye	No	Yes	No	No
1992	nal2	Orange - Continuing operations					
1992	nal2	Red - Other					
1992	nal2	Plum - Americas					
1992	nal2	Blue - Pacific Basin					
1992	nal2	Green - Europe					
1992	nal2	Green	No	No	Yes	No	No
1992	nal2	Red	Yes - red indicates "bad" in finance	No	Yes	No	No
1992	nal2	Plum	No	No	Yes	No	No
1992	nal2	Red	Yes - red indicates "bad" in finance	No	Yes	No	No

EXHIBIT 23B.20 (Continued)

The word "Charts" in this table is limited to graphs that contain financial data

Year	Code	Chart #	Section of Report	Page	Chart Title	Same Chart Last Year	Chart Type	Years	Numbers Shown	Scale Shown	Same Scale as Last Year	Scale Range (%)
1991	sta1	1	Management's Discussion And Analysis	43	Average Earning Assets	NA	VBar-Stacked	3	No, total only	No	NA	Millions
1991	sta1	2	Management's Discussion And Analysis	43	Funding of Average Earning Assets	NA	VBar-Stacked	3	No, total only	No	NA	Millions
1991	sta1	3	Management's Discussion And Analysis	49	Allowances for Loan Losses vs Net Charge-Offs	NA	VBar-Stacked	5	Yes	No	NA	Percent(%)
1991	sta1	4	Management's Discussion And Analysis	49	Loan Loss Experience vs Provision for Loan Losses	NA	VBar Cluster	5	Yes	No	NA	Millions
1991	sta1	5	Management's Discussion And Analysis	49	Average Investment Securities	NA	VBar-Stacked	5	Yes	No	NA	Millions
1991	sta1	6	Management's Discussion And Analysis	50	Composition of Average Deposits	NA	VBar-Stacked	3	No, total only	No	NA	Millions
1991	sta1	7	Management's Discussion And Analysis	52	Average Shareholders' Equity	NA	VBar	5	Yes	No	NA	Millions
1991	sta1	8	Management's Discussion And Analysis	53	Noninterest Revenues 1991	NA	Pie	NA	Yes	NA	NA	Percent(%)
1991	sta1	9	Management's Discussion And Analysis	53	Noninterest Expenses 1991	NA	Pie	NA	Yes	NA	NA	Percent(%)

EXHIBIT 23B.20 (Continued)

The word "Charts" in this table is limited to graphs that contain financial data.

Year	Code	Color Legend	Does Color Distort	Borders Shown	Other Charts Separated	Special Effects	Special Effects Distortion
1991	sta1	Black outlines with black lines to indicate stacked portions.	There is no color. The way the lines are drawn, the information is difficult to determine.	No	Yes	No	No
1991	sta1	Black outlines with black lines to indicate stacked portions.	There is no color. The way the lines are drawn, the information is difficult to determine.	No	Yes	No	No
1991	sta1	Black outlines with black lines to indicate stacked portions.	There is no color. With only two stacks, the information is not quite so difficult to determine.	No	Yes	No	No
1991	sta1	Black outlines with black lines at top with different widths to indicate different data types.	There is no color or shading to differentiate between the data, difficult to view information.	No	Yes	No	No
1991	sta1	Black outlines with black lines to indicate stacked portions.	There is no color. With only two stacks, the information is not quite so difficult to determine.	No	Yes	No	No
1991	sta1	Black outlines with black lines to indicate stacked portions.	There is no color. The way the lines are drawn, the information is difficult to determine for five stacks.	No	Yes	No	The way the stacked bars are drawn, it is almost impossible to compare the various stacks by year.
1991	sta1	Black outlines with heavy black to indicate top.	No	No	Yes	No	No
1991	sta1	Black outlines with thin black to indicate portions.	No	No	Yes	No	No
1991	sta1	Black outlines with thin black to indicate portions.	No	No	Yes	No	No

EXHIBIT 23B.20 (Continued)

The word "Charts" in this table is limited to graphs that contain financial data

Year	Code	Chart #	Section of Report	Page	Chart Title	Same Chart Last Year	Chart Type	Years	Numbers Shown	Scale Shown	Same Scale as Last Year	Scale Range (%)
1992	sta2	1	Management's Discussion And Analysis	56	Average Earning Assets	Different Colors	VBar-Stacked	3	No, total only	No	No	Millions
1992	sta2	2	Management's Discussion And Analysis	56	Funding of Average Earning Assets	Different Colors	VBar-Stacked	3	No, total only	No	No	Millions
1992	sta2	3	Management's Discussion And Analysis	62	Allowances for Loan Losses vs Net Charge-Offs	Different Colors	VBar-Stacked	5	Yes	No	No	Percent(%)
1992	sta2	4	Management's Discussion And Analysis	62	Loan Loss Experience vs Provision for Loan Losses	Different Colors	VBar Cluster	5	Yes	No	No	Millions
1992	sta2	5	Management's Discussion And Analysis	62	Average Investment Securities	Different Colors	VBar-Stacked	5	Yes	No	No	Millions
1992	sta2	6	Management's Discussion And Analysis	63	Composition of Average Deposits	Different Colors / NA	VBar-Stacked	3	No, total only	No	No	Millions
1992	sta2	7	Management's Discussion And Analysis	65	Average Shareholders' Equity	Different Colors	VBar	5	Yes	No	No	Millions
1992	sta2	8	Management's Discussion And Analysis	66	Noninterest Revenues 1992	No	3D Pie	NA	Yes	NA	NA	Percent(%)
1992	sta2	9	Management's Discussion And Analysis	66	Noninterest Expenses 1992	No	3D Pie	NA	Yes	NA	NA	Percent(%)

EXHIBIT 23B.20 (*Continued*)

The word "Charts" in this table is limited to graphs that contain financial data

Year	Code	Color Legend	Does Color Distort	Borders Shown	Other Charts Separated	Special Effects	Special Effects Distortion
1992	sta2	Green - Loans / LtOrange - Investment Securities / Yellow - Other / DkBlue Background	No	Yes, Background	Yes	No	No
1992	sta2	Turquoise - Noninterest-Bearing Sources / LtBlue - Interest Bearing Deposits / Green - Federal Funds Purchased & Repurch. / Pink - Other. DkBlue Background	Slightly, the colors are so similar it is hard to distinguish. Pink is in the Red family and indicates "bad."	Yes, Background	Yes	No	No
1992	sta2	Green - Allowance / Loans / Pink - Net Charge-Offs/Average Loans / DkBlue Background	Yes - red/pink indicates "bad" in finance.	Yes, Background	Yes	No	No
1992	sta2	Blue - Provision Loan Losses / Pink - Net Charge-Offs / DkBlue Background	Yes - red/pink indicates "bad" in finance. No consistent use of colors to indicate "good/bad"	Yes, Background	Yes	No	No
1992	sta2	Pink - Taxable / Blue - Tax Free / DkBlue Background	Yes - red/pink indicates "bad" in finance. No consistent use of colors to indicate "good/bad"	Yes, Background	Yes	No	No
1992	sta2	Turquoise - Noninterest-Bearng Deposits / Blue - Interest Bearing Demand / Yellow - Savings / Lime - Time / Pink - CD's $100M or More / DkBlue Background	Yes - red/pink indicates "bad" in finance. No consistent use of colors to indicate "good/bad"	Yes, Background	Yes	No	The way the stacked bars are colored, it is almost impossible to compare the various stacks by year
1992	sta2	Green / DkBlue Background	No	Yes, Background	Yes	No	No
1992	sta2	Green - Service Charges / Yellow - Trust Department / Red - Mortgage Administration / Turquoise - Other, Purple Background	Yes - red/pink indicates "bad" in finance. No consistent use of colors to indicate "good/bad"	Yes, Background	Yes	Yes - Pie is tilted	Yes - cannot compare size of pieces because of color and tilt
1992	sta2	Turquoise - Equipment / Green - Net Occupancy / Yellow - Foreclosed Properties / Pink - Other / Red - Salaries and Employee Benefits. Purple Background	Yes - red/pink indicates "bad" in finance. No consistent use of colors to indicate "good/bad"	Yes, Background	Yes	Yes - Pie is tilted	Yes - cannot compare size of pieces because of color and tilt

EXHIBIT 23B.20 (Continued)

The word "Charts" in this table is limited to graphs that contain financial data

Year	Code	Chart #	Section of Report	Page	Chart Title	Same Chart Last Year	Chart Type	Years	Numbers Shown	Scale Shown	Same Scale as Last Year	Scale Range (%)
1991	oru1	1	Financial Highlights	1	Net Sales	NA	HBar	5	No	Yes	NA	Billions
1991	oru1	2	Financial Highlights	1	Income from Continuing Operations	NA	HBar	5	No	Yes	NA	Billions
1991	oru1	3	Chairman's Letter	2	Income per Share from Continuing Operations Assuming Full Dilution	NA	HBar	5	No	Yes	NA	Actual
1991	oru1	4	Chairman's Letter	2	Total Debt	NA	HBar	5	No	Yes	NA	Billions
1991	oru1	5	Review of Operations	4	Cash Flow from Continuing Operations	NA	HBar	5	No	Yes	NA	Millions
1991	oru1	6	Review of Operations	5	Net Sales International	NA	HBar	5	No	Yes	NA	Billions
1991	oru1	7	Review of Operations	5	Pretax Income International	NA	HBar	5	No	Yes	NA	Millions
1991	oru1	8	Review of Operations	6	Net Inventory International	NA	HBar	5	No	Yes	NA	Millions
1991	oru1	9	Review of Operations	8	Net Sales US	NA	HBar	5	No	Yes	NA	Billions
1991	oru1	10	Review of Operations	9	Pretax Income US	NA	HBar	5	No	Yes	NA	Millions
1991	oru1	11	Review of Operations	6	Net Inventory US	NA	HBar	5	No	Yes	NA	Millions
1992	oru2	1	Financial Highlights	Inside Front	Net Sales	No	VBar	5	No	Yes	No	Billions
1992	oru2	2	Financial Highlights	Inside Front	Income per Share from Continuing Operations Assuming Full Dilution	No	VBar, with partial stack	5	No	Yes	No	Actual
1992	oru2	3	Financial Highlights	1	Cash Flow from Continuing Operations	No	VBar	5	No	Yes	No	Millions
1992	oru2	4	Financial Highlights	1	Total Debt	No	VBar	5	No	Yes	No	Millions
1992	oru2	6	Financial Highlights	1	Dividends per Share	No	VBar with partial stack	5	No	Yes	No	Actual
1992	oru2	7	Financial Section	13	Net Sales Direct Selling 1992	No	Pie	NA	Yes	NA	NA	Percent(%)
1992	oru2	8	Financial Section	13	Pretax Income Direct Selling 1992	No	Pie	NA	Yes	NA	NA	Percent(%)
1992	oru2	9	Financial Highlights	13	Effective Tax Rate	No	VBar, with partial stack	5	No	Broken Scale	No	Percent(%)
1992	oru2	10	Financial Highlights	13	Net Inventory	No	VBar	5	No	Broken Scale	No	Millions
1992	oru2	11	Financial Highlights	13	Net Sales Direct Selling	No	VBar	5	No	Yes	No	Billions
1992	oru2	12	Financial Highlights	13	Pretax Income Direct Selling	No	VBar, with partial stack	5	No	Broken Scale	No	Actual

There are other similar non-financial charts in these annual reports

EXHIBIT 23B.20 (Continued)

The word "Charts" in this table is limited to graphs that contain financial data.

Year	Code	Color Legend	Does Color Distort	Borders Shown	Other Charts Separated	Special Effects	Special Effects Distortion
1991	oru1	Light Gray on the tan paper	No	Yes	Yes	No	No
1991	oru1	Light Gray on the tan paper	No	Yes	Yes	No	No
1991	oru1	Light Gray on the tan paper	No	Yes	Yes	No	No
1991	oru1	Light Gray on the tan paper	No	Yes	Yes	No	No
1991	oru1	White on Eggplant background, set inside green paper.	No	Yes	Yes	No	No
1991	oru1	White on Eggplant background, set inside green paper.	No	Yes	Yes	No	No
1991	oru1	White on Eggplant background, set inside green paper.	No	Yes	Yes	No	No
1991	oru1	White on Eggplant background, set inside green paper.	No	Yes	Yes	No	No
1991	oru1	White on Eggplant background, set inside green paper.	No	Yes	Yes	No	No
1991	oru1	White on Eggplant background, set inside green paper.	No	Yes	Yes	No	No
1992	oru2	Light and Dark Rose sides, Gray Top	Slight - red/pink indicates "bad" in finance	No	Yes	3D triangle with points down	Yes - difficult to judge volume, points move eyes down.
1992	oru2	Light and Dark Blue sides, Gray top. shaded stack	No	No	Yes	3D triangle with points down	Yes - difficult to judge volume, points move eyes down. Stacked is not useful.
1992	oru2	Light and Dark Purple sides, Gray Top	Slight	No	Yes	3D triangle with points down	Yes - difficult to judge volume, points move eyes down.
1992	oru2	Light and Dark Plum sides, Gray Top	Slight	No	Yes	3D triangle with points down	Yes - difficult to judge volume, points move eyes down.
1992	oru2	Light and Dark Purple sides, Gray top, shaded stack.	Slight	No	Yes	3D triangle with points down	Yes - difficult to judge volume, points move eyes down. Stacked is not useful.
1992	oru2	Dark, Medium Dark, Medium, Light Plum	Slight	No	Yes	Pie with segments separated by spaces	Slight
1992	oru2	Dark, Medium Dark, Medium, Light Plum	Slight	No	Yes	Pie with segments separated by spaces	Slight
1992	oru2	Light and Dark Blue sides, Gray Top. shaded stack	Slight	No	Yes	3D triangle with points down	Yes - difficult to judge volume, points move eyes down. Stacked is not useful. Split scale prevents use
1992	oru2	Light and Dark Purple sides, Gray Top	Slight	No	Yes	3D triangle with points down	Yes - difficult to judge volume, points move eyes down. Split scale prevents use
1992	oru2	Light and Dark Rose sides, Gray Top	Slight	No	Yes	3D triangle with points down	Yes - difficult to judge volume, points move eyes down.
1992	oru2	Light and Dark Blue sides, Gray top. shaded stack	Slight	No	Yes	3D triangle with points down	Yes - difficult to judge volume, points move eyes down. Stacked is not useful. Split scale prevents use

EXHIBIT 23B.20 (Continued)

The word "Charts" in this table is limited to graphs that contain financial data

Year	Code	Chart #	Section of Report	Page	Chart Title	Same Chart Last Year	Chart Type	Years	Numbers Shown	Scale Shown	Same Scale as Last Year	Scale Range (%)
1991	hrc1	1	Annual Report of the Board of Directors 1991	6	Distribution of net sales	NA	Pie	NA	Yes	NA	NA	Percent(%)
1991	hrc1	2	Annual Report of the Board of Directors 1991	6	Net sales	NA	VBar	5	No	Yes	NA	Millions
1991	hrc1	3	Annual Report of the Board of Directors 1991	6	Regional distribution of net sales	NA	Pie	NA	Yes	NA	NA	Percent(%)
1991	hrc1	4	Annual Report of the Board of Directors 1991	7	Net income	NA	VBar	5	No	Yes	NA	Millions
1991	hrc1	5	Annual Report of the Board of Directors 1991	7	Net debt as a percentage of net sales	NA	VBar	5	No	Yes	NA	Percent(%)
1991	hrc1	6	Annual Report of the Board of Directors 1991	7	Liabilities and shareholders' equity	NA	VBar-Stacked	5	No	Yes	NA	Millions
1991	hrc1	7	Annual Report of the Board of Directors 1991	8	Capital expenditures and acquisitions	NA	VBar	5	No	Yes	NA	Million
1991	hrc1	8	Financial Statements	27	Earnings per share	NA	VBar	5	No	Yes	NA	Actual
1991	hrc1	9	Financial Statements	27	Dividend per share	NA	VBar	5	No	Yes	NA	Actual
1991	hrc1	10	Financial Statements	27	Equity per share	NA	VBar	5	No	Yes	NA	Actual
1991	hrc1	11	General Products	39	Glassfibre products, Net sales	NA	VBar	5	No	Yes	NA	Actual
1991	hrc1	12	General Products	39	Flexible packagings and consumer goods, Net sales	NA	VBar	5	No	Yes	NA	Actual
1991	hrc1	11	General Products	41	Cores and board, Net sales	NA	VBar	5	No	Yes	NA	Actual
1991	hrc1	12	General Products	41	Insulation products, Net sales	NA	VBar	5	No	Yes	NA	Actual
1991	hrc1	13	General Products	41	Glass and plastic containers, Net sales	NA	VBar	5	No	Yes	NA	Actual
1991	hrc1	14	General Products	41	Electrical accessories, Net sales	NA	VBar	5	No	Yes	NA	Actual
1992	hrc2	1	Annual Report of the Board of Directors 1992	9	Net sales	Yes - Thin Bars	VBar	5	No	Yes	No	Millions
1992	hrc2	2	Annual Report of the Board of Directors 1992	9	Net income	Yes - Thin Bars	VBar	5	No	Yes	Yes	Millions
1992	hrc2	3	Annual Report of the Board of Directors 1992	9	Distribution of net sales	Yes - Color	Pie	NA	Yes	NA	NA	Percent(%)
1992	hrc2	4	Annual Report of the Board of Directors 1992	9	Net debt as a percentage of net sales	Yes - Thin Bars	VBar	5	No	Yes	Yes	Millions
1992	hrc2	5	Annual Report of the Board of Directors 1992	9	Liabilities and shareholders' equity	Yes - Thin Bars	VBar-Stacked	5	No	Yes	Yes	Millions
1992	hrc2	6	Annual Report of the Board of Directors 1991	9	Regional distribution of net sales	Yes - Color	Pie	NA	Yes	NA	NA	Percent(%)
1992	hrc2	7	Annual Report of the Board of Directors 1992	11	Capital expenditures and acquisitions	Yes - Thin Bars	VBar	5	No	Yes	Yes	Millions
1992	hrc2	8	Financial Statements	28	Earnings per share	Yes - Thin Bars	VBar	5	No	Yes	Yes	Actual
1992	hrc2	9	Financial Statements	28	Dividend per share	Yes - Thin Bars	VBar	5	No	Yes	Yes	Actual
1992	hrc2	10	Financial Statements	28	Equity per share	Yes - Thin Bars	VBar	5	No	Yes	Yes	Actual
1992	hrc2	11	General Products	42	Glassfibre products, Net sales	Yes - Thin Bars	VBar	5	No	Yes	Yes	Actual
1992	hrc2	12	General Products	42	Flexible packagings and consumer goods, Net sales	Yes - Thin Bars	VBar	5	No	Yes	No	Actual
1992	hrc2	13	General Products	42	Cores and board, Net sales	Yes - Thin Bars	VBar	5	No	Yes	No	Actual
1992	hrc2	14	General Products	42	Insulation products, Net sales	Yes - Thin Bars	VBar	5	No	Yes	No	Actual
1992	hrc2	15	General Products	42	Glass and plastic containers, Net sales	Yes - Thin Bars	VBar	5	No	Yes	No	Actual
1992	hrc2	16	General Products	42	Electrical accessories, Net sales	Yes - Thin Bars	VBar	5	No	Yes	No	Actual

There are other similar non-financial charts in these annual reports

EXHIBIT 23B.20 (Continued)

The word "Charts" in this table is limited to graphs that contain financial data

Year	Code		Color Legend	Does Color Distort	Borders Shown	Other Charts Separated	Special Effects	Special Effects Distortion
1991	hrc1		Dark blue, gray, light blue, light gray, gray	No	No	Yes	No	No
1991	hrc1		Dark blue	No	No	Yes	No	No
1991	hrc1		Dark blue, gray, aqua, white, light blue, white, gray	No	No	Yes	No	Too many pieces of pie to be useful
1991	hrc1		Dark blue	No	No	Yes	No	No
1991	hrc1		Dark blue	No	No	Yes	No	No
1991	hrc1		Dark, medium, light blue	No	No	Yes	No	Slight, the stacked bar format does not permit comparison of same segment from year to year with three or more segments
1991	hrc1		Dark blue	No	No	Yes	No	No
1991	hrc1		Dark blue	No	No	Yes	No	No
1991	hrc1		Dark blue	No	No	Yes	No	No
1991	hrc1		Dark blue	No	No	Yes	No	No
1991	hrc1		Dark blue	No	No	Yes	No	No
1991	hrc1		Dark blue	No	No	Yes	No	No
1991	hrc1		Dark blue	No	No	Yes	No	No
1991	hrc1		Dark blue	No	No	Yes	No	No
1991	hrc1		Dark blue	No	No	Yes	No	No
1991	hrc1		Dark blue	No	No	Yes	No	No
1992	hrc2		Dark blue	No	No	Yes	No	No
1992	hrc2		Dark blue	No	No	Yes	No	No
1992	hrc2		Red, plum, blue, gold, yellow	Yes - red indicates "bad" in finance	No	Yes	No	Pieces too small to compare
1992	hrc2		Dark blue	No	No	Yes	No	No
1992	hrc2		Dark blue, orange, LtPurple, red, yellow, LtBlue	Yes - red indicates "bad" in finance	No	Yes	No	Slight, the stacked bar format does not permit comparison of same segment from year to year with three or more segments. Pieces too small to compare
1992	hrc2		Blue, orange, LtPurple, red, yellow, LtBlue	Yes - red indicates "bad" in finance	No	Yes	No	
1992	hrc2		Dark blue	No	No	Yes	No	No
1992	hrc2		Dark blue	No	No	Yes	No	No
1992	hrc2		Dark blue	No	No	Yes	No	No
1992	hrc2		Dark blue	No	No	Yes	No	No
1992	hrc2		Dark blue	No	No	Yes	No	No
1992	hrc2		Dark blue	No	No	Yes	No	No
1992	hrc2		Dark blue	No	No	Yes	No	No
1992	hrc2		Dark blue	No	No	Yes	No	No
1992	hrc2		Dark blue	No	No	Yes	No	No

EXHIBIT 23B.20 (*Continued*)

The word "Charts" in this table is limited to graphs that contain financial data.

Year	Code	Chart #	Section of Report	Page	Chart Title	Same Chart Last Year	Chart Type	Years	Numbers Shown	Scale Shown	Same Scale as Last Year	Scale Range (%)
1991	coa1	1	Financial Highlights	3	Sales	NA	VBar	3	Yes, overlaid & exaggerated	Yes	NA	Millions
1991	coa1	2	Financial Highlights	3	Trading Profit	NA	VBar	3	Yes, overlaid & exaggerated	Yes	NA	Millions
1992	coa2	1	Highlights	3	Beverages Sales Revenues	No	3DVBar Raised with shadow	5	No	Yes	No	Millions
1992	coa2	2	Highlights	3	Beverages Trading Profit	No	3DVBar Raised with shadow	5	No	Yes	No	Millions

There are other similar non-financial charts in these annual reports

EXHIBIT 23B.20 (*Continued*)

The word "Charts" in this table is limited to graphs that contain financial data.

Year	Code	Color Legend	Does Color Distort	Borders Shown	Other Charts Separated	Special Effects	Special Effects Distortion
1991	coa1	Two years dark blue, final year red. Gold letter over bars	Yes - red indicates "bad" in finance	Yes	Yes	Yes. Gold Numbers are laid on top of chart over bars and Year at bottom over bars. Gold matches gold shading on accompanying table	Yes, the size of the gold lettering negates the usefulness of the chart. When combined with the red bar, the chart gives mixed messages
1991	coa1	Two years dark blue, final year red.	Yes - red indicates "bad" in finance	Yes	Yes	Yes. Gold Numbers are laid on top of chart over bars and Year at bottom over bars. Gold matches gold shading on accompanying table	Yes, the size of the gold lettering negates the usefulness of the chart. When combined with the red bar, the chart gives mixed messages.
1992	coa2	Four years yellow, final year red, with shadowing makes sides darker.	Yes - red indicates "bad" in finance. Shadows push bars above scale.	No	Yes	Yes, 3D Bars, with shadows, pushed above the scale.	Yes, 3D pushes bars above the scales, makes it difficult to see comparative values
1992	coa2	Four years yellow, final year red, with shadowing makes sides darker.	Yes - red indicates "bad" in finance. Shadows push bars above scale	No	Yes		Yes, 3D pushes bars above the scales, makes it difficult to see comparative values

EXHIBIT 23B.20 (*Continued*)

The word "Charts" in this table is limited to graphs that contain financial data

Year	Code	Chart #	Section of Report	Page	Chart Title	Same Chart Last Year	Chart Type	Years	Numbers Shown	Scale Shown	Same Scale as Last Year	Scale Range (%)
			1991 not provided									
1992	ran2	1	Report from Management	2	Gross Revenue	NA	VBar-Stacked	5	No	Yes	NA	Millions
1992	ran2	2	Report from Management	3	Noninterest Expenses	NA	VBar-Stacked	5	No	Yes	NA	Millions
1992	ran2	3	Report from Management	4	Return on Assets & Stockholder's Equity	NA	Line w/2 scales	5	No	Yes, left & right	NA	Percent(%)
1992	ran2	4	Report from Management	4	Noninterest Expenses and Income	NA	Line and VBar - Stacked w/2 scales	5	No	Yes, left & right	NA	Millions - left Percent(%) - right

EXHIBIT 23B.20 (*Continued*)

The word "Charts" in this table is limited to graphs that contain financial data.

Year	Code	Color Legend	Does Color Distort	Borders Shown	Other Charts Separated	Special Effects	Special Effects Distortion
1992	rsn2	Plum - Net interest income Blue - Trust and investment management fees Green - Trading account and foreign exchange Red - Charge card Yellow - Service fees and charges Purple - Other operating income	Yes - red indicates "bad" in finance Too many colors makes it difficult to get information and compare performance by year	Yes	Yes	No	No
1992	rsn2	Blue - Employment Green - Net occupancy Red - Equipment Yellow - Other	Yes - red indicates "bad" in finance Too many colors makes it difficult to get information and compare performance by year	Yes	Yes	No	No
1992	rsn2	Blue - Return on average equity Red - Return on average assets	Yes - red indicates "bad" in finance	Yes	Yes	Yes - two scales	Yes - two scales makes it extremely difficult to compare the information in terms of the numbers. The use of red distorts importance of information
1992	rsn2	Purple - Noninterest expenses to gross revenues Blue - Noninterest income to gross revenues Green - Net interest income Red - Noninterest income	Yes - red indicates "bad" in finance Placing green and red together makes it difficult to determine values	Yes	Yes	Yes - two scales with lines over stacked bars	Yes - two scales makes it extremely difficult to compare the information in terms of the numbers. The use of red with green distorts importance of information. The use of lines over stacked bars prevents all but the most persistent viewer from obtaining the information hidden by the format and colors

EXHIBIT 23B.20 (Continued)

The word "Charts" in this table is limited to graphs that contain financial data.

Year	Code	Chart #	Section of Report	Page	Chart Title	Same Chart Last Year	Chart Type	Years	Numbers Shown	Scale Shown	Same Scale as Last Year	Scale Range (%)
			1991 contained no charts.									
1992	mae2	1	Highlights of 1992	4	Revenues	NA	VBar in shape of thin triangle	3	Yes	No	NA	Millions
1992	mae2	2	Highlights of 1992	4	EBITDA	NA	VBar in shape of thin triangle	3	Yes	No	NA	Millions
1992	mae2	3	Highlights of 1992	5	Net Income (Loss)	NA	VBar in shape of thin triangle	3	No	Yes	NA	Millions
1992	mae2	4	1992 Operations Report	25	1992 Revenues by Business Segment	NA	Pie	NA	Yes, including total revenue	NA	NA	Percent(%)
1992	mae2	5	1992 Operations Report	25	1992 EBITDA by Business Segment	NA	Pie	NA	Yes, including total EBITDA	NA	NA	Percent(%)

EXHIBIT 23B.20 (*Continued*)

The word "Charts" in this table is limited to graphs that contain financial data.

Year	Code	Color Legend	Does Color Distort	Borders Shown	Other Charts Separated	Special Effects	Special Effects Distortion
1992	mae2	Two years yellow, final year black.	Slight, the contrast of black to yellow on a white background reduces importance of first two years	No	No - the color selection and placement make separation difficult.	Yes - use of thin triangle with point at top	Yes, pointed triangle exaggerates the eye movement upward
1992	mae2	Two years yellow, final year black.	Slight, the contrast of black to yellow on a white background reduces importance of first two years	No	No - the color selection and placement make separation difficult.	Yes - use of thin triangle with point at top	Yes, pointed triangle exaggerates the eye movement upward
1992	mae2	Two years yellow, final year black.	Slight, the contrast of black to yellow on a white background reduces importance of first two years	No	No - the color selection and placement make separation difficult.	Yes - use of thin triangle with point at top	Yes, pointed triangle exaggerates the eye movement up or down, depending on whether there was a profit or loss
1992	mae2	Blue with pieces of pie separated by light dotted lines	Slight - dotted lines are so light, it is difficult to distinguish between the pieces	No	No - the color selection and placement make separation difficult	No	No
1992	mae2	Blue with pieces of pie separated by light dotted lines	Slight - dotted lines are so light, it is difficult to distinguish between the pieces	No	No - the color selection and placement make separation difficult	No	No

EXHIBIT 23B.20 (Continued)

The word "Charts" in this table is limited to graphs that contain financial data

Year	Code	Section of Report	Page	Chart #	Chart Title	Same Chart Last Year	Chart Type	Years	Numbers Shown	Scale Shown	Same Scale as Last Year	Scale Range (%)
1991	ikn1	Key figures	8	1	Dividend per share	NA	Surface with years separated	10	Last number	Yes	NA	Actual
1991	ikn1	Key figures	8	2	Sales proceeds beer and net turnover	NA	Two surfaces, years separated	5	Last numbers	Yes	NA	Milliards
1991	ikn1	Key figures	8	3	Trading profit	NA	Surface with years separated	10	Last number	Yes	NA	Millions
1991	ikn1	Key figures	8	4	Net profit	NA	Surface with years separated	10	Last number	Yes	NA	Millions
1991	ikn1	Key figures	10	5	Net profit in percentage of shareholders' equity	NA	Surface with years separated	10	Last number	Yes - but is broken	NA	Percent(%)
1991	ikn1	Key figures	10	6	Trading profit in percentage of total capital employed	NA	Surface with years separated	10	Last number	Yes - but is broken	NA	Percent(%)
1991	ikn1	Report of the Executive Board	15	7	Costs and profit excluding extraordinary income as percentage of the net turnover	NA	Pie drawn as a hexagon	NA	Yes	NA	NA	Percent(%)
1991	ikn1	Report of the Executive Board	16	8	Interest cover	NA	Surface with years separated	5	Last number	Yes	NA	Actual
1991	ikn1	Report of the Executive Board	17	9	Investments and depreciation tangible fixed assets	NA	Two surfaces, years separated	5	Last numbers	Yes	NA	Millions
1991	ikn1	Report of the Executive Board	18	10	Group cash flow with regard to investments in fixed assets	NA	Two surfaces, years separated	5	Last numbers	Yes - but is broken	NA	Millions
1991	ikn1	Report of the Executive Board	19	11	Group funds or percentage of total capital employed	NA	Surface with years separated	5	Last numbers	Yes	NA	Percent(%)
1991	ikn1	Report of the Executive Board	19	12	Dividend in percentage of the net profit excl extraordinary income	NA	Surface with years separated	5	Last numbers	Yes	NA	Percent(%)
1991	ikn1	Europe	24	13	Sales proceeds - Europe	NA	Surface with years separated	5	Last numbers	Yes	NA	Millions
1991	ikn1	Europe	26	14	Investments in tangible fixed assets	NA	Six surfaces, years separated	5	Last numbers	Yes - but is broken	NA	Millions
1991	ikn1	Western Hemisphere	31	15	Sales proceeds - Western Hemisphere	NA	Surface with years separated	5	Last numbers	Yes	NA	Millions
1991	ikn1	Africa	33	16	Sales proceeds - Africa	NA	Surface with years separated	5	Last numbers	Yes	NA	Millions
1991	ikn1	Asia/Australia	35	17	Sales proceeds - Asia / Australia	NA	Surface with years separated	5	Last numbers	Yes	NA	Millions

EXHIBIT 23B.20 (Continued)

The word "Charts" in this table is limited to graphs that contain financial data

Year	Code	Color Legend	Does Color Distort	Borders Shown	Other Charts Separated	Special Effects	Special Effects Distortion
1991	lkn1	Green at the beginning and shading lighter to a yellow at the final year	Yes - the light yellow on the white paper almost dis-appears for the last year	No	Yes - by scale	Yes - shading is morphed from green to light yellow	Yes - the way the surface is laid out and colored, the only way numerical relationships can be observed is by following the top of the surface The surface value is almost impossible to estimate
1991	lkn1	Green - Sales proceeds beer Yellow - Net turnover	Slight - the light yellow on the white paper is difficult to distinguish	No	Yes - by scale	No	No
1991	lkn1	Green at the beginning and shading lighter to a yellow at the final year	Yes - the light yellow on the white paper almost dis-appears for the last year	No	Yes - by scale	Yes - shading is morphed from green to light yellow	Yes - the way the surface is laid out and colored, the only way numerical relationships can be observed is by following the top of the surface The surface value is almost impossible to estimate
1991	lkn1	Green at the beginning and shading lighter to a yellow at the final year	Yes - the light yellow on the white paper almost dis-appears for the last year	No	Yes - by scale	Yes - shading is morphed from green to light yellow	Yes - the way the surface is laid out and colored, the only way numerical relationships can be observed is by following the top of the surface The surface value is almost impossible to estimate
1991	lkn1	Green at the beginning and shading lighter to a yellow at the final year	Yes - the light yellow on the white paper almost dis-appears for the last year	No	Yes - by scale	Yes - shading is morphed from green to light yellow	Yes - the way the surface is laid out and colored, the only way numerical relationships can be observed is by following the top of the surface The surface value is almost impossible to estimate
1991	lkn1	Green at the beginning and shading lighter to a yellow at the final year	Yes - the light yellow on the white paper almost dis-appears for the last year	No	Yes - by scale	Yes - shading is morphed from green to light yellow	Yes - the way the surface is laid out and colored, the only way numerical relationships can be observed is by following the top of the surface The surface value is almost impossible to estimate
1991	lkn1	Seven shades of green from dark to yellow plus two shades of lime	Slight, too many colors to make size comparisons	No	Only chart	No	Yes - too many small pieces
1991	lkn1	Green at the beginning and shading lighter to a yellow at the final year	Yes - the light yellow on the white paper almost dis-appears for the last year	No	Yes - by scale	Yes - shading is morphed from green to light yellow	Yes - the way the surface is laid out and colored, the only way numerical relationships can be observed is by following the top of the surface The surface value is almost impossible to estimate
1991	lkn1	Green - Depreciation Yellow - Investments	Slight - the light yellow on the white paper is difficult to distinguish	No	Yes - by scale	No	No
1991	lkn1	Green - Investments in fixed assets Yellow - Group cash flow	Slight the light yellow on the white paper is difficult to distinguish	No	Yes - by scale	Yes - Split legend	Split scale prevents use
1991	lkn1	Green at the beginning and shading lighter to a yellow at the final year	Yes - the light yellow on the white paper almost dis-appears for the last year	No	Yes - by scale	Yes - shading is morphed from green to light yellow	Yes - the way the surface is laid out and colored, the only way numerical relationships can be observed is by following the top of the surface The surface value is almost impossible to estimate
1991	lkn1	Green at the beginning and shading lighter to a yellow at the final year	Yes - the light yellow on the white paper almost dis-appears for the last year	No	Yes - by scale	Yes - shading is morphed from green to light yellow	Yes - the way the surface is laid out and colored, the only way numerical relationships can be observed is by following the top of the surface The surface value is almost impossible to estimate
1991	lkn1	Green at the beginning and shading lighter to a yellow at the final year	Yes - the light yellow on the white paper almost dis-appears for the last year	No	Yes - by scale	Yes - shading is morphed from green to light yellow	Yes - the way the surface is laid out and colored, the only way numerical relationships can be observed is by following the top of the surface The surface value is almost impossible to estimate
1991	lkn1	From Green to yellow, six separate stages	Yes - there are too many surfaces and colors to distinguish	No	Yes - by scale	Yes - Split legend	Too many surfaces makes volume determination impossible Split scale prevents use
1991	lkn1	Green at the beginning and shading lighter to a yellow at the final year	Yes - the light yellow on the white paper almost dis-appears for the last year	No	Yes - by scale	Yes - shading is morphed from green to light yellow	Yes - the way the surface is laid out and colored, the only way numerical relationships can be observed is by following the top of the surface The surface value is almost impossible to estimate
1991	lkn1	Green at the beginning and shading lighter to a yellow at the final year	Yes - the light yellow on the white paper almost dis-appears for the last year	No	Yes - by scale	Yes - shading is morphed from green to light yellow	Yes - the way the surface is laid out and colored, the only way numerical relationships can be observed is by following the top of the surface The surface value is almost impossible to estimate
1991	lkn1	Green at the beginning and shading lighter to a yellow at the final year	Yes - the light yellow on the white paper almost dis-appears for the last year	No	Yes - by scale	Yes - shading is morphed from green to light yellow	Yes - the way the surface is laid out and colored, the only way numerical relationships can be observed is by following the top of the surface The surface value is almost impossible to estimate

EXHIBIT 23B.20 (*Continued*)

The word "Charts" in this table is limited to graphs that contain financial data

Year	Code	Chart #	Section of Report	Page	Chart Title	Same Chart _ast Year	Chart Type	Years	Numbers Shown	Scale Shown	Same Scale as Last Year	Scale Range (%)
1992	ikn2	1	Key figures	8	Dividend per share	Yes	Surface with years separated	10	Last number	Yes	Yes	Actual
1992	ikn2	2	Key figures	8	Sales proceeds beer and net turnover	Yes	Two surfaces, years separated	5	Last number	Yes	Yes	Billions
1992	ikn2	3	Key figures	8	Trading profit	Yes	Surface with years separated	10	Last number	Yes	Yes	Millions
1992	ikn2	4	Key figures	8	Net profit	Yes	Surface with years separated	10	Last number	Yes - but is broken	No - 50 M increase	Millions
1992	ikn2	5	Key figures	10	Net profit in percentage of shareholders' equity	Yes	Surface with years separated	10	Last number	Yes - but is broken	Yes	Percent(%)
1992	ikn2	6	Key figures	10	Trading profit in percentage of total capital employed	Yes	Surface with years separated	10	Last number	Yes - but is broken	Yes	Percent(%)
1992	ikn2	7	Report of the Executive Board	15	Costs and profit excluding extraordinary income as percentage of the net turnover	No	Pie drawn with symbol and concurrent circles	NA	Yes	NA	NA	Percent(%)
1992	ikn2	8	Report of the Executive Board	16	Interest cover	Yes	Surface with years separated	5	Last number	Yes	No - four times greater than last year	Actual
1992	ikn2	9	Report of the Executive Board	17	Investments and depreciation tangible fixed assets	Yes	Two surfaces, years separated	5	Last numbers	Yes	Yes	Millions
1992	ikn2	10	Report of the Executive Board	18	Group cash flow with regard to investments in fixed assets	Yes	Two surfaces, years separated	5	Last numbers	Yes - but is broken	Yes	Millions
1992	ikn2	11	Report of the Executive Board	19	Group funds or percentage of total capital employed	Yes	Surface with years separated	5	Last numbers	Yes - but is broken	No - 10 % increase	Percent(%)
1992	ikn2	12	Report of the Executive Board	19	Dividend in percentage of the net profit excl extraordinary income	Yes	Surface with years separated	5	Last numbers	Yes	Yes	Percent(%)
1992	ikn2	13	Europe	24	Sales proceeds - Europe	Yes	Surface with years separated	5	Last numbers	Yes - but is broken	No - 1000 increase	Millions
1992	ikn2	14	Europe	26	Investments in tangible fixed assets	No - new entry added	Seven surfaces, years separated	5	Last numbers	Yes - but is broken	No - 50 increase	Millions
1992	ikn2	15	Western Hemisphere	31	Sales proceeds - Western Hemisphere	Yes	Surface with years separated	5	Last numbers	Yes - but is broken	No - 100 increase	Millions
1992	ikn2	16	Africa	33	Sales proceeds - Africa	Yes	Surface with years separated	5	Last numbers	Yes	Yes *	Millions
1992	ikn2	17	Asia / Australia	35	Sales proceeds - Asia / Australia	Yes	Surface with years separated	5	Last numbers	Yes	Yes *	Millions

There are other similar non-financial charts in these annual reports

* Both scales the same size

EXHIBIT 23B.20 (Continued)

The word "Charts" in this table is limited to graphs that contain financial data

Year	Code	Color Legend	Does Color Distort	Borders Shown	Other Charts Separated	Special Effects	Special Effects Distortion
1992	llkn2	Green at the beginning and shading lighter to a yellow at the final year	Yes - the light yellow on the white paper almost disappears for the last year	No	Yes - by scale	Yes - shading is morphed from green to light yellow	Yes - the way the surface is laid out and colored, the only way numerical relationships can be observed is by following the top of the surface. The surface value is almost impossible to estimate.
1992	llkn2	Green - Sales proceeds beer Yellow - Net turnover	Slight - the light yellow on the white paper is difficult to distinguish	No	Yes - by scale	No	No
1992	llkn2	Green at the beginning and shading lighter to a yellow at the final year	Yes - the light yellow on the white paper almost disappears for the last year	No	Yes - by scale	Yes - shading is morphed from green to light yellow	Yes - the way the surface is laid out and colored, the only way numerical relationships can be observed is by following the top of the surface. The surface value is almost impossible to estimate. Split scale prevents use
1992	llkn2	Green at the beginning and shading lighter to a yellow at the final year	Yes - the light yellow on the white paper almost disappears for the last year	No	Yes - by scale	Yes - shading is morphed from green to light yellow	Yes - the way the surface is laid out and colored, the only way numerical relationships can be observed is by following the top of the surface. The surface value is almost impossible to estimate. Split scale prevents use
1992	llkn2	Green at the beginning and shading lighter to a yellow at the final year	Yes - the light yellow on the white paper almost disappears for the last year	No	Yes - by scale	Yes - shading is morphed from green to light yellow	Yes - the way the surface is laid out and colored, the only way numerical relationships can be observed is by following the top of the surface. The surface value is almost impossible to estimate. Split scale prevents use
1992	llkn2	Green at the beginning and shading lighter to a yellow at the final year	Yes - the light yellow on the white paper almost disappears for the last year	No	Yes - by scale	Yes - shading is morphed from green to light yellow	Yes - the way the surface is laid out and colored, the only way numerical relationships can be observed is by following the top of the surface. The surface value is almost impossible to estimate. Split scale prevents use
1992	llkn2	Six shades of green from dark to yellow plus a red star in middle with red circles separating	Yes - too many colors to make size comparisons with too many distractions	No	Only chart	Yes - a gimmick chart drawn for attention, not information transfer	Yes - too many small pieces, too many distractions, no way to compare data by size of pieces. Data layout provides any information
1992	llkn2	Green at the beginning and shading lighter to a yellow at the final year	Yes - the light yellow on the white paper almost disappears for the last year	No	Yes - by scale	Yes - shading is morphed from green to light yellow	Yes - the way the surface is laid out and colored, the only way numerical relationships can be observed is by following the top of the surface. Larger scale prevents comparison with last years chart of same data
1992	llkn2	Green - Depreciation Yellow - Investments	Slight - the light yellow on the white paper is difficult to distinguish	No	Yes - by scale	No	No
1992	llkn2	Green - Investments in fixed assets Yellow - Group cash flow	Slight - the light yellow on the white paper is difficult to distinguish	No	Yes - by scale	Yes - Split legend	Split scale prevents use
1992	llkn2	Green at the beginning and shading lighter to a yellow at the final year	Yes - the light yellow on the white paper almost disappears for the last year	No	Yes - by scale	Yes - shading is morphed from green to light yellow	Yes - the way the surface is laid out and colored, the only way numerical relationships can be observed is by following the top of the surface. The surface value is almost impossible to estimate. Split scale prevents use
1992	llkn2	Green at the beginning and shading lighter to a yellow at the final year	Yes - the light yellow on the white paper almost disappears for the last year	No	Yes - by scale	Yes - shading is morphed from green to light yellow	Yes - the way the surface is laid out and colored, the only way numerical relationships can be observed is by following the top of the surface. The surface value is almost impossible to estimate. Split scale prevents use
1992	llkn2	Green at the beginning and shading lighter to a yellow at the final year	Yes - the light yellow on the white paper almost disappears for the last year	No	Yes - by scale	Yes - shading is morphed from green to light yellow	Yes - the way the surface is laid out and colored, the only way numerical relationships can be observed is by following the top of the surface. The surface value is almost impossible to estimate. Split scale prevents use
1992	llkn2	From Green to yellow seven separate stages	Yes - there are too many surfaces and colors to distinguish	No	Yes - by scale	Yes - Split legend	Too many surfaces makes volume determination impossible. Split scale prevents use
1992	llkn2	Green at the beginning and shading lighter to a yellow at the final year	Yes - the light yellow on the white paper almost disappears for the last year	No	Yes - by scale	Yes - shading is morphed from green to light yellow	Yes - the way the surface is laid out and colored, the only way numerical relationships can be observed is by following the top of the surface. The surface value is almost impossible to estimate. Split scale prevents use
1992	llkn2	Green at the beginning and shading lighter to a yellow at the final year	Yes - the light yellow on the white paper almost disappears for the last year	No	Yes - by scale	Yes - shading is morphed from green to light yellow	Yes - the way the surface is laid out and colored, the only way numerical relationships can be observed is by following the top of the surface. The surface value is almost impossible to estimate.
1992	llkn2	Green at the beginning and shading lighter to a yellow at the final year	Yes - the light yellow on the white paper almost disappears for the last year	No	Yes - by scale	Yes - shading is morphed from green to light yellow	Yes - the way the surface is laid out and colored, the only way numerical relationships can be observed is by following the top of the surface. The surface value is almost impossible to estimate.

EXHIBIT 23B.20 (Continued)

The word "Charts" in this table is limited to graphs that contain financial data

Year	Code	Chart #	Section of Report	Page	Chart Title	Same Chart Last Year	Chart Type	Years	Numbers Shown	Scale Shown	Same Scale as Last Year	Scale Range (%)
1991	ctt1	1	Year At A Glance	3	Turnover and net trading income	NA	VBar with Percent Overlay	5	The % is in center of bar	Yes, for currency	NA	Millions
1991	ctt1	2	Year At A Glance	3	Earnings and dividends per ordinary share	NA	VBar with Number Overlay	5	The DPS is in center of bar	Yes, for EPS	NA	Cents
1991	ctt1	3	Report of The Managing Director	9	Proportion of Group Turnover	NA	3 Pie Chart Cluster, each Pie shows percent, 1 division contributed	NA	The % of total is named in title	NA	NA	NA
1991	ctt1	4	Report of The Managing Director	10	Turnover and trading cash flow	NA	VBar with Percent Overlay	5	The % is in center of bar	Yes, for currency	NA	Millions
1991	ctt1	5	Report of The Managing Director	10	Turnover and net working capital	NA	VBar with Percent Overlay	5	The % is in center of bar	Yes, for currency	NA	Millions
1991	ctt1	6	Report of The Managing Director	10	Net trading income and financing costs	NA	VBar with Percent Overlay	5	The % is in center of bar	Yes, for currency	NA	Millions
1991	ctt1	7	Report of The Managing Director	10	Return on assets	NA	VBar with Percent Overlay	5	The % is in center of bar	Yes, for currency	NA	Millions
1991	ctt1	8	Report of The Managing Director	10	Ordinary shareholders' interest and net attributable income	NA	VBar with Percent Overlay	5	The % is in center of bar	Yes, for currency	NA	Millions
1991	ctt1	9	Report of The Managing Director	10	Shareholders' interest and net borrowings	NA	VBar with Percent Overlay	5	The % is in center of bar	Yes, for currency	NA	Millions
1991	ctt1	10	Report of The Managing Director	11	Proportion of Group (1) - Turnover Net trading income Trading assets employed	NA	3 Pie Chart Cluster each Pie shows different financial ratio	NA	The % of total is named in title	NA	NA	NA
1991	ctt1	11	Report of The Managing Director	13	Proportion of Group (2) - Turnover Net trading income Trading assets employed	NA	3 Pie Chart Cluster each Pie shows different financial ratio	NA	The % of total is named in title	NA	NA	NA
1991	ctt1	12	Report of The Managing Director	15	Proportion of Group (3) - Turnover Net trading income Trading assets employed	NA	3 Pie Chart Cluster, each Pie shows different financial ratio	NA	The % of total is named in title	NA	NA	NA
1991	ctt1	13	Report of The Managing Director	19	Turnover and value added	NA	VBar with Percent Overlay	5	The % is in center of bar	Yes, for currency	NA	Millions
1991	ctt1	14	Report of The Managing Director	19	Value added and remuneration	NA	VBar with Percent Overlay	5	The % is in center of bar	Yes, for currency	NA	Millions
1991	ctt1	15	Report of The Managing Director	19	Distribution of Value Added	NA	Pie	NA	The % of total	NA	NA	NA

EXHIBIT 23B.20 (Continued)

The word "Charts" in this table is limited to graphs that contain financial data.

Year	Code	Color Legend	Does Color Distort	Borders Shown	Other Charts Separated	Special Effects	Special Effects Distortion
1991	cit1	Pink in the beginning and shading darker to red at the final year, with a gray overlay on top of red	Yes - red indicates "bad" in finance. Gray overlay breaks meaning of graph	No	Yes - by scale	Yes - used % overlay on the currency bar	Yes - the use of an overlay breaks the view. A % bar laid on top of whole bar is not easily viewed. The number in middle of bar breaks ability to view volume
1991	cit1	Pink in the beginning and shading darker to red at the final year, with a gray overlay on top of red	Yes - red indicates "bad" in finance. Gray overlay breaks meaning of graph	No	Yes - by scale	Yes - used DPS overlay on the EPS bar	Yes - the use of an overlay breaks the view. A portion of whole bar laid on top of whole bar is not easily viewed. The number in middle of bar breaks ability to view volume
1991	cit1	Each pie has a different shade of red laid on top of gray pie to identify division contribution	Yes - red indicates "bad" in finance. Comparing shades of red in 3 charts not valid	No	No	Yes - 3 Pie Cluster	Yes - the 3 pie chart cluster is not normally used. When used with no legends or instructions. The viewer has to stop to see the meaning
1991	cit1	Pink in the beginning and shading darker to red at the final year, with a gray overlay on top of red	Yes - red indicates "bad" in finance. Gray overlay breaks meaning of graph	No	Yes - by scale	Yes - used % overlay on the currency bar	Yes - the use of an overlay breaks the view. A % bar laid on top of whole bar is not easily viewed. The number in middle of bar breaks ability to view volume
1991	cit1	Pink in the beginning and shading darker to red at the final year, with a gray overlay on top of red	Yes - red indicates "bad" in finance. Gray overlay breaks meaning of graph	No	Yes - by scale	Yes - used % overlay on the currency bar	Yes - the use of an overlay breaks the view. A % bar laid on top of whole bar is not easily viewed. The number in middle of bar breaks ability to view volume
1991	cit1	Pink in the beginning and shading darker to red at the final year, with a gray overlay on top of red	Yes - red indicates "bad" in finance. Gray overlay breaks meaning of graph	No	Yes - by scale	Yes - used % overlay on the currency bar	Yes - the use of an overlay breaks the view. A % bar laid on top of whole bar is not easily viewed. The number in middle of bar breaks ability to view volume
1991	cit1	Pink in the beginning and shading darker to red at the final year, with a gray overlay on top of red	Yes - red indicates "bad" in finance. Gray overlay breaks meaning of graph	No	Yes - by scale	Yes - used % overlay on the currency bar	Yes - the use of an overlay breaks the view. A % bar laid on top of whole bar is not easily viewed. The number in middle of bar breaks ability to view volume
1991	cit1	Pink in the beginning and shading darker to red at the final year, with a gray overlay on top of red	Yes - red indicates "bad" in finance. Gray overlay breaks meaning of graph	No	Yes - by scale	Yes - used % overlay on the currency bar	Yes - the use of an overlay breaks the view. A % bar laid on top of whole bar is not easily viewed. The number in middle of bar breaks ability to view volume
1991	cit1	Pink in the beginning and shading darker to red at the final year, with a gray overlay on top of red	Yes - red indicates "bad" in finance. Gray overlay breaks meaning of graph	No	Yes - by scale	Yes - used % overlay on the currency bar	Yes - the use of an overlay breaks the view. A % bar laid on top of whole bar is not easily viewed. The number in middle of bar breaks ability to view volume
1991	cit1	Each pie has a different shade of red laid on top of gray pie to identify divisions contribution	Yes - red indicates "bad" in finance. Comparing shades of red in 3 charts not valid	No	No	Yes - 3 Pie Cluster	Yes - the 3 pie chart cluster is not normally used. When used with no legends or instructions. In this case, the same format and colors are used from earlier 3 Pie Cluster, Chart 3, but the information and meanings are different. Charts 11 and 12 use same legends as this chart
1991	cit1	Each pie has a different shade of red laid on top of gray pie to identify divisions contribution	Yes - red indicates "bad" in finance. Comparing shades of red in 3 charts not valid	No	No	Yes - 3 Pie Cluster	Yes - the 3 pie chart cluster is not normally used. When used with no legends or instructions. The viewer has to stop to see the meaning. In this case, Charts 11 and 12 use same legends
1991	cit1	Pink in the beginning and shading darker to red at the final year, with a gray overlay on top of red	Yes - red indicates "bad" in finance. Comparing shades of red in 3 charts not valid	No	No	Yes - 3 Pie Cluster	Yes - the 3 pie chart cluster is not normally used. When used with no legends or instructions. In this case, Charts 10, 11 and 12 use same legends
1991	cit1	Pink in the beginning and shading darker to red at the final year, with a gray overlay on top of red	Yes - red indicates "bad" in finance. Gray overlay breaks meaning of graph	No	Yes - by scale	Yes - used % overlay on the currency bar	Yes - the use of an overlay breaks the view. A % bar laid on top of whole bar is not easily viewed. The number in middle of bar breaks ability to view volume
1991	cit1	Pink in the beginning and shading darker to red at the final year, with a gray overlay on top of red	Yes - red indicates "bad" in finance. Gray overlay breaks meaning of graph	No	Yes - by scale	Yes - used % overlay on the currency bar	Yes - the use of an overlay breaks the view. A % bar laid on top of whole bar is not easily viewed. The number in middle of bar breaks ability to view volume
1991	cit1	Gray and four shades of red	Yes - red indicates "bad"	No	No	No	Yes, four pieces of the pie are too small to compare

EXHIBIT 23B.20 (Continued)

The word "Charts" in this table is limited to graphs that contain financial data

Year	Code	Chart #	Section of Report	Page	Chart Title	Same Chart Last Year	Chart Type	Years	Numbers Shown	Scale Shown	Same Scale as Last Year	Scale Range (%)
1992	ctt2	1	Year At A Glance	3	Turnover and net trading income	Yes	VBar with Percent Overlay	5	The % is in center of bar	Yes, for currency	Yes	Millions
1992	ctt2	2	Year At A Glance	3	Earnings and dividends per ordinary share	Yes	VBar with Number Overlay	5	The DPS is in center of bar	Yes, for EPS	Yes	Cents
1992	ctt2	3	Report of The Managing Director	8	Proportion of Group Turnover	Yes	3 Pie Chart Cluster, each Pie shows percent 1 division contributed	NA	The % of total is named in title	NA	NA	NA
1992	ctt2	4	Report of The Managing Director	9	Turnover and trading cash flow	Yes	VBar with Percent Overlay	5	The % is in center of bar	Yes, for currency	Yes	Millions
1992	ctt2	5	Report of The Managing Director	9	Turnover and net working capital	Yes	VBar with Percent Overlay	5	The % is in center of bar	Yes, for currency	Yes	Millions
1992	ctt2	6	Report of The Managing Director	9	Net trading income and financing costs	Yes	VBar with Percent Overlay	5	The % is in center of bar	Yes, for currency	Yes	Millions
1992	ctt2	7	Report of The Managing Director	9	Return on assets	Yes	VBar with Percent Overlay	5	The % is in center of bar	Yes, for currency	Yes	Millions
1992	ctt2	8	Report of The Managing Director	9	Ordinary shareholders' interest and net attributable income	Yes	VBar with Percent Overlay	5	The % is in center of bar	Yes, for currency	No	Millions
1992	ctt2	9	Report of The Managing Director	9	Shareholders' interest and net borrowings	Yes	VBar with Percent Overlay	5	The % is in center of bar	Yes, for currency	No	Millions
1992	ctt2	10	Report of The Managing Director	10	Proportion of Group (1) - Turnover, Net trading income, Trading assets employed	Yes	3 Pie Chart Cluster, each Pie shows different financial ratio	NA	The % of total is named in title	NA	NA	NA
1992	ctt2	11	Report of The Managing Director	12	Proportion of Group (2) - Turnover, Net trading income, Trading assets employed	NA	3 Pie Chart Cluster, each Pie shows different financial ratio	NA	The % of total is named in title	NA	NA	NA
1992	ctt2	12	Report of The Managing Director	15	Proportion of Group (3) - Turnover, Net trading income, Trading assets employed	NA	3 Pie Chart Cluster, each Pie shows different financial ratio	NA	The % of total is named in title	NA	NA	NA
1992	ctt2	13	Report of The Managing Director	21	Distribution of Value Added	NA	2 Pie Chart Cluster each Pie shows different year	NA	The % of total	NA	NA	NA
1992	ctt2	14	Report of The Managing Director	21	Turnover and value added	Yes	VBar with Percent Overlay	5	The % is in center of bar	Yes, for currency	Yes	Millions
1992	ctt2	15	Report of The Managing Director	21	Value added and remuneration	Yes	VBar with Percent Overlay	5	The % is in center of bar	Yes, for currency	Yes	Millions

There are other similar non-financial charts in these annual reports

EXHIBIT 23B.20 (Continued)

The word "Charts" in this table is limited to graphs that contain financial data.

Year	Code	Color Legend	Does Color Distort	Borders Shown	Other Charts Separated	Special Effects	Special Effects Distortion
1992	ctt2	Red, with gray overlays shaded from light gray to dark gray over red	Yes - red indicates "bad" in finance. Gray overlay breaks meaning of graph.	No	Yes - by scale	Yes - used % overlay on the currency bar	Yes - the use of an overlay breaks the view. A % bar laid on top of whole bar is not easily viewed. The number in middle of bar breaks ability to view volume.
1992	ctt2	Red, with gray overlays shaded from light gray to dark gray over red	Yes - red indicates "bad" in finance. Gray overlay breaks meaning of graph.	No	Yes - by scale	Yes - used DPS overlay on the EPS bar	A portion of whole bar laid on top of whole bar is not easily viewed. The number in middle of bar breaks ability to view volume.
1992	ctt2	Each pie has a different shade of gray laid on top of red pie to identify division contribution.	Yes - red indicates "bad" in finance	No	No	Yes - 3 Pie Cluster	Yes - the 3 pie chart cluster is not normally used. When used with no legends or instructions. The viewer has to stop to see the meaning.
1992	ctt2	Red, with gray overlays shaded from light gray to dark gray over red	Yes - red indicates "bad" in finance. Gray overlay breaks meaning of graph.	No	Yes - by scale	Yes - used % overlay on the currency bar	Yes - the use of an overlay breaks the view. A % bar laid on top of whole bar is not easily viewed. The number in middle of bar breaks ability to view volume.
1992	ctt2	Red, with gray overlays shaded from light gray to dark gray over red	Yes - red indicates "bad" in finance. Gray overlay breaks meaning of graph.	No	Yes - by scale	Yes - used % overlay on the currency bar	Yes - the use of an overlay breaks the view. A % bar laid on top of whole bar is not easily viewed. The number in middle of bar breaks ability to view volume.
1992	ctt2	Red, with gray overlays shaded from light gray to dark gray over red	Yes - red indicates "bad" in finance. Gray overlay breaks meaning of graph.	No	Yes - by scale	Yes - used % overlay on the currency bar	Yes - the use of an overlay breaks the view. A % bar laid on top of whole bar is not easily viewed. The number in middle of bar breaks ability to view volume.
1992	ctt2	Red, with gray overlays shaded from light gray to dark gray over red	Yes - red indicates "bad" in finance. Gray overlay breaks meaning of graph.	No	Yes - by scale	Yes - used % overlay on the currency bar	Yes - the use of an overlay breaks the view. A % bar laid on top of whole bar is not easily viewed. The number in middle of bar breaks ability to view volume.
1992	ctt2	Red, with gray overlays shaded from light gray to dark gray over red	Yes - red indicates "bad" in finance. Gray overlay breaks meaning of graph.	No	Yes - by scale	Yes - used % overlay on the currency bar	Yes - the use of an overlay breaks the view. A % bar laid on top of whole bar is not easily viewed. The number in middle of bar breaks ability to view volume.
1992	ctt2	Red, with gray overlays shaded from light gray to dark gray over red	Yes - red indicates "bad" in finance. Gray overlay breaks meaning of graph.	No	Yes - by scale	Yes - used % overlay on the currency bar	Yes - the use of an overlay breaks the view. A % bar laid on top of whole bar is not easily viewed. The number in middle of bar breaks ability to view volume.
1992	ctt2	Red, with gray overlays shaded from light gray to dark gray over red	Yes - red indicates "bad" in finance	No	No	Yes - 3 Pie Cluster	Yes - the 3 pie chart cluster is not normally used. When used with no legends or instructions. The viewer has to stop to see the meaning. In this case, the same format and colors are used from earlier 3 Pie Cluster. Chart 3, but the information and meanings are different. Charts 11 and 12 use same legends as this chart.
1992	ctt2	Each pie has a different shade of red laid on top of gray pie to identify divisions contribution	Yes - red indicates "bad" in finance	No	No	Yes - 3 Pie Cluster	Yes - the 3 pie chart cluster is not normally used. When used with no legends or instructions. The viewer has to stop to see the meaning. In this case. Charts 10, 11 and 12 use same legends
1992	ctt2	Each pie has a different shade of red laid on top of gray pie to identify divisions contribution	Yes - red indicates "bad" in finance	No	No	Yes - 3 Pie Cluster	Yes - the 3 pie chart cluster is not normally used. When used with no legends or instructions. The viewer has to stop to see the meaning. In this case. Charts 10, 11 and 12 use same legends
1992	ctt2	Red, with gray overlays shaded from light gray to dark gray over red	Yes - red indicates "bad" in finance	No	No	Yes - 2 Pie Cluster	Not possible to compare values between the year
1992	ctt2	Red, with gray overlays shaded from light gray to dark gray over red	Yes - red indicates "bad" in finance. Gray overlay breaks meaning of graph.	No	Yes - by scale	Yes - used % overlay on the currency bar	Yes - the use of an overlay breaks the view. A % bar laid on top of whole bar is not easily viewed. The number in middle of bar breaks ability to view volume.
1992	ctt2	Red, with gray overlays shaded from light gray to dark gray over red	Yes - red indicates "bad" in finance. Gray overlay breaks meaning of graph.	No	Yes - by scale	Yes - used % overlay on the currency bar	Yes - the use of an overlay breaks the view. A % bar laid on top of whole bar is not easily viewed. The number in middle of bar breaks ability to view volume.

EXHIBIT 23B.20 (Continued)

CHAPTER 24A (New)

FINANCIAL GRAPHICS AS THE BASIS FOR AN INTELLECTUAL MULTIMEDIA™ COMMUNICATION PACKAGE

24A.1 INTRODUCTION

As noted in the introduction, putting charts, tables, and words together is an art. It is critical that they function together in a way that best supports the workings of the human brain. Exhibit 24.1 describes the difference between activating the brain's emotions or its intellect. We are interested in *activating the intellect,* meaning that we need to get all four parts of the brain involved in analyzing the *same* set of information at the same time.

Even though we will need to use different symbols to show the information, they should contain an identical message. For example, we will show the information in graph, tabular, and written form. All three modalities use different symbols such as numbers, alphabet, and charts.

24A.2 PAGE LAYOUT

Based on 15 years of experience, I have concluded that the page layout shown in Exhibit 24.2 is the one that best meets the brain's input requirements. The chart side of the page is on the left so that the information goes to the right side of the brain, the graph side. The tabular and the written analysis go on the right so that the brain sends the information to the left side, the tabular and written portion of the brain. There are several rules that need to be followed to make this presentation work.

THE PARADIGM SHIFT

WHOLE BRAIN INFORMATION!
MULTIMEDIA by DEFINITION.

- Emotion
  - Graphic, Animation
  - Voice, Sound
  - Human (oids)
- Right brain dominated.

- Intellect
  - Tabular
  - Written
  - Graphic
  - Voice, Sound
- Whole brain involvement.

EXHIBIT 24A.1

A. No more than two charts should be shown at once. The top chart is the primary chart used for analysis. If there is only one chart needed, it goes on the top. The second chart supports the first chart, and it should go under the primary chart. If only one chart is needed, the second space can be left blank, or the one chart can be expanded to cover the rest of the left side; that is a taste decision.

B. The tabular data should be shown on the top of the right side because tabular reports are the historical way of showing financial statements. The reports should not contain more data than the data used to create the charts. The point here is that the two numerical presentations are identical. If the numbers are not the same, the brain will try to figure out why. If the numbers are the same, the brain will try to understand the information presented.

C. The written analysis should show how the company has performed based on the data presented in the graph and tabular reports. The more consistent the analysis, the more likely it is that the reader will understand the information presented on the pages.

D. The page layouts including company logos, shading, font size, and so on, should be designed before the page design is frozen. I would recommend using a light shading over the current data that corresponds to the solid bars in the chart. This simple indexing schema will improve the reader's ability to tie together all of the information. Whatever you do, be consistent.

24A.3   HOW IS THIS MULTIMEDIA?

When you first saw the word Multimedia, a subjective interpretation came to your mind. You probably saw a full-color animated system with music, moving objects (or people), and maybe even a plot (see Exhibit 24.1). That might just be what some of the good emotion evoking presentations include. They may also have a plot with the sole purpose of creating certain emotions to cause you to behave predictably. Fortunately, that is not the purpose of financial reporting.

Multimedia financial reporting is used to help communicate the intricacies of financial reporting by properly presenting financial information. It is possible to activate all four parts of the brain with a printed report as described above, and, a verbal presentation by you! You do not need all of the technology. (See Exhibit 24.3).

Chart 1. The chart that supports the analysis. Left eye sends to right brain.

Chart 2. The chart that adds to the analysis. Left eye sends to right brain.

EXHIBIT 24A.2

The tabular presentation. Highly structured presentation. Right eye sends to left brain.

The written analysis, automatically generated. Right eye sends to left brain.

EXHIBIT 24A.2 *(Continued)*

THE PARADIGM SHIFT

"NOW THIS IS MULTIMEDIA!!!"

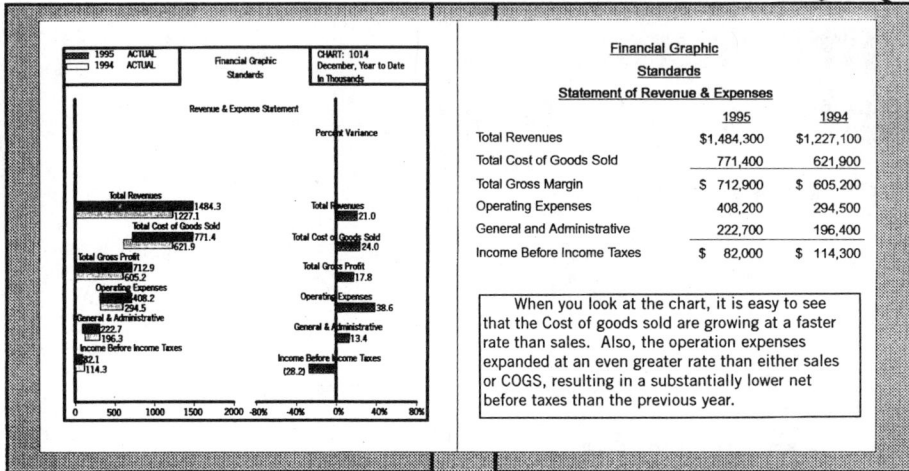

EXHIBIT 24A.3

24A.4 SAMPLES

Exhibits 24.4–24.18 are formal pages created automatically in an advanced Windows™ analysis system.[1] The charts are designed utilizing various corporate templates. The charts, the reports, and the analysis are all created automatically based on the template design. The result is a "briefing book" that not only presents the information, it analyzes it. When the financial analysts present the information to the "client," the verbal presentation cements the understanding.

The template presented here is the generic template designed for the small- to medium-sized company in various industries. The presentation is highly stylized, and the same numbers are available in all three presentation modalities. This structure has proven to work well.

---

[1] CPAnalyst™ (Charts, Presentation, Analysis), Graphic M*I*S, LLC, Chicago, Ill.

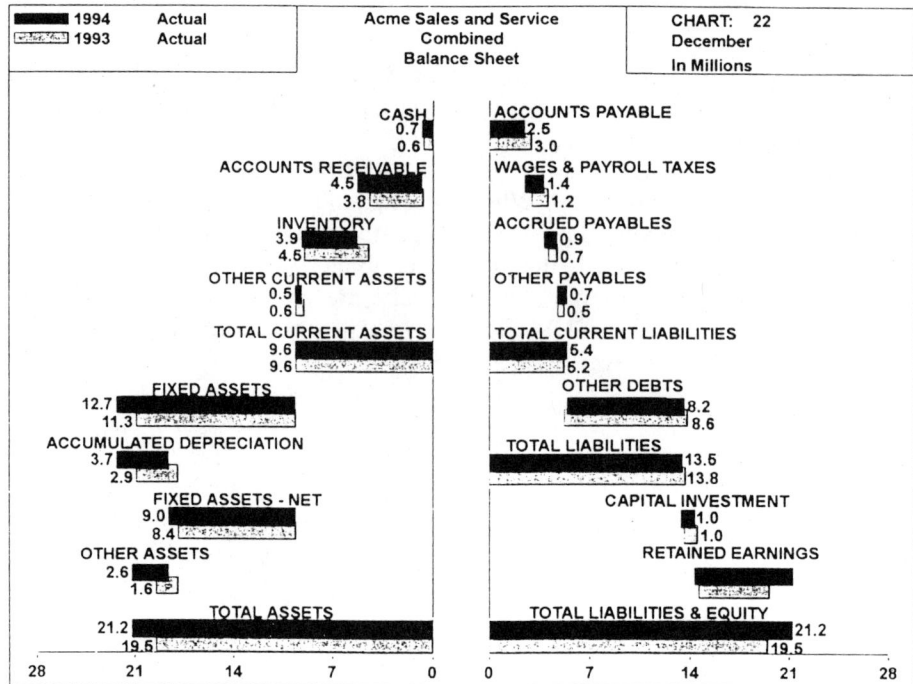

EXHIBIT 24A.4

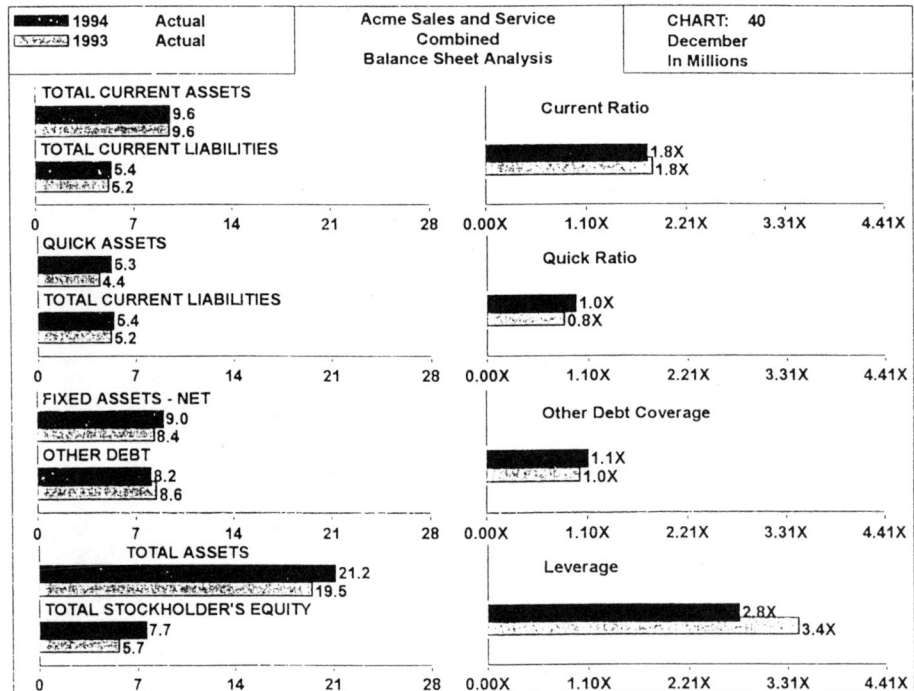

EXHIBIT 24A.5

Acme Sales & Service

Balance Sheets- For Years Ending December 31

ASSETS	1994	1993
CASH	$746,598	$645,295
ACCOUNTS RECEIVABLE	4,516,852	3,785,261
INVENTORY	3,897,659	4,521,632
OTHER CURRENT ASSETS	456,321	623,521
TOTAL CURRENT ASSETS	$9,617,430	$9,575,709
FIXED ASSETS	$12,687,232	$11,325,813
ACCUMULATED DEPRECIATION	3,652,156	2,945,631
FIXED ASSETS - NET	9,035,076	8,380,182
OTHER ASSETS	2,564,123	1,564,211
TOTAL ASSETS	$21,216,629	$19,520,102

LIABILITIES & EQUITY	1994	1993
ACCOUNTS PAYABLE	$2,456,785	$2,965,211
WAGES & PAYROLL TAXES	1,369,815	1,156,421
ACCRUED PAYABLES	896,623	652,315
OTHER PAYABLES	689,452	456,213
TOTAL CURRENT LIABILITIES	$5,412,575	$5,230,160
OTHER DEBTS	8,151,552	8,611,843
TOTAL LIABILITIES	$13,564,127	$13,842,003
CAPITAL INVESTMENT	$1,000,000	$1,000,000
RETAINED EARNINGS	6,652,502	4,678,099
TOTAL LIABILITIES & EQUITY	$21,216,629	$19,520,102

Acme Sales & Service's total assets increased 8.67% between December 1993 and 1994. This asset growth rate appears high. The Company's current ratio, a good indicator of liquidity, was 1.78 for December 1994, down from a value of 1.83 in 1993. The current ratio computes the number of dollars in the Company has invested in current assets ($1.78) to pay off every dollar raised by current liabilities. The slight reduction in the 1994 current ratio indicates a slight reduction in the Company's ability to pay current liabilities.
The Company's Quick Ratio measures 0.97 for December 1994, up from a value of 0.85 in 1993. The positive shift in the quick ratio shows that the Company has shifted the current asset investment mix to the more liquid current assets. Based on the data provided, the current and quick ratios considered together indicate an acceptable ability to pay current liabilities.
The Company's Other Debt Coverage ratio measures 1.11 for December 1994, up from 0.97 in 1993. This increase means that during 1994, the Company invested $0.14 more in long-term assets for every dollar of long-term debt. Based on the data provided, Long-Term Debt Coverage seems low and may put too much pressure on earnings and current assets to service the debt.
The Company's Leverage Ratio lowered from 3.44 in 1993 to 2.77 as of December 1994. This decrease in Leverage means that during 1994 $0.67 more equity was used to finance the increase in total assets. Considering the two debt ratios together indicates that management is shifting their funding strategy from debt to equity. Leverage and debt coverage are more industry specific than most other ratios. Some industries with a large Fixed Asset base depend on higher leverage. Companies with a high asset turnover can support higher leverage. Leverage is best explained in context with the other DuPont ratios, see Company Performance Review.

EXHIBIT 24A.6

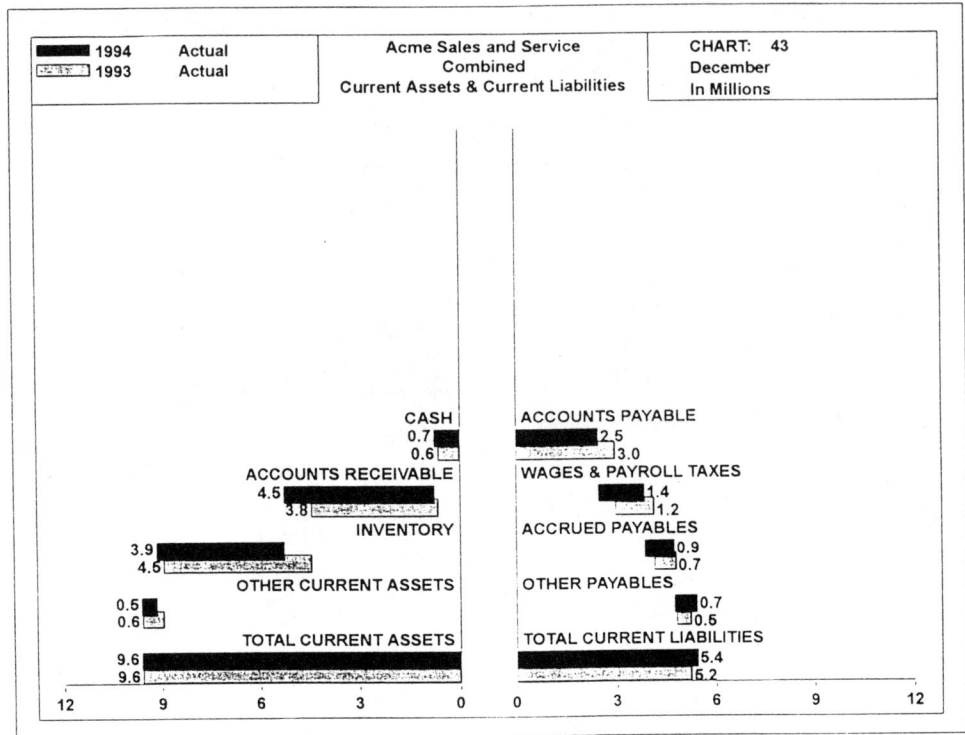

EXHIBIT 24A.7

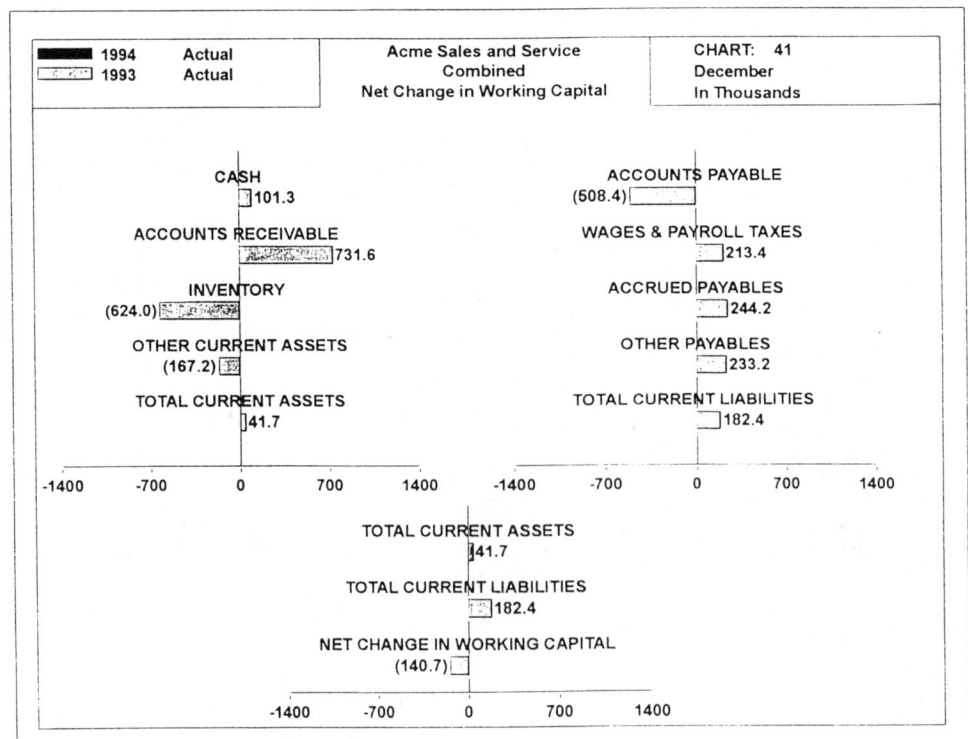

EXHIBIT 24A.8

Acme Sales & Service

Current Assets & Current Liabilities For Years Ending December 31

ASSETS	1994	1993	Variance
CURRENT ASSETS			
CASH	$746,598	$645,295	$101,303
ACCOUNTS RECEIVABLE	4,516,862	3,785,261	731,591
INVENTORY	3,897,659	4,521,632	(623,973)
OTHER CURRENT ASSETS	456,321	623,521	(167,200)
TOTAL CURRENT ASSETS	$9,617,430	$9,575,709	$41,721

LIABILITIES & EQUITY	1994	1993	Variance
CURRENT LIABILITIES			
ACCOUNTS PAYABLE	$2,456,785	$2,965,211	($508,426)
WAGES & PAYROLL TAXES	1,369,815	1,156,421	213,394
ACCRUED PAYABLES	896,523	652,315	244,208
OTHER PAYABLES	689,452	456,213	233,239
TOTAL CURRENT LIABILITIES	$5,412,575	$5,230,160	$182,415

Acme Sales & Service experienced a $140,694 decrease in working capital for the year ending December 31, 1994. Working capital is the net difference between the current assets and the current liabilities, $4,345,549 in 1993 and $4,204,855 in 1994. The larger the working capital, the more likely a company will be able to pay off their current liabilities in a timely manner.

The Net Change in Working Capital is a statement designed to show the components of change. The net change in working capital is the difference between the net changes in Current Assets, $41,721, less the net changes in Current Liabilities, $182,415, a net change of ($140,694). The ($140,694) reflects a 3.35% decrease from 1993. The net changes in Current Assets and Current Liabilities are described in the statements by the net changes in their respective components.

EXHIBIT 24A.9

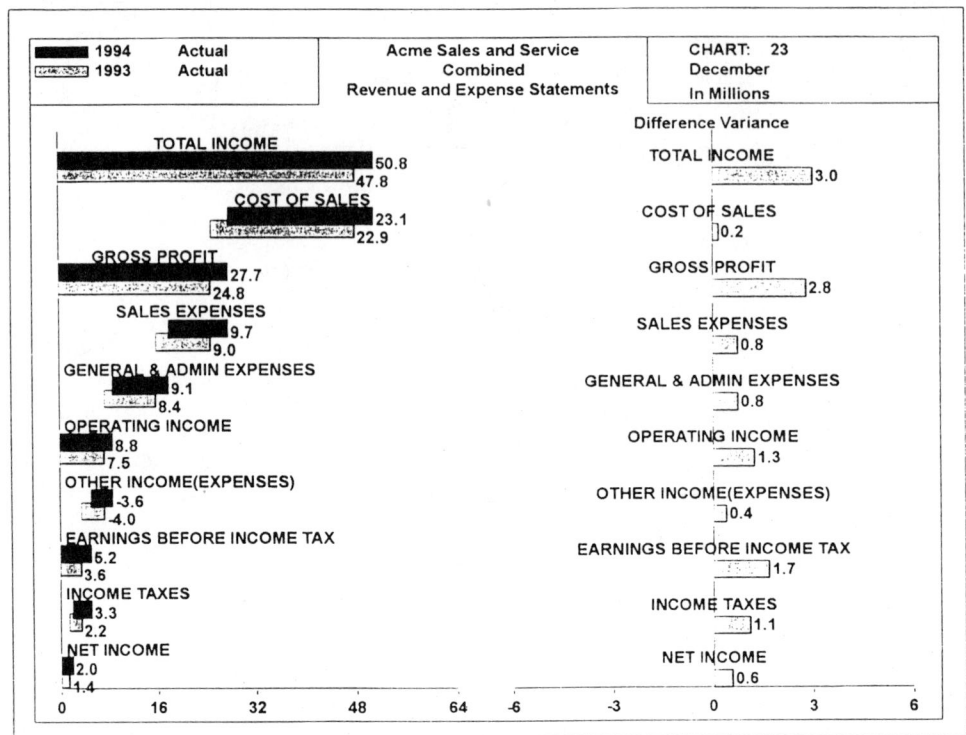

EXHIBIT 24A.10

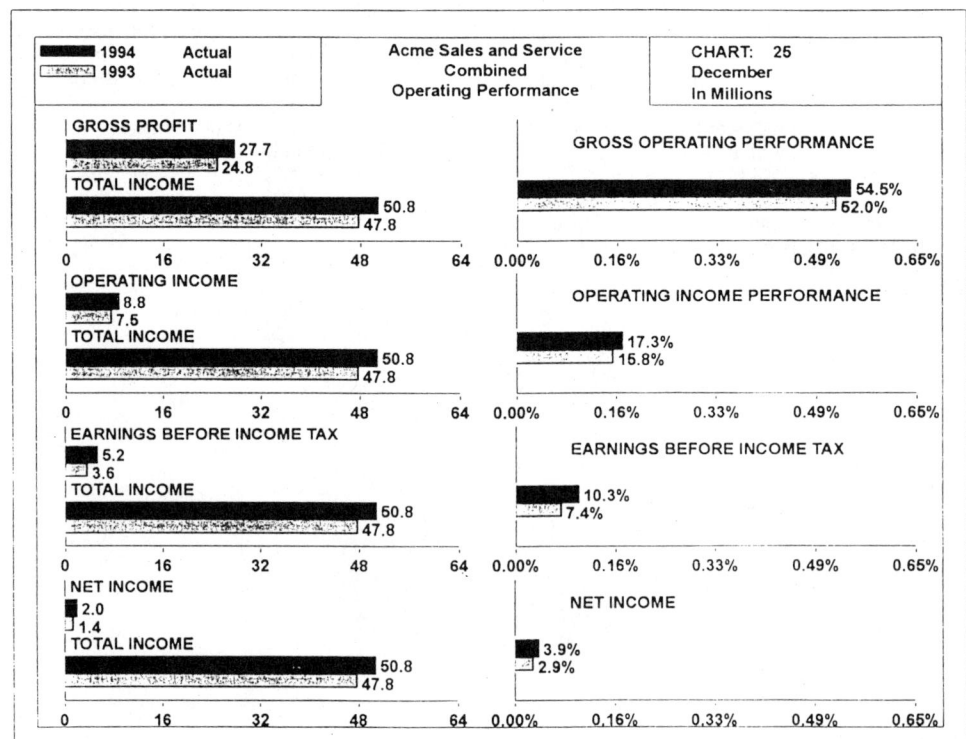

EXHIBIT 24A.11

Acme Sales & Service

Revenue and Expense Statements - For Years Ending December 31

	1994	1993	Variance
TOTAL INCOME	$50,793,000	$47,785,000	$3,008,000
COST OF SALES	23,135,782	22,936,800	198,982
GROSS PROFIT	$27,657,218	$24,848,200	$2,809,018
SALES EXPENSES	9,725,963	8,956,231	769,732
GENERAL & ADMIN EXPENSES	9,125,628	8,352,156	773,472
OPERATING INCOME	$8,805,627	$7,539,813	$1,265,814
OTHER INCOME(EXPENSES)	(3,562,141)	(3,985,623)	423,482
EARNINGS BEFORE INC. TAX	$5,243,486	$3,554,190	$1,689,296
INCOME TAXES	3,269,083	2,156,871	1,112,212
NET INCOME	$1,974,403	$1,397,319	$577,084

Acme Sales & Service's Revenue and Expense statements describe a Net Profit of $1,974,403 for the year ending December 31, 1994, up from $1,397,319 in 1993. The 1994 Sales increased 6.29%, from $47,785,000 in 1993 to $50,793,000 in 1994. The Cost of Sales in 1994 increased 0.87% resulting in an 11.3% increase in Gross Margin, from $24,848,200 in 1993 to $27,657,218 in 1994. The COMPANY's Gross Profit percent was 54.5% in 1994, up from 52.0% in 1993.

Sales Expenses increased $769,732 in 1994, and General & Administrative expenses increased $773,472 in 1994.

Operating income increased from $7,539 813 (15.8% of Total Income) in 1993 to $8,805,627 (17.3% of Total Income) in 1994, a 16.79% increase. Other Income & (Expenses) in 1994 netted out at ($3,562,141), $423,482 less than 1993.

The Earnings Before Income Tax increased from $3,554,190 (7.4% of Total Revenues) in 1993 to $5,243,486 (10.3% of Total Revenues), a large 47.53% increase. Income taxes increased from $2,156,871 in 1993 to $3,269,083 in 1994, a 51.57% increase. The 1994 Net Income increased $577,084 over 1993 income, a 41.30% increase. Such results are extraordinary.

EXHIBIT 24A.12

	1994	Actual	Acme Sales and Service	CHART: 42
	1993	Actual	Combined	December
			Retained Earnings	In Thousands

Difference Variance

RETAINED EARNINGS - BOY
4678.1
3280.8

NET INCOME
1974.4
1397.3

DIVIDENDS
0.0

RETAINED EARNINGS
6652.5
4678.1

0   2000   4000   6000   8000

RETAINED EARNINGS - BOY
1397.3

NET INCOME
577.1

DIVIDENDS
0.0

RETAINED EARNINGS
1974.4

-3400   -1700   0   1700   3400

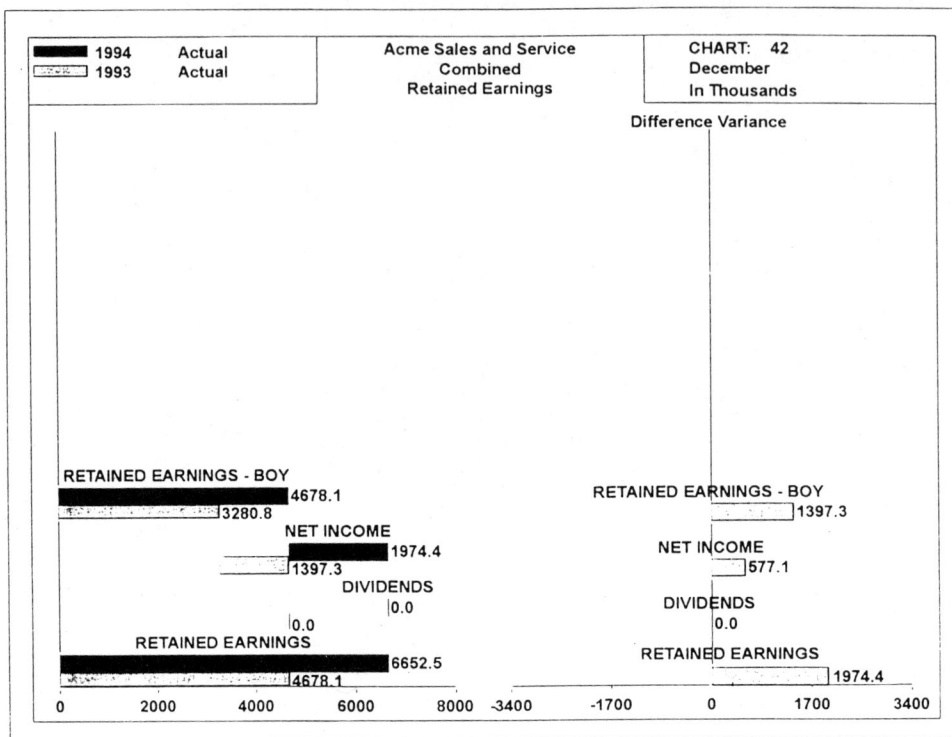

EXHIBIT 24A.13

Acme Sales & Service

Statement of Retained Earnings - For Years Ending December 31,

	1994	1993	Variance
RETAINED EARNINGS BOY	$4,678,099	$3,280,780	$1,397,319
NET INCOME	$1,974,403	$1,397,319	$577,084
LESS DIVIDENDS	0	0	0
RETAINED EARNINGS EOY	$6,652,502	$4,678,099	$1,974,403

Acme Sales & Service increased Retained Earnings by $1,974,403 in 1994. The Statement of Retained Earnings is the one statement that ties the Revenue & Expense Statement to the Balance Sheet. Notice that the Retained Earnings EOY (End Of Year) is the same Retained Earnings that is in the liabilities and equity side of the balance sheet. This statement shows how much of the earnings management decides to reinvest in the firm.

In the current statement, the Company has decided to reinvest all of the earnings into the company and to pay no dividends to the investors. To pay or not pay dividends is a funding decision. If dividends are not paid, then the company has the use of those funds to reinvest in company assets. If dividends are paid, then management may have to use other funding methods to support company investments. It is management's responsibility to earn more from such use of those funds than the investors could make from their own investments.

EXHIBIT 24A.14

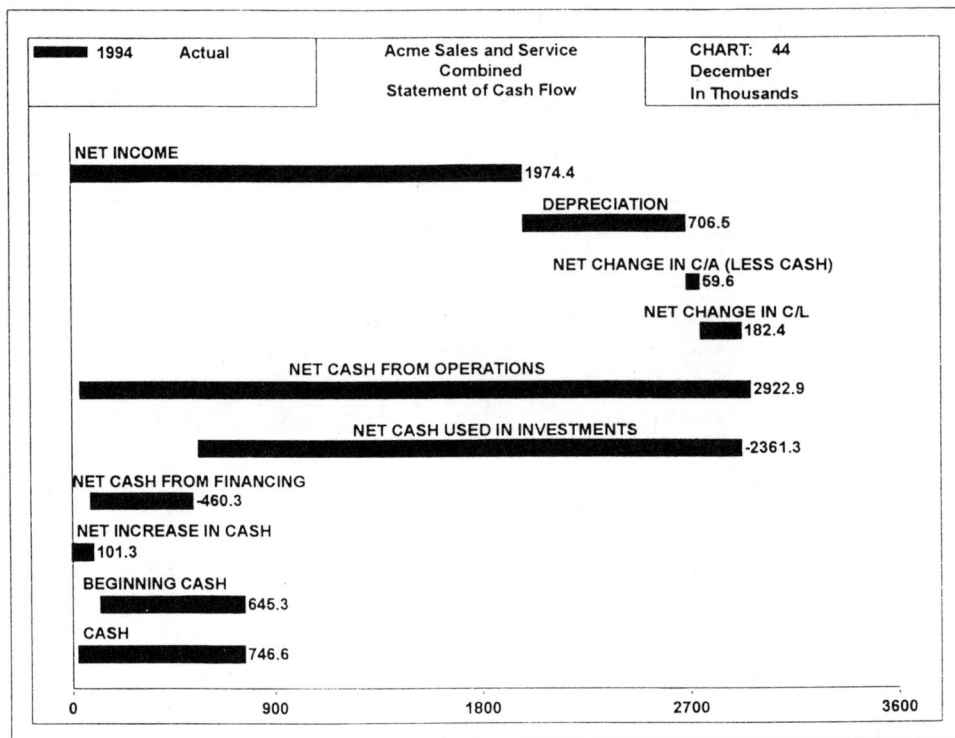

| 1994 Actual | Acme Sales and Service Combined Statement of Cash Flow | CHART: 44 December In Thousands |

NET INCOME — 1974.4
DEPRECIATION — 706.5
NET CHANGE IN C/A (LESS CASH) — 59.6
NET CHANGE IN C/L — 182.4
NET CASH FROM OPERATIONS — 2922.9
NET CASH USED IN INVESTMENTS — -2361.3
NET CASH FROM FINANCING — -460.3
NET INCREASE IN CASH — 101.3
BEGINNING CASH — 645.3
CASH — 746.6

0   900   1800   2700   3600

EXHIBIT 24A.15

Acme Sales & Service

Statement of Cash Flow- For Year Ending December 31, 1994

NET INCOME	$1,974,403
PLUS: DEPRECIATION	706,525
NET CHANGE IN CURRENT ASSETS (WITHOUT CASH)	59,582
NET CHANGE IN CURRENT LIABILITIES	182,415
NET CASH FROM OPERATIONS	$2,922,925
NET CASH PROVIDED BY INVESTING ACTIVITIES	(2,361,331)
NET CASH PROVIDED BY FINANCING ACTIVITIES	(460,291)
NET INCREASE IN CASH	$101,303
CASH BEGINNING OF YEAR	645,295
CASH END OF YEAR	$746,598

Acme Sales & Service generated $101,303 cash in 1994. Many analysts believe that the cash flow statement is the most important of all the operating statements. The ability to operate a profitable company and maintain a cash flow sufficient to support the operating and investment needs of the company is the sign of a seasoned management team. Cash is the fuel that keeps the company operating. Normally cash comes from Operations or from Financing. Normally cash is used to invest in the assets that generate profits.

The Company generated $2,922,925 cash from operations in 1994.

Cash from operations is computed by adding back non cash expenses deducted from Net Income. In 1994 Depreciation expensed was $706,525. Net changes in Current Assets (without considering Cash) and Current Liabilities are then reconciled to reflect their impact on cash. A net increase in Current Assets is deducted from Net Income because the increase reflects expenses that were paid for but not used in operations; net decreases (are added to Net Income because they are expenses that were used in Net Income but not paid for.

In 1994, Current Assets not counting cash decreased $59,582.

Net increases in Current Liabilities are added to Net Income because they represent expenses used but not paid for; net decreases are subtracted because they reflect cash paid that did not impact Net Income. In 1994, Current Liabilities increased $182,415. Net cash provided by investments is the amount of cash that was generated or used by activities that affect the long term assets on the balance sheet.

In 1994 the Company used $2,361,331 to invest in Fixed and Other assets. Net cash provided by financing activities is the cash generated or used to obtain cash for the company. Financing comes from Other Debt and Capital (Equity). In 1994 the Company used $460,291 of the funds generated by operations to pay off Other Debt. They raised no funds through Capital or Equity activities.

The net result is that the Company increased Cash by $101,303 in 1994. The increase in Cash occurred even though the Company invested $2,361,331 in Fixed and Other Assets and reduced their Other Debt by $460,291. All of the activities were supported by cash generated from operations. Such a performance is outstanding.

EXHIBIT 24A.16

▬▬▬ 1994 Actual	Acme Sales and Service	CHART: 24
▭▭▭ 1993 Actual	Combined	December
	DuPont Ratios	In Millions

NET INCOME
2.0
1.4

TOTAL INCOME
50.8
47.8

0   16   32   48   64

RETURN ON SALES
3.9%
2.9%

0.00%   0.08%   0.15%   0.23%   0.31%

TOTAL INCOME
50.8
47.8

TOTAL ASSETS
21.2
19.5

0   16   32   48   64

ASSET TURNS
2.4X
2.4X

0.00X   1.10X   2.21X   3.31X   4.41X

TOTAL ASSETS
21.2
19.5

TOTAL STOCKHOLDER'S EQUITY
7.7
5.7

0   16   32   48   64

LEVERAGE
2.8X
3.4X

0.00X   1.10X   2.21X   3.31X   4.41X

NET INCOME
2.0
1.4

TOTAL STOCKHOLDER'S EQUITY
7.7
5.7

0   16   32   48   64

RETURN ON EQUITY
25.8%
24.6%

0.00%   0.08%   0.15%   0.23%   0.31%

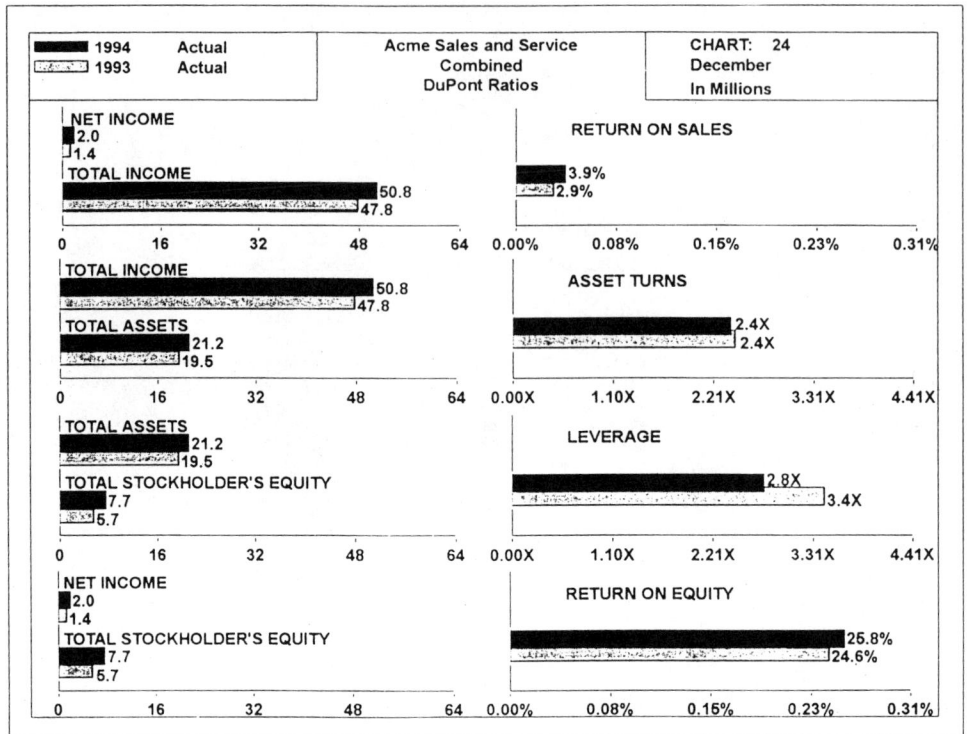

EXHIBIT 24A.17

Acme Sales & Service

Corporate Performance - For Years Ending December 31,

	1994	1993
NET INCOME	$1,974,403	$1,397,319
TOTAL INCOME	$50,793,000	$47,785,000
TOTAL ASSETS	$21,216,629	$19,520,102
TOTAL STOCKHOLDER'S EQUITY	$7,652,502	$5,678,099

The overall performance of a company is best measured by seeing how well the company uses the investments they have made utilizing the financing methods they employ. The DuPont ratios are used by a wide range of managers and financial analysts to provide such an overall measure. People who start and invest in a business expect to receive a better than average return on the money (and efforts) they put into the firm.

Acme Sales & Service provided a 25.8% Return on Equity in 1994, up from 24.6% in 1993. The 1.2% increase in Return on Equity is explained by the other three ratios shown. The first three DuPont ratios multiply against each other to equal Return on Equity ("ROE"). Return on Sales ("ROS") is the percent of Net Income earned by the company as compared to their Total Revenues. Acme Sales & Service returned 3.9% on their Total Revenues in 1994, up from 2.9% in 1993.

The relatively small amount of ROS, however, can be enhanced by the two multipliers that are used to compute Return on Equity.

The first multiplier is Asset Turns. Asset Turns measures the number of times the company turns their Asset investment as compared to the Total Revenue. The Company has managed to turn their assets an impressive 2.4% in both 1993 and 1994.

The next multiplier is Leverage. Leverage describes how much of the assets are funded by equity and how much by debt. The more debt that is used, the higher the leverage and the more ROE. The problem with expanding ROE with a high leverage multiplier is that assets in various industries require a minimum amount of equity for proper operations. As recent history has shown, when companies are too highly leveraged, they tend to go broke with the debt service.

The Company has managed to increase Asset Turns with a bigger Asset base and to lower Leverage from 3.4 times in 1993 to 2.8 times in 1994. The Leverage ratio is moving in the appropriate direction. The Return on Sales multiplied by Asset Turns and Leverage is a most acceptable 25.8% Return on Equity.

EXHIBIT 24A.18

INDEX